RECREATION and Leisure:
Issues In An Era of Change

RECREATION and LEISURE:

Issues In An Era of Change

edited by

Thomas L. Goodale

University of Ottawa

and

Peter A. Witt

North Texas State University

(formerly University of Ottawa)

VENTURE PUBLISHING

State College, Pennsylvania

Distributed outside North America by
E. & F.N. Spon Ltd
11 New Fetter Lane, London EC4P 4EE

ISBN 0 419 12980 4

Printed in the United States of America

Venture Publishing, Inc.
1640 Oxford Circle
State College, Pa. 16801
U.S.A.

Cover Design by Marilyn Shobaken

Library of Congress Card Number 79-92646

CONTENTS

Preface

Thomas L. Goodale and Peter A. Witt

The litany of problems which confront and confound us in this quarter century can begin at any point and proceed in any sequence. The problems are complex and interwoven. Together they suggest that a variety of crises may be at hand; together they spur us to think about needed changes and transformations as dramatic as at any time in our history. Because of its presumed centrality to peoples' lives, the park and recreation movement cannot escape this kind of scrutiny, reflection, and questioning. Indeed, the park and recreation movement needs large doses of these processes to help deal with some of its basic dilemmas, contradictions, and incongruities.

Too little is said about current philosophic and directional difficulties which face the movement. In cataloguing our current status, too little attention has been paid to the essential issues of *raison d'etre* and the impact of burgeoning social issues and ills on current and future practices. Too little is said about the basic forces that are shaping society and generating questions about the park and recreation purpose. There are exceptions, of course. Still, most of the questioning is about issues like proliferation of programs and services, clarification of mandates, sources of financial support and the like. Many reviews of the park and recreation movement have concentrated on cataloguing numbers, current legislation or the size, location, and responsibilities of park and recreation services and educational curricula.

Although allusions are often made to such issues facing the profession *and* the movement (for these are different), more energy seems to be given to extolling the virtues of legislative victories and programmatic successes. Professionalism, registration/certification, accreditation and professional preparation receive more attention than issues of "where to what next, how do we get there from here" and more importantly, "why." The search for stability via institutionalization draws attention away from currents of flux and change, shades of dissatisfaction and misgivings, and the forces within our political, social, and economic systems which can hinder or help us be what we purport to be. A few examples are briefly sketched below.

Gradually but unstintingly, our modes of living and thinking must change. Especially at the individual level, there is already much change in evidence. Change, inevitably, is more difficult and consequently slower for our agencies and institutions. From this pattern, as from others, emerges a sense of lag, and for many, a diminution in congruity.

We are, in the main, certain that the agencies which we serve and which serve us must change markedly. But we are much less certain of what those changes should be. Still, we would like to respond of our own volition since we know unabated problems only make matters worse up to the time alternatives are shrunk and change forced upon us. Too, there is no virtue in doing the right or required thing under duress.

There is much current interest in community development, local autonomy and control, returning resources and responsibility to neighborhoods and local associations in the recreation field. There is also heightened interest in volunteers serving the field in various capacities. But how do we weigh the antecedents of this rebirth of interest? Surely some weight must be given to economic restraints. Perhaps some of this interest is only recognition of a growing spirit of independence among the people, or at least a growing disenchantment with organizational and institutional provisions of service. Surely there is some basis for the renewed interest in the philosophy of individual workers and agencies in the recreation fields; perhaps there is a growing feeling of uncertainty, inadequacy, and humility in the face of so much to do. Still, that is received with equanimity since there are still so many so dedicated to building the recreation "profession." Such issues as these point to serious and difficult questions which the movement and profession must ultimately address. For example:

A.–There is a growing concern in many areas of human services over the proliferation of service providers, the overlapping of service provision efforts, and the scope and breadth of service involvements in the everyday lives of individuals. Coordination, integration, systems planning have all been mentioned as potential means for controlling, limiting, and making service efforts more efficient. Thus, the question naturally arises: Where do recreation and leisure services fit in the overall scheme of human services delivery systems?

B.–Basic to the above is the question of who are or should be the prime recipients of leisure services: the poor, the middle class, urban dwellers, institutional residents? If leisure services increasingly come under the ruberic of enabling services, should efforts be directed toward those who are the least fortunate? Who is to be enabled–and enabled to do what?

C.–What are the expected outcomes of leisure experiences? How do these relate to concern for the quality of human existence? Can we mandate what people should do according to some notion of social utility, personal well-being, wholesome involvement, human experience? Can we trust that people know what they want or do they need to be told (led or directed or counseled)?

D.–How can the powerful establishments which shape our values (the advertising establishment, the welfare establishment, the corporate establishment) be made to understand the vital nature of recreation, creative involvement and all forms of endeavors promoting spiritual, emotional and social development? Can the more traditional sources of values such as the family and the church be revitalized? Does the recreation movement have a stake in all this? Does it matter whose values prevail?

E.–Do recreation services create a self-perpetuating need for continued service provision? To what extent are recreation services used as instruments of social control? To what extent do recreation organizers create or manipulate needs? To what extent should they? And on whose behalf?

F.–Should recreation agencies devote the bulk of their energies to stimulating and supporting those recreational opportunities which are least demanding of elaborate and specialized facilities and which are least consumptive of durable and nondurable goods? Perhaps we have become so enchanted with things that we have lost sight of the fact that the greatest recreational resource we have is ourselves and our families and friends, and there is little else that we need. Are we culpable for that?

G.–Have we abandoned ourselves as resources in favor of resources provided by the collective, thus willfully becoming dependent on agencies only too happy to foster dependency as it contributes to the agency's growth and longevity? Exclusive of those whose roles change due to political and economic forces, where is there a park and recreation agency consciously striving to reduce its size but not necessarily its significance?

H.–Is it enough for a park and recreation agency to print its annual report on recycled paper, when the report resembles last year's in other respects? Or should the agency become the community's outstanding example of harmoniously living in and parsimoniously sharing our finite resources? A commitment to the later course would effect nearly every service and every operation of the agency. It may even mean a shift in emphasis from parks to the whole environment.

I.–With the environmental as well as monetary cost of energy, especially fossil fuels, how much longer should we build and maintain artificial ice rinks, heated swimming pools, and other facilities and operations which make heavy energy demands? Even assuming the financial means to continue such practices, they cannot be sustained ethically as it only forecloses options for those who follow. Further, it tacitly endorses the right of the wealthy, whether individuals, communities, or nations, to consume resources critical to the well being of all. Should any agency, by providing facilities at no matter how large a fee, encourage use of "recreation vehicles," some of which travel but a few miles on each gallon of gas?

J.–Given the current economic situation (perhaps we could label it "slow growth") and projections of it well into the future, what responses are required of the recreation field? Increased reliance on revenue generated by fees and charges may further imbalance services in favor of those with the ability to pay. Increased reliance on high salaried, full-time staff along with increased professionalization and unionization of what was previously volunteer, part-time, and seasonal work may deprive many of involvement which could add meaning to their lives. It may also deprive many of needed, however limited, income. It most certainly drives up the cost of service. Whatever the case, clearly the economics of the steady state or the conserver society will require major changes in the park and recreation field.

K.–What is the balance of benefits to the public, as opposed to an individual "professional," from accreditation, registration, and certification? Whose interests does a profession serve? What are the advantages of professional versus volunteer leadership? Are there personality and socialization factors that selectively bias the perception and attitudes of recreation professionals?

Questions about the recreation and park field, then, come pouring out. The essence of them all is, "How do we respond to the many problems which confront us all and how do we provide leadership in ameliorating these problems and establishing new modes of living and thinking? How do we turn problems into opportunities and capitalize on them for the common good?

In some ways it is easy to agree with Gray and Grebin when they state that: ". . . our contribution (as a movement) has been somewhat minimal in terms of providing leadership for the main current of social progress in America and somewhat marginal to where the action is."[1] It is also easy to agree when they express their view of the plight of creative leaders in the movement who "describe their sense of isolation because they dare to be innovative and because they defy the party line."[2] Although these observations are relatively recent, the problems raised are long standing. They remain unresolved still.

It is no wonder, then, that "value crises" has become such a fashionable, if not always fully fathomed topic. It is no wonder, then, that our age is characterized as one of uncertainty and anxiety. A spate of books are addressed to the end, decline, demise, twilight, challenge, crisis, and failure of one (damn) thing after another. The term "relevance" has been on every lip, so much so that we tired of it, and use it no more. But it concerns us still.

We are fortunate to have such concerns as they are reserved only for those who can afford them. Our affluence, our conveniences, our transportation and communication ability, our high levels of education, our ability to produce beyond our ability to consume; these are prerequisites to our anxiety. These attainments have always been viewed as ends, and in the main we have attained them, however poorly their benefits may be distributed. Now we regard them as means to an end. And the question before us is, "to what end?" That has been the main item on our agenda for at least the last quarter century. Answers, typically, refer to freedom, releasing human potential and creativity, and the like.

How much agreement there is on such answers is a mystery, given the mega-structures and mountainous proprietary interests contingent upon the absence of freedom and the atrophy of human potential and creativity. And we must look further to determine what it is we have the freedom, potential, and creativity to do. To "do your own thing" avoids the question, rather than answers it.

That leisure and recreation are important to attaining new ends, whatever those ends might be, is widely recognized, or, perhaps more precisely, is widely assumed. Even that assumption could bear review, along with most others.

So whether we speak of the economy, energy, population, or urbanization; growth or stasis; the rights of the collective or those of the individual; the virtues of work or of leisure; the search for escape or for identity, meaning, and involvement; we are speaking of the right things. No doubt we will continue speaking of these things for some long time. Meanwhile, some outlines for leadership and action are before us, ill-focused though they may yet be. It is time to begin addressing the important issues and responding to them, particularly among those engaged in parks, recreation, and leisure services who have joined hands in holding out the promise of a new, and somehow better order for us all.

THUS THIS BOOK

Some three years ago, in the midst of a discussion about the literature in the recreation field, we uncovered a mutual and long-held interest in trying to put together a book about issues facing the field. In recent years we have witnessed the publication of some very good books on recreation and leisure—and some very bad ones. However good or bad one judges some or all of the literature in the field to be, still there remains a gap in that too seldom are issues raised or argued forcefully enough that they cannot be readily dismissed. We believe the task of presenting issues an important one, whatever the subject or applied field.

For that reason we are particularly indebted to Venture Publishing, Incorporated (an apt name?) for supporting our venture and thus making it their own. Together, the editors and publishers believe this book will help fill a void in the literature of the recreation and leisure field. Most books in the field are introductions, regardless of titles or prefactory claims. The periodical literature, with few and recent exceptions, has been oriented toward practical program and administration matters or toward data based and quantitative research. Again, one's opinion of the literature is not our concern; rather it is the absence of issues and arguments on matters that concern us.

The textbook approach may be ill-suited to a time in which the concensus on nearly every subject, including leisure and leisure services, is shrinking. Most extant views and underlying assumptions are being challenged by professionals, students, and an increasingly aware citizenry. A renewed humanistic spirit seems to be both cause and effect of the questioning attitude, along with the sobering effect of environmental degradation, energy consumption, urban congestion, slowed economic growth, and related phenomena. There is still some "living in the past," or in a present shored up by optimism and perhaps naivete.

To help deal with these issues, each of the twenty-nine chapters in this book is presented in a manner to be perceptive and timely, being based on wide-ranging study and experience of an objectively viewed North American scene. Each is forward looking as well as a reflection on our present and past experiences. Much of the material also has a timeless quality as some of the issues and concerns are related to, if not in fact derivatives of such enduring themes as Mill's liberty, Rousseau's social contract, Marx's class struggle, Veblen's leisure class, Durkheim's anomie, Riesman's lonely crowd, Jacob's cities, Ward's habitat, Weber's protestant ethic, Ellul's technological society, and much more.

The book is unique in another way. Each chapter is a mini-treatise. In that sense, it is analytical but not methodological; empirical, but not laden with data on a cross-section of the population at a given time. In each piece, the reasoning for the view taken is developed in order to generate thought, reflection, and even argument. No one (including ourselves) will agree with all of the positions or arguments here. That is as it should be.

This is neither a "how to" book nor a mere compendium of current thinking or practice. Neither diatribe nor mainstream, it is an exploration of concerns, issues, assumptions, values, and perceptions which underlie our efforts to serve. There are no answers; there are no easy answers anyway. But there are many suggestions, and much to think about.

The book is divided into four sections which contain a total of twenty-nine chapters. The four sections of the book raise and explore all of the issues (and more) outlined above. The authors represent a variety of backgrounds and experiences and geographically encompass almost every corner of North America. The contributions are the outgrowth of each author's concerns and convictions and could easily stand alone as separate, important contributions to the overall literature in our field. Together they are able to form a whole that should contribute significantly to understanding and working through the vital and important issues that face our field in an era of change.

Some three years ago, when we began inquiring among potential contributors, we drafted several pages to indicate both the tone and reasons underlying this project. It stirred a number of reactions. Many received it warmly and wanted to be a part. Others thought we were describing "a bunch of misfits," and declined the invitation as a result. Not all of the contributors to this book would accept the characterization we drew of them. Some never read it. But we repeat it to indicate where many contributors, at least, and especially the editors, "are coming from." We wrote:

Perhaps in every field, the field of recreation and leisure services being no exception, there are people with a decade or two of dedicated involvement, at least a modicum of success, modest reputations, and established careers who are wondering what they'd like to do—or be—when they grow up. Periodically, at meetings and conferences, while some are exercising the liberty of being away from home and others are straining to be busy, visible and important, still others gather in small groups to talk quietly about their concerns and misgivings, their dreams, their simple pleasures, and the little things that bring meaning to their lives.

The authors here fall increasingly in the third group when they meet, although the meetings seem less frequent now, a reflection not so much of economic restraint as of *deja vu.* And that is consistent with the shared feeling of being, for the moment at least, in an eddy aside from the rapid current of mainstream thinking and acting.

Perhaps the contributors are only too familiar with the large genre of current literature describing an assortment of crises, the need for major transformations in the way we think and act, and the anxiety and general malaise that seem to characterize the era. Perhaps the literature's content is too familiar to the authors, it being an ordered expression of what so many think and feel in moments of reflecting about the unfolding of ordinary days.

Being still in the water, aside from the main current, is not cause for alarm but rather invigorating for anyone unhappy or, more likely, unsure about where the main stream may transport us. So there is no angst, alienation, or anomie among the contributors. Rather there is hope and confidence, not so much in things as they are, nor any clear notion of what they should be. It stems from an appreciation of what can be; of what human beings being human can achieve. There is shared belief among the contributors that recreation is central to that process. Most, then, are recreation professionals reluctantly, and friends of recreation intuitively.

There is no felt need to level a broad side from inside the field of recreation, although there is a tradition of that in every field. Rather, the contributors feel that the time has come for a wider sharing of reflections, reconsiderations, concerns, second thoughts and misgivings about where we've been, where we are, and where we seem headed.

When one finds one's self in an eddy aside from the mainstream, one generally feels alone. Any who feel that way now can rest assured that there is much company. In fact the eddy may be crowded; it may even be the new mainstream. If so, perhaps it will run slower and deeper. If in it there is some groping for principles and purposes around which to order congruent personal and professional lives, then fine. It may result in less drifting with the current, or thrashing about.

TLG
PAW

REFERENCES

1. Gray, David S. and Greben, Seymour. "Future Perspectives." *Parks and Recreation.* 1974(July). p. 31.
2. *Ibid.*, p. 32.

SECTION ONE

Clarifying Concepts: The Ongoing Struggle for Understanding

Introduction

Thomas L. Goodale and Peter A. Witt

Most books on almost any subject begin by defining the basic terms to be utilized and making distinctions between key concepts that need to be introduced. Books on recreation and leisure follow this general pattern. Unfortunately, after reading presented definitions of terms like recreation, play or leisure, the reader is often left with the vague sense that though a lot has been said little has been communicated and definitional and conceptional understanding continues to be elusive.

Perhaps the haze surrounding the terms and concepts essential to understanding the field of recreation and leisure provides a convenient hiding place for those who prefer the status quo or who cannot admit to their confusion. But it seems clear that if the field of recreation and leisure is to advance and mature, we must continue the struggle for clarity; concepts must become more than the academic interest of scholars and philosophers. It is a process that ultimately forms the basis for practice and evaluation of whether services or systems have met stated goals and objectives.

One of the purposes, then, of this opening section is to focus attention on some of the basic words and concepts that are used in our field. For example: Arnold (1) delves into the background and interrelationship of recreation, leisure and play; Farina (2) examines time and free time; Goodale (4) and Bregha (3) analyze freedom and obligation; Smith (5) looks at pleasure; and Bishop and Jeanrenaud (7) and Michaelis (6) assess play and creativity. Their combined efforts add considerable support to material contained in later sections of the book which notes the crippling consequences of failing to come to grips with defining our terms or clarifying our concepts. For example, Burton (29) notes how conceptual and definitional problems restrict the effort to attain maturity as an interdisciplinary field, especially regarding, though not limited to, recreation and leisure research; Westland (27) describes how difficult policy formation is when the framers of policy neither understand nor can agree upon basic terms or concepts. Thus, the wrestling with meaning sets the stage and tone for efforts in the other sections of the book to describe needed services, professional practices, and research and policy issues.

Several other themes emerge through the articles in this section. One of these is the necessity to balance objective and subjective conceptualizations and evidence for our key concepts and terms. Farina (2), for example, points out the extraordinary complexity of the concept of time. In a society such as ours–technologic, inter-related, and interdependent–time as a quantity is inescapable. As a commodity measurable with uncommon precision, we know the mechanistic, objective side of time well. Godbey's (13), discussion of "time deepening" or Sessoms' (14) delineation of life span, life cycle concepts are examples of further efforts to catalogue the use of time and the patterns of time usage that occur over a person's life.

On the other hand there is the subjective, aesthetic and experiential side to time. While more difficult to grasp it may be far more important because the "problem of leisure" is perhaps not so much a problem of quantity of time but the quality. This is clear, as Farina (2) points out, in the two most common qualifiers attached to the word time, as in "free" time and "leisure" time. Beyond any objective meaning these adjectives are laden with qualitative, evaluative and emotive content. Ultimately, Farina suggests that leisure is probably better understood in relation to freedom rather than time.

Freedom thus becomes another dominant theme of this section. Bregha (3) raises the issue of whether we are dealing with freedom *from,* i.e. free from work and other obligations, or freedom *to,* i.e. freedom to choose what to do. Bregha ultimately asks: How much freedom do we really have? What are the conditions of freedom? What are the internal as well as external barriers to choosing freely?

The fragile nature of freedom *to* becomes a dominant issue for several other authors in this section as well. For example, Michaelis (6) describes the conditions that can deteriorate playfulness as one moves through childhood and into adulthood, while Bishop and Jeanrenaud (7) discuss the many potential roadblocks to creativity and the difficulty in its preservation. In Section Three, Reynolds (18) points to the social control potential of our service system as a significant negative influence on the freedom *to,* while Lord, Hutchison and VanDerbeck (17) chastise professionalism per se for presenting significant restraints on leisure and the ability to choose.

The goal of leisure is another dominant theme. Bregha (3) notes that goal-less leisure is a contradiction and the choices made are not equal in quality, morality or social relevance. Smith (5) makes a similar observation in stating that not all intellectual pleasure (thinking) is good because the product of it may be twisted or destructive. This is also noted by Goodale (4) in his discussion of the strong link in Aristotle's philosophy between leisure, ethics and the exercise of virtue. Thus, we are once again involved in the age-old task of distinguishing means from ends. To Aristotle, happiness was the end and leisure in the sense of freedom *to* was an essential means. But Aristotle clearly separated leisure from amusement and recreative past-time.

In the words of poet Alexander Pope: "Amusement is the happiness of those who cannot think." That is one way to summarize Aristotle's philosophy on that subject. It is also an appropriate summary of Smith's (5) analysis of the "Biological Basis of Pleasure" and its implications. Smith raises several issues related to the goal of leisure and its end, pleasure, by discussing the neuro-physiologic evidence which points to human beings as distinguishable from other animals by their ability to derive pleasure from thought. He describes the fact that too many of us involve ourselves in sensate, hedonistic and even narcissistic pleasures, increasingly ignoring the potential of deriving pleasure through thought. These pursuits he sees as sub-human and not in the best interests of human development and purpose. Whether this is only a value judgement or has basis in declining culture and fulfillment is a matter of opinion. Those who seek sensory pleasures, which probably includes us all to greater or lesser degrees, could reply to the effect that we are, after all (or merely) human. But then there are those who have suggested that in light of the many problems and challenges confronting man being only (or merely) human may not be enough.

Smith's discussion of the biological basis of pleasure also points to the potential for recent research into brain functioning to supply important new information about the purpose and value of play and leisure. Michaelis (6) also sees the potential descriptive value of this emerging information, noting the primacy of the right brain and of the affective, non-rational model of thinking to play and creativity. The ultimate need to integrate right and left, cognitive and affective, and rational and non-rational elements also brings us back to the objective-subjective distinction regarding what is leisure noted earlier.

As a fitting conclusion to the section, Mannell (8) raises questions concerning the emergence of "experience" as the focus and objective of recreation and leisure services. Psychic rather than material gratification has increasingly become the motivation of what advertisers tell us is the "now" generation and social critics tell us is the "me" generation. Mannell thus warns us against the "Psychologization of Leisure Services" where "experience engineers" manipulate "psychic loadings" and the like. How far is it from here to the "freebies" and solidarity services of Huxley's *Brave New World?*

In total, the time has come to think seriously about what and how we think, what we mean, what we intend, what we do and what happens as a result. Leisure, recreation and play can and often do mean and imply different things; means and ends of service delivery need to be distinguished; and the disparity between objective and subjective experience resolved.

TLG
PAW

Chapter One

The Dilemma of Meaning

Serena Arnold

Almost everyone believes that he or she has an adequate understanding of leisure, recreation and play. Most people have a ready definition and will argue that leisure is time off the job, time free from requirements of life and time in which they may choose to do what they like. Recreation will be reported as closely allied with sports and games, and if you ask people to identify their recreations, more often than not you'll be provided with the name of an activity perceived as a means of escape from routine. It will be asserted that play is an activity of children, the opposite of work or the antithesis of attention to duty. Some might even suggest that play is the *work* of children. How frequently we hear that Americans work hard at their play and their work is their recreation. At the same time, some persons will assert that they have no *time* for leisure.

Such descriptions of these terms, whether from a sample of citizens or authors in the field of recreation, clearly indicate that our concepts are fuzzy and misleading. The ambiguity is counterproductive when we attempt to analyze and interpret, for example, the function or process of recreation and leisure services. If we are to communicate with any degree of understanding, then we must come to grips with our semantic representations.

Ability to communicate through symbols is one of the important attributes that separate human beings from other creatures. Words are symbols, just as the number two is a symbol. If we fail to understand the symbols we use, we cannot hope to reach any degree of understanding among ourselves. The basis underlying our ability to conceptualize leisure, recreation and play is the meanings of the symbols used. The influence symbolization exerts in human affairs through language is fundamental to thought. Within words can be found tracings of taboos, fetishes, and value judgments in a civilization. For these reasons, an investigation into semantics is essential for understanding—before we undertake developing ideas related to our terms.

To assert that recreation is a condition of re-creation, leisure is free-time and play is a non-productive activity for children, and that all are opposites of work, is to compound many past errors in reasoning. Tracing origin and conceptualization of words associated with the study of recreation can offer an improved comprehension of our developing body of knowledge and practice. Such endeavors can assist in clarifying transitions which have occurred and perhaps those that are inevitable in the future. What we are today as individuals is tied to what we were yesterday, and so it is with words and the meanings they have.

Only recently have there been serious attempts to discretely analyze the meanings of leisure, recreation and play. For the most part these terms have been utilized with emotive intent rather than by reason of their significance. Many of us have not recognized that there is a difference between what is loosely meant by a term and its symbolic meaning or significance. The two approaches are often confused, just as we often confuse the difference between a definition of a word from a description of what it represents. Some college students find it hard to accept that a standard dictionary does not contain definitions, but rather synonyms.

Culminating from centuries of usage and changing moral codes, the terms play, recreation and leisure have undergone a variety of adaptations resulting in a mix of impreciseness. To bring concrete thinking out of generalizations and to separate meanings presents a formidable task. While the English language is generally considered to be rich and expressive in a literary view, ambiguous terms with varying connotations are precarious for planning or scientific purposes. So much of what has been written concerning recreation, leisure and play fits more precisely into journalistic convenience than into scientific explanation. Temptations to coin new terms should be approached with caution, however. For a time I advocated, with some logic, the proposition of coining the term Ludinetics for the study of recreation (ludas, Latin for play; etics, study), but soon discovered that even with such esoterics, I could not avoid coming to grips with the hackneyed terms I wished to evade.

The field of recreation is not alone in its semantic difficulties. Traditional disciplines are still fraught with the agonies of accepted designations. In medicine, for instance, the term disease has no precise meaning, and even more perplexing is the word sick. Recently, 15 physicians were interviewed in an attempt to find agreement as to what was meant by "sick." Interestingly, conclusions from the responses for a definition resulted in sick being "something is not working." For physicians, the word has meaning only to the extent that it is broken down into referents and these referents isolated and made definitive through laboratory investigation. Viability and respectability of any field is not found in its designation *per se,* but rather by the preciseness of its concepts and concreteness of its research.

One of the immense challenges for those in recreation is to delimit our area of concern and study. Yet, only a few efforts have been made to establish discrete boundaries and few agreements have been reached. As long as recreation is anything done in free time and described by activities pursued for pleasure; as long as leisure is welded to time and as long as play is viewed as games of fun, there are no boundaries. We may find solace in centering our interests on designing facilities or developing and managing parks, but in avoiding clear definitions of terms we meet our ultimate dilemma. For example, the very connotation of freedom with which we have traditionally interpreted our field may have some bearing on the maddening misuse of park amenities. There are differences between play and display, leisure and license, recreation and diversion.

The focus of this chapter, therefore, is an historical review of sources from which terms attached to recreation have emanated. Such an overview may yield some insights for those concerned with meaning. Those who say, "let us get on with what we are doing and stop the old-age argument of what is meant by recreation," should recognize that the problem will not resolve itself.

Academic study of leisure, recreation and play is little more than a few decades old and during this time research has been largely devoted to descriptive studies depicting the *status quo*. Considerable emphasis has been placed on administration and management practices as well as leadership, but these studies have been predicated upon the premise that recreation was universally understood and comprehensively defined. Too often we read or hear that recreation or leisure is among the leading American industries, yet such assertions are made without information as to criteria or rationale for whatever was included. The case can be extended for studies involving play. In reviewing 123 recently published research articles related to aspects of behavior termed play, only 19 authors were found who attempted to define what they meant by play. To say that we know what is meant by recreation and subsequently attach terms such as attitude, way of life, or state of mind as our explanation, may well provide richness through ambiguity for literary purposes, but it is asking too much of an inquisitive thinker. Such statements may be perfectly true, but to explain a phenomenon by unsubstantive and emotive phrases adds little to knowledge. Our dilemma, therefore, lies in subjectivity without definition. That recreation is descriptive of a *thing* which can be counted or an objective state of being that can be measured has not yet been established. There is, however, instructive value in knowing and admitting our problems.

Symbolization in human affairs and language is fundamental to thought. With words whose referents are as precise as possible, we enable ourselves to think more effectively, thus reducing conditions that give rise to misinterpretation or sheer error. As instruments of thought, words are used for reflective purposes as identifying things as well as affecting emotions which have non-symbolic influences.

Ogden and Richards stated the problem concisely when they wrote:

> "...the approach to Meaning, far more than the approach to such problems as those of physics, requires a thorough-going investigation of language. Every great advance in physics has been at the expense of some generally accepted piece of meta-physical explanation which had enshrined itself in a convenient, universally practiced, symbolic shorthand. But the confusion and obstruction due to such shorthand expressions and to the naive theories they protect and keep alive, is greater in psychology, and especially in the theory of knowledge, than elsewhere; because no problem is so infected with so-called metaphysical difficulties—due here, as always, to an approach to a question through symbols without initial investigation of their function."[1]

The authors could have written equally well for recreation. It is only within recent years that we have become acutely aware of our own "symbolic shorthand."

When a field such as recreation has evolved out of the issues within society and developed by and through a type of missionary and moralistic appeal on the part of non-specialists, generalizations become habitual. So it has been with recreation, leisure and play. To sever such semantic ties becomes an arduous undertaking. In the case of recreation, there has been a willing dependency and attachment to the applied professional practice of recreation in communities. Leaders have, in turn, been dependent upon the attitudes, tastes and concepts held by their clientele who support or participate in their programs. Contagion in language and attitudes has long been recognized, and only a few iconoclasts will question or resist this prevailing influence. When one is busy "doing," to be concerned with reasoning out word symbols in order to better understand meaning is to be obstructive at best—a bore is one who insists on clarity.

RECREATION AS AN ABSTRACTION

The term recreation is an abstract symbol and thus resists modeling into a series of sub-referents without resorting to further abstractions. In this sense, it could be argued that recreation has no meaning because it doesn't represent a thing or an object to exact description or quantification. Furthermore, its boundaries are unlimited by the number of referents that can be brought to mind. The word is a conditional symbol of varying magnitude, as on a continuum. It raises issues not dissimilar to those associated with defining such words as pleasure or beauty.

If we assert that recreation represents revitalization of the individual because he or she has participated in certain activities, we place upon the symbol qualitative meaning assigning a degree of worth or value, hence a morality. How did the connotation of good and bad arise? As far as I have been able to determine, recreation as an English word arose from Middle English of the 14th century and was adopted previously from Old French. Originally, we may assume that it stemmed from Latin *recreatio*.

In the history of the English language, we find that literary words stemming from French and incorporated into English were probably words of the upper classes. In England of this period, French was the literary language of "polite society" while Anglo-Saxon, considered vulgar and inferior by upper class members, was the idiom of commoners. After the Norman Conquest, in the process of political unification, it became expedient for members of the ruling class to have command of both Anglo-Saxon and French. Through the slow process of language fusion, the English language made its beginnings as a strange assimilation of several languages and idioms, but predominately Anglo-Saxon, French and Latin.

It can be deduced that recreation was a word incorporated into English from French and retained as an expression of the upper class. Thus, recreation had use not to peasants and laborers but to those who enjoyed the privileges of "recreation." If there was a word in the idiom of commoners that connoted recreation in the sense of refreshment, revitalization, or entertainment, it has eluded me. All of these words, including amusement, were of French-Latin extraction. On the other hand, the word "rest" is probably from the Germanic "rast" which referred to ceasing work or the absence of motion—to be at ease.

In Latin, *recreatio* carried a connotation of restoration or recovery from something. Its root is in the word *re-creo* (to create again) to refresh, invigorate, or revive. Further references include such inferences as to amuse oneself after obligation: *laxandi levandique animi gratia*, having to do with pleasant respite. Without neuro-scientific evidence, the word with which we are dealing has a metaphysical quality. If we are to accept the various synonyms given, we would need to substantiate activity as a means for attaining relaxation or rest. The assumption indicated would produce a dichotomy: rest from activity or a cessation of movement on the one hand and diverting activity on the other.

In the study of word meanings, and accepting the canon that thought is dependent upon symbols, we should try to find a word to mean the opposite of recreation. If we selected the referent, revitalization or refreshment, the antonyms fatigue and exhaustion would come to mind quickly. If, however, we accept the Latin root *creare*, the antonym would be exterminate or annihilate. Further the Latin word *creo* has the meaning of bringing forth and quite clearly symbolizes work (fabricate). With the root word for recreation relating to work, it would require considerable imagination to establish re-creation as the antithesis of work. Furthermore, words carry emotive overtones and for centuries the word create was associated in usage with the Divine Creator, and re-create with being born of the Spirit; of being made anew spiritually. In this sense, the word recreation was ontological, rather than a name for some activity as such.

During the 16th and 17th centuries, recreation began to be used to represent activities that provided both spiritual and physical refreshment for industrial workers after hours of delibitating toil. It was during the industrial revolution when the word became a referent for both a state of being and activities of a diversionary nature which were espoused by advocates as essential to maintaining health of workers confined in factories for the majority of their waking hours. In Germany, and to a lesser degree in England, physical exercise was promoted and took root among groups outside of factory workers *per se*. In England, field sports became widespread means for diversionary activity. In the United States, problems associated with factory work and crowded living conditions led to the play movement for children. During the early 19th century, this evolved to the recreation movement, thus including all ages and more than sport activity. Recreation did not lose its moral connotation. With secular support, it was often seen as an antidote for many social ills. The term recreation became useful to satisfy the tastes of entrepeneurs, the moralistic interests of reformers, and the literary proclivities of intellectuals. From these early stages, Patrick proposed what was to be known as the "recreation or relaxation theory," and recreation as the opposite of work became an engrained notion.[2] While I find no support for such liberties with word meanings, and no precedents set in the Greek Language, we seem to persist in choosing work as the antonym for recreation.

LEISURE IDEALS

We turn to Greece and particularly the writings of Aristotle for discourses on leisure and its ideal, a highly significant component of culture. Historically and profoundly, leisure was a way of personal and cultural life for the citizens of Greece, particularly in Athens during the 5th Century B.C. This was the period often referred to as the Golden Age or The Age of Pericles; the time during which the Parthenon was constructed and various intellectual and aesthetically centered advances were made. The importance of Greek culture to any study of Western civilization and Occidental thought cannot be minimized. Our system of reasoning is of Greek origin to say nothing of political influences in democracy and the arts and sciences. Approximately ten per cent of the English language is Greek, including much of the nomenclature associated with leisure. The Greek term *okole* (leisure) has since evolved into words such as school, scholar, scholastic, and a host of other terms which we use daily. Curiously, however, we possess no counterpart to the Greek *asxolia* (un-leisure) which of course was the antonym and fit nicely the Greek penchant for clarity.

Athenian society particularly was centered around leisure or, in our terms, centered around freedom from labors associated with everyday necessities. The social system was supported by a slave population which was rationalized as essential to a citizen's freedom to reach a state of *arete* (the nearest English translation being virtue). *Arete* represented "excellence in all things" and, in the Homeric period, symbolized the ideal for which all citizens should strive: attainment of the highest good for which humans were capable. Leisure, therefore, was the "opportunity" for realization of that ideal. The complexity and universality of leisure was in the wholeness that the term evoked. Jaeger, in his scholarly works, explored these concepts fully, relating them to the central meanings of culture.[3] Peiper asserted that leisure was the basis of culture and implied that recreation, commonly used to reflect activity, was erroneously attached to the term.[4] DeGrazia also supported that contention.[5]

In classical Greece, leisure was not time available to be employed, nor was it a means to an end outside and apart from itself. It would have been incomprehensible to Aristotle for a person to state, "Now I have leisure to do some activity." Neither was work considered the opposite of leisure, for our word work in Greek was *erg*, the root meaning for expenditure of energy. Also, a state of toil, or our term labor can be found in the Greek counterpart for slave. Thus, we draw from early Greek culture our emotive referents associated with distaste for work and labor, representing somewhat less than the good life for ourselves. Although we cling with passion to the idea of freedom, we also center our lives around work, and in our attempt to integrate the two concepts we have created a dichotomy of semantic complexity which entangles us in inconsistencies. Somehow those framers of our Constitution, many of whom were scholars of Greek who held that the pursuit of happiness was the American ideal, did not anticipate that Americans would become slaves to technology rather than technology replacing the slaves of Athens. We have great difficulty conceiving of a period of history where work was not the center of life.

Referents by which to clarify the Greek meaning for leisure requires study of the first chapter of Aristotle's *Metaphysics*.[6] There it is evident that the important referent for *schole* (leisure) is found in the word contemplation. This term does not symbolize inactivity in the sense of posturing oneself in the position of the Thinker, but rather it meant to observe, view and behold. Contemplation has a close association etymologically with Greek *theoria* from whence we draw our word theory. *Theoria* referred to being a spectator at festivals and it is interesting to recall that during the Periclean period, poor people were given money or "passes" by government to attend the theater. The *theorikos* were those who traveled to see men and things and reflect upon them as one would speculate or postulate an explanation of a phenomenon. In the modern sense, it would apply if we attended a World Series baseball game and reflected on the scene to gain insights into the character of our culture. But, contemplation meant more than reflecting on phenomena and perceiving man's place in the scheme of things. One must be both spectator and participator to see the environment and envision one's relationship with it; to establish self-identity. Attendance at a festival was a highly religious experience and a culmination of all that was Greek. The *theorikos* were persons of action, and through their beholding of phenomena, innovations within the culture arose. To dissuade ourselves of the notion that contemplation did not result in action and that leisure was inaction, we need only to turn to archaeological discoveries that clearly reveal the Greek's contribution to technology. Brumbaugh published an impressive account of machines, gadgets and a variety of inventions that were precursors of our clocks as well as mechanical toys.[7] Leisure, then, fits well into the Greek scheme of aesthetics as experiential integration of thought and action.

In Latin derivations of leisure we find that important diversions occurred which affected our current concepts. The dominance of Rome over Greece was more military and economic than intellectual. Greek philosophers and teachers perpetuated their system of education and left lasting marks on Roman literature, religion and language. While the Greeks were profoundly aesthetics and idealists, the Romans were above all else practical. Therefore, any infusion of ideals held in regard to leisure by the Greeks was to resolve finally into a Roman application.

Leisure came to use through the Latin word *licere* by way of the French, *leisir*, the Middle English *leisere* and finally to its present spelling, leisure. The root word, *licere*, meaning to be permitted, evolved into another word—license. The word leisure literally meant exemption or permission as applied to opportunity afforded that was free from legal occupation. Most Roman writers, however, invoked *otium* as signifying the idea of leisure. *Otium* was associated with contemplation and opportunity for freedom *from time* as well as freedom from occupation. As we have the adverb, leisurely, to describe a manner, there was the Latin *otiose*. There was also the word *vaco* which symbolized emptiness, to be free from, and as Cicero used the word, to have occasion for something, or to have leisure. Our word vacation comes from the same root. The English phrase, "free living" could be represented by *licentia* which for Ovid implied dissoluteness or licentiousness.

The counterpart for the Greek term, *schole* was the Latin *schola* and, according to classical dictionaries, *ludus literarum* and *ludus discendi* literally meant to be free of books. Later, schola was to become associated with a sect of scholars or disciples, and thus the word discipline referred to activities at *schola*. In this sense, learning and scholarship were representative of leisure as well as the absence of any legal occupation. Much later, *schola* came to indicate a place where learned lectures and discussions took place, where disciplines were undertaken as studies. For some time after Greece was conquered by Rome, young Roman patricians were sent to Athens for schooling, and *ludus* (play) became a referent for schooling and learning. Hence we find our word campus to mean playground.

Connotations, both Latin and Greek, related to leisure were linked closely to education or learning. Contemplation or reflection could take place only when a condition of leisure was experienced. Leisure could not be forced, it could not occur under servitude, it was a non-materialistic and non-business like condition and it was opportunity for knowledge and learning. *Artes liberales* has the meaning of leisure in the finest sense.

We must remember that Roman writers such as Ovid, Seneca, Virgil, and Cicero were profoundly influenced by Greek culture, and therefore reflect a selective point of view. Their philosophies do not necessarily reflect the thinking of either the populace or the ruling classes. It was after disintegration of the Roman Empire that *otium* was considered circumspect in terms of Christian moral codes. Christian writers had witnessed license within leisure and condemned festivals and spectacles during the waning years of Roman civilization. On the other hand, *otium* was to fuse with the contemplative life within monastaries and continued to have an association with learning. Leisure was strictly controlled within monastic life and the doctrine of work was to become associated with cleansing of the spirit.

Centuries later, the economist Thorstein Veblen attached to leisure the notions of free time and economic advantage characteristic of what he termed the "leisure class."[8] From this disclosure, considered a classic especially among sociologists, Veblen left his mark on our thinking. At this juncture, connotations of leisure became associated with free time, unproductiveness and absence of necessity to work, in fact even an unwillingness to work. Many became disdainful of the wealthy who had freedom from maintenance necessities, a popularized notion not unlike that held by Puritans of New England. It may well have been, as Hall suggested, that opposition to pursuits of the wealthy was not so much that the pursuits themselves were evil, but that envy resulted in recriminative acts against the group that had opportunity to do many of the things the less advantaged would have liked to do.[9] Veblen's influence may be cause for the common definition of leisure, as found in Fairchild's Dictionary of Sociology,[10] in which leisure is defined as time remaining after the necessities of life are attended to; hence the notion that leisure as time is given a quantitative distinction. Semantic faithfulness to leisure as a term has been abrogated. Without removing from it the commodity connotation, investigations of leisure, recreation and play which employ time as a referent for leisure will continue to compound errors in reasoning. We should abandon the use of such phrases as "leisure time," "free time," "use leisure," and a host of other phrases propositional to quantities of time. I do not suggest that we eliminate use of the term leisure, but encourage us to recognize the meaning of the word. Time and leisure are anomalies, just as "good leisure" or "bad leisure" have become anachronism for today's students of leisure, recreation and play.

PLAY AS A SYMBOL

There is no single idea to be expressed by the word play, any more than for the words discussed previously, but the concept of play is far more universal than either leisure or recreation. While the other two terms applied only to humans, play extends to include animals. It is therefore instructive to keep in mind the associative juncture with the gambolling and frolicing of animals as well as of humankind.

The English word play etymologically came from the Anglo-Saxon *plega* and *plegan*, literally symbolizing play and *to* play. The word came from the commoners of Britain and not from the literature aristocracy, therefore it has no equivalent in French, Latin or Greek roots. While I know of no author that has undertaken an analysis of recreation and leisure to any exhaustive degree, Huizinga has provided us with a classic treatment of play.[11] My own research tends to support his contentions that the word, stemming from German idioms and fusing with English, provides us with many more referents than simply to move swiftly, frolic, or play a game for amusement. Etymologically, the word encompasses the whole spectrum of ways of playing, moods of playing and conditions of playing. Bringing together referents from a variety of languages, the case may be established that play has a focal meaning of a harmonious mix of sheer fantasy and powerful realism. A review of the 52 referents offered in standard English dictionaries supports the assertion.

There appears to be no generic term for play that represented all play and all forms of play. The basic Greek word was *paidia* (play), which referred to the play of children, with its roots in child *pias*. In literary usage, however, *paidia* had an extended meaning to represent the belief that one must be as a child to play. This influence is illustrated by Plato when he wrote, ". . .man is God's plaything, and that is the best part of him." He noted that, "Life must be lived as play, playing certain games, making sacrifices, singing and dancing, then man will be able to propitiate the gods. . ." In this discourse, Plato was referring to a much higher order of play than mere "child's play." We find the same extended usage for play in association with education, the term for which *paideia*, contains the root word for child. There is no doubt that the Greeks considered education as a life-long concern that was integrated into culture. According to some authorities the word *paideia* literally referred to culture.[12] It is apparent from Plato's writings that learning and play were bound together and that the former was a natural outgrowth of a play motive in life, that play extended from the child's level to the highest realms of aesthetic and religious experience. Symbols referring to play were for the most part derivations of *paidia*. Suffixes were to indicate playing, playful, plaything, playfulness, attendance at school, rearing or bringing up children, teaching and instruction, as well as to take part in festivals. Included also was playing as with music or a musical instrument. They had no word equivalent to our word game or sport. There was no morality attached to play and no antonym to connote "un-play." The conceptual as well as the linguistic evidence supports the premise that although they may not have understood play any better than we, they recognized it and nurtured it.

Not unlike the classical Greek, but more inclusive, we find that Latin had one universal word to express the whole realm of play: ludud. The word stems from *ludere*, of which *ludus* is the referent. Play was not drawn from the root for child, but rather from a breadth of concepts and at all ages and all levels of society. *Ludus* covered aspects of drama, gambling, games, festivals, athletics, school and learning, satire and comedy, as well as activities associated with parades and public celebrations for amusement. Other derivations cover the realm of unreality or conditions illusionary or fanciful. Cicero used the word *ludimagister* or schoolmaster, hence a direct link with education or learning.

The word *alea* represented a game of dice and later was to become a referent for chance or hazard. To play, or *ludo*, indicated that one could play in a variety of ways including dice, dance, for purposes of amusement, to banter in conversation, or deceive or delude another with tricks. In classical Latin, there was no word for game in the literal sense, only *ludus*. Game is of English origin as is the term sport. Although we loosely term festivals and circuses of Roman times as "public games" they are in Latin not games, but literally play.

Curiously, we find only faint tracings of the original, classical Latin *ludus* in the Romance languages. Our words ludicrous, ludibrious and other derivations carry overtones of play, but in a limited sense. Interestingly, we have a game called Ludo, which is related to parchisi and bears ancient relationship to backgammon. Backgammon is often given as the source for game, or originally gammon.

It seems that in our search for meaning of recreation, leisure and play, we find a central theme among characteristics indicated in the historical tracings of those languages most nearly associated with our own. This theme converges in play, the phenomenon most interesting to the researcher. It would appear then, that play is the experience attributed to recreation and sought from leisure. By systematized observation and autobiographic investigations, we are able to distinguish play from among other animal or human behaviors. When you and I play, we are conscious of the experience and are not self-deceiving. By focusing on play to understand concepts associated with leisure and recreation, there is no linguistic violence committed against the other terms. The major handicap that I have found is in derisive connotations of an emotive nature among those who fail to understand the universality and significance of play. I am convinced that these handicaps will pass as we become more oriented to a research approach.

Of the three terms, play is the most visually action oriented. It is the most universal among all peoples in the world, for all languages have a symbol for the behavior; no group of people has ignored it. If we accept the root meanings for work as in energy, we cannot rationally or logically accept work as the antithesis of play. In the literal sense, we can understand what should be meant by "Americans work hard at their play." That the word play comes through the language of common folk and subjected peoples helps explain emotive responses to the word by intellectuals and upper classes in England and thence America. It might be said that, historically, only the disenfranchized persons played (including animals and children) while the wealthy and powerful recreated and had leisure.

CONCLUSION

With this very cursory review of the evolution of terms it becomes apparent that we have been subjected to strangely contrived interpretations of leisure, recreation and play and, due to these inconsistencies, we have been thwarted from defining them logically, undermining the search for knowledge, scientific evidence, and clarity. Just as the word "sick" literally means something is not working, it has come to have specific referents to explain what is not working. The thrust of students of recreation must be to remove as much of the ambiguity as possible from whatever terms we apply to the phenomenon of play behavior. Would that reports, essays, or investigations in which any of the three terms are used allowed the reader to be privy to what was meant by them.

The causes or influences which have brought about such confusion in meaning are various. Not the least of our dilemmas stems from emotionally justifiable sources and poetic attitudes held by early leaders and founders of recreation as a social movement in America. In the early stages of any social movement, energizing emotional responses is more productive to draw attention than intellectual stimulation. Today, however, since recreation has gained acceptance as an institution in America, the time for dispassionate analysis is here.

In recreation, our laboratories are as broad as life itself and our tools an abundant collection of desires to invite, if not produce, happiness. In themselves, these laboratories and tools are not necessarily illigitimate and should not be degraded. But they are no longer adequate to give the field of recreation a sound foundation and body of knowledge on which to base a specialized discipline. Research as we know it, is dependent upon systematically obtained and objectively analyzed data which researchers anticipate might throw light upon some aspect of a certain phenomenon. If, as early leaders believed, recreation, leisure and play contribute to the fulfillment of life's purposes and increases appreciation of life processes, then the field is of infinite worth in a society fraught with uncertainties about the nature and purpose of man. In consequence of our acceptance of play as a phenomenon, we need to exert every effort to explain this phenomenon and attempt to understand its relationship to other human endeavors. This is case enough to support any attempt to unravel the warp and woof that others have woven for us and consider each and every thread. In light of the present, however, we must not only recognize the holes in others' symbolic systems of reasoning, but also in our own.

REFERENCES

1. Ogden, C. K. and Richards, P. A. *The Meaning of Meanings, A Study of the Significance of Language Upon Thought and of the Science of Symbolism*, New York: Harcourt Brace, 1923. p. 12.
2. Patrick, George T. W. *The Psychology of Relaxation*. Boston: Houghton Mifflin, 1916. p. 15.
3. Jaeger, Werner. *Paideia: The Ideals of Greek Culture*. (Gilbert Highet, Trans.) New York: Oxford University Press. 1939.
4. Peiper, Josef. *Leisure: The Basis of Culture*. New York: The New American Library, 1963.
5. deGrazia, Sebastian. *Of Time, Work and Leisure*. New York: The Twentieth Century Fund, 1962. p. 264.
6. Aristotle. *Metaphysics*, Chapter I.
7. Brumbaugh, Robert S. *Ancient Greek Gadgets and Machines*. New York: Thomas Cromwell Co., 1966. p. IX-X.
8. Veblen,, Thorstein. *The Theory of the Leisure Class*. New York: The Macmillan Company, 1899.
9. Hall, Thomas Cuming. *The Religious Background of American Culture*. Boston: Houghton Miffin, 1930. Chapter I.
10. Fairchild, Henry Pratt, (Ed.). *Dictionary of Sociology*. New York: Philosophical Library, 1944. p. 175.
11. Huizinga, Johan. *Homo Ludens: A Study of the Play Element in Culture*. Boston: Beacon Press, 1955. Chapter II.
12. Jaeger, *Op.Cit.*

Chapter Two

Perceptions of Time

John Farina

Time, as a concept, has caused insomnia to philosophers, artists, social and physical scientists from the beginnings of recorded thought. Yet for the ordinary man the concept itself presents no problem. He knows what time it is – he received a watch for Christmas. He knows when he starts and quits work – he punches in. He knows when the buses, trains and aircraft come and go. He has a fair sense of what sixty miles per hour means both objectively and subjectively. The calendar gives him some idea where he is on the continuum of history. On occasion he has too much time and, perhaps more frequently, he has not enough time.

It seems, however, that the most illuminating observations on time have been recorded not by common men but by uncommon men, not by scientists, social or physical, but by artists and philosophers.

Lao-Tse the Chinese mystic simply noted that, "Time is a state of the mind." Omar Kayam indicated the finality of the progress of time in his beautiful verse:

> The Moving finger writes, and having writ,
> Moves on; nor all your piety nor wit,
> Shall lure it back to cancel half a line,
> Nor all your tears wash out a word of it.

In a related vein Henry Dobson answers a rhetorical question regarding time. "Time goes you say? Oh no! Alas, time stays, *we* go."

Omar Ibn Al Halif notes that regardless of whether we go or time goes, time does not come back:

> "Four things come not back:
> The spoken word
> The sped arrow;
> Time past;
> The neglected opportunity."

Einstein speaking of visiting friends lingering (this is the artistic Einstein) states; "They remind me of time – always going but never gone."

The pace of time is beautifully contrasted by Shakespeare and Oscar Wilde speaking of its slowness and Herrick and Tennyson speaking of its inexorable speed.

Macbeth laments:

"Tomorrow and tomorrow and tomorrow,
Creeps in this petty pace from day to day,
to the last syllable of recorded time:"

And Oscar Wilde's sad, sad lines from the "Ballad of Reading Gaol":

"All that we know who lie in gaol,
Is that the walls are strong;
And every day is like a year,
A year whose days are long."

Contrast this tragic slowness of time with the light hearted challenge of the swiftness of time as presented by Herrick in his cavalier sonnet:

"Gather ye rosebuds while ye may,
Old Time is still a-flying,
And this same flower that smiles today,
Tomorrow will be dying."

Tennyson's *Ulysses,* referring to the swift passage of time, bemoans the brevity of opportunity that the limits of just one life time imposes:

"Life piled on life were all too little;
And of one for me – little remains,
And vile it were for some three suns,
To store and board myself:"

Marcel Proust lucidly explicates the relativity of time:

"The time which we have at our disposal every day is elastic;
the passions that we feel expand it, those that we inspire
contract it; and habit fills up what remains."

In this day of such concepts as space-time, time-motion and the theory of relativity, the most appealing literary reference to time comes from Lewis Carrol. In *Alice in Wonderland,* that rich source of creative thought, the Mad Hatter speaks with Alice:

"If you knew Time as well as I do you wouldn't talk about wasting it. It's him."

"I don't know what you mean," said Alice

"Of course you don't" the Hatter said, tossing his head contemptuously, "I dare say you never spoke to Time."

"Perhaps not," Alice cautiously replied; "but I know I have to beat time when I learn music."

"Ah! That accounts for it," said the Hatter. "He won't stand beating. Now if you only kept on good terms with him, he'd do almost anything you liked with the clock. For instance, suppose it were nine o'clock in the morning, just time to begin lessons: you'd only have to whisper a hint to Time and round goes the clock in a twinkling! Half-past one, time for dinner!"[1]

What, then, is this slippery concept time which has been so diversely described? A half facetious (and therefore more than half wise) definition states that: "Time is the diminution of the future by the accumulation of the past."[2]

Historically man has in fact judged time by periods or intervals. The earliest such intervals were marked by natural events such as: night and day; Spring, Summer, Winter; full moon, new moon; planting and harvest; etc. It is somewhat ironical that just as man achieved precision and accuracy in the measurement of intervals by the development of chronometers and by observations of the solar system, the concept of the relativity of time (subjectively recognized by artists throughout history) was proposed by physical scientists. It is therefore necessary to attempt to relate the views of the philosopher-artists on the one hand and the physicists on the other hand before we can present a comprehensive social concept of time.

While physicists have long used time as a basis for measuring motion – miles per hour for speeed of motion or feet per second as a measure of acceleration – they now view time as a concept without which motion and change cannot exist. Time by definition now represents rather than simply measures change or motion. Two or more differing and non-simultaneous images are required in the perception of motion; non-simultaneous means time. For the physicist, time is inextricably bound to change and motion. For the social scientist this change and motion is also seen in terms of the activity of people, of process, of social change and interchange, and of the interaction of people.

Yet the social concept of time seems inextricably bound to our value system. Thus George Woodcock, writing on the tyranny of the clock, suggests that the clock was the most important instrument of the Industrial Revolution.[3] George Soule, suggests that "The American Attitude" includes enslavement by and reverence to the clock. This he relates directly to economic attitudes characteristic of the Protestant Ethic.[4] Thus we spend, waste, exchange, buy, hoard, sell, forget, save, use, kill, structure, beat, and pass time. Time itself; marches, flies, plods, creeps, passes by, and escapes. All these terms relate directly to action and process. While to the economist and worker time is money to be saved, spent or wasted just as material goods, but time is also a dimension of activity, change, or process. In turn, time has several dimensions, including duration, intensity, extensity and quantity, and quality.

DIMENSIONS OF TIME

Duration

This attribute of time may be viewed as a continuum extending from the infinite past to the infinite future. The present is an infinitesimal moving interval proceeding at a regular and unfailing pace from the past to the future. Time as the accumulation of the past by the diminution of the future fits this notion beautifully. Thus duration is measurable in terms of the regular passage of the present along the continuum of duration. Indeed this measurement has been so operationally accurate and economically useful that it has been literally reified in terms of an interval scale – the clock. This approach to time synchronizes smoothly with the notion of money, also an interval scale, to represent materially the value of man's time. Thus a man might say, "My time is worth $10.00 an hour."

There is, however, a subjective aspect of duration. The psychologists point out that time which is occupied with much pleasant activity tends to seem shorter than time which is devoid of meaningful activity. For example: one hour of playing baseball seems shorter than one hour of waiting for a bus. In retrospect, however, the reverse is true. The time which was occupied seems longer on recall than does that time which was relatively unoccupied.

Intensity

Since time is inextricably bound up with action, the subjective experience of any given action over a period will vary in intensity. What we must recognize is that regardless of the precise indices of time we use we are in fact dealing with perceptions and feelings. De Grazia notes:

> "Thus by using a strictly quantitative assembly-line conception of time – time as a moving-belt of equal units – one ignores the significance of much activity. A moment of awe in religion, or ecstasy in love, or orgasm in intercourse, a decisive blow to an enemy, relief in a sneeze, or death in a fall is treated as equal to a moment of riding on a bus or shovelling coal or eating beans."[5]

We can note the same intensity differential almost daily: – bases full, two out, last of the ninth inning, the home team 2 runs behind, the count on the batter 3 and 2: – is a significantly more intense moment than a ninth inning with 2 out nobody on and the home team leading 10-0. The subjectivity is clear in this illustration for in addition to the different intensity potential which is inherent in the setting and structure of the activity there is a distinguishable subjective intensity difference for the pitcher and outfielder, for the team managers and the umpires, for the players and the spectators, and among the spectators depending upon their emotional commitment to either team or the amount of their bet on the outcome of the game.

Extensity and Quantity

Under this heading consideration is given to the extent to which identifiable blocks of time are available. For example that block of time called a life time has doubled in western civilization during the past 1,000 years. This greater life expectation is increasing in extensity, i.e. it is becoming available to more people in more areas of the world.

Again – in western civilization – that block of time we identify as "work-time" is becoming more brief and this shortening of work time as a quantity of time is becoming more extensive. The obvious corollary is that non-work time increased in direct proportion to the decrease in work time. Again, speaking in terms of extensity, if we view non-work time as being mostly leisure time (as some do) we can state that, in Western Civilization at least, this is the age of Mass Leisure. No longer, as in Veblen's day is leisure so restricted in extensity or so limited in quantity that we can speak of the leisure class. There is no longer a class identified by the fact that it alone has quantities of leisure.

Thus when we speak of time in terms of extensity we are referring to the extent of the distribution of identifiable blocks of time. When we speak of time as quantity, we are speaking of the variations in measurement of particular blocks of time. Thus the 35 hour work week refers to the quantitative aspect of work time. The availability of the thirty hour work week to a given number of office workers refers to the extensity of this particular block of time.

Quality

The quality of time refers to those conditions that make it possible to classify a period as: work, leisure, free time, idleness, etc. To a great extent the quality of time is culturally determined and inextricably dependent upon values. Most societies tend to dichotomize time and the tendency of western civilization is to do so in terms of work and non-work. To a large extent this particular dichotomy dates from the Industrial Revolution and is a reflection of the Protestant Ethic.

Other societies employ different dichotomies: e.g.

African Bushmen – Women's activities and Men's activities.
Plains Indians – Peace and War.
Baluchi of Pakistan – Obligatory and time of free will. Here the

emphasis and status is on the latter.

In one respect the Baluchi point of view is easier for us to understand than is the view of the Plains Indians; for, like us, they distinguish between an area of sober, mundane, practical activity and an area of play or free will.[6]

Work and Obligated Time

Work time in our society is that time required for maintenance of or for material improvement of self and dependents. It is literally time spent in return for money or its equivalent. It is time *spent* to fulfill the obligation of monetary reward. One man spends his money for another man's time while reciprocally the other man spends his time for another man's money.

Obligated time may be divided into two types although these are not always mutually exclusive:

1. Sleep and personal maintenance time. This would include time involved in personal toilet and for eating. Non-essential eating time can, however, on occasion be viewed as free time, leisure or recreation.
2. Non-work obligatory time. This involves time committed to one's primary role expectations outside the sphere of gainful employment. It is adequately illustrated by such characteristic suburban activities as upping and downing storm windows and screens, mowing the lawn, driving junior to his music lesson, the trip to the shopping centre and sundry obligatory "voluntary" activities. These may or may not be satisfying modes of behavior. No judgment is being passed on the value of these activities. For some they may challenge the mentality or spirit or simply be pleasant in themselves; for others they may be dull and "plonking."[7]

IDLENESS, RECREATION, FREE TIME, LEISURE

Idleness

In general use, idleness is a term of eprobrium although it can be an alternate for recreation, free time and leisure. It found wide currency following the Protestant Reformation when it was generally used in reference to non-workers. As recreation came to be viewed as a contributor to greater productivity, the term idleness was reserved for those non-workers who were not refreshing or recreating themselves for more efficient work. Today the term has lost currency outside puritan oriented religious groups.

All four of the terms listed above represent the non-work side of our time dichotomy. We must recognize, however, that leisure is not the antonym for work but rather is the positive counterpart. The opposite of work is unemployment.

Recreation

This term in our society has been implicitly identified with the work category of time although it is popularly believed to represent the non-work category of time. Professional recreation workers identify recreation as activity indulged in voluntarily for the satisfaction derived from the activity itself and leading to revitalization, or re-creation, of mind, body or spirit. In fact this is a limiting definition in terms of pre-determination as it is only by the result (re-vitalization) that recreation can be identified.

Nonetheless – our society assumes that certain types of activity are potentially recreative – music, sports, drama, cinema, social events, etc. Public, private and commercial organizations providing opportunities for these types of activities have proliferated in recent years. The question raised by the definition of recreation is: recreation or revitalization for what? Recreation promoted by business and industrial concerns, recreation as a medical prescription, and recreation as an adjunct to our educational system all emphasize the potential of such activities for revitalizing the individual so he can work more efficiently.

Will the role of leisure in relation to work undergo a basic change? Up to now our leisure as well as most other activities of our life has been work-oriented. Leisure is often thought of in terms of "recreation" –i.e., activities to be engaged in during non-work hours which will refresh or "recreate" the individual so that he may be a more effective worker upon his return to his job. Otherwise, it is regarded as idleness. With increasing leisure, will new types of pursuits emerge – goal-directed, useful, long-term, satisfying in nature – around which man may also focus his energies and ambitions? Will work once again in human history become a means to other ends – as visualized in Thomas More's *Utopia* – rather than an end in itself.[8]

Free Time

In general usage free time is considered as residual time after we take account of work-time, sleep-time and time for personal care. More precisely, free time may be considered as that time during which one is relatively free of primary role expectations. This approach ties the concept of free time into the theoretical framework of role theory.

It derives from the notion that free time is time which is not restricted by occupational and family duties and obligations. Other obligations and duties then are considered secondary to an individual's family and occupational roles. Indeed occupational role may be considered as subsidiary to family role or as a specific aspect of that central role. Free time, then, is time during which one is relatively free of economic, social, or physical restriction or compulsion.

As with duration, free time and obligatory time can be conceived as the extremes of a continuum. Thus we may view time as relatively free or relatively obligatory. In terms of this conceptualization, absolutely free time is an ideal and probably unattainable.

Free time allows for relatively preferential behavior while obligatory time involves the expectation of a particular kind of behavior. During obligatory time an individual acts with reference to the norms and primary expectations of his occupational and family roles. While role expectation is not absent in free time there is not the same intensity of obligation to assume specific role behavior. If obligations to assume specific roles or to meet specific role expectations are present then the time during which such a role is performed is less free than when such obligations do not exist. During free time there is a greater opportunity for a person to select from a wide range of choices of behavior as he or she may pursue goals not necessarily related to economic or family expectations. It must be recognized that the individual is seldom, if ever, free of structural expectations. During free time he comes under the pressure of different norms which might be quite as restrictive as those operating during obligatory time.

Free time then presents the opportunity to exercise preferential behavior. The range and quality of choice may vary considerably in terms of the quantity and quality of time available. There is a difference in the quality of behavioral opportunity after ten hours of strenuous work and after eight hours of refreshing sleep. Also there is a great difference in the range of choice offered during a 15 minute free period at a factory ten miles from home and a free afternoon at a summer resort.

Leisure

Leisure, as opposed to recreation, does not describe activities and as opposed to free time is not time. The term "leisure time" as differing from "leisure" describes a particular type of time. On this basis *leisure* should perhaps be more logically compared with *freedom,* i.e. the two modifiers in the terms "free time" and "leisure time" warrant comparison.

Leisure has become a recent concern of the modern social science scholar whereas previously it was primarily the domain of the philosopher. We are not, however, dealing with a new concept but rather with a reconceptualization of a construct which has been a subject of philosophic discussion since the Golden Age of Greece. Most discussions of leisure take Aristotle's ideas as the point of departure.

Aristotle viewed leisure as, "a condition or state, the state of being free from the necessity to labor."[9] On occasion he used the term in such a manner as to suggest that it involved a time element, that is, the time during which one was in the particular condition or state referred to as leisure. The essential terms in this definition are "freedom" and "necessity." We must not be misled into believing that labor, in the sense of strenuous physical activity, is excluded from Aristotle's notion of leisure. What is excluded is the *necessity* or obligation to labor.

It must be noted, however, that freedom from the opportunity to labor does not constitute leisure if the necessity to labor is present. Thus the unemployed do not necessarily have leisure.

Pieper, commenting on Aristotle's view noted: "The provision of an external opportunity to leisure is not enough; it can only be fruitful if man himself is capable of leisure and can as we say occupy his leisure."[10] This suggests a value placed on the manner in which leisure is occupied: i.e. "fruitfully." Leisure thus has a positive connotation. If a man is free from the necessity to labor and does not employ himself "fruitfully" he is more likely referred to as idle than as at leisure.

A definition of leisure devoid of value is that offered by the Oxford English Dictionary: "The state of having time at one's disposal; time which one can spend as one pleases; free or unoccupied time."[11] This definition includes the notion of leisure as a state and of its freedom. It adds, however, the non-judgmental element of choice of use of time without specifying that the choice must be "fruitful" in order to qualify as leisure.

Thus we find a consensus that leisure is characterized by freedom, a sense of freedom that is in the mind of man as differing from environmental or socially determined freedom. This freedom can be considered an opportunity to act as one pleases with the limits imposed by environment and social context. The idea that the action must be "fruitful" appears too judgmental and value oriented to be an essential aspect of the concept. In given circumstances, if we leave the judgment of leisure to criteria external to the concept, then we may speak of fruitful or non-fruitful leisure according to context.

When we divest the view of Aristotle and its restatement by Pieper of the value element, there remains the clear implication that activity is an aspect of leisure. The time during which one is in the state of leisure must be "occupied."

This occupation of time may include overt activity and also such "leisurely" pursuits as counting clouds on a sunny afternoon, or quiet meditation, or contemplation, Indeed Pieper considers the notion of non-activity an essential of leisure.

> "Leisure is a form of silence, of that silence which is the prerequisite of the apprehension of reality: only the silent hear and those who do not remain silent do not hear. Silence, as it is used in this context, does not mean 'dumbness' or 'noiselessness'; it means more nearly that the soul's power to 'answer' to the reality of the world is left undisturbed. For leisure is a receptive attitude of mind, a contemplative attitude, and it is not only the occasion but also the capacity for steeping oneself in the whole of creation."[12]

Pieper adds that this ideal state of leisure contributes to happiness. The element of freedom as a precondition to leisure is explicated by Kaplan[14] in terms of social role obligations. He suggests that during leisure a man can choose to assume obligations "voluntarily, and with pleasanter expectations than, for example, going to work on January 2 to which he is formally committed for a long period of time."[13] Our conceptualization of free time borrows the notion of freedom from social role obligation. We are, however, impressed with de Grazia's concern regarding the loss of free time by increasing family role expectations.[14] Our notion of leisure, however, goes further. Leisure is that time when one is free from the necessity of fulfilling primary role expectations. This means time not restricted by the demands of occupational and family duties and obligations. Clearly this concept does not limit leisure to free time.

It is possible to achieve leisure within the context of primary role obligation if the need or demand to act in a particular manner is not present. Thus a professional man may choose an activity while performing his professional role which is not necessary or demanded of him at that time. A worker on an assembly line lacks this choice. Similarly a father may feel obliged to play ball with his son, which we would consider non-leisure, or he may choose to join his wife on the patio for a gin and tonic which would be leisure. The differentiating factors are the element of necessity and the element of freedom of choice.

Man is faced with an ever increasing block of time which is potentially free. Whether he keeps it free and is able to free himself to enjoy leisure is the challenge of our age. Meeting this challenge will not be facilitated by simplistic and often contradictory notions of time, of leisure, and of freedom. Conceptual clarity is essential in the use of designations. Games, play, idleness, contemplation, leisure, recreation, sports and cultural activities are clearly related terms. Yet just as clearly they are not synonymous or interchangeable when we want words to work with the precise denotations that are essential to knowledge building.

A more hopeful factor that might contribute to meeting the challenge is how man chooses to occupy his ever increasing potential inherent in free time. In a society of increasing unemployment, rapid replacement of workers by automation, earlier retirement, later entry to the work force, innumerable make-work jobs, and increasing income maintenance programs, it seems ridiculous to be concerned with full employment. Rather, maximum non-employment might be a more reasonable goal for a post industrial society. Certainly, this would satisfy an essential precondition to a leisure society and free man's potential to occupy his time constructively and productively in terms of the quality of life. Towards this end, *time* is of the essence.

REFERENCES

1. Carroll, Lewis. *Alice's Adventures in Wonderland.* New York: The Modern Library, 1920, p. 94.
2. Author unknown.
3. Cited in: Kaplan, Max. *Leisure in America: A Social Inquiry.* New York: John Wiley and Sons, 1960. p. 265.
4. Soule, George. "The Economics of Leisure." *The Annals of the American Academy of Political and Social Science,* (September, 1957). pp. 16-24.
5. de Grazia, Sebastian. "How People Spend Their Time." In: Kleemeier, Robert W. (Ed.). *Aging and Leisure.* New York: Oxford University Press, 1960. p. 142-43.
6. Donahue, Wilma, et.al. (Eds.) *Free Time.* Ann Arbor, Michigan: University of Michigan Press, 1958. p. 10-11.
7. A favorite Stephen Potter word meaning just what it sounds like.
8. Donahue, *Op. Cit.* p. 130.
9. de Grazia, Sebastian. *Of Time, Work, and Leisure.* New York: The Twentieth Century Fund, 1960. p. 11.
10. Pieper, Joseph. *Leisure: The Basis of Culture.* New York: Pantheon Books, 1952. p. 71.
11. *Oxford English Dictionary.* Toronto: Leland Publishing Company, 1957.
12. Pieper. *Op. Cit.* p. 52.
13. Kaplan. *Op Cit.* p. 23.
14. de Grazia. *Op. Cit.* Chapter III.

Chapter Three

Leisure and Freedom Re-examined

Francis J. Bregha

In reviewing some current definitions of leisure, one finds that many link leisure with freedom, even if only in the form of "free time." Two examples will suffice. De Grazia describes leisure as "the state of being free from the necessity to labor."[1] Neulinger affirms: "Leisure has one and only one essential criterion, and that is the condition of perceived freedom."[2]

Whether freedom is analyzed as an actual state of being or as a perception by an individual or a group, as suggested by Neulinger, it is evident that for many conceptual thinkers in our field, there is a profound and intimate relationship between leisure and freedom. How free do we need to be to enjoy leisure? Is professional intervention in leisure services enhanced or limited by the ethos of freedom? Does freedom, in fact, mean the ability of doing what one wants to do when one wants to? And if so, is leisure one of several possible outcomes of such an ability? Where do such questions lead us?

At this point, a word of caution: The purpose of this chapter is to raise questions more than to suggest answers. It is quite true that this old philosophical method of inquiry is rather unfashionable in our technological age in which answers have market value whereas questions tend to irritate. Moreover, we live at a time in which most believe that there must be an answer to everything, the growing evidence to the contrary notwithstanding. Therefore, this text should be read as an invitation to stop, to think, even to look into our own spiritual mirror and to reflect on the questions and answers that we find there.

It is a generally accepted belief that, as children, we first discover freedom, its delights and dangers, in playing. As formal education gradually replaces play, we all experience constraints, some of us rebelling, some adapting. Our freedom, as grasped and developed in childhood, is beginning a long process of adjustment that will last our entire life. But it is particularly in the world of modern work that the freedom of most of us will be subjected to its most severe restrictions. Whether because of standardization and uniformization of both products and production or whether because of the complex hierarchies of our bureaucracies, we can seldom, if ever, do what we would like. There is little place for a free, creative act, except perhaps one that brings in a new routine. Opportunity to do that is reserved for only a few. Hence, some people are actually unlearning the little freedom that may have survived their preparation for the working place. Freedom, like anything that is not exercised, atrophies. In Max Weber's words, "one does not work to live, one lives to work."[3] Marx spoke of alienation and Pieper brilliantly exposed the modern situation in *Leisure: The Basis of Culture.*[4] Finally, in old age many of us fall victim to institutional confinement, poverty or unkindly restrictive expectations of the younger generation. By that time, freedom may not have survived, even in memory or dreams.

If leisure and freedom are as closely related as current descriptions suggest, how can leisure survive whenever freedom is progressively curtailed, shrinking from birth to death? There is no freedom and therefore no leisure for those subjected to a routine, be it at work or elsewhere. Nor is there leisure for a prisoner, whether of conventions, social pressures or exhausted imagination. There is no leisure for anyone who has not maintained his freedom. Would, therefore, the maintenance of freedom throughout our lifetime not be the first and most important precondition of leisure; a sine qua non for its successful practice? Similarly, does such reasoning not suggest that, to be a professional in leisure services, means, among other things, the urgent need for helping people to rediscover their freedom, to define and maintain it? Surely a noble task, yet also one that is bound to lead to confusion if performed by those who are not free themselves.

ABILITY TO EXPERIENCE LEISURE

Going back to our initial question, whether leisure be the outcome of an ability to do what one wants to in a specific situation, one discerns the pivotal importance of the term "ability." It means several things: firstly, the possession of those qualities that enter into being able to do what one wants, essentially knowledge to compare options and then physical and spiritual capability to act on them; secondly, it suggests the availability of means required by such an option; thirdly, it connotes power and strength necessary for acting at all and living with the outcome of our own actions.

Let us look more closely at all three. Firstly, the possession of qualities that enter into being able to choose what one wants to do includes more than information on what is available or permissible. Something deeper is required: the knowledge of oneself as well as of one's milieu; the knowledge of what is good and what is wrong; the knowledge of various possibilities and of their consequences. Indeed, were such knowledge absent, then every choice would of necessity be a blind one, contradicting the very ability that is required. Thus leisure is linked to knowledge and to wisdom, both of which form part of the ability to choose with intelligence and responsibility. Furthermore, this analysis suggests the need of education for leisure. Throughout history we have increasingly accepted education for work: in fact, the working force in our century is vastly better prepared, more educated for work than ever before. Can humanity be left to its own devices in regard to leisure if we wish to occupy our leisure with intelligence and responsibility?

Secondly, there is the question of means. Throughout history, wealth was perceived as leading to leisure. The poor classes were excluded. Property and leisure went hand in hand, as noted in the expression "the leisure class." Leaving aside, then, the necessity for providing means to everyone who aspires to leisure, still a considerable undertaking even in our prosperous society, there remains the problem of our ability to use available means effectively and responsibly. The presence of means, however, is not sufficient. On top of it, man must have mastery over the means that his concept of leisure demands. Hence leisure cannot exist without training, apprenticeship, or whatever form of preparation the mastery over means may call for. Nor can it exist without a socially conscious management of means, especially for their conservation.

Thirdly, the ability to do what one wants is related to power and strength to act. Since few forms of leisure, except contemplation, can be practiced without at least passive consent of our neighbors or civic authorities, the ability we are seeking here addresses itself to the need for such power arrangements that permit the seeker to proceed without fear or punishment. The incapacity to enjoy leisure may in many instances be due to the constant pressures exercised by modern states and their authoritarian institutional structures upon individuals, especially if those states are totalitarian or collectivist in character. Therefore, beyond knowledge, both practical and ethical, beyond accessibility to means and mastery over them, the ability that gives birth to leisure must also be based upon our secure power and strength to enjoy leisure in peace.

Assuming for a moment that such an ability can be developed and maintained through our lives, a phenomenon of extreme rarity in all history, what are the critical points at which our present world threatens to separate leisure from its roots in individual freedom? this is the most difficult part of our analysis as it forces us to reach beyond symbols with which we are increasingly bombarded in our communications-mad society, and to pierce through the thousand and one mirrors used by politicians, salesmen and propagandists of all hues to disorient us.

MANIPULATION AND LEISURE

The most obvious threat to leisure comes from manipulation of any kind, the problem being simply that few people know how much they are being manipulated. Many people do not know what they want. Quite practically, they want what they know – or what someone else shows or tells them. Although education may be presented sometime as an attempt to "draw out" the best that there is in us, in its actual form of schooling, training, or apprenticeship it clearly implies the transmitting of knowledge and skills from the outside to a more or less willing and ready learner.

Our economy may be painted in the bucolic colors of a free market in which free agents freely compete for the best supply-demand interaction – yet a moment of observation shows the ruthless manipulation of everyone by everyone else, the weakest, i.e. the poor, the unemployed, the consumers, holding the short end of the stick while the strongest, i.e. vertically integrated monopolies, are getting richer. One does not need to study Galbraith; personal experience is sufficient to show that, in our economy, there is little place for leisure rooted in freedom. In fact, all known economic systems use blatant manipulation to achieve their ends.

In politics, of course, manipulation parades as propaganda, lobbying, pressure groups and, in extreme cases, as brainwashing or psychiatric treatment. At a more subtle level, none of us is exempt from some degree of political manipulation since we all deal in power relationships in our daily lives. There is no reason to think that leisure services are less receptive to bribery by politicians than other services, or that leisure professionals would confuse persons and principles or policy and expediency less frequently than anyone else. The freedom to act politically in Canada and the United States often reduces itself to biased reacting, to voting against rather than for something, to fighting first for self-interest and only second for common good. In short, manipulation in politics is easy because we offer it great opportunity and expect, even perversely enjoy, being manipulated by our leaders.

Manipulation, besides going unrecognized fully by many, presents, the further threat of succeeding so well in some instances that the Orwellian 1984 is suddenly perceived as having arrived prematurely. "War is Peace," "Freedom is Slavery," and the brainwashed public is no longer able to discern even the sharpest value opposites. Manipulation, of course, thrives on gullibility and aims at the total elimination of all freedom, hence of all leisure, however cleverly labeled in the new doublespeak. The emergence of religious and ideological cults of exotic nature, effectively enslaving their adherents in a web of preposterous and sometimes dangerous beliefs; the amazing scope of phony commercial and financial operations; the readiness to accept as true the most clearly distorted news stories – an acquired taste to which a whole new industry is catering – are only a few current examples of the extreme situations created by successful manipulation in our midst.

We can now perceive the importance of what used to be called "inner strength," "independent judgement," even "character" before our times produced more ambiguous terms. These qualities constitute our defense against manipulation. Hence the ability to be independent, self-sufficient in judgement and its expression, is a fundamental condition of both freedom and leisure.

Beyond the massive manipulation by major forces to which we are subjected as learners of life, as consumers and as citizens, a variety of threats can make enjoyment of leisure problematic or impossible. A host of them reside actually in our very minds. Feelings of guilt, especially when not working at something useful, fears reflecting religious or moral norms that appear contradicting what we wish to do, even the prosaic lack of imagination that instead of leisure in freedom generates idleness in boredom. These obstacles are as difficult to overcome as the more visible ones, created by explicit manipulation. Yet, no one is free who fears freedom; no one can be at leisure who feels guilty before an offered opportunity. The Greek advice of knowing oneself first of all remains valid today since the true independence needed for satisfying pursuit of leisure can never be achieved unless we get rid of what distorts us from within. Thus leisure frequently has to take the form of liberation, starting inside oneself.

Finally, environmental factors have to be considered. In a city where there are insecurity, noise, pollution of all sorts and hectic activity in all public places, leisure will be difficult, if not impossible, as no one can be at one with oneself in such conditions. Nor will a sensitive human being be able to enjoy leisure wherever nature is destroyed, exploited and beauty denied by functional utilitarism. This describes so many of our modern surroundings that one can well raise the question: What chance for leisure here? There may be freedom though that freedom may only mean freedom to adapt or undertake the titanic task of environmental change. There may be "leisure activities" and "leisure facilities" – and yet, little leisure can ever be experienced there. It is so because true leisure, like true freedom, can exist only in peace, in peace with oneself but also with one's surrounding.

LEISURE: AN IMPOSSIBLE GOAL?

The picture of leisure that is emerging from this discussion shows how difficult, fragile, almost impossible leisure is for modern man. Much less free than superficially believed, much more manipulated than publicly admitted, much less educated than generally thought, modern man appears to be lacking precisely those components of leisure that make it such an exacting state of being: self-knowledge and inner peace. Yet, were these two qualities added to those that we have identified as the basis of freedom, leisure would still not automatically follow. Bordom could still be with us, because leisure, to express freedom, requires choice; choice, in turn, requires awareness of preferences, hence a sense of direction, ultimately a goal. In other terms, leisure is as much freedom *to* something as it is freedom *from* something. Goalless leisure, then, is a contradiction which illustrates, even in our times, the differences between leisure and idleness.

These goals, of course, can be many. It is precisely the essence of leisure that they be almost without number since they define what is most personal, most unique in every one of us. At the same time, one suspects that these unique goals are not equal – in quality, morality or social relevence. Nor are they defined out of a vacuum. Besides individual predispositions, they reflect cultural influences and values constantly being absorbed and transformed. Leisure goals thus illustrate a state of a society, probably better than any other single indicator. Obversely, the state of a society is perhaps the greatest determining factor in shaping the leisure goals of its members. Using other terms: how well freedom fares in a given society will be the first measure of leisure opportunities in it.

One indirect result is that this diversity of leisure goals makes leisure as a social phenomenon so hard to grasp, to analyze and to classify. The study of commonalities leads to the development of theories – the study of unique particularities tends to resist scientific approach. Therefore, those social sciences that deal with leisure should not be astonished when their attempts at predicting or controlling, valid as these goals may be in regard to other phenomena, produce quite problematic results.

Much more important, though, is the inability of modern man to conceive worthwhile goals for himself. And yet, without a goal, he is condemned to an unleisurely life. As abhorrent as such a sentence might be to him, he falls victim to the all pervasive sickness of our times: the confusion of means and ends.

He starts with viewing education as a means to obtaining a job, then sees a job as means to securing a livelihood, considers work as means to getting rich, uses money as means to buy what he deems necessary or what would give him status and, finally, even that hardly acquired status becomes means to differentiating himself, a means to establishing his identity. Such a man lives in the world of means. There are no ends in his life that he does not use as means to still other ends and so, in growing confusion, his life results in what a poet once quite rightly described as "one damn thing after another."

Leisure, like freedom, is an end in itself. If perceived as means, it should be called recreation – a worthwhile but quite utilitarian concept. We do not occupy our leisure in order to become healthier or more productive. Leisure allows us to be free, to be what we want to be. Hence the importance of examining our own thoughts, desires and hopes and reflecting whether our lifestyle translates them or not into a coherent, meaningful life: an enterprise in which leisure counselling and education for leisure ought to play a role. The invitation to look into a spiritual mirror, issued at the beginning of this essay, is in fact a daily challenge. The questions that we shall find there, may not be answered immediately or by our effort alone. We need others as others need us. Beyond individual answers, we require societal ones and the understanding of their meaning. In this perspective, leisure professionals are both interpreters and builders of their communities.

It is for this reason that Aristotle's remark in his *Politics* remains so pertinent: "That is the principal point: with what kind of activity is man to occupy his leisure."[5] He, over 2,000 years ago, as well as Pieper more recently, saw that activity related to divine worship. Leisure was part of celebrating God, exactly as Psalm LXV, II has it: "Have leisure and know that I am God."

This view is no longer shared by most contemporary analysts of leisure. Leisure's link to religion has been gradually weakened as religious festivities, rites and feasts occupy less and less of a place in our lives. Instead, modern technology has multiplied the means available for the pursuit of secular leisure while saying very little about their value or moral direction. It should be clear that we are possibly the first generation that faces a peculiar problem in regard to our leisure. As long as leisure found its origin in God and its expression in partaking in worship, its morality was beyond reproach. Now that a divorce has taken place and leisure is linked to freedom rather than to God, a vast question mark as to its ultimate purpose is before us. Who is to guide us through the maze of good and evil now that God is absent and freedom is perceived in many ways? This brings us back to the dichotomy of freedom *from* and freedom *to*. Historically, we have found it easier to define and to fight for freedom *from.* Although this process is far from finished in most of the world, in Canada and the United States the emphasis is slowly shifting towards the consideration of freedom *to*. Since the 1960's, significant sections of our population, particularly women, youth and some minority groups have raised new questions that can be answered only in terms of freedom *to* – hence the considerable increase in conflicts over values. And also, therefore, such an explosion of new, morally untested leisure pursuits.

Is one type of leisure activity as good as any other? Are we to assume that, since leisure is the highest expression of our freedom and freedom, in turn, thrives best in our leisure time, there is not – there cannot be – an ethical conflict? Are leisure and freedom so good per se, in their essence, that neither can give birth to evil, under any circumstances? These questions flow naturally from linking leisure with freedom and necessarily lead into an examination of the moral dimensions of leisure. To say that modern leisure derives its meaning from personal self-fulfillment reached in various ways during free time is clearly no longer sufficient. All of us who in the past have been tempted into perceiving the ultimate goal of leisure in the Maslowian concept of self-actualization surely realize by now that such a self-actualization cannot take place in a moral vacuum. The ethics of leisure, including the reconciliation of individual and collective goals within a coherent value system, thus form part and parcel of every serious inquiry into the nature of our freedom.

To sum up: leisure undoubtedly is the most precious and also most fragile expression of our freedom. Freedom remains leisure's pre-condition, its rewards being that freedom can flower best in pursuits that are leisurely. Whereas the maintenance of freedom becomes, then, our constant task and the defining of freedom *to* our greatest challenge, leisure itself still depends as much on the knowledge and wisdom entering into our options, on our ability to choose goals that will bring use happiness, on our inner strength and independence that affirm our unique character, and finally on an environment that is conducive to leisure because it offers peace, per chance beauty and quiet enjoyment.

REFERENCES

1. DeGrazia, Sebastien. *Of Time, Work and Leisure.* New York: The Twentieth Century Fund, 1962. pp. 13-14.
2. Neulinger, John. *The Psychology of Leisure.* Springfield, Illinois: Charles C. Thomas, 1974. p. 15.
3. Cited in Joseph Pieper. *Leisure: The Basis of Culture.* (Tr. by Alexander Dru). New York: Pantheon Books, Inc., 1952. p. 20.
4. *Ibid.*
5. Cited in *Ibid.*, p. 55.

Chapter Four

If Leisure is to Matter

Thomas L. Goodale

Judging from the number of new periodicals with "leisure" in the title, or the pervasive use of the term in the literature and in conversation, or the jargon of leisure studies, leisure education, leisure research, leisure counseling, leisure services, etc., we are moving into the age of leisure at last. Unfortunately, that would be a hasty judgement because leisure is more common in our literature than in our lives and because the term leisure is usually used as little more than a substitute for words we have grown tired of.

Frequently, leisure is used where recreation would serve better; as in the phrase leisure services. Often leisure means no more than free time; as in the phrase leisure time. In addition, the term has been resurrected from antiquity to refer to a state or condition; that is, where one is at. When one is at leisure one is in a relaxed, contemplative condition. If we convey no more than one of these meanings when we say leisure, then we burden ourselves with being concerned about what is, per se, not very important. If this is all we mean, then leisure doesn't matter – not yet.

MISAPPROPRIATING ARISTOTLE'S THOUGHT

There is deeper meaning which does not come to the surface in most talk and writing about leisure. To find it requires a more careful examination of Aristotle's thought, and the thoughts of those like Pieper[1] and de Grazia[2] who have tried to guide us to and through Aristotle's philosophy. With few exceptions, our encounters with Aristotle's thought, as interpreted by many of those writing about leisure, are not very satisfying. Leisure seems simple, impossible, and unrelated to our lives. There is too little congruence between what we read and hear of it and what we experience everyday.

Seldom do we reflect on the complexity and subtlety of philosophical thought. Understanding Aristotle's writings is at best difficult. His style, as his subject, does not readily yield understanding. Too, there are few among us who read him in the original. Rather, what we read are translations, of which there are many, and notes and interpretations, also in great number. Indeed, Aristotle spawned an industry, as the shelves of any respectable library attest. Obviously, there are differences in the translations, notes, and interpretations. As a simple example, depending on the translation, Aristotle wrote either "one swallow makes not a summer" or "one swallow makes not a spring." The message, if not the season, is of great importance to us as is noted later. Surely, "leisure" is a much more complex notion than spring or summer. In fact, one of the better known translators, Benjamin Jowett, notes that Aristotle's "leisure" is "one of the most difficult notions to translate into English words and modes of thought."[3]

Aristotle was a product of a milieu so foreign to ours as to seriously tax our ability to comprehend. Consequently, it seems folly to wrench small bits of his writings from their context, transport them over twenty-three centuries, and set them down in an inhospitable place. This is especially hazardous as it is frequently noted that in Aristotle's thought, the existing order – that is what was – was an essential element in his thinking about what ought to be. The result is that there is much in Aristotle's writing that, quite simply, doesn't fit our time at all, some notions about women, friendship and love, slavery and citizenship, for example. He argues that friendship is a relationship between men exclusively, since it requires awareness and return of mutual affection. In relations between unequals, such as rulers and subjects or men and women, "the more useful" of the two should receive more love than *he* gives."[4] And he writes, "Domestic authority is the best model for aristocracy, for the authority of the husband is founded on the superiority of his abilities and virtues."[5] One of Aristotle's contemporaries, a man named Aleman, in wishing to compliment some girls, could find no other way to refer to them except as "female boyfriends."[6] In Aristotle's Greece, women were simply not men's equals.

But all men were not equal either. Clearly leisure was not possible for all; or even many. As is widely known, Aristotle's concept of leisure, indeed many argue Greek civilization itself, was built on the backs of slaves. In most Greek cities of the time, slaves, plus a few thousand non-voting metics and freemen, out-numbered citizens by ratios varying between 4:1 and 20:1.

In the context of the times, that posed no ethical dilemma. Citizens, in order to have time for government, war, literature, and philosophy, must have someone attend to their material concerns. To have leisure, one must be free from economic tasks. It is not necessary to be wealthy, but one must have means. Aristotle, if anything, was a preacher of moderation. To him slaves were animate tools, and he foresaw the machine age in recognizing inanimate slaves. He was, by all accounts, good to his slaves and to his women. But leisure was not for them; it was only for citizens. "Because mechanics and laborers cannot practice virtue while leading the life of mechanics and laborers they will not be included in the category of citizens."[7] Further, while slaves could enjoy "inferior pleasures," . . . "who will ascribe the happiness of a man to him who by his character or condition, is disqualified from manly pursuits?"[8]

THE IMPORTANCE OF WORKING WELL

In the literature about recreation and leisure, one brief passage from Aristotle's voluminous writings is frequently cited. It is from *Politics, Book VII.*

> Nature herself . . . requires that we should be able not only to work well, but to use leisure well; for as I must repeat once again, the first principle of all action is leisure. Both are required but leisure is better than occupation and is its end.[9]

Translators differ. Elsewhere one finds:

> Nature requires not only that we should be properly employed, but that we should be able to enjoy our leisure in an honorable way.[10]

There is agreement, however, that being able to work well, or to be properly employed is so evident as to be a foregone conclusion. Although that part of the passage is often neglected in the recreation and leisure literature, we are reminded of it in so many other ways.

It is said, for example, that Aristotle died of a stomach ailment aggrevated by overwork." Pieper, in referring to Aristotle's maxim, "we are unleisurely in order to have leisure," writes that the maxim is more weighty because Aristotle was, " . . . a cool-headed workaday realist."[12] Further, there is no mistaking the closing verses of Genesis, Chapter I and the opening verses of Chapter II. On the sixth day God reviewed his work and saw that it was good; on the seventh day, he rested from his work. Too, it seems clear that Jesus was proud of the fact that he could make a table because he was a carpenter.[13]

In *Politics, Book X,* Aristotle notes the role of rest and recreation. They are good, but not the highest good.

> Happiness then, cannot consist in mere recreative pastime; for it is absurd to think that all our serious exertions and strenuous labors

should terminate in so frivolous an end. We do not labor that we may be idle, but, as Anarchis justly said, we are idle that we may labor with more effect; . . . The weakness of human nature requires frequent remissions of energy; but these rests and pauses are only the better to prepare us for enjoying the pleasures of activity. The amusements of life, therefore, are but preludes to its business, the place of which they cannot possibly supply; and its happiness, because its business, consisting of the exercise of those virtuous energies which constitute the worth and dignity of our nature.[14]

Rest and amusement are preludes to, and cannot replace business or happiness, the latter flowing from the former if by business we understand the exercise of virtuous energies.

VIRTUE, ETHICS AND LEISURE

Matters of virtue are found throughout Aristotle's *Politics*. This is so because Aristotle wrote *Politics* in conjunction with *Ethics*. He considered them part of one work. It is in *Ethics* that he identifies happiness as the highest good, it being an end in itself. And the wellspring of happiness is virtue. Happiness doesn't come cheap; one has to be virtuous. That is the often repreated message of *Nicomachean Ethics;* happiness derives from a lifetime of virtue.

> The proper good of man consists then in virtuous energies, that is in the exercise of virtue continued through life; for one swallow makes not a summer; neither does one day, or a short time constitute happiness . . . The multitude, indeed, pursue different pleasures, because they do not rightly apprehend in what true pleasure consists. But pleasure, strictly so called, is the delight of a virtuous man whose life needs not an appendage of false joys, containing the perennial spring of true pleasure in itself . . . In the estimation of a wise man, virtue is pleasant because it is honorable and good; his happiness is one regular whole; not broken and disjointed.[15]

Of course, Aristotle did note that leisure was better than work, or at least better than work done by non-citizens, and he clearly linked leisure with the contemplative life but, again, in far more complex ways than we generally understand, because contemplation was inextricably bound to the divine in man; to the somehow transcendent soul. Difficult a time as scholars have had with the notion of leisure, it is as nothing compared to this. For Aristotle's notion of contemplation was linked to his notion of God and God's own sense of pleasure. To illustrate:

Contemplation . . . is possible only by virtue of the divine element in man. We ought then not confine our thoughts to the ephemeral, but so far as possible we ought to seek immortality.[16]

The life of good conduct – of morally good action – is the best human life, the completest expression of human nature . . . But there is in man an element which is either itself divine or the most godlike of elements in man: vous, or whatever that should be called whose nature it is to rule us and to take thought of things noble and divine. And in the activity of this element – in contemplation – man experiences the completest felicity.[17]

Work, leisure, contemplation and happiness are not the simple matters, at least in Aristotle's argument, that we sometimes make them out to be. In most contemporary discussions or writings about leisure, little is said about virtue and less about the divine. The omissions destroy the meaning.

We Without Means

Leisure in the Aristotelian sense is troublesome enough for us on the most secular of grounds; i.e. having means. If to be at leisure one must have means then what are we to do? Those without means, which is nearly all of us, are simply going to have to work. If, as de Grazia suggests, work and leisure live in two different worlds and free time lives in the world of work,[18] then what are we to do? We live in a world of work and we have no reason to think we should not. We are workers and have no reason to think we should not be, not because Calvin walks in the land but because the world's work (dare we say God's work?) remains to be done. Quite evidently, then, work will require us to exercise our virtuous energies more so than in the past.

If as Pieper writes, "Leisure . . . (is) utterly contrary to the ideal of 'worker' in each of its three aspects . . . as activity, as toil, as a social function,"[19] then what are we to do? We have no recourse but to reject Pieper's characterization of the "worker."

The 'worker' it has been seen in our brief analysis of that significant figure, is characterized by three significant traits: an extreme tension of the powers of action, a readiness to suffer in vacuo unrelated to anything, and complete absorption in the social organism, itself rationally planned to utilitarian ends.[20]

The description is not without merit, historically at least, including the recent past. It seems ill-fitted to the present and in any case there is no reason to cling to the characterization. Where it still fits perhaps it should not. Perhaps one of our major tasks is to assure that it does not. As long as we must work we must rid ourselves of hostility toward it. If leisure is to be a possibility for us, then it must infuse our work. Much more is involved here than the concepts of fusion or extension between work and non-work activities and roles. Our work should be what we choose to do; what we and others consider important. It should so absorb us, as W. H. Auden suggested, that in doing it we are, in essence, praying.[21] Would that Gibran's phrase, "Work is love made visible," was applicable. For if it is not, there seems little hope for leisure.

THE DIVIDING OF TIME . . .

A world of work such as ours suggests, a priori, that the most we can attain is free-time. So leisure as free-time becomes the focus. But free-time is not a goal; per se it is not important and it cannot shoulder the burden too readily placed upon it. What is usually meant by free-time is time free from work and other obligations. But even if by leisure we mean nothing more than free-time, ours is still not an age of leisure and there seems little prospect of it. "One widely current illusion about the future needs to be dispelled. This is the illusion of great affluence and leisure . . . obtained via projections of increased productivity."[22] Productivity gains have not matched expectations for the past several years. Unemployment in mature economies has been increasing. The inanimate tools that Aristotle anticipated have not set us free; they have set us to work as servo-mechanisms. Sometimes they have set us aside. People now become redundant, a presumably sophisticated but actually grotesque way of saying unemployed. Economic and material growth was to have solved the problems of the unemployed and the poor. It has not, and it cannot, even if growth were to continue as in previous decades, and that seems most unlikely.

Free-time unavoidably carries with it a connotation of subservient worth and value. That is a handicap and a burden. It is undermined by its own definition; it is unobligated time and it is free from work. But who is ever free from work and other obligations? Because one has some discretion about how his or her time may be used does not make it unobligated. In fact, the reverse is true. It is only when we have the opportunity to choose that our obligations become fully apparent. That, as noted later, is consistent with Aristotle's thought. Surely there is no end to the worthwhile work that must be done. Besides, do not each of us always have obligations to ourselves and to the cosmos and to most everything in between? Further, and particularly disconcerting about the notion of free-time, is that it perpetuates the dichotomy between work and leisure as free-time. The dichotomy deals leisure a heavy blow; probably a fatal blow. Jacques Ellul notes it well, among literally scores of other commentators.

> To assert that the individual expresses his personality and cultivates himself in the course of his leisure is to accept the suppression of half the human personality. History compels the judgement that it is in work that human beings develop and affirm their personality . . . When the human being is no longer responsible for his work and no longer figures in it, he feels spiritually outraged . . .The annihilation of work and its compensation with leisure resolves the conflicts by referring them to a subhuman plane . . . To gamble that leisure will enable man to live is to sanction the dissociation I have been describing and to cut him off completely from part of life.[23]

The work leisure dichotomy does violence to our nature in so many ways, ". . . for one swallow makes not a summer; neither does one day, or a short time constitute happiness. . ." Evenings, week-ends and holidays, however, lengthened, are insufficient. A recent study in England revealed that a disproportionate number of suicides were committed on Sunday. Psychologists suggested that perhaps some of the victims of their own hand were not capable of facing another week of work.

AND OF LIVES

Much of the difficulty we face has been attributed to the factory system and the dehumanization of work, but people in comfortable high-rise office towers show signs of a similar malaise. The factory system is, however, partly responsible for "the leisure problem" and for creating the work-leisure dichotomy, because it forced a separation; where one lived and where one worked became quite distinct, making the division of time a simple matter. Since then, the separation has been carried much further. Now we believe that working and living should be separate. One appeal of the suburbs, for many at least, is that they are not close to work. The space, and the time needed to traverse it, provides insulation between home and work, leisure and work, living and working. We are not supposed to take our work home; what goes on at the plant or office is supposed to be left at the plant or office. We can and do work at home, but that is a different matter. It is more imperative that one does not take home to work in the sense that one's activities and affairs outside of work are not to influence work at the plant or office. So half our lives, for a period of 40 years or more, is supposed to be unrelated to the other half. It is errant nonsense of course. It is probably impossible as well. And to be constantly suppressing half of one's life inevitably carries a heavy psychological cost.

This is not just a matter of playing different roles. Even if it were, why must we be constantly playing roles? The main difficulty is that the roles have become not simply unrelated but worse, incompatible. Ruben Nelson makes the case powerfully, illustrating it with the story of a space engineer caught up in a project requiring long hours of hard work. On returning home, he was always surprised to find that his wife seemed just as tired as he was. He didn't think she had much to do but she claimed she had more to do than she had time for. So he arranged to take a day off and spend it with his wife – not on a dinner or family picnic, however. He did a time and motion study of her day. He determined conclusively that his wife's complaints of being overworked were unjustified, and henceforth paid no attention whatever to her complaints.[24]

PERSONS OR OBJECTS

Surely we all recognize how inappropriate was his response. But we also recognize that his response was not inappropriate to the world of work. So we have come to see ourselves and others in two lights – as persons in our private lives, and as things or objects in our public or working lives. We have come to live by two sets of rules – those for the role of worker, functionary, agent, official or whatever role we play in our public lives, and those for the role of parent, friend, spouse, lover or whatever roles make up our private lives. But the roles are incompatible. We can't reconcile them.[25]

Publicly, as objects, we seek to maximize our profits, importance, and status; in part by externalizing our costs and wastes. "Let the buyer beware." Don't require the vendor to be forthright. That is why we're advised not to do business with friends or relatives; the roles are incompatible. Privately, as persons, we share our profits and strengths, and internalize our burdens and those of others – that is what friendship is about. To Aristotle, the first characteristic of friendship was, "the promotion of another's good for his own sake."[25] Publicly, we are unrestrained except by law and regulation: sometimes not even that restrains us. For surely billions of dollars are spent each year to change, avoid or circumvent the law, always to the spender's advantage. Sometimes we are merely rule obeyers ("I'm only doing my job. Don't blame me, I don't set policy.") which is "an organized form of non-responsible behavior."[27] Publicly, as objects, we know only institutional restraint and avoid even that when we can. Privately, as persons, we restrain ourselves; we recognize and exercise personal responsibility. A place where personal responsibility no longer exists would be a good working definition of hell.

MEANING AND MATTERING

The notion of free time diverts our attention from problems which free time can't resolve. The dichotomy of work and leisure as free-time, the abandonment of people to incompatibly split lives, and the subsidiary value of free time is destructive as it recognizes – even emphasizes – selves as public "things" rather than private "persons." This creates not only confusion but also cynicism because we know that much of our work has lost its meaning; much of what we do doesn't seem to matter and so with our lives. That applies as often to those engaged in providing human services as it does to those providing goods or services for profit. Galper,[28] for example, notes that social workers are aware that many social services are of little benefit to people, thus they experience a sense of the limited value of their work. While individuals often feel the urgency and crisis, their institution often does not. As persons, they often feel that whatever they do will make little difference and they become dissatisfied with their own inadequate performance. Still, as things, they receive recognition and promotion in the system, perhaps for having resigned themselves to making the best of a situation which may be impossible. They learn not only that much of what they do may not matter, the institution conveys to them that it doesn't matter that it doesn't matter. Is it any wonder then that fatalism is on the rise, with not only more bingo and gambling in the usual sense but also with astrology and Tarot cards, religious and other cults (some of which have remarkably nasty streaks) and in privately and, increasingly, publicly sponsored lotteries, nearly all of which have been vastly more productive than their sponsors ever dreamed? There are even state organized lotteries for getting children into decent schools and those with too limited income into decent housing. What an incredible perversion. The losers are expected to blame their desperate situation on luck rather than on the failure of systems and institutions. As Cohen notes:

> In the context of competitive culture the idea of luck may serve as a convenient stabilizer, convenient, that is, to the "lucky ones" at the same time stultifying initiative and independent thinking.

> Daily emasculation of the reflective processes of millions, whose horoscopes are cast in the daily press, produces a potentially pliable mentality that sees the futility of social intervention if everything is ordained in the stars.[29]

Perhaps Cohen has cause and effect in reverse order, but it does seem that fatalism and a sense of futility go together.

Finally, the dichotomization of work and free-time, the subservience and the abandonment suggested in the notion of free-time; the fractioning of whole persons and whole lives as though no more than whole numbers, exacerbates what is generally regarded as the period of crisis in which we now find ourselves. Walter Lippmann addressed the issue directly, as noted in the editor's preface to his *A Preface to Morals.*

> Thus, Lippmann indicates, business, the family and the other preoccupations of men's daily lives are, in effect, religion's "lost provinces." This loss has inevitably made life seem less meaningful to many men. For with each province now autonomous, each having its own standards and its own modes of thought, there is no longer any strong central theme in men's lives; nothing seems to be organically related to anything else, and so nothing seems to be terribly important.[30]

Tillich, in *The Courage To Be,* comes to the same conclusion. He notes that the anxiety characteristic of our era is that of emptiness and meaninglessness, placing us " . . . under the threat of spiritual nonbeing."[31]

So the final problem with the notion of leisure as time free from work and other obligations is that it doesn't matter. It is without value or meaning. If we have a leisure problem it is not because we have too much free time, or too little work. What we have is too little meaning in our free time and in our work; in sum, in our lives.

In only one sense is free-time a useful notion: the sense of discretion about its use. The opportunity and ability to choose is important. There is no other road to virtue because, to cite Aristotle once more, when he summarizes his argument about the relation between virtue and voluntary and involuntary acts: "The habit of moral virtue implies the deliberate preference of one kind of conduct to another; and deliberate preference implies freedom of choice."[32]

IF LEISURE IS TO MATTER

Leisure is a useless notion if by it we mean merely free time or some contemplative state. Still, the Aristotelian view may inform and encourage us if we keep his context. The context is virtue. The world of action is an essential corollary. If happiness is the highest good and the product of contemplation, so it is also the result of action; the exercise of virtuous energies. Well being and well doing are parts of a whole; complementary and synergistic. That, not surprisingly, is more compatible with our experiences than merely contemplating, even though such experiences may be pitifully infrequent. For who has not felt the peace and joy of having done something truly worthwhile, having done it well, and knowing it?

Aristotle concerned himself with whole men leading whole lives. He saw clearly that happiness was unattainable otherwise. Only if we conceive our lives, including our work, holistically, can we come to grips with Aristotle or with an endless collection of scholarly thought since his time.

What those in the recreation or leisure service fields should do about all this is not entirely clear. It is characteristic of our time, perhaps because we are only beginning to understand the crises before us, to have some ideas about what needs to be done without yet knowing what to do. The recapture of selves as persons rather than things; the exercise of virtue through a lifetime; the reintegration of all aspects of life into a varied but congruent whole; the recovery of meaning; these are the tasks before us all.

If leisure is to matter, these tasks must be addressed more directly, and probably more radically, than in the past. Until then, the judgement that leisure has arrived is not only premature but also misleading, with consequences which can only be dire.

REFERENCES

1. Pieper, Joseph. *Leisure: The Basis of Culture,* (Alexander Dru, trans.) New York: Pantheon Books, 1952.
2. de Grazia, Sebastian. *Of Time, Work and Leisure.* New York: The Twentieth Century Fund, 1960.
3. Steward, J. A. *Notes on the Nicomachean Ethics,* New York: Arno Press, 1973. p. 446.
4. Kierman, Thomas P. (Ed.) *Aristotle Dictionary,* New York: Philosophical Library, 1962. p. 137-138.
5. Gillies, John. *Aristotle's Ethics.* (John Gillies trans.) London: Routledge, 1886. p. 138.
6. Durant, Will. *The Life of Greece* (The Story of Civilization: Part II), New York: Simon and Schuster, 1939. p. 301.

7. Kierman, *Op. Cit.*, p. 149-150.
8. Gillies, *Op. Cit.*, p. 361.
9. Kaplan, Justin (Ed.). *The Pocket Aristotle.* (W. E. Ross trans.) New York: Pocket Books, 1958. p. 336.
10. Durant, *Op. Cit.*, p. 533.
11. Kierman, *Op. Cit.*, p. xii.
12. Pieper, *Op. Cit.*, p. 21.
13. Nash, J. B. *Philosophy of Recreation and Leisure,* Dubuque, Iowa: Wm. C. Brown Co., 1973. p. 222.
14. Gillies, *Op. Cit.*, p. 360.
15. *Ibid.* p. 169-170.
16. Ferguson, John. *Aristotle.* New York: Twayne Publishers, 1972. p. 138.
17. Rees, D. A. (Ed.). *Aristotle: The Nicomachean Ethics,* (A Commentary by the late H. H. Joachim) Oxford: Oxford University Press, 1951. p. 287.
18. de Grazia, *Op. Cit.*, p. 7-8.
19. Pieper, *Op. Cit.*, p. 40.
20. *Ibid.*, p. 39.
21. Auden, W. H. "Culture and Leisure." *Ekstics,* (144, Feb., 1966). p. 418-420.
22. Boulding, Kenneth. "The Future of Personal Responsibility." *American Behavioral Scientist,* (15:3, Jan./Feb. 1972). p. 352.
23. Ellul, Jacques. *The Technological Society.* (John Wilkinson, trans.) New York: Random House, 1964. p. 339-400.
24. Nelson, Ruben F. W. *The Illusion of Urban Man,* Ottawa: Information Canada, 1976. p. 34.
25. *Ibid.*
26. Ferguson, *Op. Cit.*, p. 137.
27. Nelson, *Op. Cit.*, p. 56.
28. Galper, Jeffrey H. *The Politics of Social Services,* Englewood Cliffs, New Jersey: Prentice-Hall, 1975. p. 58.
29. Cohen, John. *Chance, Skill, and Luck: The Psychology of Guessing and Gambling.* Baltimore: Penguin Books, 1960. p. 66.
30. Lippmann, Walter. *A Preface to Morals,* New York: Time Inc., 1964. p. xiii.
31. Tillich, Paul. *The Courage to Be,* London: Nisbet and Comp., Fontana Library, 1952. p. 57.
32. Gillies, *Op. Cit.*, p. 194.

Chapter Five

On the Biological Basis of Pleasure: Some Implications for Leisure Policy

Stephen L. J. Smith

More often than not current speculations about the nature and value of leisure are either variations on a theme by Aristotle or a quantitative simulation of Veblen's observations of society. Many of our ideas about leisure are still strongly rooted in a school of thought 2300 years old or in the much more recent and mechanistic view that leisure is the leavings of time. We find ourselves in this condition because, it seems, we have forgotten a fundamental aspect of leisure: pleasure. Examine any recent article on any aspect of leisure and you will likely find a discussion of human rights, human dignity, social improvement, environmental quality, political action, holism, humanism or any of a shoal of other currently popular phrases and ideas. But you will find few, if any, references to pleasure. To ignore pleasure is a serious flow. Pleasure is not trivial. It is absolutely essential to leisure, recreation and play, and we know very little about it. It is the answer to "why people play"; it is the reason for leisure and recreation. In this sense, "pleasure" has a much broader connotation than it does in Freud's concept of the "pleasure principle" or in Aristotle's distinction between "pleasure" and "joy." Pleasure is used here to include happiness, joy, fun, sensuality, amusement, mirth and tranquility. These diverse emotions share one common quality – they make a person "feel good"; that is, they give pleasure.

Too often we try to better understand *why* humans play and recreate by ignoring pleasure and instead concentrate on the social structures that merely *shape* play, recreation and leisure. Much that has been learned by social scientists is useful for solving certain problems, but their work is neither fundamental nor universal. The subject which seems to offer more for the etiology of recreation, and thus pleasure, is neurophysiology.

Neurophysiology, the study of the nervous system, treats physical processes which are independent of the temporarily prevailing economy, political system or social mores. These external forces will result in different stimuli being perceived by the nervous system and in different material being learned, but the neurological processes of a person in the United States are the same as those of a person in the People's Republic of China. There is a common denominator in recreation which makes historical and cross-cultural studies academically meaningful and intriguing. That common denominator is pleasure – and pleasure is a neurophysiological phenomenon.

SOME BACKGROUND OF THE STUDY OF PLEASURE

A major step forward in the objective study of pleasure was made in 1954 as the result of an experimental error. James Olds,[4] a psychologist, was working on the mechanisms involved in the alerting response, the changes in an animal when it goes from a drowsy state to an alert state. Olds already knew that the process was due to some sort of electrical activity in a portion of the brain called the reticular activating system. He was working with a group of rats in which electrodes had been implanted in the reticular system to study in detail certain aspects of their alerting responses. The stimulation was not a particularly pleasant experience – with one apparent exception. One rat, when its electrodes were activated, showed no signs of alerting. It did exhibit a peculiar form of behavior, however, that caught Olds' attention. When removed from the corner of the cage where the electrodes were activated, the rat would try to return to that corner. Olds began to close the switch that excited the electrodes whenever the rat was in the corner and observed that the rat never wandered very far away. It stayed in the corner – apparently waiting for the next charge to its brain.

Examination of the rat by a curious Olds and his research team revealed that the electrodes had been incorrectly positioned. Instead of exciting the reticular activating system, they were stimulating an adjacent area called the limbic system. Very little was then known about the limbic system; some researchers, though, suspected that this primitive part of the brain was involved in several forms of behavior. This bit of serendipity implicated the limbic system as the biological basis of pleasure. In fact, a portion of the limbic system is now called the pleasure area of the brain. The process of pleasure-seeking the rat exhibited is called intra-cranial self-stimulation.

This form of direct pleasure stimulation of the limbic system quickly became an exciting new field for experimenters. For example, Olds devised an experiment to test the relative strength of the pleasure drive in rats. He gave the test animals one hour a day to obtain intra-cranial stimulation of the pleasure area or to eat. They consistently chose self-stimulation. The drive was so strong that the test animals completely forewent food. One animal starved to death; the researchers discontinued their experiments when other animals lost up to a third of their body weight.

The limbic system, with little change in structure and virtually no change in function, also exists in the human brain. So, as one would expect, work on other species eventually led to studies on human beings. Some notable experiments were with mental patients of Robert Heath at the Tulane School of Medicine. Heath provided his patients with a set of implanted electrodes and a button. He noted that the patients used the buttons frequently. According to them, it felt good and made them feel happy. The improvement in their moods ranged from general pleasure, through intense excitement, to a profound euphoria that lasted anywhere from a few hours to several days. The variation depended on the strength and duration of the charge and the portion of the limbic system being activated.

Years of work and experimentation on these pleasure areas have determined that the pleasure drive is one of the strongest drives in animals (at least for vertebrates). Direct limbic stimulation offers the most powerful drive seen in animals, in the sense that "with the electrodes squarely in a pleasure area and a lever to activate them, the animal wishes to do nothing but press the lever and has no desire to engage in any other behavior whatever."[5] Direct stimulation of the pleasure areas is such a powerful drive that it overwhelms the desire for water, food, mating or protection of the young. What is being observed is "not merely pleasure in any parochial sense but what is clearly the ultimate pleasure, the font of all behavior."[6]

Intra-cranial self-stimulation clearly represents a totally new type of behavior although the idea of seeking pleasure is well-known in psychology and philosophy. However, no one could seriously suggest this kind of stimulation is "normal" behavior. Yet the pleasure areas of the brain, whether that of rat or man, are normally stimulated through our senses and internal nerve receptors in our daily round of activities. Indeed, the idea of seeking pleasure is a well-known idea of psychology and philosophy.[7]

SENSORY PLEASURE STIMULATION

Common experience tells us that not all sensory stimuli are pleasurable. Many mild stimuli and very sharp, intense stimuli are unpleasant; even painful. These forces activate another part of the limbic system which registers pain, but since we are dealing with recreation, and thus pleasant feelings, our focus is on the pleasure area. It was a similar interest in voluntary behavior (motivated by pleasure) which led Campbell, who had been studying intra-cranial stimulation (along with many other experimenters), to consider peripheral or sensory stimulation of the limbic system.

This new line of work didn't rely on wires and electrodes or the conventional rewards of food, water or sex for a deprived animal but on mere sensory stimulation of a healthy animal in a homeostatic environment. Campbell hoped to prove experimentally that animals would voluntarily engage in some behavior which would yield no reward other than the pleasure of doing that particular act. In humans we can call this play, leisure or recreation. Campbell's experiments included successful sensory stimulation (using a small external electrical "tickle") of fish, newts, terrapins and a crocodile. The most significant successes, however, were with squirrel monkeys. His animals were kept in a light environment with food, water, room to play and mate, noise and human activity. Campbell provided his monkeys with a 500 watt lamp that would light whenever the monkeys touched a capacitance rod. The advantages of the rod included the fact that it had no moving parts to wear out, but most importantly, it made no noise and, in general, was a rather dull plaything. During the initial test sessions when the lamp was not attached to the rod the monkeys touched the rod about 30 times in 15 minutes. As Campbell describes their behavior, "unless it (any new object) proves edible or can be made love to, the new object is soon tired of and ignored."[8] After the lamp was attached, the monkeys required several sessions to learn how to "operate" the switch and the lamp. Once this education was accomplished they began touching the rod at the rate of 300 to 500 times in a 15 minute test.

The lamp used provided pure white light, which is not a stimulus readily analogous to the monkeys' usual range of experiences. There is no reference or symbolism to meat or mate or to free existence in the wild. All that was operating was a meaningless flash of white light directly into the eyes. Unlike intra-cranial stimulation which so absorbs an animal that it never stops voluntarily, peripheral or sensory stimulation will eventually become boring. When a white light was made available continuously the monkeys stopped flashing it within two hours. The same tapering-off or boredom was observed with any color light of equal brightness. However, when the colors of light were changed every 15 minutes the monkeys kept flashing the light for over four hours. Such behavior is not unknown in humans. Manufacturers in recreation and other fields understand the value in bringing out the same old product in a new container or new form. Boredom haunts all forms of recreation from television to sex.

Psychologists, too, have discussed motivation based on intrinsic factors and pleasure seeking. White's conceptualization is one of the most insightful, although not physiologically based.[9] White notes that conceptualization of intrinsic motivation is needed to account for both actual behavior and the improvements in behavior animals and humans learn as they cope with their environment. The new conceptualization White suggests is "competence" – the ability of an animal to effectively cope with its environment. Learning, exploring, playing and thinking are among the activities that increase competence. White described these competence-increasing activities as "motivated in their own right;" that is, there is no motivation for them other than the feeling of satisfaction derived from their performance. White is heading straight for the recognition that pleasure is basic, that it is an element that cannot be simplified or explained by a still simpler concept. However, he stops short and calls the satisfaction of activity not pleasure or fun, but a "feeling of efficacy." This phrase obscures the fundamental reality of fun and the fundamental importance of pleasure. White does acknowledge however that efficacy shows itself most clearly in the fun of play.

The point to be drawn from these ideas is that animals do engage in behavior solely for the pleasure derived. In fact, most activities in which an animal engages in the natural world, eating, copulating, or exploring, are done for pleasurable stimulation only. Fortunately, some of these activities keep the animal alive. The pleasure derived from eating concomitantly provides nourishment. But, and it is a critical distinction, an animal does not eat to get nourishment; it eats to get pleasure. If an animal's mouth is "numbed" so that there is no taste or feel of food sensed during the eating, an animal may starve to death. Research by Ziegler[10] indicates that over-eating may be due to a malfunctioning of the trigeminal nerve which registers oral tactile sensations such as kissing, smoking and eating. In his experiments the destruction of the trigeminal nerve not only stopped the sending of the pleasurable feelings of eating, but also stopped any interest in eating. The strength of the drive for pleasure through other forms of behavior, especially exploration, has been experimentally documented as early as the 1940s and 1950s by researchers such as Whiting and Mourer,[11] Montgomery and Markman,[12] and Berlyne.[13]

When a healthy animal reaches satiation (stops receiving pleasure) from eating or any other activity, such as looking at a flashing light, it doesn't stop behaving; it seeks out something new. If it did not constantly seek new stimuli that lead to pleasure it would die. For however pleasurable or beneficial any single act may be, it will not maintain homeostatis for the animal over any length of time (i.e., keep it alive). This is the fatal characteristic of intra-cranial self-stimulation: animals will push a lever until they drop. This also suggests, physiologically, the fundamental reason for most (perhaps even all) animal behavior – it is an unending search for renewed pleasure. Survival is not the motivation for the actions of an individual animal; the motivation is the seeking of pleasure.

The biological basis of pleasurable feeling (sensory and proprioceptive stimulation of the limbic system) is the same for all vertebrates and this necessarily includes man. Whatever one's feelings about an immaterial part of humans, a spirit, soul or whatever, man in his body and its processes is an animal. We feel pleasure in the same way that animals do.

THE HUMAN DIFFERENCE

There is one difference, however, in the ways that humans can attain pleasure. This is a way of seeking pleasure which makes some of us most of the time, and all of us part of the time, different from animals. We can obtain pleasure from thought, from the use of the tertiary portion of the human cortex – that part associated with creative thought and symbolic reasoning. Animals do not because they cannot. This includes the dolphins and whales whose large cortices are the subject of much popular speculation. There is no evidence that the crustaceans use their large convoluted cerebrums for pleasure; they are too busy using their brain for the pursuit of the simpler pleasures of food, breathing and the companionship of their own kind.

The potential of conscious thought to control the older parts of the brain is a common experience. Almost all of us have experienced psychogenic insomnia – those nights when excited or angry thoughts have overwhelmed the call for sleep. This same barrage of electrical activity can be directed into the pleasure areas.

This organization and function of the brain provides the only unqualified, non-solipsistic and non-mystical difference between man and animal. The unique characteristic of Homo sapiens is that members have the potential for achieving pleasure from thought. To the degree that someone actualizes this potential and seeks pleasure from mental activity, he is acting human. To the degree he seeks sensory pleasure he is acting subhuman. These are unpleasant words, but we must face the truth, even if unpleasant, if we are to progress as human beings. The truth is: members of Homo sapiens often engage in decidedly sub-human acts.

With this simple distinction we can now perceive a pattern in recreation activities which is more basic than existing classification schemes such as the familiar indoor/outdoor dichotomy. Recreation activities, or anything else an individual does for fun or pleasure, can be placed on a continuum from purely sensory to purely intellectual and thus on a spectrum of sub-human to human activity.

This difference is not, in the first place, a philosophical one but an objective one (although there are many philosophical implications). In a rather over-simplified way the difference between acting human and acting sub-human is how you seek pleasure: stimulation by the cortex (human) versus stimulation by the peripheral receptors (sub-human).

While pleasure-seeking runs the gamut from sensual to intellectual, it can be approximated by three separate types of behavior. These three ways of pursuing pleasure have rather indistinct boundaries, but still provide a useful scheme for identifying different forms of pleasure-seeking behavior which is independent of prevailing social and political conditions. The three types of pleasure-seeking can be given the labels of (1) sensory, (2) expressive-cortical and (3) intellectual cortical. The basis for differentiation is the relative importance of the cortex in generating the feelings of pleasure.

SENSORY RECREATION

Sensory activities include many popular and traditional activities: eating, some forms of children's play, much music (especially such primitive forms as rock), vandalism, hunting, sports, snowmobiling, flirting and rape. These apparently unrelated activities are grouped together because a person finding pleasure in any of them does so because the activity stimulates the peripheral receptors. Physical play, sports, hunting and snowmobiling involve the pleasurable use of muscles which is sensed by the proprioceptors (nerves sensing muscular movement).

Eating, drinking, loud rhythmic music and similar activities provide direct stimulation of the senses and, with allowances for variations in personal tastes, provide pleasure for all people. Other activities are enjoyable because of the visceral or autonomic pleasure they provide. David Klein, a professor at Michigan State and a commentator for National Public Radio in the United States, has suggested the great popularity of snowmobiling in states like Michigan is due to the feeling of danger and personal confrontation with power it provides. These visceral pleasures (such as the tightening of the stomach) offset the blandness and tedium of jobs such as those on Michigan's automobile assembly lines. Klein suggested that snowmobiling could be greatly reduced (if this were deemed socially or environmentally desirable) by making snowmobiles safe, slow and quiet. Similarly, Campbell observed that the pleasure of mountain climbing comes primarily from the danger involved. Although the use of muscles, eyes, ears and nose must also provide pleasure it is the difficulty and challenge which draws climbers to their sport; thus "despite its apparent masculinity it reduces to the fairground mentality."[14]

Much so-called sexual pleasure also stems from the "fairground mentality." Caressing, kissing and intercourse provide many pleasurable stimuli, but not all apparently sexual activity is truly sexual. The first adolescent contacts between boys and girls generate great feelings of excitement and pleasure, but these are largely autonomic, arising from the pleasurable sensations in changes in the heart rate, respiration rate and movement of the stomach and intestines. Because these early pleasures (which also typically accompany any new contact between adults which has sexual overtones) are primarily autonomic, they inevitably decline as the two people become more familiar with each other. The mystery and intrigue is gone; sex becomes routine; the flame has gone out of their romance. Some change is necessary to rekindle the feelings: having sex in more exotic or naughty ways, in semi-public places or with new partners. Truly sexual feelings intensify with familiarity as the couple begins to draw together emotionally and become more skilled in their caresses. In brief, much so-called sexual attraction is basically pleasurable fear – like a roller coaster ride. In fact, a roller coaster is a not-unknown analogy in describing many love affairs.

EXPRESSIVE-CORTICAL RECREATION

The next group of recreation activities, expressive-cortical, are based on a mingling of man's sensory and intellectual characteristics. The expressive-cortical activities are those which use creative thought to produce something which also gives sensual pleasure (e.g., classical music) or which adds a major intellectual dimension to a sensory experience (e.g. winetasting). The arts and crafts: painting, sculpture, composing music, film-making, calligraphy and all the rest; sex based on emotional closeness; and certain occupations such as medicine and engineering provide this type of pleasure. Physical artifacts are used to give expression to an activity which is predominantly intellectual.

This category has especially confused borders. A composer of a piece of classical music will probably be closer to enjoying an intellectual-cortical pleasure than a sensual pleasure although his music can give sensual pleasure. The performer of that piece and the audience will tend to be successively more drawn to the sensual character of the music. However, some mathematicians, for example, who have a taste for classical music have occasionally described perceiving profound mathematical structures in a musical movement. On the other hand, Einstein described some of his early ideas about relativity as mental dance images. His intellectual reveries took on, in his mind, sensual qualities. Beethoven, near the end of a lifetime composing powerful, sensual music, completed several works while deaf. His pleasure in the Ninth Symphony could hardly be called sensual since he lacked the sense to appreciate it. Similarly Adolf Gottlieb, a 20th century abstract expressionist, produced some of his best pieces after he became blind.

Some types of children's play are expressive-cortical. Any parent who has watched children play has seen them first enjoy physical activity with a plaything and then grow bored as they exhaust the initial possibilities for pleasure. Children will then attempt to renew the fun of the activity or plaything by increasing its complexity, by changing the rules of play, by using the toy for fantasy or, if all else fails, by taking the toy apart to see how it works. The phenomenon is one where a child can easily obtain pleasure from sensory stimulation, and when he grows bored, will seek new pleasure by changing the form of play. The change that overcomes boredom is the change that allows the child to use his intelligence and creativity. These observations are probably the objective origins of the play theories of Berlyn, Maddi, and Ellis.

INTELLECTUAL-CORTICAL RECREATION

Intellectual-cortical, the final category of pleasurable behaviors, seems to belong to the realm of the thinkers. Actually, everyone obtains some pleasure from intellectual activities – those activities which provide pleasure without the use of sensory stimulation. Only a few people, however, derive most of their pleasure from such sources. They form an elite in any society which is regularly singled out for admiration or, as often happens, suspicion and ridicule. These are the philosophers, theologians, linguists, mathematicians, logicians, certain historians, theoretical physicists, mystics, and, at times, politicians. Any motor behavior associated with their seeking pleasure is only ancillary. Some physical action is necessary to obtain information, education or the resources to keep alive; their pleasure comes from their minds and not their actions.

The development and nurturing of a human mind capable of human pleasures is one of the greatest responsibilities a society faces. It would be a mistake, though, to believe that all intellectual pleasures are necessarily lofty and virtuous. There are a great many bad philosophers and theologians. Many intellectuals are as silly as non-intellectuals. The vast potential of the creative intellect can also be turned to fantasizing and daydreaming, which are surrogates for sensory pleasure. Still, other humans develop elaborate, twisted political philosophies which give intellectual pleasure but all too often find ultimate expression in sub-human, destructive terrorism and war. Fascism and the twisted science developed under Hitler are probably the major examples from this century.

Not all intellectual pleasure is constructive, creative, enduring and socially desirable. Only intellectual activities, however, have the potential for becoming so. Sensory pleasure virtually never does. Apparent exceptions are individuals such as the Wright brothers who experienced an exquisite aesthetic reaction as well as physical thrill in their early experiments with flight. But even in such cases the work is preceded by long periods of intellectual study and analysis which either gave or promised future pleasure and contributed the requisite scientific basis for a lasting contribution.

A FEW IMPLICATIONS

The identification and classification of phenomena is basic to any discipline, profession or body of practitioners. Researchers and academics are still searching for a paradigm which will help guide work and provoke questions for future study of recreation, leisure and play. Such a paradigm may be built out of the common denominator of these phenomena or pleasures. This chapter has described in brief terms some of the physiological importance of pleasure and in doing so pointed out an important dichotomy in the search for pleasure, vis., an objective difference between human and sub-human pleasures. This difference is based on the origins of the stimuli received by the limbic system.

If a society holds the philosophy that the state not only exists to make people happy, but to bring out the best in its citizens, to make them as human as they can be, to emphasize and nurture good and enduring human values, then those social institutions that provide leisure services should take a careful look at their programs. Public recreation agencies, park departments, athletic leagues, youth groups, churches and schools (including universities) have the responsibility to evaluate their offerings in terms of their location on the sub-human to human spectrum. Few people would seriously suggest that we should not worry about preserving open-space natural beauty; nor would they suggest that we can completely ignore physical health. The issue is one of relative emphasis, of budgets and of program resources. A flat statement that all recreation and park agencies are emphasizing the sub-human in us by virtue of their sensory-oriented programming is unwarranted. But we do have the responsibility to take a critical look at programs and honestly evaluate just what part of our human/animal personality we are developing and whether this is the appropriate role of a public or educational agency. Surely, the magnitude of sports programs in most schools deserves special attention. A comparison of the institutional support for intercollegiate and intramural sports with cultural recreation at the same institutions should be made and interpreted in light of the concepts argued in this paper. Societies and governments which provide so much support and place so much attention on events such as the Olympic games are highlighting and promoting sub-human behavior. Considering the recent events of terror, retribution, resource boycotts and other global acts of sensory pleasure-seeking (in the name of whatever ideology), the emphasis given the Olympics and world-champion prize fights is disturbing, to say the least.

The same pattern can be found at local levels. Recreation is often claimed to be a deterrant to juvenile delinquency. The causes of delinquency, as with most social problems, are diverse and diffuse. But it seems almost paradoxical to think that a recreation program which emphasizes some forms of sub-human behavior is going to have broad success in eliminating other forms of sub-human behavior. Fights and riots which too often accompany sporting events and rock festivals are evidence that sensory recreation may not be such a cure-all for socially undesirable forms of sensory recreation. On the other hand, rare indeed are plays, classical music concerts, lectures or other intellectual events which are followed by violent forms of sensory-oriented behavior.

All this is but one aspect of the new approach to recreation. There are many others, some philosophical, some scientific. A biological approach to recreation will place many familiar phenomena in new contexts and will challenge quite a few of our old comfortable beliefs about sports, athletics, arts, the humanities and science. It suggests that there is indeed something special and unique about being human – and that many people (perhaps most) don't act "humanly" for much of their lives. We have much, much more to learn about pleasure, the manifold ways people pursue it and the implications for fields of inquiry from management to evolution to theology. Through it all, the image of man as constantly striving to be happy, and being most human when he is pursuing "human" pleasures is an optimistic and hopeful image of humanity.

REFERENCES

1. A few of the many different approaches can be read in the works of the following authors: Veblen, Thorstein. *The Theory of the Leisure Class.* New York: The American Library, 1953; de Grazia, Sebastian. Of *Time, Work and Leisure.* Garden Center, New York: Doubleday and Company, 1964; Pieper, Joseph. *Leisure: The Basis of Culture.* New York: Pantheon Books, 1952; Linder, Steffan. *The Harried Leisure Class.* New York: Columbia University Press, 1970; Brightbill, Charles. *The Challenge of Leisure.* Englewood Cliffs, NJ: Prentice-Hall, 1960; Dumazedier, Joffre. *Toward a Society of Leisure.* New York: The Free Press, 1967; Martin, Alexander Reid. "Leisure and Our Inner Resources." *Parks and Recreation.* March, 1975, pp. ia-ff.
2. Kuhn, Thomas. *The Structure of Scientific Revolutions.* Chicago: University of Chicago Press, 1970.
3. A recent example is the debate over the acceptability of hang-gliding in the National Parks. Questions on appropriateness were raised in a *New York Times* editorial by Ronald Taylor, November 11th, 1975, "National Park Policy."
4. Olds, James and Milner, Peter. "Positive Reinforcement Produced by Electrical Stimulation of Septal Area and Other Regions of Rat Brain." *Journal of Comparative Physiology and Psychology,* 47, 1954, p. 419. See also Olds, James. "Differentiation of Reward Systems in the Brain by Self-Stimulation Techniques." In *Electrical Studies on the Unanesthetized Brain.* New York: Hoeber-Harper, 1960. pp. 17-49.
5. Campbell, Herbert. *The Pleasure Areas.* New York: Delacorte Press, 1973. p. 25.
6. *Ibid.*, p. 24.
7. Among these would be Freud, Sigmund. *Beyond the Pleasure Principle.* James Strachey (Translator). New York: Liveright, 1961; Szasz, Thomas. *Pain and Pleasure.* New York: Basic Books, 1975; Heath, Robert (Ed.). *The Role of Pleasure in Behavior.* New York: Hoeber-Harper, 1964.
8. Campbell, *Op. Cit.*, p. 49.
9. White, P.W. "Motivation Reconsidered: The Concept of Competence." *Psychological Review,* 66, 1957, pp. 297-333.
10. Ziegler, H.P. "The Sensual Feel of Food." *Psychology Today,* August, 1975, pp. 62-67.
11. Whiting, J.W.M. and Mourer, O.H. "Habit Progression and Regression – A Laboratory Study of Some Factors Relevant to Human Socialization." *Journal of Comparative Psychology,* 36, 1945, pp. 229-253.

12. Montgomery, D.C. and Markman, J.A. "The Relationship Between Fear and Exploratory Behavior." *Journal of Comparative Physiology and Psychology,* 48, 1955, pp. 254-260.
13. Berlyne, D.E. "Novelty and Curiosity as Determinants of Exploratory Behavior." *British Journal of Psychology,* 41, 1950, pp. 68-80.
14. Brown, Evelyn. "An Ethological Theory of Play." *Journal of AAHPER,* September, 1968.
15. Berlyne, D.E. *Conflict, Arousal and Curiosity.* New York: McGraw-Hill, 1960.
16. Maddi, S.R. "Exploratory Behavior and Variation-seeking in Man." In *Functions of Varied Experience.* Edited by D.W. Fiske and S.R. Maddi. Homewood, Illinois: Dorsey Press, 1961.
17. Ellis, M.J. *Why People Play.* Englewood Cliffs: Prentice-Hall, 1973.

Chapter Six

Fantasy, Play, Creativity and Mental Health

William Michaelis

> ". . .with my anti-experimental bias I don't save myself from trouble, but it does have a lot of sideways opening effects."
>
> Gregory Bateson[1]

The United Nations International Year of the Child was 1979. But shouldn't every year be the year of the child? One of the ten rights of children as declared by the United Nations is the "right to full opportunity for play and recreation." To discover what this means, it is important to reexamine the nature of play and to ask if our services are in line with our professional and theoretical knowledge. Our job as play professionals is not just to provide activities or to fill people's time, but to educate people for leisure. Everything that we do, from the way we use our tools, to the environments that we create for people and the type of leadership that we provide, should have this focus. The objective of leisure education is for people to have an understanding and actualization of the play experience in their lives. But what is play?

There are strong threads of interconnection between play and several other important concepts, notably fantasy, creativity, mental health and the "flow" phenomenon. Each of these has its own intracacies and muddled complexity, and each has relevance for human happiness. This chapter will explore those connections and suggest specific implications for the leisure services field.

PLAY AND MENTAL HEALTH: THE PRIMARY OF RIGHT BRAIN PROCESSES

David Gray, in a classic article, suggested that recreation was primarily an existential state. It was an experience that one received from, or an attitude that one brought to, particular episodes in one's life. It was a way of looking at the world that was not tied to specific time blocks or activities.[2] Play might also be viewed this way as some of its most significant components are fantasy, imagination and openendedness.[3]

Although play may be very intense, there is a healthy air of "unreality" about it. But there is more.

There has been much recent research on left and right brain functions. Psychologists tell us that we have primarily two modes of thinking. They are: (1) our right brain *primary* processes—our non-rational, dreamlike, emotional symbolizing modes; this is the powerful stuff of our tears, laughter, anger, hopes, fears, loves, loneliness and, yes, our play. And (2) our left brain *secondary* processes—our cognitive, reality-based, rational modes; this is our organizing, planning self. Although play certainly contains aspects of rational planning, its magic and power lies in its attention to right brain, primary process elements. Eli Bower noted, ". . .that, for play and life in general, it is the primary process mode that is generally the more powerful, pervasive and satisfying of human symbolizing experiences, although secondary processes do serve an important organizing and planning function in our lives."[4] Bower goes on to point out that a *balance* of both primary and secondary modes is necessary for mental health.

Erik Erickson confirms that play serves a very important mental health function. He reports that in a 30-year follow-up of people who had been studied as children, those subjects who had the most interesting and fulfilling lives were the ones who had managed to keep a sense of playfulness at the center of things.[5] The sad fact is that our institutions give very little attention to play and right brain functions. Most people are taught to put away "the child" as they are subtly socialized into mass society.

PLAY AND CREATIVITY

Arieti describes the creative act in similar terms. He, too, uses the dualism of primary and secondary processes, but he postulates a third mode which he calls the *tertiary* process. He states that the task of this process is to fuse the irrational with the rational processes and thus produce an integrative balance and the magic synthesis of creativity. Both Bower and Arieti advocate that greater attention be paid to primary process development—the stuff that is the magic and power of play. Arieti states it this way: ". . . A society that urges the young to 'stop daydreaming and pay attention,' to 'stop playing and get to work,' is not one that encourages magic at all."[6]

Further evidence linking the right brain elements of play to creativity comes from systematic research and the identification of blocks to creative lifestyles. Psychologists identify some of the main blocks to creativity as (1) the reluctance to play, (2) sensory dullness, (3) impoverished fantasy life, (4) the reluctance to "let go" and (5) an impoverished emotional life.[7]

Corrine Hutt, in a series of longitudinal studies of 3-7 year olds, has shown that the opportunity for inventive and exploratory play affects a child's later creativity and social interaction. Feitelson and Ross also found that play experiences influence creativity.

> ". . .after a period of play training, their experimental group significantly increased their scores on a battery of creativity tests. Children who become more imaginative in play can apparently transfer some of that imaginativeness to their responses on conventional tests of creative thinking, such as completing unfinished pictures in a way no one else would think of. The most obvious reading from this study is that creativity is encouraged by the development of imaginativeness in play."[8]

Bower summarizes our task when he states that ". . .a society concerned with producing a fair amount of creative and imaginative adults must protect the play modalities of childhood."[9]

PLAY, DREAMS AND FANTASY

Dreams and Daydreams as Play

Internalized fantasy or dreaming as a form of "play" has long held validity among many play theorists. Sutton-Smith speaks of adult daydreaming as playing around in the head.

> "Play seems to parallel dreams in that it contains at least two types of processing: on the one hand the quite mundane assimilation of daily events and on the other the fairly elaborate and vivid construction of imaginary companions and the like."[10]

As children, most of us lived in a "never never land" where we externally acted out our fantasies. It may have been the backyard, the imaginative worlds of dolls or cars, the forts built on bunk beds, the pickup games where the rules constantly changed, or the abandoned lot down the street. In many ways the whole world was accessible and limited only by imaginations. We were not locked into narrow conceptualizations of everyday objects. A table could be a fort or, turned upside down, a ship or a motorcycle. But as we grew, powerful social forces buoyed by peer and adult pressure told us (overtly or covertly) to put aside that childlike freshness and creativity. Expressions of external fantasy were generally no longer legitimized or encouraged and play became more structured and reality-secondary process oriented. Bower suggests that much of the pain in growing up is the pull between the childlike fantasy and feelings of primary process and the demands of rational secondary process realities. It is clear, however, that as children grow to adulthood more of their fantasy and primary process activity is relegated to dreams and daydreams or *internalized play*. But these are still play and they do serve an important subconscious and conscious right brain function. But what if they are blocked?

Blocked Dreams (Internal Play) Lead to Disfunctional Behavior

Recent dream research indicates that smooth functioning in the "awake, rational reality state" is influenced by the integrative primary process function that is performed while we sleep. During sleep there are times when we wiggle our eyes and possibly dream a little. This wiggling has been called by sleep researchers rapid eye movement (REM).

> "First, accepting the REM behavior as an indication of dreaming, researchers have found that people dream about every 90 minutes or so during normal sleep, though very few of these dreams are remembered. In other words, as human beings, we go through a kind of thinking in our sleep which seems to be very necessary. REM's can be monitored so that when the eyes start to wiggle, the person can be awakened by a bell and prevented from dreaming. . . .When dreaming is persistently blocked, so that primary process thinking is continually interrupted, it becomes very difficult for such individuals to function in their waking state. Humans whose REM thinking periods are consistently blocked become hostile, irritable, and a little disoriented. . . . Our sleeping state probably allows us a kind of rendezvous and sorting out of rational and non-rational thinking so we can awaken fresh for new experiences and concepts. Research on sleep confirms the need by man for increasing opportunities for integrating primary and secondary modalities of thought."[11]

This sorting out and integrating process that night dreams accomplish occurs in a subconscious state. But isn't the day dreaming that Sutton-Smith describes as one form of adult play also accomplishing this "sorting out" (bridging) process in a more conscious awake state? And isn't the spontaneous make-believe fantasy play that children externally act out also accomplishing this?

The Importance of Daydreams, Fantasy and Make Believe Play

Jerome Singer states that the nurturing of fantasy in our lives is vital for mental health.

> "Fantasies and daydreams, far from being irrelevant and insubstantial, may be the foundation of serentity and purpose in our lives. . . .

Those who have trouble using fantasy to enrich their experience or as a substitute for aggression run the risk of serious trouble at each stage of their lives. . . .A well developed fantasy life seems to be partly responsible for independence, tranquility and realism."[12]

But the encouragement of fantasy still frightens a lot of people. Sutton-Smith, however, suggests strong linkages between fantasy and the development of creativity.

> "Teachers, even of middle-class background, still ask me whether a child with high levels of fantasy is not in danger of a nervous breakdown. The answer is no; in most cases, he is only in danger of becoming an outstanding scientist, writer, scholar, or perhaps even an international chess player."[13]

But what if people have difficulty with daydreaming, fantasy and make believe play?

Blocked Fantasy and Make Believe Play Leads to Disfunctional Behavior

Singer details studies with aggressive delinquents, drug abusers, and overweight people, among others, that seem to indicate close realtionships between their "problems" and their lack of elaborated fantasies. He suggests that the aggressive group may never have had the early contacts with adults that allowed them to try out playfully and in fantasy the complex and relatively self-controlled behavior of adults. The drug (including alcohol) abusers more than nonusers were found to be much more

> ". . .subject to boredom and mind wanderings and their fantasies, though frequent, tend to be fleeting and undeveloped. They are not as interested in inner consciousness as in blotting things out or developing external sensations. Marijuana users were found to be the exception to this research and were generally found to be interested in expanding both their internal and external awareness."[14]

Singer also reports studies of school-age children and adults which indicate relationships between healthy fantasy development and behavior.

The development of imaginative play, which allows the exercise of right brain functions, becomes increasingly important in light of the often reported negative effects of heavy television viewing on children. Dr. Lawrence Friedman points out that regular television viewing has rendered children passive, thus denying them normal outlets for their fantasy and aggression. "All television, except in small doses, feeds children ready-made fantasy, at a time when fantasy making is crucial for their development. . . ."[15]

It has been suggested that the power and magic of play lies in its attention to primary process right brain functions, and the balanced integration of these functions is necessary for health and creativity. Final evidence for this position comes from the phenomenological investigations of the psychologist Mihaly Csikszentmihalyi into "flow" experiences. Simply put, "flow" is enjoyment, and although enjoyment is made up of both rational (left brain) and non-rational (right brain) elements, it is argued that "flow" is also mostly influenced by the primary process mode. A look at the reported experiences of the phenomena suggests why.

TOWARD HIGHER CONSCIOUSNESS – THE FLOW EXPERIENCE

Csikszentmihalyi was interested in the feelings that emerged from activities found to be rewarding in and of themselves. He studied people in a variety of work-play settings–surgery, different sports, rock-climbing and artistic pursuits–and discovered that as individuals became totally immersed in a sport or creative act, they lost a sense of time and the external world and they experienced an ecstatic "flowing" feeling. His investigations indicated that this feeling approximated an "altered state of being" for those subjects.[16]

> "In this state the person loses a self-conscious sense of himself and of time. He gains a heightened awareness of his physical involvement with the activity. The person in flow finds, among other things, his concentration vastly increased and his feedback from the activity enormously enhanced."[17]

Certain core elements always emerged from the different descriptions. One of them was a merging of self with the environment:

> "One of the rock climbers put it this way: 'You are so involved in what you are doing you aren't thinking of yourself as separate from the immediate activity.'. . ."[18]

Another core element was the dreamlike sense of time.

> "In flow there is a sense of being lost in the action. . . .'Time passes a hundred times faster. In this sense it resembles the dream state,' said a chess player. Sometimes the centering of attention produces a spatial alteration akin to the changed sense of time."[19]

What is the relevance of the flow phenomenon? It appears to be closely related to the existential attitude by which play and re-creation were defined earlier. It is one of the higher forms of enjoyment, and Csikszentmihalyi's research points out that this enjoyment can occur in a wide variety of activities and is not limited to any particular time frame. The application of the flow experience principle may have tremendous potential for integrating the "ideal play state" into all aspects of every-day life, thereby helping facilitate the holistic merger of traditional work-play spheres. And it can be learned.

Csikszentmihalyi states that in addition to changing environments (i.e., home, job, associates) there are four requirements for increasing people's potential for flow.[20] They are:

1. A need to fit the difficulty of the task to our skill levels. This is an external prerequisite that people can control and it relates strongly to the arousal theory of play described by Ellis.[21] If the demands of the activity are too slight a person will feel bored. Industrial psychologists have long pointed to this factor as a key contributor to the alienation of the assembly line worker. To use a recreation example, try being in flow by playing tic/tac/toe with a friend for three hours. It just isn't likely to happen.

   On the other hand, if the challenge is too great for a person's ability, he feels anxious and this blocks the potential for flow. It would seem that this fact alone proves a strong argument for multi-skill level intramural approaches at all age levels, and for rules and leadership flexibility in leisure service programs. These are not new ideas but certainly increase the probability of people experiencing the play state. In addition, this match of skills and tasks provides a strong argument for more holistic work approaches. This is the only external prerequisite for flow: the remaining three are internal.

2. A need to focus attention and merge one's awareness with the activity that one is involved in. . .to become totally absorbed in the moment of concentration on the activity. Did you ever get caught up in the energy of a good ping pong rally?

3. A need to forget time. This involves people allowing themselves to focus on the moment, to put away clocks and stop racing from one thing to another. These times are often when re-creation or leisure is truly experienced.[22]

4. A need for people to relax more and to become more aware of their bodies and senses. Flow depends on a relaxed body and an alert mind. There are many techniques for developing this. The growing holistic health movement is in the forefront of promoting this concept. Dr. Jim Polidora, a professor at the University of California-Davis Medical School and a holistic play practitioner uses such things as dance therapy, the eastern martial arts, massage, yoga and many other techniques to help people actualize the play experience in their lives.[23] These methods have tremendous implications for the leisure service profession, but are rarely utilized.

All of the above steps that Csikszentmihalyi identifies are key elements of leisure education. They are practical ways to help people grow by enabling them to be more comfortable and aware of themselves, to be less chained to time and to be more relaxed. By incorporating these steps into their lives people can maximize the play state—the higher consciousness of flow. The ultimate result of the understanding of "the fun in fun" may be an increase in healthier, happier people and a redefinition of the work ethic.

The flow experience is a form of higher consciousness accessible to all people. At least part of its power comes from its relationship to the right brain, primary process mode of symbolizing. The chess player, described earlier, referred to the time alteration experience in flow as a dream-like state. And dreams are primarily a right brain activity. If dreams and daydreams are forms of internal play that serve an important integrative mental health function in human beings, then it may be logical to assume that make believe play and flow serve some of the same functions in a more activity oriented conscious state. Even the surgeon who loses himself in the flow of the moment of the operation, and who certainly is attending to rational reality states, is experiencing something beyond that reality. It may, in fact, be that "pure play state" that fosters the total immersion into the activity, the heightened awareness and feedback, and the dreamlike loss of time. Further suggestive evidence for the connection of flow to such primary process activities as dreams, daydreams and make believe play comes from looking at what happens to people when their flow is blocked.

Csikszentmihalyi discovered that when the people he studied attempted to inhibit their preferred forms of flow, for example daydreaming, talking, gaming, or watching, or when they were blocked in some other ways, they became very irritable.[24] This mental health disfunction is consistent with research cited earlier on blocked primary process activities such as dreaming, fantasy and make believe play.

INTERRELATIONSHIPS

It has been suggested that the power and magic of play lies in its attention to the primary process mode of symbolizing, and that the active functioning of this mode, as evidenced in such things as dreams, daydreams, fantasy, make believe play and flow, is crucial for mental health. Also, the playful exercise of this mode is a key element in creativity. Mental health then might be more broadly defined as the actualization of creative lifestyles—lifestyles that are open to growth, sensitivity, the universal quest for love and human happiness. Each of the concepts of fantasy, play, creativity, and mental health is complex, but they are indeed interrelated as illustrated on the accompanying schematic diagram. It should be clear that one common denominator for creative lifestyles is play.

The understanding of the nature of play has important implications for enriching our lives and improving practices in the leisure services field. The job of all professionals in the field, as noted earlier, is to be leisure educators. If leisure service professionals are to help in the facilitation of creative lifestyles and human happiness, the environments and programs that they provide and the tools and leadership techniques that they use must be consistent with the theoretical understanding of play.

IMPLICATIONS: BRIDGING THE GAP BETWEEN THEORY AND PRACTICE

It is clear that more people today are engaging in more activities that have leisure potential.[25] But it is also clear that our society is experiencing an accelerating cultural lag that makes the job of educating people about play that much more important. Too often the values of play that are professed by the leisure profession are not reflected in its services. One of the strengths of the recreation profession has always been its pragmatic problem solving ability, and it is important for professionals to understand their clients' needs and to help meet them. But for leisure educators there is a greater task: to provide not only for *what is* but also models of *what can be*. All programs, in reality, should be geared to educating people about healthy play values. Leadership in this area is increasingly important because it is clear that the people that take part in leisure service activities are also constantly being influenced by strong social forces that often confuse or distort healthy play values. For example, in an increasingly rapid-paced, depersonalized, technological, consumer oriented society such as ours; forces such as conspicuous consumption, escapism and self-destruction through the media of drugs, and obligatory mass leisure all have an influence on play values. Urbanism, the highly structured product orientation of capitalism, sexism, cultural stereotypes of such groups as the disabled, and early parental mixed messages such as withholding play as a punishment or using it as a reward, also confuse the conceptions and values of play for many people.[26] And although it is changing, the work ethic is still alive and well. Leisure education cannot be viewed in

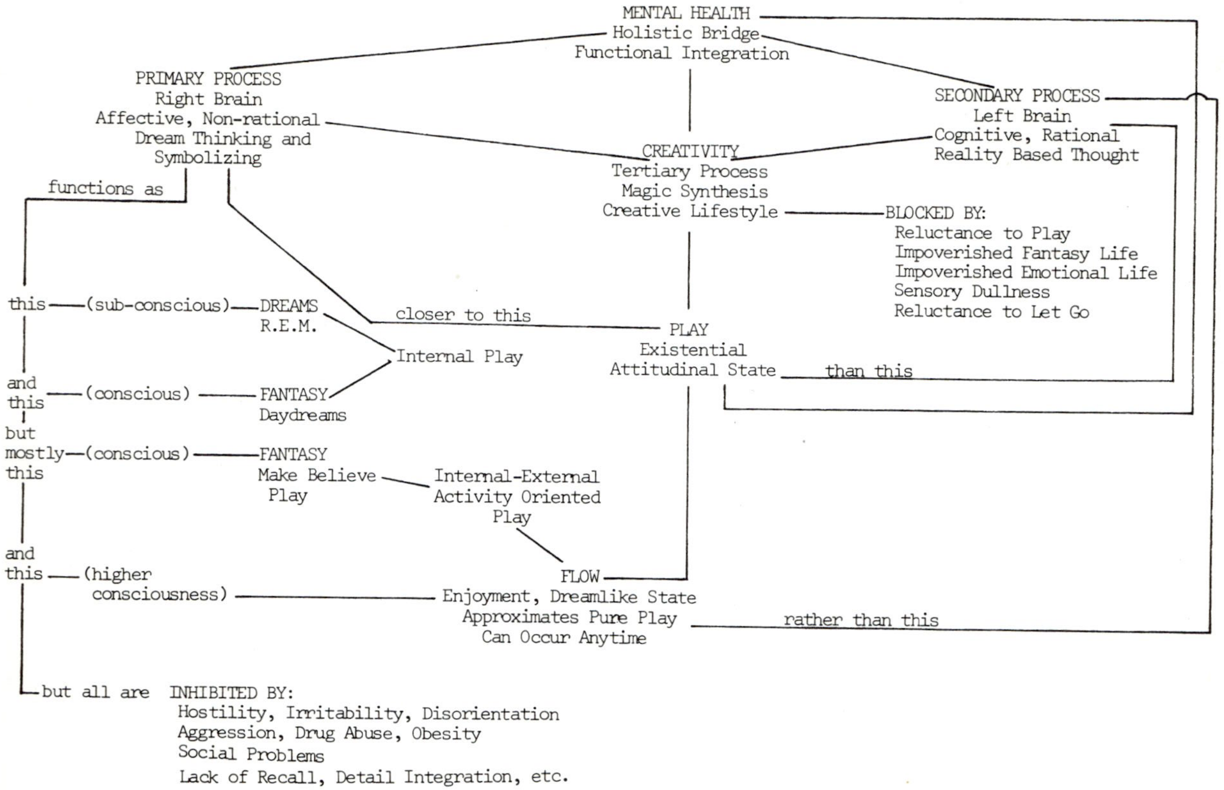
MENTAL HEALTH
Holistic Bridge
Functional Integration
PRIMARY PROCESS
Right Brain
Affective, Non-rational
Dream Thinking and
Symbolizing
SECONDARY PROCESS
Left Brain
Cognitive, Rational
Reality Based Thought
CREATIVITY
Tertiary Process
Magic Synthesis
Creative Lifestyle
BLOCKED BY:
Reluctance to Play
Impoverished Fantasy Life
Impoverished Emotional Life
Sensory Dullness
Reluctance to Let Go
functions as
this
(sub-conscious)
DREAMS
R.E.M.
closer to this
PLAY
Existential
Attitudinal State
than this
Internal Play
and this
(conscious)
FANTASY
Daydreams
but mostly this
(conscious)
FANTASY
Make Believe
Play
Internal-External
Activity Oriented
Play
and this
(higher consciousness)
FLOW
Enjoyment, Dreamlike State
Approximates Pure Play
Can Occur Anytime
rather than this
but all are INHIBITED BY:
Hostility, Irritability, Disorientation
Aggression, Drug Abuse, Obesity
Social Problems
Lack of Recall, Detail Integration, etc.

a vacuum, and all of the above factors, as well as many others, make the job of value leadership that much more important. A more careful look at children's play and socialization further illustrates this point.

PLAY AND SOCIALIZATION

Recall that Bower suggested that a society concerned with producing a fair amount of imaginative adults must protect the play modalities of childhood. As children we had tremendous potential creativity within us and exercised it because in a very existential way we knew what play was all about. We had adventures, challenged ourselves, played made-up games with made up rules, explored new areas of the world in our heads and in activities. We knew what play was about because it included such elements as flexibility, change and spontaneity. Fantasies were allowed and feelings were exercised. Play had a healthy air of unreality about it; often loose and open-ended. Play wasn't without its "serious" moments, difficulties or hurt feelings, but things were worked out because we wanted to keep playing. For the most part we provided support for each other's play.[27] If lucky, we might have had support for playfulness from some significant adults in our lives. But something happened—to many of us, at least.

As we grew older, powerful social forces began to influence playtime and thus conceptions of both play and the world. The message was to grow up and put aside that child self.[28] The abuses of two forces in particular have a very strong influence on children. The first is the existence of very structured, highly competitive, adult dominated youth sports leagues that emphasize a win-at-all-cost ethic. And the second is the power of the plug-in drug, television. Both of these forces, youth sports and television, can be playful, positive educational tools, but there is increasing evidence of their abuse and this abuse has had a strong influence on childrens' abilities to conceptualize and operationalize play alternatives.

For example, by the time a high school student graduates he or she will have spent more time in front of "the tube" than in the classroom, and most children as young as five years old watch television for more than 25 hours a week. In addition more and more evidence continues to accumulate about the negative effects of heavy viewing on such things as creativity, the development of reading skills, the communicative emotional climate of the home, self-image, and healthy nutritional habits. Studies have also suggested links between heavy viewing and increased fears, violence and reality distortion.[29]

The abuses of youth sports are also well documented. The "pro model" of big money, rigid levels of structure and a narrow definition of winning that includes only those with the highest score has filtered down to youth, with a strong push from the media. Although there are many well-meaning, caring adults in youth sports, there are also those whose expectations of children are too high, and they crush individuality and promote conformity by attempting to create little five and six-year old warriors. They lose sight of the playful developmental *process* that is the power of youth sports, and often their 'products' are increased violence, cheating, concern with bigger trophies and an increasing number of young athletic dropouts. Those who most need the positive reinforcement of healthy activity are often the first cut or spend most of their careers on the bench. Too often this aspect of childhood play has become over-institutionalized and "adultocentric."[30]

Most professionals would state that they would like to have a hand in facilitating more creative, independent individuals. However, most recreational leadership and programs foster dependence on structure and experts and create a group think mentality. This is indeed the era of the expert. Witness the rise of, for example, racquetball clubs and the variety of recreational skills classes. Certainly much good can come from these, for without them, many are lost. They don't know how to play on their own, and the roots of the national disease of boredom grow deeper. All people have the potential for creative, playful independence, but they are subtly socialized out of that magic, creativity, flexibility and individuality that is play; the stuff that is vital for healthful growth and development. And children buy into the media, youth sports and other influencing social forces (even the abuses) because they perceive very few alternatives. After all, adults *are* modeling their options. So children begin to perceive play as a narrow set of behaviors. Self-developed fantasy and pick-up games are things to be put aside. Play is to be structured to provide instant gratification or is something to pay for. Although there are many positive exceptions, unfortunately recreation services, despite a potentially strong theoretical play base, still mostly reflect the confusing social forces influencing leisure rather than leading to a healthier future.

AND A CHILD SHALL LEAD. . .

The main job of the leisure service profession is values leadership and that must include the nurturing of the positive child self and right brain elements for old and young alike. Education, for example, for all its innovations, is still mostly cognitive and career oriented and based on faith and fear; drill and grill. Yet the development of the affective-primary process mode is crucial for creativity and mental health. And the operationalization of this leadership challenge will take many forms.

Not only is there a need to revitalize the traditional offerings of most recreation departments, but the future demands that a variety of playful leadership, programming and environmental alternatives be provided to people. Children, teens and grownups alike need to perceive real options and most programs are, in reality, very similar to each other. No one model can meet the diverse needs of all individuals and groups.

There is much to be done. In the broad sense the profession must refocus its attention on play as seen from the child's perspective. Traditional offerings even of the most competitive type, still have an important place in the scheme of things. But the abuses must be eliminated and the values focus must once again be on the *process* of enjoying, on the playfulness that is central to our profession. Leaders must ask what's best for the development of mental health, human happiness and creativity. What messages are we giving people? Rather than running the serious risk of duplicating the left brain secondary process in their 'free' time, and the stresses and anxieties that may accompany it, people need to be reminded not to take play too seriously. The non-rational unreality of it is important. The magical right brain elements are the factors that free us from the boxes that we are in.

This will require leadership; leadership that does not just provide what people want, but expands into the areas where there is presently very little being done. There is still, for example, a paucity of cultural arts offerings in most public programs. It is clear that the full range of arts provide the much needed exercise of the right brain elements. They need as much (if not more) attention as sports programs. Related activities such as movement education, theater, imagination and fantasy games, and the acclimatization movement in outdoor education all have much potential to put people in touch with themselves and with the total environment. Important leisure education messages come from all of these activities. That is, "It's okay to touch, to move, to feel, to dream, to giggle to play and to create adventure in one's daily life."

THE FUTURE: THE CREATION OF DIVERSE MODELS

People need options, and it is interesting to note that some of the most innovative models for the encouragement of healthy play values come from outside the mainstream of the leisure services profession. These alternatives not only provide some future direction for the parks and recreation movement, but also help to remind those in leadership of the nature and importance of play.

Adventure Playgrounds

The adventure playground movement has been alive and well for a number of years in Europe and it is growing in North America. What adventure playgrounds do is provide the space, materials and caring supervision of children to create and own their play experiences. They are environments for validating the powerful primary process elements of play. Some of their values are that (1) they encourage social and moral growth because there is a lack of adult prescribed structure, (2) they provide for change and flexibility, (3) they provide for fantasy making, (4) they provide for physical and psychological development through self-selected risk taking, (5) they are a good vehicle for mainstreaming and integrating diverse groups and, (6) they are a great setting for the modeling of play behavior for children by adults.

At adventure playgrounds, children learn to interact cooperatively to solve problems, and to deal with change, perhaps some of the most important survival skills in a "future shock" world.[31] Girls learn the message that it's okay to learn building skills or to roughhouse. There is not only a low key adult to supervise, but the same adult might be painted by the children or slide down the mud slide with them. This "modeling," which research tells us is a crucial aspect in the development of playfulness in children, gives an important message: "Big people can play too!"[32]

Adventure Games/Project Adventure[33]

The recognition of the need for and value of adventure type activities for both young and old people helped spawn the Adventure Games movement. Stemming originally from the outdoor education movement, Project Adventure uses games and activities that involve cooperation, initiative, challenge, risk and fantasy. Although one person described Adventure Games as a "fun form of anxiety," the ultimate goal is to put people in touch with their physical selves, their abilities and their feelings as well as to connect with the people around them. Project Adventure's attention to both the realistic elements of risk and challenge and the playful primary process elements of fantasy and feelings provides a healthy integrative learning experience. One of the most successful juvenile diversion programs uses adventure activities as a major part of its approach in self-concept development.

Project Adventure can be viewed not only as an alternative physical education program, but it has also developed resources and provided consultation for schools to use adventure activities to teach traditional subject matter in an engaging way.

This integration of leisure education into the schools is vital. In addition to Project Adventure there are regional and national programs that provide useful models. The "Play and Games for Learning" and the "Play Express" programs in the San Francisco Bay Area are two examples.[34] And the National Recreation and Park Association's Leisure Education Advancement Project has a variety of excellent resource materials available.[35] All of these programs educate teachers, students, and community groups about the integration and importance of healthy play experiences. We need this advocacy, even if it takes place in the street.

New Games[36]

New Games is about playing for the fun of it. It was begun a few years ago by the New Games Foundation of San Francisco; its purpose was to foster and communicate a style of play encouraging participation, community and creativity. Since that time it has become an international movement to help people refocus on the process of enjoying the play experience. A variety of techniques are used to make this happen, including cooperative games, trust games, theater and expressive activities, icebreakers and constructive, competitive "soft war" outlets for aggression. In fact almost anything can be "New Games" because it's not so much *what* people play but *how* they play it. The goal is to re-acquaint people with the creative child-self that is within them; to exercise that right brain; ultimately to build a community of caring players where everyone is a "winner."

New Games is also about breaking down the barriers that divide people in their play. People of all ages and abilities can come together in joyful celebration. In one sense it is a revitalization of the family recreation concept, and in another sense, like the Adventure Playground, New Games activities provide a setting for mainstreaming and integration. Fathers, mothers, sons, daughters, able-bodied and disabled people can come together and play and learn from each other. This is accomplished by providing choices for people to opt in and out of, and through game change and flexible leadership. In an open, trusting and democratic play community people can share a game, change the rules of an activity to make it "work" for all the players, or create an entirely new game. This concept of "ownership" is central to the New Games philosophy, because it gives people the message that they have the power to "referee" themselves and to actualize the creative play experience in other aspects of their lives.

Cooperative Games[37]

A similar movement that is an excellent model is the Cooperative Games Movement led by Terry Orlick at the University of Ottawa. Like New Games, Orlick's focus is on the process of enjoyable challenges. In a recent book he shares a wide variety of resources including international games, self-refereed intramural programs, cooperative games for all ages, and academic learning experiences. The focus is on playing and winning *together* to build positive self-concepts.

. . . AND MANY MORE: CONCLUSIONS

These are just a sampling. There are many similar models that concerned recreators should be aware of. The Children's Museums movement, devoted to making the visitor a participant by touching, exploring, manipulating, and testing, is among other notable examples. More than 20 such museums have been established in recent years. Organizations and movements like the Game Preserve, the Play Factory, the Human Service Movement, the Eastern Cooperative Recreation School, the Esalen Sports Institute, the Power of Play, the Big Apple Circus, Dancing Bear Theater and others are all doing important pioneering work that deserves attention and support. In fact there are so many organizations that a national clearinghouse is needed to connect them and provide information about them to interested parties.

Their common strength lies in the promotion of healthy play values and a recognition that the magic of play comes mostly from its attention to non-rational primary process modes of symbolizing—the fantasy, the imagination, the feelings, the sensory awareness, the power of that right brain and its connections to creativity and mental health.

We are entering a new era of multi-discipline Playshops, as well as an era of tight budget constraints. It is not without significance that most of the above models are low cost alternatives. People need a variety of play options, and the gap between theory and practice needs to be bridged if the profession is serious about helping people actualize the play experience, and ultimately achieving greater "flow" in their lives. Initially people may demand just "more of the same" but once they appreciate the excitement, fun and energy of these options, they will demand more. And leisure services will be transformed into a more viable vehicle for human happiness. This is a challenge for a humanistic profession. Each year should be the "year of the child" for big and little people alike.

"Teacher, let me swim in a puddle,
Let me race a cloud in the sky,
Let me build a house without walls,
But most of all. . .
Let me laugh at nothing things."[38]

REFERENCES

1. Bateson, Gregory. "Both Sides of the Necessary Paradox: Meditations on George Bateson and the Death of the Bread and Butterfly." *Harpers*, 1973.
2. Gray, David. "This Alien Thing Called Leisure." In: Gray, David and Pellegrino, Donald P. (Eds.). *Reflections on the Recreation and Park Movement.* Dubuque: W. C. Brown, 1973. p. 7.
3. Berlyne, D. E. "Laughter, Humor and Play." In: Lendzey, G. and Aronson, E. (Eds.). *Handbook of Social Psychology*. Reading, Massachusetts: Addison Wesley, 1968.
4. Bower, E. "Plays the Thing." In: Bower, E. *Games in Education and Development*. Springfield: Charles C. Thomas, 1974. pp. 10-11.
5. Bruner, Jerome. "Play is Serious Business." *Psychology Today*. 8, (January), 1974. pp. 81-83.
6. May, Charles. "Study of Creativity and Sense of Magic." Review of: Arieti, S. *Creativity: The Magic Synthesis.* In: *Sunday Los Angeles Times Book Review Section*, January, 1977.
7. Kaufman, Lynn. "Blocks to Creativity." Handout in E. Bower's Class, University of California, Berkeley School of Education, 1970.
8. In: Sutton-Smith, Brian. "The Useless Made Useful: Play as Variability Training." *School Review*. 83, (February) 1975. pp. 197-214.
9. Bower, *Op.Cit.*, p. 11.
10. Sutton-Smith. *Op.Cit.*
11. Bower, E. et.al. *Learning to Play/Playing to Learn.* Berkeley, California: University of California, Berkeley Creative Arts Printing, 1974. pp. 8-21.
12. Singer, Jerome. "Fantasy, The Foundation of Serenity." *Psychology Today*. 10, (July) 1976. p. 32.
13. Sutton-Smith. *Op.Cit.* pp. 197-214.
14. Singer, *Op.Cit.*
15. Caplan, Frank and Caplan, Theresa. "Creativity Through Play." *The Power of Play*. Garden City: Anchor Press, 1973. pp. 149-179.
16. Csikszentimihalyi, M. *Flow: Studies of Enjoyment*. Public Health Service Report: University of Chicago, 1974.
17. Furlong, W. "The Flow Experience: The Fun in Fun." *Psychology Today*. 1976 (June). pp. 36.
18. *Ibid*. p. 37.
19. *Ibid*. p. 37.
20. Csikszentmihalyi, M. *Beyond Boredoms and Anxiety*. San Francisco: Jossey-Bass, 1976. See also Csikszentmihalyi, *Op.Cit.*, 1974 and Furlong, *Op.Cit.*, 1976.

21. Ellis, M. J. *Why People Play.* Englewood Cliffs, New Jersey: Prentice Hall, 1973.
22. deGrazia, S. *Of Time, Work and Leisure.* Garden City, New York: Anchor Books, 1964.
23. Polidora, James. *Course Syllabus and Reading Guide for Behavioral Biology 451*. University of California, Davis Medical School, 1977.
24. Csikszentmihalyi, M. *Op.Cit.*, 1974 and Furlong, *Op.Cit.*, 1976.
25. Glasser, W. "Needed for America: The Kind of Recreation that Frees the Mind." *U.S. News and World Report*. (May 23) 1977. pp. 74-76.
26. Gunn, Scout Lee. "Blocks to Play." National Recreation and Parks Association Congress. Las Vegas, Nevada. October, 1977.
27. See, for example: Hawes, Bess Tomax. "Law and Order on the Playground." In: Bower, E. *Games in Education and Development.* Springfield, Charles C. Thomas, 1974. pp. 12-22.
28. Montague, A. "Don't be Adultish." *Psychology Today*. 11 (August) 1977. p. 46.
29. Comstock, George. *Television and Human Behavior: The Key Studies*. The Rand Corporation, 1975.
30. Orlick, T. *Winning Through Cooperation*. Washington, D.C.: Acroplis Book Co., 1978.
31. Sutton-Smith. *Op.Cit.*
32. Feitelson, D. and Ross, G. "The Neglected Factor: Play." *Human Development*. (16) 1973. pp. 202-223.
33. Project Adventure, P. O. Box 157. Hamilton, Massachusetts 01936.
34. Michaelis, W. "Have You Ever Thought That. . . .?" *California Parks and Recreation Magazine*. (August) 1975. pp. 25-26.
35. National Recreation and Park Association. *Leisure Education Advancement Project*. Arlington, Virginia: The Association, 1978.
36. See, for example: Fluegelmar, Andrew. *The New Games Book.* Garden City, New York. Dolphin-Doubleday, 1976.
37. Orlick, *Op.Cit.* 1978 and Orlick, Terry. *The Cooperative Sports and Games Book.* Westmaster: Pantheon, 1979.
38. Cullum, A. *The Geranium on the Window Sill Just Died, But Teacher Went Right On*. Holland: Harlin Quest, 1971.

Chapter Seven

Creative Growth Through Play and its Implications for Recreation Practice

Doyle Bishop and Claudine Jeanrenaud

A cherished belief among many play specialists is that play enhances the development of creativity.[1] The fact is, the paths to play have many dead ends, detours, and debris that discourage instead of enhance the development of creativity. These bad road conditions are numerous and often not easily visible until it is too late. The traffic engineers, road crews, and patrolmen who manage the journey through play (i.e. parents, teachers, recreation leaders, therapists, and others) must work hard to remove these roadblocks. If they do not, play experiences will almost certainly help to make non-creative children and later adults.

We propose to demonstrate these roadblocks with a general model of the stages, or choicepoints, involved in play. This model is the authors' integration of diverse ideas about play as well as some that, up to now, have not been closely linked to play. The model is the result of the authors' many discussions between themselves and with students. The detailed ideas included in the model are not novel; we have borrowed heavily from previous research and theory. What is original is the particular ways in which we have tried to integrate the ideas to provide one view of play and its link to creativity.

It seems to us that our emphasis, in the model, on the importance of exploratory behavior and its balance against too much or too little directiveness and structure, as a path to creative growth, provides a focal point for examining some possible limitations of current recreation practice. In the last part of the chapter we explore those limits. But first it is important to look at the path to creative growth and the ways in which it can be blocked.

The main ideas from previous work that we have relied on are those of Hutt[2] and Linford and Jeanrenaud,[3] who laid the groundwork for viewing play as a series of critical stages; reinforcement theorists such as Hull[4] and Skinner[5], whose principles of learning help to show how movement through the stages of play can be enhanced or retarded; arousal theorists, particularly Berlyne,[6] and Fiske and Maddi,[7] whose ideas about concepts like novelty, complexity, curiosity, and exploration help to define the distinctive crossroads on the path through play;

personality and development theorists like Piaget,[8] Harvey, Hunt and Schroder,[9] and Eysenck,[10] whose ideas illustrate how different combinations of persons and environments, for both players and managers, can produce different outcomes at the different stages of play; and some investigations of play and creativity such as those by Torrance," Lieberman,[12] Sutton-Smith,[13] and Bishop and Chace,[14] which have demonstrated that play is a powerful medium for inhibiting or enhancing creative potential. These authors and works are mentioned here so that the rest of the paper can proceed without continual reference to previous literature.

Refer to the diagram in Figure 1. For our purposes, a journey through play begins at:

THE ATTENTION STAGE

There is a story about an old farmer who used to periodically whack his mule on the snout with a stick of firewood. When asked why he did this, the farmer replied, "I can't l'arn him nuthin if'n I don't first git his attention!" Now, we do not recommend the whack-between-the-eyes method to get a kid started at play. But the farmer's wisdom, verified repeatedly by psychological research, is sound in principle: In order to begin learning anything, the person must first pay attention to some object or situation. No attention, no learning. No learning, no creativity.

NOVELTY

Novelty, or the extent to which an object differs, relatively or absolutely, from what has occured before, helps to gain one's attention. So does the *intensity* of the object or situation – how much it stands out from the rest of its environment. Things that are familiar or plain will not grab our attention very often or for very long. How many of you have noticed the light bulb in your ceiling lately? If you have, our guess is that it had stopped producing light. When was the last time you marvelled at a gray cement wall that you passed?

Those with an economic motive, like toy manufacturers, understand very well the old farmer's wisdom. Have you ever seen a child in a department store, grasping towards a brightly-colored toy and throwing a temper tantrum, because his mother is trying to pull him away? If so, you have witnessed first hand the significance of the attention stage of play.

Figure 1

Model of the Behavioral Stages and Blocks to Creativity Through Play

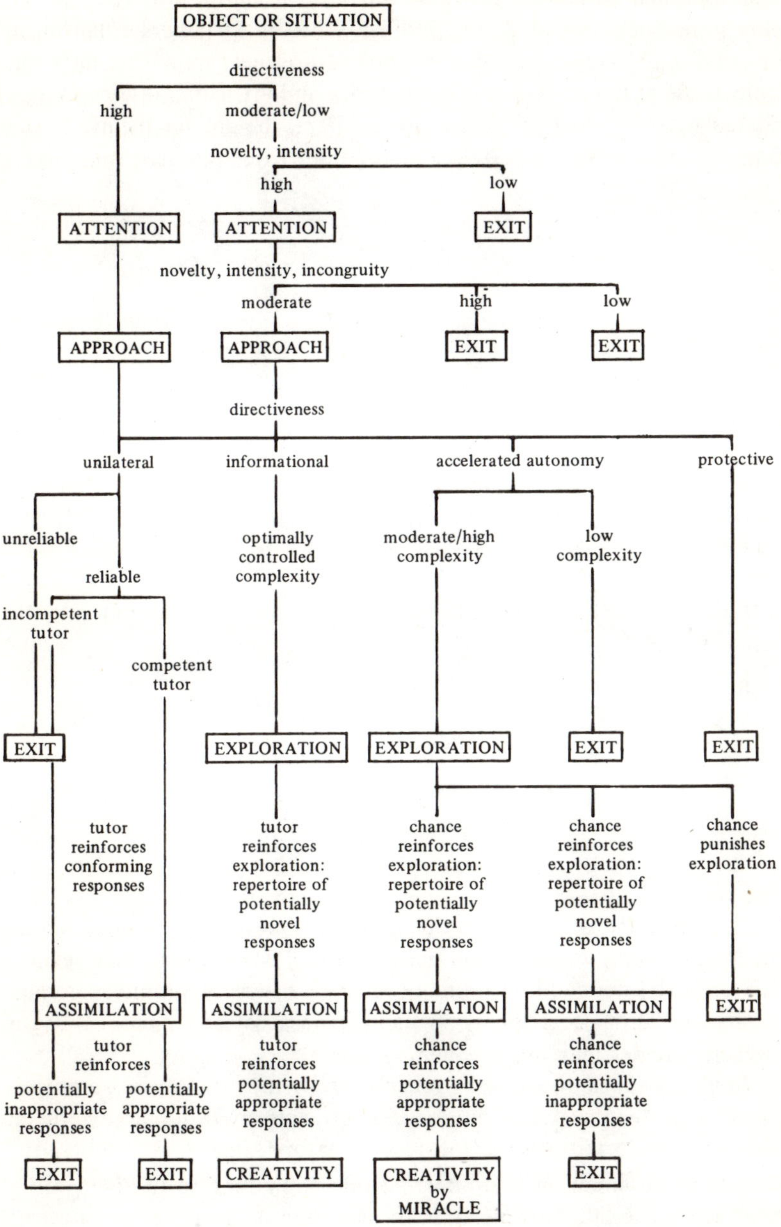

CURIOSITY

The *approach-avoidance conflict,* must be resolved into approach if play is to occur. Novelty and intensity also make a person approach or avoid a play object or situation. But their effects are a little different from those at the attention stage. Novelty and intensity are increasingly related to attentiveness: The more of them, the greater the attention. But they have an "inverted U" relation with avoidance-approach.

Figure 2

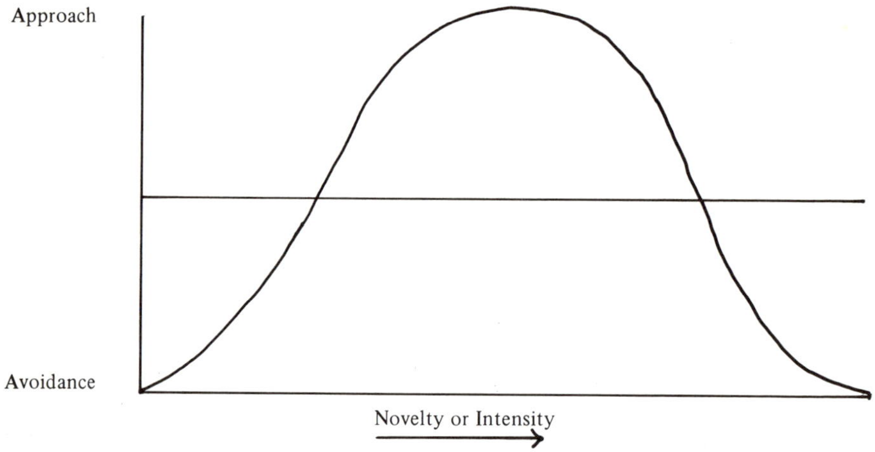

More novelty or intensity, up to a certain level, increasingly makes the person want to approach the play thing or situation. But beyond this critical level, adding more novelty or intensity produces greater avoidance. This effect seems to happen because too much novelty or intensity creates fear, not wonder.

Approach does not have to mean literally moving toward an object. It can also mean sustained interest, or not actively avoiding the object. This is an important distinction for spectator forms of play, where the play thing or situation is supposed to do something to the person, instead of him to it. This meaning of approach is illustrated by a circus performance that one of the authors attended. In part of the show, a gorilla escaped from his cage and his trainer to create havoc and fear among the other circus performers in the arena. This display riveted the interest of the children in the audience, who seemed delighted by these antics, until the gorilla leaped over the arena wall into the spectator section! The younger children, terrified, then began crying, clinging, and in some cases running for the exit. Soon the "gorilla" took off his hooded mask to reveal a man in a gorilla costume. The children immediately composed themselves and either returned to their seats or went over to the man-gorilla to get a closer look. Clearly, the children's approach tendency was close to or at the peak of the "inverted U," before the "gorilla" jumped out of the arena. Then, novelty and intensity were just too high and avoidance reactions followed. Finally, the object was transformed to one that was relatively familiar but still somewhat novel – enough to produce literal approach and even touching.

This example demonstrates that approach (or avoidance) can be psychological as well as physical. The example also shows that distance between player and object and the presence of barriers between them can affect the amount of approach or avoidance.

In summary, if you present a child with optimum amounts of novelty, intensity, distance, and barriers in a play situation, he will be inclined toward curiosity; he will resolve the approach-avoidance conflict in favor of approach.

EXPLORATORY PLAY

Exploration is the manipulation of the new object or situation in order to discover its properties. Berlyne distinguishes between two kinds of exploration: a) specific exploration, aimed at finding a single answer to a problem or challenge and b) diversive exploration, aimed at finding in the environment elements that can produce excitement or distraction. Exploration is the means (not necessarily conscious or deliberate) by which the individual acquires a wide range of information; it adds to the person's repertoire of possible ideas and responses. The availability of this repertoire at a later time makes it possible for the person to produce many ideas or actions in a given situation; this potential is a necessary, though not sufficient, condition for creativity to occur.

The *complexity* of the play thing or situation determines how much the person will explore it. A complex thing has many different parts and/or unusual arrangements or combinations of parts; so certain kinds of novelty affect exploration too. An object or situation that has many things to see, hear, touch, smell, taste, and manipulate, especially in unusual ways, is more complex than one with fewer of these features and is more likely to encourage exploration.

Imagine a cuckoo clock with a dial that permits choosing the cycle in minutes with which the cuckoo sounds. Now add complexity by providing three doors and three "cuckoos" – a bird, a lion, and an old car – with an unpredictable pattern of which one will come out of which door. Add more by allowing the three cuckoos to do different things when activated – the lion can croak like a frog or toot like a car's horn, the bird can roar like a lion or moo like a cow, and the car can bark as well as squirt water from a radiator leak. As more and more features like these are added and the child has some way of influencing, though not precisely determining, their occurence, the frequency and duration of exploratory play should increase.

These rules about complexity and exploration hold, of course, only if the parts of the object did not produce so much intensity or novelty that an avoidance reaction occured. Given that approach takes place, then complexity should be increasingly related to exploration.

ASSIMILATION

Assimilation or Consolidation play is the repetition of behaviors or situations, which, during the exploratory stage, appeared challenging or were reinforced; such repetition permits the child to assimilate or master the behavior or situation. As a rule, unless other people impose the constraints that we discuss later, the child's assimilation play does *not* involve 100% repetition. Complete repetition of behavior, all the time, would seem to discourage the development of creative abilities. The natural tendency of the child, according to Freud and Piaget, would be to make subtle transformations in his play or the situation. These transformations are the child's attempts to bring the object or situation within his range of comprehension or ability. These attempts are not diversive exploration but are forms of specific exploration that result in *mastery*; this word, although a good one to describe the outcome, does not necessarily mean that the child is diligently striving to master some specific skill, like a high school student strives to memorize the parts of the body for an anatomy course. Mastery or comprehension tend to follow (if not interfered with) not necessarily by the child's design or intent but often simply as a result of practice.

Assimilation play, along with formal training, helps the individual acquire proficiency in various responses; this proficiency is the other necessary condition for creativity.

CREATIVITY

Creativity is the production of *novel* responses that have an *appropriate* impact in a given context. If several truckloads of creativity were dumped in your front yard, this definition probably would not help you to identify it. But the definition does neatly summarize, if somewhat cryptically, the essence of extensive research and writing about creativity. Most people would probably agree that redundancy of ideas or products is not creative, but neither is novelty for novelty's sake; if the idea or product does not resolve some problem or affect established beliefs or practices, it is regarded as *not appropriate* and thus not creative, *for the given context,* although it might be appropriate in another place or time.

Our concern is to outline the general conditions that are likely to enhance or, more often, inhibit the person's ability to make novel *and* appropriate responses. According to the definition, if either of these abilities fails to develop, the person will be incapable of creative performance.

The first condition for creativity, the ability to make novel responses, comes primarily from the *exploratory-play* experiences of the person; the attention and approach experiences are critical as well, but mainly because exploratory play cannot occur without them. In exploratory play the child learns the many different things that the environment can "do" and the many things that he can do to it. Over time, in many exploratory play situations, he accumulates a repertoire of potential responses that he can call upon, if and when he needs to. The more responses he accumulates, the greater the probability that at least one of them will be novel in some context, sometime. Also, the more there are the greater the possibility of combining several to yield a novel pattern of behavior, even though one response would not be novel in the given context. In short, exploratory play, by providing many potential responses, helps make the person *potentially creative,* in that he is able to emit those responses in some future context.

Exploratory play probably also increases the person's *motivation* to make novel responses, or at least reduces his fear of making them. Studies of humans and other animals suggest that fear of novelty is an acquired drive and that it is greatest in animals whose early environmental experiences are impoverished. We believe it was Piaget who said, "the more a child has seen and heard, the more he wants to see and hear." And we would add that this probably applies to the stimuli produced by the child's own responses.

The second condition for creativity, the ability to make appropriate or useful responses, comes primarily from the *assimilation-play* experiences of the person. It is during assimilation play that the person develops, through repetition and transformation, specific, known skills. He is not trying to find out all the things that the environment can do or that he can do to it, as in exploration; he is perfecting, within the limits of his existing abilities, his understanding of or skill at some particular situation or task. He is figuring out how to hammer a nail, throw a football, ride a bike, or why mother insists that he eat with a fork, not his hands, why he goes to the dentist, or later how a barometer, carburetor, or electric motor works.

In short, there is a kind of learning, distinct from exploration, that results in the acquisition of particular performance skills that are, or are intended to be, thorough and permanent. The more thorough and permanent the skills developed in a given domain of performance, the more likely it is that the person can make *appropriate* responses, and thus is *potentially creative,* in that domain. And the more frequently specific-skill learning is concentrated in one domain, the less potential creativity the person has in other domains: It is not likely that a professional novelist will help to invent a new breed of computers, and we would not expect an electronics engineer to win the Nobel prize for literature.

To briefly summarize, these are the major stages. By successfully progressing through these stages repeatedly, on many encounters with the environment during development, the person would become creative. Progression can be blocked, however, by environmental, social, and personality factors; the more often this happens, the less creativity will develop. We have seen how the degree of novelty, intensity, incongruity, and complexity affect these stages. Now we will look at some other factors that can block the development of creative ability.

BLOCKING PROGRESS TOWARD CREATIVITY

Control can be exercised by parents, older friends or relatives, teachers, etc. For lack of a better word on which most people can agree, they will be referred to as tutors. Tutors, then, can exercise control either directly on the child by means of directives and/or reinforcements (rewards and punishments), or indirectly through manipulation of the child's play environment, including its degree of novelty, complexity, intensity and incongruity.

Control can be exercised with over-directiveness, underdirectiveness or moderate directiveness. Over-directiveness can take several forms. The tutor can draw the child's attention against his will, and show him how to handle an object or situation *before* the child has had time to be curious about it or to explore it. For instance, the tutor may say this to the child: "Here, come with me, I want to show you something: see this plane? I want you to play with it, and I'll show you how to hold it . . . " This condition is called unilateral since all the information passes from the tutor to the child, and none from the child to the tutor. If the plane flies and does not crash, the condition is considered as reliable.

Under this form of over-directiveness, reinforcement is contingent upon conformance to directions. So punishment might sound like this: "How many times must I tell you not to hold your ball with your left hand?" Because both curiosity and exploration were circumvented, the behaviors displayed during assimilation play are limited to the motions dictated by the tutor. Consequently, the child becomes fearful, dependent upon his tutor's instructions, initiative, conforming and non-creative.

If the tutor's directives are unreliable, i.e. produce undesirable outcomes or contradict previous directions, the child faces a multiple conflict: following directions does not necessarily lead to desirable outcomes; not following them certainly leads to punishment. Besides having missed exploration, the child has no alternative solutions to the tutor's instructions. Consequently, he reacts with distrust and anger towards the tutor, and might try to oppose him. Often, therefore, behaviors opposed to directions and that escaped punishment are perceived as rewarded, even though they may be regarded as inappropriate by his society. So, the child might become rigidly anti-authoritarian and non-conforming – but not creative.

The tutor can also provide unnecessary assistance. For example, he might say this: "Here, this is too hard for you, I'll do it!" Under these *protective interpersonal* conditions, the tutor is over-responsive to the child's wants. While the tutor might interfere at any stage of the child's experience, he tends to do so mostly when the child meets his first obstacle during exploratory play, thus preventing assimilation play. Therefore, while the development of novel responses might not have been affected as severely as under unilateral conditions, acquisition of proficient responses, whether appropriate or not, will have been inhibited.

One response, however, will have been fully explored and assimilated: manipulation of the tutor in order to elicit his assistance. The child might, therefore, become an expert at social manipulation, but without confidence in his own ability to achieve anything. So, he remains dependent on others to be creative in his place.

Under-directiveness occurs when the tutor exercises no control over the child. This is considered to be the *accelerated autonomy* condition. Spontaneous attention, curiosity, exploratory and assimilation play all occur, but in the absence of any guidance by the tutor. Reinforcement is dispensed by the environment. Behavior is rewarded whenever environmental consequences are pleasant, and punished whenever environmental consequences are adverse.

For instance, a child's attention has been caught by a toy which is lying on a table. He decides to explore the toy. Because he is too small to reach it, he grasps the table cloth and pulls on it until the toy falls on the floor. If the toy breaks, the child's behavior has been punished. If not, the child's behavior has been rewarded and table cloth pulling might become one of his favorite play activities.

As this example illustrates, the absence of adult guidance makes it difficult for the child to learn about his society's sense of appropriateness. So while he might have developed a wide repertoire of novel responses, few of them will be appropriate, thus limiting his creativity.

Moderate directiveness, as in the *interpersonal informational* condition, is most likely to lead to creativity. The tutor manipulates the environment so as to provide the child with an environment structured in such a way that the child will almost always proceed through a progression of experiences.[15] Although the child's approach and exploration are experienced as spontaneous, they actually follow a predetermined path leading to the discovery of appropriate responses.

For instance, if the tutor decides that the child will learn about cooperation, he sets up a game where success depends directly on the degree of cooperation between the players. He does not tell the child what to do. The child's desire to succeed motivates him to test alternative approaches, including the cooperative one. The consequences of the various approaches are compared. This information is stored and thus becomes available for combination with previously stored information, so that conceptual links can be drawn. In other words, the seeking of alternative solutions has been elicited, and concept formation made possible.

To that, the tutor may add social reinforcement by congratulating profusely the child for cooperating or initiating exploration. So, the behaviors likely to be learned during assimilation play are those rewarded during exploration as well as exploration itself. The child thus develops a wide range of appropriate and novel responses, the two necessary skills for creativity.

Table 1

Illustration of the Skills Developed under Each Control Condition, and the Resulting Creativity

Control Conditions	Creative Skills Novelty	Appropriateness	Resulting Creativity
Unilateral			
reliable	–	+*	–*
unreliable	–	–	–
Protective	+	–	–
Accelerated Autonomy	+	–	–
Informational	+	+	+

*Note: + means existing skill; – means absent skill.

In summary (see Table 1), of the control conditions discussed above, only the last one offers the opportunity to develop both novel and appropriate responses. The unilateral condition, by bypassing exploratory play and emphasizing assimilation play, encourages the development of appropriate responses (at least when the tutor is competent), but discourages the development of novel responses. The protective condition allows some exploration, but no assimilation. Therefore, while some novel responses might develop, neither appropriate nor inappropriate learning occurs. Finally, in the accelerated autonomy condition, exploration and assimilation both take place, but the absence of guidance results in the learning of many inappropriate responses.

PERSONALITY OF PLAYER AND TUTOR

The environmental effects and tutoring practices that we have outlined are probably determined, in part, by the personality characteristics of both learner and tutor; some effects of personality are undoubtedly independent of what is actually present in the environment or what the tutor intends *at any given time.* On the other hand, the stages that we have discussed obviously help to shape the personalities of people in some ways. So movement through the stages and the participants' personalities are in a dynamic relationship; they influence one another. This dynamic interplay continues throughout development, which, though concentrated in one's early years, probably is a lifelong process.

The player or learner will be motivated or able to notice, approach, or explore things depending, in part, on his past experience in doing so. Some kids will approach and explore things that other kids will not even notice or will be frightened by. Piaget's phrase, "the more he will want to see and hear," is highly relevant to this point; so is the added notion: the more he will *be able* to see and hear. Fiske and Maddi's idea of high- and low-activation people (seekers or avoiders of stimulation) could be an example of a pertinent personality characteristic, which presumably develops out of experience.

Eysenck's introverted and extraverted types, which he believes are largely inherited, are other examples. The introvert has a nervous system characterized by high levels of cortical arousal and low levels of reactive inhibition (mental fatigue or boredom); the extravert is just the reverse. These differences suggest that introverts should be less impulsive, more conscious of details, more persistent at various tasks, and more capable of long-term memory than extraverts; these hypotheses have been supported by a variety of studies. Extraverts, because of their high boredom potential, presumably would attend to and approach novel stimuli more than introverts but would engage in less detailed exploration and less consolidation play. This reasoning would conclude that, given the same developmental circumstances, introverts have a better chance of becoming creative than extraverts.

Now consider the personality of the tutor. Even with the best of intentions for the outcome of his tutoring, what he can actually *do* will be partly dictated by his own personality. In fact, his intentions – what he thinks should be done – will be somewhat pre-conditioned by his personality. This, to us, is a vital point for the management of play experiences: A tutor, say a recreation leader, cannot simply decide to manage play for the betterment of the player and expect to do so entirely on the strength of his own motivation and game skills. His personality might be such that he cannot recognize or manage the delicate balance between exploratory and consolidatory play. If his aim is the enhancement of creativity, he will almost certainly fail (unless someone else plugs the holes that he leaves).

A highly extraverted tutor, for example, if Eysenck's meaning of extraversion is correct, would probably emphasize a great variety of novel but, for learning purposes, superficial experiences in play. This approach, if prolonged or used often enough, seems likely to produce a jack-of-all-trades-but-master-of-none kind of player. Such persons, though often interesting, are hardly models of creative production.

Because tutors were once players and learners, their personalities have been shaped by the developmental experiences that we have described. The methods of control used by tutors, outlined previously, were derived largely from the childhood training conditions described by Harvey, Hunt and Schroder.[16] Those authors claim that the different training conditions produce distinctive adult personalities, ranging from the highly concrete, authoritarian, rigid person to the highly abstract, open-minded, adaptive one. What this means, in our terms, is that tutors who were frequently exposed to directive, unilateral methods of control in their development are likely to become concretistic, authoritarian personalities who, as tutors, will employ directive, unilateral methods of control.

SUMMARY

We have not tried to give a precise and exhaustive rendering of relevant personality characteristics. We have merely attempted to point out the importance of personality, for both player and tutor, and to suggest a few directions for further thought and research. The reader might have concluded by now that in order to promote creativity in others a tutor must be creative himself. We do not disagree with that conclusion. Unfortunately, telling would-be tutors to "be creative" is about as helpful as telling an alcoholic that he really ought to stop drinking. Clearly, it is easier said than done.

We have presented a model of stages of play, which is really a view of developmental experience adapted to play, in order to reveal various roadblocks to creativity. Figure 1 summarizes this model. We have not often referred to Figure 1 throughout our discussion. We hope that the figure, bolstered by the text, adequately summarizes our major points: a) the critical stages of play or, more generally, development, b) the dynamics between these stages and personality development, and c) the many roadblocks to creativity as well as the nature of the singular path that is likely to lead to it.

Recreation rhetoric sometimes extols the joys and wonders of play and its role in creative development. And researchers, including ourselves, have often looked to play as one source of creative behavior. We do not wish to squelch pretty thoughts or discourage positively-oriented research. But perhaps an alternative view should be heard and researched: If our model is somewhere along the right lines, the greater miracle is that anybody at all ever becomes creative.

IMPLICATIONS

This chapter has referred to childhood learning and experiences and their effects on later creativity. But "later" actually never comes. Recent research findings are beginning to re-emphasize what many individuals have always known but some of our institutions forgot: the need for creative development continues throughout the life cycle right up until death and, so far as we know, perhaps beyond it. Thus, fundamental ideas about the paths to creativity are relevant to adult behavior and development. And the recreation professionals who develop recreation institutions, programs, and the training of other recreation professionals are heavily implicated in that process, whether they want to be or not. Sometimes it seems that they do not want to be.

Recreation personnel are supposed to be "people-oriented." In their personal lives they most clearly are. Both casual observation and psychological test data show that recreation personnel are about as extraverted as you are likely to find. But in their professional lives – what they do on the job, what they write books about, and what they try to teach others to do – many seem to show greater concern with things like organizational charts; staff assignments; budget preparation, defense, and allocation; facility or resource design and maintenance; and the rules and regulations that shall govern people's recreation behavior. These activities smack of a love for *things* and their orderly arrangements rather than a genuine concern for people as such. It is fair to ask whether anyone, recreation professional or otherwise, can really be genuinely concerned with *people.* Perhaps most of us are only capable of being genuinely concerned with a person or two. As is often suggested, if you discover that your true friends can be counted on one hand, do not be dismayed – feel fortunate.

Nevertheless, one must wonder what this heavy emphasis on things and abstract processes is doing to recreation's potential for fostering creative growth in child and adult participants. In the terminology of the model presented above, the recreation field sometimes seems like the unilateral, reliable (?), competent (?) tutor who reinforces conforming responses and expects participants to assimilate the response alternatives proffered. The sterility of many recreation programs and places and the apparent lack of concern for exploration (by professionals or by the public they serve) is notable. Perhaps most or all recreation professionals occasionally allow, consciously or unconsciously, exploratory behavior to appear. But, often, these instances seem too infrequent and too superficial.

Some counter arguments to this characterization of the recreation field need to be acknowledged. First, organizational charts, budgets, rules, etc. are necessary and serve valuable functions. It is hopelessly idealistic to imagine that parks, playgrounds, recreation centers, and some resources can manage themselves. We might be surprised, however, at the positive outcomes that would follow a loosening of the reins in some instances. Total loosening, or a *laissez-faire* philosophy, in addition to being disastrous in some ways, will not promote creative growth in participants, as we tried to show by the accelerated-autonomy form of directiveness. Partial loosening of the tight structure of planning and programming might, of course, lead to *less well-managed* outcomes. But as our model also shows, well-managed tasks constitute only a necessary, not a sufficient condition for creative development of players.

Second, there is the claim, related to that of poorly managed outcomes, that people will "muck things up" (the environment, facilities, other participants' recreation) if recreational experiences are de-controlled. This rationalization for emphasizing institutionalized processes in recreation reminds us of the one used by some hunters to justify the killing of other animals for "sport": The hunted animals, it is claimed, are deficient in natural predators or sustenance; so if men do not kill them, they will die anyway from overpopulation or competition for scarce resources. Some of these benevolent-minded sportsmen do not appear to question how their prey came to be in this unnatural predicament in the first place. Perhaps because of the actions of previous "benevolent-minded" men? To what extent does the perceived need to regulate recreation experiences stem from some consequences of having regulated them in the past? Is it possible that some "mucking up" behaviors are exploratory forms of protest against institutionalized processes that were conceived in order to prevent people from "mucking things up"? There is evidence that this is exactly what happens in some types of regulated work situations, such as assembly lines. It is ironic that the recreation profession promotes itself as the opposite of such situations, as the guardian of people's leisure – the freedom from constraints and from the necessity to be occupied. Exploratory behavior is an important quality of leisure, and, if our model is correct, is essential to one of the outcomes of leisure – creative growth. Yet, such behavior is often blocked by the very people who claim to be leisure specialists.

The irony of the discrepancy between recreation's words and deeds can be seen another way. It can be fairly said that recreation is not alone among the service professions in its bureaucratized ways. Medicine treats patients' diseases pretty well but often makes the recipients feel degraded and helpless in the process; many teachers teach well but seem unable to help students learn (and there is a difference); school administrators sometimes appear to forget both teaching and learning; counselors sometimes devote enormous energy to describing their clients' problems in terms of some personality model rather than help solve the problems; and some policemen are good at enforcing the law but forget to help and protect the public.

An important difference between recreation and these other fields is the distance between rhetoric and reality. Most doctors know that they are highly trained technician-scientists who can remove your ulcers, prescribe the right antibiotic for your infection, or possibly repair your malfunctioning heart. They do not claim to do more. Recreation is one of the few fields, along with certain branches of mysticism and Sunday-morning evangelism, that claims significant effects on crime reduction; family functioning and unity; social and community development; physical fitness; mental health and therapy; the development of attitudes, values, leadership, and character; psychological and spiritual growth; and "self-actualization."

One wonders how a field can know or do anything about family problems when it seems blissfully unaware that in this explosive, exploratory world there are two-parent families, one-parent families, no-parent families, nuclear families, extended families, childless families, living-together-but unmarried families, married-but-living-apart families, homosexual families, communal families, and probably many more. As for self-actualization, Abraham Maslow's eternal sleep might be fretful indeed, if he knows that the existing practice of recreation is being touted as the pathway to that ultimate state of personality development.

People, especially in America, are today exploring a large variety of lifestyles and leisure pursuits. Much of this is moved by an urge for creative growth. Some do not participate much in the hubbub but, instead, observe it, investigate it, try to understand it. Whether as participants or observers, people in other fields appear to be more aware of leisure, its current stirrings, its myths, its possible futures, than many recreation professionals.

In a recent issue of *Psychology Today,* a sociologist investigated the rapid growth of around-the-clock activity in American cities. He showed that banks, supermarkets, garages, restaurants, discotheques, theatres, tour agencies, laundries, and other privately owned facilities were adopting all-night hours to cater to this nocturnal life. No mention was made of public recreation facilities. Are they involved in this latest trend? Many recreation personnel can tell you who won last year's Orange Bowl game and the exact score or the latest attendance figures at the community swimming pool. But do they have a clue, or do they care, what people are seeking by wandering about in the middle of the night?

Economists and other social scientists are investigating possibilities for completely revising the calendar and work-leisure cycles – for instance, a nine-day week with alternating 6 day-3 day, on-off cycles. The way in which we structure and allocate time goes to the heart of what leisure is all about. Yet, where are the recreators – the leisure specialists – in thinking innovatively about this most fundamental commodity?

It is perhaps in the area of research that the reluctance of many recreators to engage in or encourage exploratory behavior is most noticeable. Recreation practitioners often complain of the irrelevance of research, the researcher's apparent lack of concern for "meeting" the practitioner's needs. Despite decades of thought and careful research into the nature of creative thinking, these complainers still are unaware of a fundamental fact: Relevance is not something that is given; it is something that is conceived or created in an individual mind. The internal creative flame often needs external sources of fuel to feed it. But the sources, in themselves, are neither relevant nor irrelevant. It is an exploratory attitude and behavior that make them so.

After these critiques, it is appropriate to acknowledge that there are some changes, which perhaps signify exploratory thinking, in the recreation field. There is a growing emphasis on the leisure problems of special populations that are not in the mainstream of American or Canadian life; there is increasing recognition of the importance of personality, the individuality of leisure, and the possible need for individual lifestyle counselling; in a few communities, recreation departments are "opening up" facilities to multiple and unusual uses, dictated by the felt needs, or whims, of the participants. These approaches had to grow out of some exploratory thinking, because they show a recognition of the idiosyncracies of human needs – those that cannot be handled by the standardized operating procedure given by organizational charts and activity schedules. In a field that claims to deal in a quality, leisure, that represents freedom from constraints and uniformity, these kinds of approaches should be the rule, not the exception.

REFERENCES

1. The part of this paper that describes the model of play and creative growth originally appeared in Jeanrenaud, Claudine and Bishop, Doyle. "Road Blocks to Creativity Through Play." In Wilkinson, Paul (Ed.) *Play in Human Settlements,* London: Croom and Helm, Ltd., 1979. We gratefully acknowledge the cooperation of Paul Wilkinson and Croom and Helm, Ltd. in allowing a different and expanded version of our original paper to appear here.
2. Hutt, Corine. "Exploration and Play in Children." In *Symposium of the Zoological Society of London,* 18, (1966). pp. 61-81.
3. Linford, Anthony G. and Jeanrenaud, Claudine. "A Behavioral Model for a Four-Stage Play Theory." In Kenyon, G. S. (Ed.) *Contemporary Psychology of Sports.* Chicago: Athletic Institute, Chicago, 1970. pp. 446-450.
4. Hull, C. L., *Essentials of Behavior.* New Haven: Yale University, 1951.
5. Skinner, B. F., *Science and Human Behavior.* New York: McMillan, 1953.
6. Berlyne, D. E., *Conflict, Arousal and Curiosity.* New York: McGraw-Hill, 1960.
7. Fiske, David W. and Maddi, Salvador. *Functions of Varied Experience.* Homewood: Dorsey Press, 1961.
8. Piaget, Jean., *Play, Dreams and Imitation in Childhood.* London: Routledge and Kegan Ltd., 1951.
9. Harvey, O. J., Hunt, D. E. and Schroder, H. M., *Conceptual Systems and Personality Organization,* New York: Wiley, 1961.
10. Eysenck, Hans J., *The Biological Basis of Personality.* Springfield, Illinois: Charles C. Thomas, 1967.
11. Torrance, E. P., "Education and Creativity." In C. W. Taylor (Ed.), *Creativity: Progress and Potential.* New York: McGraw-Hill, 1964. pp. 49-128.
12. Lieberman, J. Nina. "Playfulness and Divergent Thinking: An Investigation of Their Relationship at the Kindergarden Level." *Journal of Genetic Psychology,* 107: (1965). pp. 219-224.
13. Sutton-Smith, Brian. "The Role of Play in Cognitive Development." *Young Children,* 22: (1967). pp. 361-370.
14. Bishop, Doyle and Chace, C., "Parental Conceptual Systems, Home Play Environment and Potential Creativity in Children," *Journal of Experimental Child Psychology.* 12(2), (1973), 212-232.
15. Harvey, et. al., *Op. Cit.*
16. *Ibid.*

Chapter Eight

The "Psychologization" of Leisure Services

Roger C. Mannell

Today we are often exhorted to think of leisure as a state of mind or as a subjective experience. Unfortunately clear and unambiguous descriptions of this state or experience are all but non-existant. Most of us would be unable to say with conviction whether or not we had encountered one of these mysterious experiences. While "experts" have dodged describing the characteristics of the leisure experience, some view it as being achievable by only a select few,[2] yet others consider it approachable by anyone at almost anytime.[3] Most agree that it is *pleasurable*, yet criteria have not been forthcoming to allow us to distinguish between leisure and non-leisure states.[4] Are religious, mystical, aesthetic, amusement, intense competitive sport, and experiences during altered states of consciousness leisure experiences? With these questions unanswered it is not surprising then, that leisure services have not developed planning strategies specifically to encourage and promote experiencing during leisure or developed evaluation techniques to assess the success of such efforts. Similarly, leisure research, until quite recently, has all but ignored examining the factors which affect the experiential component of leisure.[5]

Now we find ourselves on the threshold of an *experience revolution* – a revolution for which our leisure service delivery systems may be unprepared. Numerous Canadian studies by futurists predict that we will devote increasing amounts of time and energy to creative activity, personal growth and self-actualization endeavors.[6] Over the last few years there has developed a tremendous interest in esoteric eastern philosophies and psychologies, western psychotherapies and personal development programs on the one hand, and high risk outdoor pursuits and the hunt for fantasy and amusement experiences on the other. These trends, if they continue, may mean an increase in the search for and collection of exotic, novel and exciting blends of experiences. This experience revolution has many potentially positive aspects, yet like the failure of increases in discretionary time and affluence to lead inevitably to a leisure society, the emerging experience revolution may bring us no closer to achieving leisure lifestyles or self-development.

We must, then, explore the notion of an experience revolution and some of its implications for the delivery of leisure services. And we must look critically at the notion of an ideal human condition or personality and the "experience vendors" who are emerging to meet the demand for experiences that will lead to this state of development. Should leisure services become experiential and compete with the private entrepreneur for their share of the "experience" market? Is there another role that leisure services can play? Will the current interest and efforts in a psychology of leisure result in information that will serve as a basis for some form of "leisure experience engineering" to support leisure services in providing experience oriented (psychologized) services?

DO WE NEED A MAN-OF-LEISURE PROTOTYPE?

In more optimistic times, times pre-dating the energy crisis and the appearance of ecological and environmental concerns, the eventuality of a leisure society seemed assured. Though the details of the nature of such a society have always been obscure, the need to do little or no work, accompanied by abundant amounts of discretionary time and resources to pursue a wide variety of interests seem to characterize this vision. The psychological, economic, political and social changes necessary to support leisure lifestyles for our citizens have not been considered comprehensively other than through the occasional writer's literary construction of a utopian community or society. Similarly the phrase "leisure lifestyle," so frequently used these days, has not been defined, or the types of activities or behaviors comprising this mode of living agreed upon.

During the last decade there has emerged a growing concern that the movement toward a workless society has not resulted in a shift to a leisure society. Increases in discretionary time and affluence have not guaranteed the adoption of leisure lifestyles–whatever they are! Some social critics have argued that one of the major barriers to the achievement of a leisure ethic, besides a lingering work ethic, has been its subversion by the consumer ethic.[7] The consumer ethic, a refinement of Veblen's notion of conspicuous consumption, suggests that we have not become leisurely but rather have used increases in discretionary time and resources to purchase and expend more. This consumption oriented lifestyle supposedly allows us to "shore up" our personal identities and establish our social status on the basis of what we spend rather than on the basis of our work. The achievement of a "true" leisure lifestyle would seem to infer that social status needs are to be abandoned and self-esteem result from the personal development allowed one in a leisure society.

More recently there has even been a loss of optimism that we can sustain a continued movement away from a work society, with the appearance of energy crises, population pressures and economic competition with newly developing nations. Yet, in spite of these problems and the spectre of economic collapse the consensus of futurists is that developments in Canada for the next 20 years still hold the possibility of a society with a substantial amount of leisure. Fewer young people, smaller families, shorter working hours, increases in discretionary time are familiar predictions that continue to be made. However the authors of these reports hasten to caution us that prosperity is not assured, and that our consumption patterns must be made a little more modest since we may be obligated to redefine our concept of prosperity.

Of particular interest is the apparent consensus in the predictions of changes in our values:

> "New values will gradually take over as the dominant, decision-making values of our society. There will be a decline in values associated with materialism, private ownership, capitalism and unqualified economic growth. Increasing emphasis will be placed on concepts such as the quality of life, self-actualization, creativity, individualism and humanitarism."[8]

The one recurring theme of most futurist predictions is that there will be an increasing demand or need for opportunities to be more creative and self-actualized, that is, for opportunities for personal development. Apparently then, it is still possible that if man fails to "cremate himself equal" in a nuclear holocaust or crowd himself off the earth, he may be condemned to the horrible fate of a workless society—the victim of automation. What type of person shall inherit this leisure world? Will the survivors possess a huge arsenal of recreation skills and the surviving society be one populated with Renaissance men—the ultimate recreators? Is there a suitable prototype for all members of a leisure society? Is a life based on intellectual and rational pursuits, the pursuit of the cultural arts and recreation able to sustain the total population or only a small elite segment of the population?

We have a need for a "man-of-leisure" prototype, and for a clearer notion of the types of activities and experiences that will sustain this individual and contribute to a meaningful lifestyle. Is this to be a leisure lifestyle? Leisure service professionals are being urged to devote more organizational time to leisure counseling and education which are espoused as suitable mechanisms for shaping the prototype man of the future. What are the features, options and capabilities of this new model of man? What exotic blend of experiences will be needed to "power" leisure man in his search for happiness and self-development?

Today we encounter a variety of competing views regarding the appropriate model for living. These views have been at various times stated in terms such as oneness with the universe, Christian virtue, manhood, proper taste, or self-actualization.

Ideas about the *ideal person* and how he should relate to his world come from many sources. In Western society Christianity contributed to the ideal of *Spiritual Man* whose present life is a preparation for an afterlife where people are to be free and equal. With the European Renaissance the ideal of *Intellectual Man* evolved with the belief that our salvation was to be found in this world and achieved through the application of human intelligence to our problems. The extension of this belief into the political sphere fostered the ideal of a *Political Man* who was to be actively involved in modifying the political institutions of his society to further the quality of life. With the industrial revolution the image of *Economic Man* evolved with the belief that man would achieve the good life through his contributions to economic growth and development.[9] Of course, during this evolution of various notions of the ideal man the development of the scientific method and science contributed to the belief that man could solve all his problems with an objective, rational, and scientific approach. Most recently it has been suggested that a new ideal of *Psychological Man* has emerged with the belief that we are moving into an era in which we are achieving a clearer understanding of human needs and will more completely meet them.[10] Psychological Man is contemporary man with a developed self-awareness who has shifted his attention from the external world to his own nature. Much has been written over the last thirty years concerning the barriers preventing contemporary man from achieving a "free," "self-actualized," and "happy" existence. Numerous models of the ideal orientation to life and means to self-development have been suggested, supposedly based on modern psychological principles.

Other models for the ideal person also exist: the hero/intellectual, the artist, the mystic, the saint and the prophet. These models all suggest different emphases on what are desirable or ideal human traits. While most models of man recognize the need for some kind of psychological growth, there is no universal view of the ideal human condition.[11]

Unfortunately, we are faced with a bewildering array of models of the ideal person which does not help us decide what prototype we should be encouraging in leisure counseling and education. We are not even sure that a society in which most persons did not have to work would be a society where man could survive and adapt in such a way that his life would be perceived by himself as happy and fulfilled. Is a man-of-leisure prototype suitable for all persons, only for an elite, or for no one? Implicit in many of our activities and thinking is the assumption that man—the masses—can be counseled or educated into adopting a leisure lifestyle which will sustain him, provide meaning and purpose in his life, prevent him from becoming a social nuisance, and he and his fellows collectively from becoming a social problem.

The essence of a *leisure problem* would seem to be a question: can man, when biological survival is no longer problematic, adjust his goals and find activity in which to engage that allows him to perceive himself as happy. When work and consuming no longer preoccupy us, we may finally have to personally confront the purpose of our lives. What new goals shall we seek? Can man convince himself that the exploration of his own psyche, the search for self-actualization or personal development is sufficient to provide direction, meaning and importance for his life? How are leisure services evolving to provide for these needs of Psychological Man?

THE EXPERIENCE INDUSTRIES AND THE PSYCHOLOGIZATION OF LEISURE SERVICES

Critics have been pointing out the need to focus a concern not on how much we consume or participate but on the quality of our experiences. As a result leisure is currently viewed by those in the "know" as a state of mind or a subjective experience. Pessimism has been expressed about the possibility of the masses being able to achieve this state. More optimistic futurists predict that the future will see an increasing concern for personal development. Toffler, writing before the appearance of the energy crisis, predicted an experience revolution. He was optimistic that the current preoccupation with acquiring goods and material possessions as an avenue to happiness would pass as merely a stage in the adaptation of man to an affluent society where his needs were readily met.

> As rising affluence and transience ruthlessly undercut the old urge to possess, consumers begin to collect experience as consciously and passionately as they once collected things.[12]

Toffler predicted that the manufacturing sector would direct more resources into the conscious design of "psychological distinctions and gratifications" with the development of experiential industries which would also keep the economy growing as the production of goods went beyond our material needs. "We are moving from a 'gut' economy to a 'psyche' economy because there is only so much gut to be satisfied."[13] The term "psychologization," coined by Toffler, labels this predicted shift from providing goods and services simply to meet functional needs to also generating experiences:

> We shall go far beyond any "functional" necessity, turning the service, whether it is shopping, dining, or having one's hair cut, into a pre-fabricated experience.[14]

Writing before the advent of the energy crisis and our current economic difficulties, Toffler's predictions are still relevant. We will need to focus more and more on psychological or psychic gratifications (experience) because excess materialism beyond a "comfortable" level will be wasteful and costly in a world of scarce resources and large populations.

Will the shift from the acquisition of material goods mean that suddenly we are going to achieve a happy and satisfying life as a society? Toffler, himself, wondered what would happen when industry began to produce experiences for their own sake that ". . .blur the distinction between the vicarious and the non-vicarious, the simulated and the real?"[15] As well, we may give up our need to possess more and more material goods only to replace it by a similar fascination with collecting experiences. One would expect that the simple clamoring after experience does not mean that the road to self-development will be better guaranteed.

THE SEARCH FOR EXPERIENCE

What is the nature of a lifestyle that is centered around the pursuit of experience? Are we now not continually experiencing our surroundings every waking minute? To say there will be an experience revolution seems to suggest that greater concern will be given "engineering" our experiences and the situations which give rise to them. The purpose of this "experience engineering" would be to create experiences that are somehow of greater quality than in the past, that are perhaps more memorable, that give greater satisfaction, and that perhaps lead to a fuller life or more complete personal development. What types of experiences are likely to attract man if he is given the opportunity to pursue experience for its own sake?

Education and the Search for Knowledge

The formal educational institutions of the West have not fostered the "development of the mind" through intense and exotic experiences.

Personal development has been viewed as based on the slow and gradual acquisition of factual information and the development of intellectual, rational and scientific modes of thought. The education system has been very work oriented.[11] Unfortunately, universities have backed themselves into a corner by stressing their ability to place graduates in jobs instead of the less fashionable and tangible ideals of a liberal education. They are now scrambling to develop and market continuing education programs as self-development opportunities to meet the problems of shrinking enrollments as the number of young people in our population decreases and also they avoid university since its brand of experience no longer guarantees jobs.

Experience Seeking: Growth or Addiction

A current psychological view of man is that he is constantly motivated to maintain an optimal level of arousal. That is, man attempts to maintain enough change or novelty in his life to avoid boredom or anxiety from too little or too much change respectively. When the challenge of survival is no longer available to provide this arousal as would be the case in a leisure society, man will play or leisure to maintain the optimal level of arousal.[16] When this physiological model is translated into subjective or experiental terms the conditions providing for an optimal level of arousal often lead the human organism to experience "flow" or a peak-like experience which is pleasurable and highly involving.[17] In a workless society many people are likely to search out situations which will provide this type of experience. What role do these types of experiences play in the development of psychological well-being and personal development? For example, the pursuit of high risk activities appears to generate intense and highly involving experiences. Contemporary psychological theory has generally viewed this type of behavior as negative or abnormal, particularly the behavior of those who devote a whole life to its pursuit. Is this merely a hold-over from the protestant work ethic?

If one engages in activities in which one's skills develop so as to make that activity less challenging or novel, then higher risks or novel forms of the activity must be found. In the case of high risk sports this cycle has been seen as addictive:

> Stimulus addiction implies the derived need to expose oneself repeatedly to situations where the balance among fear, danger and anxiety remain within the boundaries of personal control. The cyclical need to extend oneself to the absolute physical, emotional and even intellectual limits is the quest to escape from bland tensionless states associated with everyday living.[18]

We might expect increasing numbers of people when freed from the constraints of work and thoughts of survival, no matter how indirect, turning to a more immediate and direct flirtation with survival. Experiences derived from balancing on the edge of survival/non-survival may produce an intoxication that cannot be provided by any other type of activity. The removal of the need to work for one's living or survival, no matter how indirect the connection in our society, may lead us to erect artificial barriers which we then challenge in the face of fear. This activity must take a form that is accepted by society such as play and sport. The endless search for novelity and experience is already underway.

> There is a whole set of leisure environments that are becoming a part of American life. These "ultra mod" settings include: electronic game parlors; computor games in people's homes; amusement parks which offer the latest in simulation and fantasy; and lazer light and music entertainment centers.[19]

The Mind Field or the Consciousness Technologies

While our educational institutions have stressed the rational, intellectual and logical approaches to understanding, there has been a trend to seek experiences which provide for self-development and knowledge through more intuitive and experiential modes. Many persons in our society in the search for this self-development are sampling western psychotherapies and encounter groups as well as various degenerate forms of the esoteric eastern psychologies currently being marketed. We have embraced transcendental meditation, astrology, biofeedback, gurus and trantrum yogas. The need to explore the intuitive side of our natures has caused many ". . .to flock, unthinkingly, to rudimentary spiritual sideshows, which are quick, cheap, and often flashy"[20] . . .and an earnest individual ". . .encounters innumerable freaky, peaky psychologies and associations, advertisements in the Sunday newspapers for courses in instant self-improvement . . .and tiresome loonies of almost every persuasion."[21] While the types of experiences provided by these "growth" fads are undoubtedly self-indulgent and sensational, recent physiological and psychological research on brain function and human cognitive capabilities suggest that man has two modes of thinking or knowing and a variety of techniques that have evolved in many esoteric eastern psychologies may allow us to explore one of these ways of knowing.[22] As a nonverbal, nonlinear, nonintellectual approach to knowing ourselves and the world, this mode sharply contrasts with the usual Western approach which utilizes rational, intellectual and verbal modes of thought. Is the search for mystical, religious and peak experiences synonymous with the search for leisure experience? What role will leisure services provide to potential experience consumers?

LEISURE EXPERIENCE ENGINEERING

Toffler has argued that the psychologization of services will mean that ". . .no important service will be offered to the consumer before it has been analyzed by teams of behavioral engineers to improve its psychic loading."[23] Psychological research on leisure is only now beginning to study mental experience during leisure. The field of psychology abandoned the study of consciousness early in its own history and has only recently begun to consider these processes as legitimate areas of inquiry. The small amount of leisure research done has focused on the motives or needs for leisure and recreation preferences, while leisure experiences have been overlooked. The view of leisure as a state of mind or experience has made it difficult to study from the perspective of the social sciences with their emphasis on the collection of objective data. A handful of studies though, have emerged over the last several years attempting to measure leisure experiences themselves. Several studies have measured recreators' moods over the course of a recreation engagement using measures of the changes in positive and negative moods as unidimensional indicators of leisure experience. In my own research I have attempted to develop several parallel measures of leisure experience. By monitoring changes in subjects' moods, time perception and awareness of their surroundings, I and my colleagues have been able to monitor the impact of environmental factors such as the degree of freedom to participate and the level of competition in the setting on experiences during leisure. As well, the effect of personal characteristics on one's leisure response to these environmental factors can be examined.

> . . .the identification and monitoring of these experiences (leisure) will hopefully lend itself to a systematic effort to discover those features of situations, activities, and persons which inhibit or enhance the experience of leisure. The impact on leisure experiences of such factors as freedom of choice, intrinsic and extrinsic motivations, work and leisure attitudes, personality, and man-made and natural environments could be tested experimentally.[24]

Unfortunately or perhaps fortunately, the research output is far behind any attempt to formalize scientific planning and design principles which could provide the tools for leisure service professionals to become "leisure experience engineers."

THE ROLE OF LEISURE SERVICES IN THE EXPERIENCE REVOLUTION

Is there a role for public leisure service agencies in a society in which experiences and consciousness technologies are marketed and sold? Should public leisure services jump into the race and compete for a "piece of the experience market"? Perhaps the private sector should be allowed to evolve unimpeded to meet these experience needs. Public leisure service agencies are unlikely to have the investment monies needed to pioneer the development of the facilities and programs that will be demanded to provide exotic experience opportunities. Perhaps public leisure service agencies should become monitoring and consumer protection bodies to ensure that the experiences entering the market are "safe," "sanitary" and "enriched." We will then need to have knowledge concerning what experience contribute to growth states and consciousness raising and to discern leisure from non-leisure states. We will have to establish criteria for what are "good" experiences and develop standards. A complementary role to the consumer protection and product monitoring role would be to take responsibility for leisure counseling and public education to ensure that people become wise "experience consumers."

Our professional preparation programs in the universities and colleges would have to adapt to these changes. What skills should our students depart with, and where will our students find jobs? Should we be training "leisure experience engineers" able to apply leisure experience principles that have been developed by researchers in the social sciences concerned with human experience and leisure? If we are to take this route there is a need to train some of our students to be behavioral and experiential researchers. Also the majority of the jobs for our students, certainly the most exciting jobs, will be in the private sector, therefore we should better train them to operate and function in the commercial sector both as innovative inventors of experiences and as knowledgeable private entrepreneurs. To ensure the quality of commercial leisure services and the availablity of jobs for our graduates, we should press the government to pass legislation requiring the licensing of leisure experience engineers. It would be expected that the designer of a leisure experience would be suitably trained as would be the designer of a bridge. Commercial leisure service firms would, as a matter of course, hire our "engineering" students. There also would be positions in government. Leisure experience inspectors would be needed to police and monitor existing services and new varieties of experience introduced to the market. The experience revolution will mean a whole new role for leisure service professionals and leisure services as they are psychologized.

REFERENCES

1. Toffler, Alvin. *Future Shock*. New York: Random House, 1970. p. 188. Toffler coined the term "psychologization."
2. deGrazia, Sebastian. *Of Time, Work, and Leisure*. New York: Twentieth Century Fund, 1962.
3. Gordon, C., Gaity, C., and Scott, J. "Leisure and Lives: Personal Expressivity Across the Life Span." In: Binstok, R. and Shanas, E. (Eds.), *The Handbook of Aging and the Social Sciences*. New York: Van Nostrand Reinhold, 1976.
4. Mannell, Roger, "A Conceptual and Experimental Basis for Research in the Psychology of Leisure." *Society and Leisure/Loisir et Societe*, (in press).
5. Mannell, Roger. "Social Psychological Techniques and Strategies for Studying Leisure Experiences." In: Iso-Ahola, S., (Ed.), *Social Psychological Perspectives of Leisure and Recreation.* New York: Charles C. Thomas, 1980.
6. Balmer, Ken. *The Elora Prescription: A Future for Recreation*. Toronto: Ontario Ministry of Culture and Recreation, 1979.
7. Kando, Thomas. *Leisure and Popular Culture in Transition*. Saint Louis: Mosby Co., 1975.
8. Balmer, *Op. Cit.*, pp. 9-11.
9. Drucker, Peter. The End of Economic Man: *A Study of the New Totalitarianism*. New York: John Day, 1939.
10. Tolman, Edward. *Behavior and Psychological Man: Essays in Motivation and Learning*. Berkeley: University of California Press, 1951.
11. Coan, Richard, *Hero, Artist, Sage, or Saint*? New York: Columbia University Press, 1977.
12. Toffler, *Op. Cit.*, p. 193.
13. *Ibid.*, p. 201.
14. *Ibid.*, p. 192.
15. *Ibid.*, p. 201.
16. Ellis, Michael. *Why People Play*. Englewood Cliffs, New Jersey: Prentice-Hall, Inc., 1973.
17. Csikszentmihalyi, Mihalyi. *Bdyond Boredom and Anxiety*. Washington, D.C.: Jossey-Bass, 1975.
18. Ogilvie, Bruce. "The Stimulus-Addicts, A Psychosocial Paradox." In: Schwank, W. (Ed.), *The Winning Edge*. Washington, D.C.: American Association for Health, Physical Education and Recreation, 1974. pp. 49-50.
19. Fridgen, Joseph. "Leisure Behavior: An Environmental Perspective." *Leisure Information Newsletter*, 5:4 (Spring, 1979). pp. 6-9.
20. Ornstein, Robert. *The Mind Field*. New York: Pocket Books, 1976. p. 11.
21. *Ibid.*, p. 20.
22. Ornstein, Robert. *The Psychology of Consciousness*. Markham, Ontario: Penguin Books Ltd., 1972.
23. Toffler, *Op. Cit.*, p. 209.
24. Mannell, "Social Psychological. . .," *Op. Cit.*

SECTION TWO

Changing Services and Resources: Doing More With Less

Introduction

Thomas L. Goodale and Peter A. Witt

The past few decades have been laden with important political, economic, and social developments which have already begun to impact upon the recreation movement, the nature of recreation services and the way those services are presented. We are faced with tighter limits and must make harder choices. We are faced with the task of doing more, better, and often different than what has been done in the past. And this must be done with fewer of the resources, especially financial, that we have been relying upon. This is especially the case for government sponsored or public recreation services which have grown so prolifically over the past few decades.

This is quite clear in the chapters comprising this section, "Changing Services and Resources." In the opening chapter, Dunn (9) discusses and documents changes taking place, especially in municipalities, as a result of diminishing resources. Competing and conflicting interests, system complexity, and difficult decisions and choices increasingly characterize the milieu within and surrounding the recreation movement. She identifies a number of implications of these changes which weave throughout other chapters and sections in this book: conceptual clarity, research and policy, and the role of the profession and professionals. Dunn concludes with some difficult questions about professionals' roles in the future and shares with Mannell, (8) Godbey (13) and others a concern about our seemingly unlimited ability to produce goods and experiences without criteria for judging their worth.

Many of these issues are developed by Gold (10) with particular reference to the urban environment. Here, as elsewhere, many significant changes are recognized: decreased faith in institutions, taxpayers' revolts, demographic change, austerity and pinched incomes in all quarters–individual as well as institutional. Efficiency and effectiveness become the watch words of responses to this relatively new set of circumstances. Changes in the age structure of the population, alternative family structures, shifts in values, and a plethora of life styles increase the challenges, as is noted also by Godbey, (13) Sessoms, (14) and Murphy (15) particularly. Re-conceptualization of services, resources, alternatives and being less presumptuous about peoples' needs and the ability of planners and programmers to meet them also seem to be important criteria for recreation service as it continues to evolve.

Irene Spry's discussion of "The Prospects for Leisure in a Conserver Society" (11) is particularly interesting because of her background as an economist extensively involved in studying resources for the future. She is clearly hopeful that the recognition of limits will result in conserving resources and environmental quality by limiting highly consumptive and destructive pursuits. In their place will (hopefully) emerge activities which are more parsimonious, constructive and creative—in a sense more gentle and human. Spry also expresses the hope, like Goodale (4) Smith (5) and others that recreational pursuits can be a source of self-esteem and respect from a life that has some significance. In concert with other economists concerned with our resource future, she is hardly saddened in saying "bye, bye to buy, buy" (the title of an article by her colleague Dr. Arthur Cordell) or to those activities which consume space and destroy beauty.

Certainly Carls (12) would not be saddened either. The technical ability to produce and the advertising and marketing ability to sell recreational equipment has other effects than consuming goods and space. Particularly with various outdoor recreation pursuits, increased participation has not always been accompanied by increased appreciation. In many respects, money and machinery has replaced sensitivity and skill and de-valued both the outdoors and those values and experiences traditionally associated with it. This subject is heavily laden with the conflicts and hard choices which Dunn (9) particularly, described. And to note the pleasure of killing may add cogency to Smith's (5) argument.

This subject also illustrates many of the concerns expressed by Godbey (13) as well as others. The seemingly endless quest to acquire both goods and experiences and the economic and technical ability to consume them quickly and conveniently has a number of consequences, good and bad, depending on the value base for judging. The liberating affects of an emerging pluralism, carried too far, result in less freedom rather than more. Godbey notes clearly that value disputes, the difficulty of ethical judgments and the dependence on law to define limits can be problematic in a pluralistic society.

Conversely, the last two decades have clearly demonstrated that a single set of what are usually called "traditional" values is no longer adequate anymore so than monolitic structures or unilateral decisions handed down from the top. It seems clear that planning for leisure must be a more open, participatory, decentralized, patient, tolerant exercise. How much each one of us can accommodate is an open question. How present systems and institutions can accommodate that exercise is another. And while we know the limits must be extended, we don't know how far.

Sessoms' (14) shows clearly that the concepts and values widely accepted in the past, and the mandates adopted in keeping with them, narrowed our perspective and shortened our vision. Gold (10) and Murphy (15) also address that problem, and all three authors, along with Michaelis (6) Goodale (16) and others note alternatives and objectives responsive to the changing environment. Sessoms focuses particularly on the impact of demographic shifts and on the rediscovery that adults are people too. He finds in the concepts of life style and life cycle a hopeful conceptual base for an expanded view of recreation and leisure service and shifting and expanding roles and mandates for the recreation movement.

Like Sessoms, James Murphy (15) finds the seeds for reconceptualizing recreation and leisure services in developments of the last several years. Ecology, conservation, limited growth, a holistic view of man and his surroundings, pluralism and humanism are among recent movements not only suggesting but forcing change. Clearly resource limits make it impossible, especially for governments, to be direct providers of all the needed, or demanded, facilities and services. It has also become clear that such a service model may create dependency and destroy initiative. These are antithetical to philosophic and programmatic intent. From this comes the recognition that major role shifts are required from that of provider to advocate and educator; and to enabler, facilitator and catalyst.

The chapters in this section are similar in that the necessity for and inevitability of change underlies each. Just as the future is uncertain, the outcome of change, whether chosen and pursued or coerced and resisted, is also uncertain. And that is a source, however great or little, of anxiety for us all. In the concluding chapter of this section, Goodale (16) notes that it is easier to anticipate and discuss change than it is to experience it–much less instigate it. But it seems clear that the reality of social, economic and political forces point in the same directions as the emerging, more humanistic philosophy of recreation and leisure service. He argues that the burden of change and the responsibility for it ultimately rests with each individual. Obstacles and opportunities abound, as is evident throughout the chapters in this and other sections. It is also evident that within the recreation movement or (arguably) profession, much re-thinking is underway and much is needed.

TLG
PAW

Chapter Nine

Future Leisure Resources

Diana R. Dunn

During the past dozen years, first world nations have been jolted from an assumption of abundance to a new awareness of resource limits and scarcities. The 1960's were exuberant, expansive, and expensive. In the United States, public services proliferated and public recreation flourished. Near the end of the decade, the country reached the moon, and discovered that "spaceship Earth" was indeed finite, as environmentalists had been proclaiming.

By 1972, the authors of a small, controversial book reemphasized that the planet had measurable limits; that if population growth and resource depletion continue unabated, our way of life will change dramatically. *The Limits to Growth*[1] tried to persuade a comfortable public that the Golden Age of Affluence would soon end. Many rebutted the "doomsday book," charging variously that it was too simplistic or was flawed in assumptions, methodologies, findings, or conclusions. Others yawned.

In 1974, however, incredulous Americans were astonished by lines at gasoline pumps; the Energy Crisis was identified and labeled. That phenomenon precipitated several new threats to lifestyle, including double-digit inflation which led to soaring real estate values and taxes. Reluctantly, Americans began to change some long-held beliefs and behaviors. They started to bag their own groceries, pump their own gas, recycle their papers and cans, and entertain such formerly subversive thoughts as "smaller is better."

It was difficult for recreation professionals to reconcile these seemingly extraneous events with increasingly grim professional developments. They were skeptical, for example, when a major investigation of recreation and open space in U.S. cities conducted between 1970 and 1973 concluded:

> Municipal austerity has had a profound negative impact on the maintenance of city recreation and park system facilities. In some cities, recreation facilities are crumbling, staffs have been cut back, and services have been slashed. Public park and recreation systems in America's big cities are in critical financial condition.[2]

In 1975, Americans winced at New York City's financial fiasco, and recreation professionals shuddered sympathetically at the effect it had on the public recreation and park system in that megalopolis. They were further shocked when 40 percent of local and state public recreation agencies responding to a manpower survey that same year reported job freezes in effect.[3] By 1977, professionals simply nodded numbly when the U.S. Department of the Interior published the first of 16 "inferences" drawn from its preliminary study of urban parks:

> Virtually every standard metropolitan statistical area (SMSA) studied appears to have a serious problem in providing urban recreation. Whether it be a need for setting aside additional open space, poor access to parks, or the inability to operate, maintain, or develop protected lands, nearly all the SMSA's scrutinized in this study have a major problem (generally fiscal) in providing their residents with recreation.[4]

In June 1978, some 4¼ million Californians revolted and voted to cut and limit property taxes. Tax reform dealt a widespread and fundamental fiscal blow to that state's human services, and the revolt spread across the nation. By 1979, it was clear that public services had entered a new era of limits, destined, most believe, to extend through the 1980s. Public recreation services have not been exempted.

Around the globe, water, food and housing continue at the top of the hierarchy of urgent needs and will undoubtedly stay there. Realistically, the allocation of scarce and non-renewable resources directly for recreation purposes begins the newly recognized "era of limits" very low on society's priority list. Some will contend that pessimistic predictions are premature, but leisure resource scarcity, in the broadest sense, is touching everyone now. Evidence mounts that both space and facilities will be increasingly inadequate and insufficient. It is probably an understatement to suggest that a fundamental challenge confronting all nations in coming decades will be which leisure activities can or should be continued or encouraged, which discontinued or discouraged, which modified, and which new experiences need to be devised or invented.

In developed countries, finite natural resource limits have been reached simultaneously with the achievement of new leisure possibilities. Later labor force entry, shorter work weeks, longer holiday weekends, extended vacations, year-round school plans, more generous sabbaticals and leave programs, earlier retirement options, and longer life spans are among many contemporary phenomena contributing to more leisure or discretionary time for many of the increasing numbers of us. The clash between limited resources and limitless leisure confronts concerned recreation professionals with the certainty of an escalating insufficiency of funds, personnel, information, space, facilities and equipment.

SOME DIFFICULT GOVERNMENT TASKS

Resolution of the perplexing search for balance occasioned by the ironic scenario will be determined largely by governments, for it is in the political realm that decisions are made which affect resources, the antecedents of free time, and what can be done during it. These include policies concerned with international relations, energy, environmental quality, housing, food and water, as well as those influencing work, education, mobility, affluence, accessibility of recreation resources, and the quantity of leisure and its distribution.

The heterogeneity of governmental units, private and voluntary agencies, and commercial enterprises which own and operate resources complicates efforts to determine the dimensions of the total leisure resource base of any nation. In the United States, national and state parks, public beaches, bicycle trails and school playgrounds can be identified readily, and, with effort, enumerated. But the total leisure resource system of the nation is far broader. It includes commercial as well as public facilities, man-made as well as natural resources – the backyard swimming pool, bowling alley, sport stadium, amusement park, culture center, campground and resort. (Philosophic debate about what is "recreation" also tends to complicate enumeration.)

Needed is a benchmark assessment of the total leisure resource base available and a determination of a set of alternative leisure futures based on both likely resources and identified human needs. When hobbies, television, adult education, cross country skiing, playgrounds, off-road vehicles, Las Vegas, Disney World, professional, semiprofessional, amateur arts and sports; outdoor recreation and tourism are viewed under the same umbrella, intelligent choices regarding their relative merits and legitimate demands upon the resources of a nation or the world will be more likely. Conceptually and mechanically, such planning seems remote, but growing resource limitations and scarcity will eventually mandate it.

In metropolitan areas of the United States, where over two-thirds of the nation's population is concentrated, only 25 percent of the nation's recreation facilities and only 3 percent of public recreation lands are reasonably accessible. From these urbanized areas come early warning signals regarding overused recreation resources. For example, Los Angeles officials have estimated there are 115,000 golfers for every course, and over 1,700 tennis players for every court. Across the country in New York City, applicants for permits to play on that city's 522 tennis courts must present a passport-size photo of themselves when applying.

In many industrial nations, leisure is regarded as a social and economic tool, with resources provided accordingly. In the United States, profit motives and tradition influence present and future leisure resources far more than undetermined human or social benefits. One result is that in most American cities, national minimum standards are not met for many types of recreation facilities, including parks, playgrounds, tot lots, swimming pools, tennis courts, and basketball and volleyball courts. Some of these average less than 20 percent of the very conservative national minimum standards, and, with widespread austerity, the percentage is diminishing. However, despite their popularity (perhaps largely a function of the resources which are provided), there is no evidence that any of the activities are essential to Americans (indeed, there is growing scientific support contending some may actually be harmful in certain respects). On the other hand, there is no evidence that other kinds of facilities might be more beneficial to more people at less cost – and perhaps even more fun. With the exception of spin-off information accruing from heart disease prevention research, no new knowledge is being systematically sought which might help better utilize increasingly limited fiscal, spatial, and nonrenewable resources for recreation purposes.

COMPLEX AND COMPETING FORCES

Competing leisure interests complicate decisions regarding the allocation of resources. Should limited assets be committed to acquiring precious open space, developing playgrounds for children, building bicycle or jogging trails, supporting the performing arts, providing senior citizen centers, transporting handicapped persons to special programs, underwriting subventions for adult education, or constructing new stadia? Disputes are increasingly fierce. Paradoxically, many urban recreation facilities are under-utilized, particularly in inner city areas, due to inadequate maintenance, poor or uninspired leadership and programs, stifling summer heat, poor accessibility, vandalism and padlocked cyclone fences.

United States leisure resources are maldistributed in nonurban areas as well. Nationally, recreation acres are not located where the people are; no amount of manipulation can equalize a situation in which only 15 percent of the population lives in the West with 72 percent of the nation's recreation acreage. (Despite this inequity, one-eighth of the total land area of the United States is currently set aside for public recreation, although many relatively remote resources are used far beyond reasonable carrying capacities.)

The second home and resort industry is a growing dilemma to leisure professionals. Residents near prime outdoor recreation resources adjacent to metropolitan areas contend they need industry to survive; vacationing, conservation-minded urban residents prefer their leisure environments to remain pristine. Battle lines are drawn along ocean shores, rivers, canals, and in mountain and desert environments as well. Achieving a balance between preservation and utilization is one of the most difficult challenges confronting leisure resource managers. Whether protecting oceans or wilderness areas from poachers, city parks from freeways, or great works of art from madmen, the problems and issues are fundamental, profound, interrelated and international.

When the planet's first national park, Yellowstone, was established in 1872, Congress directed that it "provide for the preservation from injury or spoliation of all timber, mineral deposits, natural curiosities, or wonders within said park, and their retention in their natural condition." Yet the park was also "dedicated and set apart as a public park or pleasure ground for the benefit and enjoyment of the people."

A century later, at the second World Conference on National Parks, experts agreed that rationing is the only alternative to destruction of national parks around the world. Overuse is a condition reported in every country, not just in the industrial nations. But in too many outdoor recreation areas, obsolete practices are still encouraged. Such practices may have been appropriate years ago, but are now increasingly untenable environmental insults. Textbooks and teachers reflecting nostalgic unawareness that stoves have replaced campfires and that tents have superseded pine bough lean-tos can no longer be tolerated. "Take nothing but pictures" still pertains, but "leave nothing but footprints" is inoperative.

Congestion at national parks and other popular leisure resources during peak use seasons has become an expected, if vexing, aspect of vacation planning for families in most industrial nations. Several public and private leisure resources in the United States have banned private automobiles from specific areas in an effort to permit people to see and enjoy attractions. It is difficult to prophesy at what point the pleasure of enjoying a resource becomes less than the frustration attendant to visiting it. Queues and crowds at zoos, popular films, ski lifts, and national historic sites and monuments surely repel a growing would-be user-visitor group. One can conjecture cynically that rationing wilderness use, requiring reservations at state campgrounds, and mustering tour-groups may soon seem Utopian rather than an intrusion upon personal freedom.

ALTERING EXPERIENCES

A cartoon depicted the entrance to "Perma Park," which advertised "fiberglass flowers, polystyrene turf, plasta grass, recycled water, styrofoam rocks, asbestos trees and shrubs – a carefree oasis in an anxious world." Such speculation is perhaps not as amusing as the artists intended. The "old swimming hole" is already among romantic memories of days when water pollution and the population explosion were largely undiscovered; today, concrete, fiberglass, vinyl, and gunite swimming pools are respectable replacements. Denuded picnic areas, beach dunes, deserts, and hillsides testify that there comes a time when natural vegetation is defeated by masses at leisure.

Experience modification has become a popular intervention for many leisure resource managers faced with such problems. An ironic example comes from Philadelphia, location of one of the nation's most historic buildings, Independence Hall. The Hall was the site of the signing of the Declaration of Independence and the United States Constitution; it is now the home of a very famous British product, the Liberty Bell, an emblem of freedom known throughout the world. Until 1973, individuals could enter this building at leisure on any day to relive its history and to view and perhaps touch the Bell. Since then, however, freedom has been restricted, for too many were coming. Now, one's only option is a guided tour.

Duplication of a popular resource or attraction to eliminate bottlenecks caused by overuse is sometimes feasible. Often, however, it is impractical, or, as with the Liberty Bell, impossible. From around the world come examples of similar dilemmas. The French have been pondering the problems of "green leprosy," caused by the humid breath of tourists which stimulates a furious growth of a destructive green fungus on the prehistoric wall paintings in the Lascaux Caves. The solution seems to be to build "new" caves under the old one, containing facsimilies of the Stone Age hunting murals. In Italy, complex problems attending the willful destruction of Michelangelo's Pieta perplex custodians no less than the restoration experts. And in Cairo, Egyptian officials are increasing tourist fees to raise funds needed for care and restoration of the Pyramid of Cheops and the Sphinx.

ALTERING ACTIVITIES

Activity modification is a typical response to increasing pressures in a variety of settings. Softball and baseball batters in several countries now approach the plate with a "given" 2-1-2 count (2 balls, 1 strike, and only 1 foul ball to go). Games are shortened, more teams are accommodated, personnel and utility costs are lower per game played, and play moves faster.

An increasingly important aspect of leisure resource planning and management is that of interchangeability between and among leisure activities. Can equal benefit and satisfaction be derived by an individual or society from among a subset of leisure options? Intuition suggests the affirmative, but specific prescriptions for governments and citizens do not exist.

If one's life meaning has been derived largely from the cultural opportunities existent in a great metropolitan area, what replacement options should be explored if relocation to the hinterlands becomes necessary? If team sport participation has been paramount, what might replace it in case of incapacitating illness or injury? What alternatives should be prescribed for children in a city which can no longer afford to operate a summer recreation program or provide traditional facilities? Gamblers who cannot afford to lose any more money? Persons afflicted with depression? Tourists when the dollar declines? Bathers when the ocean is polluted? Vacationers when fuel prices soar or gas shortages are rampant? Industries when raw materials and labor costs push the costs of recreation products above the public's willingness to buy? Nations whose flagging tourist industry contributes to a deficit balance of payments?

The interchangeability dilemma is closely related to a favorite chicken-or-egg exercise practiced by recreation professionals: does recreation demand create justification for leisure resources, or do resources themselves create demand? Popular corollaries suggest that skills, attitudes, and peer expectations (most often transmitted through educational programs) create demand. Less often considered is the likelihood that the market-place creates demand and tradition maintains it. Absolutely omitted from discourse is the possibility that demand is a reflection of basic human need, that is, the absence of a specific resource or activity will exacerbate some social, psychological, or physiological pathology among some segment of the population.

Should public policymakers react favorably to all new leisure industries and provide incentives or make other accommodations on their behalf? How should they determine if a new product has been developed with no social conscience or obligation beyond the dollar, mark, or yen? These issues will continue to confound governments across the country and around the world for the foreseeable future.

A budding new area of interest offers some promise. Education for leisure demands consideration of probable limits of future resources. Teaching children and adults skills, values, and attitudes with no regard to likely future recreation opportunities is at best professional malfeasance. The public will rightly question school and recreation programs which emphasize the development of expectations which cannot now be met and will be increasingly frustrated. It will correctly identify the professions dealing with leisure services as self-serving retainers of the status quo. More important, leisure education must enable individuals to participate successfully in the process of dealing with rapidly changing leisure options. Within the life span, recreation seems destined to be more varied and dynamic in an increasingly complex and changing world.

The lack of sufficient leisure resources is regrettable and the depreciation of their quality unfortunate. Dramatic population growth and acceleration of the rate of social and environmental change made the conditions progressively intolerable. Old practices require critical reexamination; answers must be sought to such fundamental questions as "why are we teaching activities and building facilities as we are?" If the nation's resources cannot support all forms of leisure expression, who will determine priorities and on what basis: cost benefit analysis? physical fitness needs? cultural values? Answers may enable us to prophesy with some confidence whether physical educators and recreation professionals will be leaders or technicians in the twenty-first century.

Leisure resource scarcity is not a precisely predictable phenomenon. Status and trend information exists, however, which permits us to regard it as one which can be ameliorated or exacerbated by professional action or inaction. Both time and opportunity exist for those concerned with the broad array of recreation options to develop and implement strategies which will minimize dysfunctions between recreation demand and leisure resources in the twenty-first century.

It is appropriate to search seriously for reasonable and realistic alternatives to shortsighted "what-we-will-need-then-is-more-of-what-we-have-now" attitudes. There is opportunity to retain what will be feasible and desirable and to replace what will be obsolete and quite possibly now is indefensible. Discriminatory efforts must address space, facilities, and equipment as well as the more important and controversial area of activity form.

THE CHALLENGE FOR PROFESSIONALS

The recreation professional of the future will be confronted by a panoply of role choices. The management of facilities and transmission of activity skills will most likely be continuing traditional functions. Of growing significance, however, will be options which might be classified as advocate and leadership roles. These include active efforts to devise and determine the most beneficial and feasible sport and physical activity forms for individuals and the larger society, to inform the public of alternatives and their relative costs and benefits, and to aggressively solicit citizen support for needed resources. Some may be reluctant to assume such leadership roles; they must resolve the moot question: who should?

If recreation professionals do not assume such functions, who is best qualified to assess present resources and probable future resource limitations facing every popular leisure activity? Who should document scientifically the relative merits of various activities for citizens of every age? Who should devise and popularize new high-density participant sport forms? Who should endeavor to maximize potential use of present and future resources and facilities around the clock and around the calendar? Who should minimize environmental impacts of physical activities and their attendant facilities, equipment, and transportation requirements? Who should insist that the rhetoric of lifetime sports conform realistically to probable future resources as well as beneficial activity forms? Who should be certain that skills, values, and interests fostered and encouraged through formal and informal education programs will not be frustrated by lack of accessible resources and facilities?

The responsibility for curriculum and program change in light of probable future resource scarcity must be assumed largely by those leading the fields of physical education and recreation. The alternative to dynamic and aggressive professional leadership is intervention and control of the leisure destiny of the nation by anyone who will assume leadership and responsibility. One might speculate that local, state, and national policy-makers in 1980 or 2000 will demand an end to the teaching of many sport forms and physical activities because insufficient leisure resources exist. There is no reason to expect an overworked elected official to be concerned with eliminating the less beneficial activity, or to make efforts to replace those discarded with more feasible ones.

As our automobiles slow to 55 miles per hour, there is time to ponder options, and to determine if our personal and professional best course is to act or to react. For many reasons, it seems propitious for professionals to aggressively seek leisure alternatives which will be not only responsive to human needs, but also feasible in the future.

REFERENCES

1. Meadows, Donella H. et. al.. *The Limits to Growth: A Report for the Club of Rome's Project on the Predicament of Mankind.* New York: Universe Books, 1972.
2. Dunn, Diana R.. "Leisure Resources in America's Inner Cities." *Parks and Recreation,* (March), 1974. p. 56.
3. Henkel, Donald D. and Godbey, Geoffrey C.. *Parks, Recreation and Leisure Services Employment in the Public Sector: Status and Trends.* Arlington, Virginia: National Recreation and Park Association, 1977. p. 65.
4. U.S. Department of the Interior, *A Preliminary Urban Parks Study.* Washington, D.C.: (January), 1977, pp. 11-12.

Chapter Ten

Future Leisure Environments in Cities

Seymour M. Gold

It is a time for great optimism in the field of parks and recreation because, after years of romanticism, professionals are beginning to cope with reality. Changing values, technology, the energy crisis and inflation are forcing cities to do out of necessity what they might have done by choice. The traditional approach to providing open space and leisure services, long dominated by the use of arbitrary standards, outmoded concepts and conventional wisdom is being challenged as never before in the literature and in practice.

A new generation of recreation spaces and programs is evolving that presents some hopeful alternatives. These alternatives are based on the ideas of a small group of professionals who have been: (1) calling for a redefinition of leisure services in cities, (2) describing the phenomenon of nonuse of local parks, (3) alerting us to a *cost-revenue crisis* in government, (4) urging realistic citizen participation in the planning and decision process for urban parks, (5) pleading for more research and demonstration programs in park planning and management, and (6) suggesting it is not how much, but how good urban parks are. These people have been telling us the major problem in this field has been, and will be, coping with *change*.

REALITY CHECKS ON THE PRESENT

A critical review of the literature and practice yields these reality checks on the present:

Recreation Planning

The current state of the art is characterized by tradition. Recreation planning and design has been dominated by the use of arbitrary standards, and irrelevant concepts. Most of the ideas in current use are premised on 1930's thinking about recreation and open space preservation in cities.

Most recreation plans still assume an emphasis on youth, unlimited growth, increasing personal income and mobility, cheap energy and unlimited public budgets. They project a past and present that may not be realistic in light of current trends toward an aging society, growth management, decreasing real income and a growing energy crisis.

Problem-Solving

The Park and recreation field is essentially retrospective and romantic in the way it approaches problem-solving. Most recreation plans do not acknowledge or accommodate significant changes or trends in leisure lifestyles, legislation, technology or values.

Demonstration and innovation are the exception in most communities. Studies of user behavior are not evident in most recreation plans. Parks and recreation is still not considered an experimental field with credible solutions, measures or a theoretical foundation. It has not applied sophisticated planning or management techniques such as: systems analysis, performance budgeting, critical path method or gaming simulation to assess the future impact of options or programs on people, cities or the profession.

People Orientation

The objectives of many public park and recreation systems better accommodate the needs of the supplier than the user. Public participation in the planning process is still viewed with professional skepticism and given token attention. Nonuse, especially of neighborhood parks, is common in most communities because these spaces do not accommodate the recreational needs of people.

Advocacy and pluralism are becoming accepted dimensions of the planning and decision-making process. It is no longer enough for government to do things for some people. It must do things for and with all people and be able to rationalize this effort in human terms. The needs of special populations, e.g., racial and ethnic minorities, senior citizens, the poor, physically handicapped and mentally retarded, have not been met in most communities that have yet to meet the needs of the general population.

FUTURE TRENDS AND EVENTS

Philosophical and pragmatic changes in American society, the recreation movement and evolving public policy reveal these changing perspectives, trends and events which will have a significant impact on urban parks and recreation and open space.

Lifestyle

A cultural revolution is taking place in thought about environment, leisure, work and sense of community. It is concerned with the consumer, physical health and the quality of life. Translated into space or services, this revolution demands a more enlightened view of the way people use leisure time and space in cities. It implies rethinking our conceptual distinctions between space and services, public and private opportunities or indoor and outdoor spaces.

The idea that urban parks are for all people and established for the pleasurable use of leisure time is in contradiction with the lifestyles and leisure behavior of a growing number of people. Many types of leisure behavior are labeled as "deviant" because of outmoded laws, arbitrary policies and conventional thinking. Urban parks are one reflection of reality in an increasingly plastic world. The notion that they should be used by only "normal" people for the "constructive" use of their leisure time may be in violation of human rights.

Professionals have begun to redefine recreation in terms of human development. In the emerging view, it is not activities, facilities or programs that are central, it is what happens to people. Recreation is not a specific event, point in time or space. It is a dimension of self-development that has little to do with activity.

Self-Sufficiency

A new spirit of self help, volunteerism and community involvement is emerging in many places. This spirit recognizes the limits of government in solving many human problems. It senses a degree of commitment, responsibility and resourcefulness that can be used by people to help design, develop and maintain urban parks. The ideas of self-generated and self-maintained urban parks have yet to be tested in most communities. The expectation of professionals or government doing everything may be passe, fiscally impossible or not serve the best interests of people.

The logic of voluntary simplicity, self-sufficiency and self-directed leisure is the wave of the future. This idea, coupled with the philosophy of alternative, noncompetitive recreation programs such as "New Games," implies drastic changes in our approach to program leadership. It casts the professional as an enabler or resource person and the citizen as a volunteer leader.

Frugality and Austerity

Taxpayers, faced with a decline in real income, are not likely to approve bond issues or tax increases for local parks. They are developing a serious interest in the effectiveness of leisure services to obtain the best value for their dollar. Parks and recreation must now compete as never before for budget. The days of rationalizing public budgets with rhetoric instead of facts are gone.

Local governments are experiencing a cost-revenue crisis that will not diminish in a steady state economy coupled with rapid inflation, high levels of unemployment and a federal policy of indifference to the critical problems of American cities. Cities cannot expect needed financial help from the states or counties for the same reasons. Drastic cuts in municipal services will be necessary just to keep pace with inflation.

The existing system of recreation spaces in most communities will be all they can afford to operate and maintain. Funds will not be available for new spaces which implies making the best use of existing spaces that need renewal. *Recycling* urban parks in the same way we recycle newspaper or glass is the only strategy for many communities, and it makes good sense.

The traditional priorities of land acquisition, development and programs are being reversed in some cities that are beginning to sense the entire city as a recreation place in which voluntary program leadership in private or quasi-public spaces are more effective than extensive public investments in land and facilities.

Consolidation and Integration

A consolidation of government services is rapidly combining the park and recreation department with other social or environmental services. In both cases, the traditional "fun and games" or "housekeeper" images of these departments is dramatically broadened toward human development and environmental management.

The "withering of city hall" and "strategy for attrition" of local government is an irreversible trend in the 1980's. Park and recreation agencies that cannot justify cost-effective leisure services will be replaced with private contractors. Many professionals will shift from the public to the private sector, if they wish to stay in this field. Public leisure services that are not self-supporting or subsidized by charitable donations or voluntary efforts will become endangered species.

Limits

An "era of limits" is being defined in politics, science, government, and industry that says small is beautiful, less is more, that we have reached the limits of unqualified growth and must make more rational use of existing resources. In a materialistic society, it is "Economics as if People Mattered" based on a lower set of expectations and conservation of human and natural resources.

The energy crisis is real and beginning to show an impact on disposable income, mobility patterns, and lifestyles. The choice of work or leisure places is being conditioned by the price of fuel. The increased cost of gasoline or the prospect of fuel rationing may force many people to drastically change their priorities and seek energy conserving ways to spend their leisure time in or near cities. The option of personal transportation will be replaced with mass transit alternatives or bicycle or pedestrian access to local recreation opportunities.

Municipal austerity programs have had a profound effect on the maintenance, development and redevelopment of urban parks. These park systems would be unable to accommodate the sustained levels of increased use which could result from a prolonged energy crisis without substantial increases in funding. At the very time urban parks are needed to provide energy conserving leisure options for many people, these systems are in jeopardy. The "energy connection" represents the last best hope to justify a significant federal and state commitment to the direct support of urban park systems.

These future trends will have a significant and sustained impact on the nature of urban leisure patterns, public services and the profession. However, there are several current conditions which may have an even greater impact on the future. These conditions should influence our thoughts, plans and actions. They represent restraints and opportunities for coping with change and reality. For example, these items can have profound implications on future leisure environments in cities:

1. People's trust in institutions is at an all time low. Most people do not trust authority. The credibility of government and professionals is being questioned as never before. At the very time we need credibility, it would seem few people are listening. The legacy of Viet Nam, Watergate and a host of events such as the Three-Mile Island nuclear accident or DC-10 engine mountings failure have eroded public confidence in authority.

2. The taxpayers' revolt is real. There is widespread overt and latent national support for balanced budgets from both political parties. People have embraced this as a new cause or religion. They are angry at big government, excessive tax burdens and waste. Their mood is reactionary and uses the only initiative left which is to cut public budgets or remove politicians who will not do so. Public agencies that cannot justify their existence in credible human terms that have political support have dim prospects of survival in an era of scarce resources and competing needs.

3. Society is aging. The post-war baby boom of the 1950's has become the baby bust of the 1980's. The "Greening of America"[2] has changed to the "Graying of America." Surplus schools are being

turned into nursing homes as the youth culture fades. The median age will pass 30 in 1981, reach 35 by the year 2000 and approach 40 by 2030. During this period, the number of people over 65 will more than double to 52 million, one out of every six Americans. The demographic facts are irrefutable.

4. Working wives, moonlighting and late retirement as a way to cope with inflation or declining family income are causing significant changes in leisure patterns. Many people have less leisure time or flexibility which implies peak use of limited facilities or use rationing. The recreation demand projections of the 1980's based on increasing levels of leisure time may not reflect the work and leisure of the 1980's. For most people, the recreation use patterns of the 1980's may, of necessity, parallel the patterns of the 1880's with weekends and holidays being the major source of leisure time.

5. Individual and family income is declining in terms of purchasing power. The gap between the rich and poor is widening. Many people will have less disposable income for leisure services at the same time most communities are considering significant increases in fees and charges to make these services self-supporting. A severe economic recession is likely in 1980. The length and depth of this recession will depend on this country's ability to become more self-sufficient and energy conserving which has a direct relationship to the way we use leisure time and space in cities.

These perspectives call for drastic changes in the current approach to urban recreation and suggest a radical departure from the traditional approach of applying arbitrary standards to the past or present recreation activities of a mythical population to rationalize the allocation of recreation space or services. They imply a sophisticated understanding of urban living, leisure, behavior and the future not common in this field.

In a planning context, these changes imply it is necessary to move beyond a narrow focus on recreation activities, buildings and parks toward a mission of improving the quality of life and environment. At the policy or operational level of local government, these concepts place park and recreation services in the broader context of a social service delivery system which emphasizes a humanistic approach to problem solving. They recognize the interrelation of recreation and park services to the social and physical environment of cities.

This emphasis on cities, people and the future will require the bold vision and sense of social purpose which characterized the early years of the park and recreation movement. It will also require a commitment to research and demonstration to find new ways to think about leisure in cities. Most important, an emphasis on the future will require an understanding of social or technological change and innovation.

CHANGE AND INNOVATION

If change were to take place with equal force or speed, it might allow projection or, at least, prediction. But now change is uneven and subject to great forward leaps. A breakthrough in one area can have profound impact in other areas. Who anticipated the consequences of these items we now take for granted:

automobiles, space flights, income taxes, billboards, air conditioning, frozen foods, computers, penicillin, hydrogen bombs, Kentucky Fried Chicken, paper wedding dresses, dune buggies, neon lights, disposable diapers, color television, collective bargaining, credit cards, nuclear power, affirmative action, social security, vending machines, mobile homes, supermarkets, jumbo jets, detergents, tranquilizers, revenue sharing, shopping centers and suburbia?

Each item has had some influence on urban life. Combined, they have created a need for people to adapt to or cope with change which is the fundamental cause of most issues or problems. Some of these problems include:

an energy crisis, racial polarization, juvenile delinquency, traffic congestion, water and air pollution, urban blight, inflation, diminishing open space, crime, flight to the suburbs, water shortages, inadequate schools, bankrupt cities and slums.

Beyond the present is an uncertain future where innovation and technology may solve some problems, but create still more. Who is considering the future impact on leisure patterns of:

increased lifespan, disease eradication, psychedelic drugs, weather control, cybernation, guaranteed minimum wage, and flextime work schedules?

In the context of urban parks and recreation just 10 years ago, who envisioned:

skateboard parks, racquetball centers, mainstreaming the handicapped, unisex toilets, inflatable buildings, water scooters, giant slides, electronic games, hang gliders, roller skates, astro turf, surf machines, and solar heated pools?

Most important, who is thinking about the possible impacts on the park and recreation experience or agency of:

legalization of marijuana, nude beaches, an aging society, social impact reports, surplus schools, television games, growth management, mopeds, a major recession, a sustained energy crisis and zero-based budgeting?

SCENARIOS OF THE FUTURE

One way to focus on the possible implications of change and innovation is with four scenarios of the future that can be translated into two options for people and professionals to consider. For example, these scenarios of the future seem possible:

Traditional View

The traditional view projects trends which may no longer be true.[3] For example, by the year 2000 population density, mobility and personal income will double, the work week will decline and people will retire at 60. An energy crisis and economic depression will not occur. Growth and affluence will continue with an unlimited consumption of resources. Simple forms of outdoor recreation will continue, but more specialized and expensive activities will gain mass appeal. The work ethic will prevail and leisure time will be used to escape from cities to the country.

Humanistic View

The humanistic view envisions a future where there is little distinction between work and leisure.[4] Work in an affluent society may become a privilege for a few and mass leisure will be socially acceptable. Work will become people-oriented instead of object-oriented. The emphasis of society will be on human services instead of things. Education systems will prepare people for a life of leisure instead of work. A leisure ethic will replace the work ethic and humanism will replace materialism. The question will no longer be the production of wealth, but the fair distribution of wealth. Open space will be a public trust for future generations instead of a speculative commodity to be exploited for profit.

Pessimistic View

The pessimistic view sees the future as one of complexity, scarcity and turmoil with mass leisure as a problem in an industrialized world with diminishing resources and competing needs.[5] Technology, combined with an accelerating pace of change, will subject recreation to "Future Shock."[6] Our relationship with things will become more temporary and the throwaway culture and transience described by Toffler will become a way of life for many. His descriptions of items like: portable playgrounds, modular fun palaces, experience-makers, life environments, fun specialists and leisure-based subcults would boggle the minds of most park and recreation commissions. Open space preservation will be an opportunity foregone or a luxury beyond the reach of most communities.

Optimistic View

New work attitudes, lifestyles and ethics will shape our leisure patterns. Three-day work weeks and flextime schedules will level peak use. Work sharing, extended vacations, sabbaticals and early retirement will allow extensive travel and participation in local recreation programs. Work will be done at home or workers will live close to where they work in new or recycled cities. Cottage industries will bring work and leisure environments together again. Gasoline shortages will force people to rediscover urban parks. Inflation and declining real income will force people to rediscover simple activities. Managed open space will create the environmental framework and social focus of cities. Open space and parks will be considered an essential of urban living to be provided by community action and sophisticated long range planning.

These views imply significant changes in our mission, meaning and nature of urban parks. They require a critical evaluation of existing policies, acknowledgement of reality and radical changes which will not be easy to initiate or accept. These changes can be described with two coping strategies:

Urban Parks (Status Quo)

A business-as-usual attitude of delay and obfuscation of the real facts and issues. Tokenism and attempts to solve problems by treating the symptoms or effects instead of the causes. Bureaucratic finger-pointing and prolonged studies to evade the questions of responsibility. A naive hope and idealism that urban parks are a necessary "good" to be justified on their own merits. A posture of status quo, defensiveness to criticism, and assumption that the current and future changes or challenges will magically vanish with time.

Urban Parks II (Survival)

An attempt to change the situation based on the real facts and issues. Bold innovation, demonstration, and full commitment to solve problems by treating the causes. Bureaucratic honesty and immediate or interim policy statements to fix the questions of responsibility. Sober reflection and reexamination of the role and value of urban parks as they relate to other public services. A posture of reasoned change, humility instead of arrogance, and conviction that the current and future changes or challenges will accelerate with time.

The predictable result of strategy I is the demise or deterioration of existing urban parks. The impact of this scenario is unthinkable to many who have long considered this public service or institution impregnable. The result in human and economic terms seem catastrophic for this field which has never experienced public censure or had its professional survival threatened. This scenario is tragic and needless. Its impact on urban America would be profound and regretful.

The predictable result of strategy II is the survival and improvement of urban parks. The impact of this scenario would be to sustain, strengthen, and justify the provision of leisure services as a vital American institution. The potential results in human and economic terms seem impressive, considering the level of investment already in public open space. Most important, the potential of parks and recreation to contribute to the quality of urban life and the urban environment could be realized. The impact of this scenario on urban America would be dramatic and hopeful.

NEW DIMENSIONS OF RECREATION

Regardless of which events or scenarios occur in the long range future, a spectrum of new activities, institutions and concepts is evolving that should be considered now in the preparation of recreation plans. These items represent some dramatic alternatives for the provision of leisure opportunities in cities. They illustrate what is needed and possible.

New Activities

A new generation of activities will become common in or near cities. These activities will require new spaces, management techniques and sophisticated leadership. Many of these activities will be self-directed, noncompetitive and energy conserving in the use of land or facilities. They will symbolize dramatic changes in lifestyle, ethics or attitudes toward people and the environment. A sampling of these new activities includes:

ballooning, ski-touring, windsurfing, put/take fishing, land sailing, psychodrama, PONG, turf-skiing, spinnaker flying, New Games, water-walking, ski-bobbing, hot tubbing, flingbee, snurfing, spelunking, para-sailing, camera hunting, par-course fitness, yoga, Rolfing, wind skating, flickerball, disco skating, and swingball tennis.

New Institutions

A new type of institution will develop to accommodate the lifestyles and leisure needs of the future. Human development and environmental management will become the expanded focus of public parks and recreation agencies. The arts, culture and education will be closely coordinated in departments of life enrichment. Among the new or expanded institutions of the future will be:

1. Public Utilities–To provide leisure services in the same way as gas, water, electricity and mail are delivered to local communities.
2. Recreation Franchises–Private contractors will provide revenue producing services, e.g., tennis, golf or marinas.
3. Contract Services–Private contractors will provide many of the planning, design, management, maintenance and program services now provided by the public sector in most communities.
4. Commercial Enterprises–Private concessionaires will provide community and regional theme or amusement parks on public land.
5. Company Resorts–Private corporations will provide special park and recreation opportunities for their employees in or near cities.
6. Leisure Cooperatives–Individuals, neighborhoods and organizations or social groups will join together to provide specialized leisure opportunities or equipment for their members, e.g., sailboats or swimming pools.
7. Leisure Counselors–Public and private specialists will advise people on alternative ways and places to use their time budgets in the same manner as investment counselors now advise people on how to spend their discretionary money.
8. Day Care Centers–Public and private places to provide supervised care for children while parents are participating in recreational activities will become common at the neighborhood level.
9. Community Colleges–Local colleges will assume a dominant role in providing arts, cultural and human development programs for adults. Their facilities will be integrated with park and recreation facilities to serve the entire community.

New Concepts

We need new ways to think about leisure in cities. For example, we have traditionally considered only public land and water for outdoor recreation, but new or expanded use of approaches to design, management and program offer these exciting possibilities:

1. Air Rights–Using space over public and private urban development for leisure opportunities. We can deck over freeways, railroad yards, warehouses and parking lots for recreational use.
2. Underground Spaces–Developing underground malls, plazas and pathways that have multiuse recreational potentials.

3. Risk Recreation–Providing activities and places that encourage physical and mental challenge or self-confidence.[7]
4. Self-programmed Recreation–Encouraging simple, energy-conserving, noncompetitive activities such as New Games[8] or Parcourse fitness.
5. Recycling Existing Parks–Renewing existing parks that no longer meet the needs of users to include a major emphasis on adventure playgrounds, community gardens, and water or energy conserving landscapes.
6. Reuse of Existing Buildings–Converting abandoned or obsolete buildings to public or private recreational uses, e.g., theaters, schools, factories, or supermarkets.
7. Self-generated Parks–Encouraging residents to help design, develop and maintain neighborhood parks.
8. Rooftop Spaces–Making intensive use of rooftops for public and private recreational opportunities.
9. Recreational Retailing–Combining amusement parks with shopping centers.
10. Reuse of Cemeteries–Redeveloping or opening cemeteries for passive recreational use, arboretums and wildlife preserves.
11. Urban Campgrounds–Providing campgrounds in urban parks for tourists.
12. High Rise Recreation Structures–Building or redeveloping high rise structures for recreational use, e.g., tennis clubs, hostels or play areas.
13. Pneumatic Structures–Providing large air supported structures for special events or temporary facilities in changing neighborhoods.
14. Joint Use of Facilities–Using private clubs, marinas, golf courses, shopping centers and industrial parks for public programs.
15. Public/Private Opportunities–Considering the entire city as a recreation place to include places such as streets, theaters, bars, restaurants, libraries, museums, historic districts, private plazas and flea markets where people can experience diversity, pleasure or enrichment.

We can build cities in parks instead of parks in cities. The idea of parks or recreation as an isolated set of spaces or experiences in cities is passe. Past distinctions between indoor and outdoor spaces and public vs. private opportunities are fading with new concepts that integrate space and service to serve the needs of people at the lowest possible cost.

A NEW AGENDA

It is time to rethink the future of urban parks. A new agenda is necessary to cope with the present and shape the future. This agenda will require an unparalleled sense of urgency, innovation and professional sophistication. There is no substitute for these ingredients. The positive or negative results of our actions or indifference are predictable on the quality of urban life and environment.

There has never been a better time for innovation and demonstration in the parks and recreation field, if we will try to understand and shape the future. There is much to be done. Here are some places to begin:

1. Study the future as well as the past and present to see if we are thinking boldly enough about current issues and trends. We teach courses in the history of recreation, why not the future?

2. Develop a more humanistic or people-serving concept of urban parks and recreation. It is time to balance our emphasis on the resource with a serious concern for the user.

3. Broaden our interpretation of urban recreation in time, space and attitude. There is no rule that says parks must be public, square, horizontal, and dull places that do not relate to people.

4. Encourage the private sector to provide high quality services. Government cannot and will not do the whole job.

5. Consider parks and recreation an experimental field with a major emphasis on research, demonstration and innovation to develop new products and services. It took thousands of experiments to develop birth control pills or color television, surely we can find an alternative to competitive sports or traditional play areas.

6. Link our efforts to improve the quality of urban parks to the energy crisis, changing needs, priorities, and lifestyles of people living in cities to include those with the greatest need for leisure services, e.g., the poor, senior citizens, physically handicapped and mentally retarded.

7. Challenge the assumptions, concepts and standards traditionally used to provide leisure opportunities in cities. One mark of professionalism is self-criticism.

8. Understand the best way to preserve wilderness areas from overuse is to improve the quality of life and environment in cities. By placing a priority on urban open space we can solve instead of perpetuating these two problems.

9. Develop objective measures to assess the need for and effectiveness of urban leisure services. It is difficult to do research or rationalize public funds for the support of parks and recreation without credible measures.

10. Train or retrain a new breed of enlightened professionals in Parks and Recreation to meet the challenges and opportunities of the future.

The impact of a taxpayers' revolt and energy crisis will probably do more to increase the effectiveness and appreciation of urban parks and recreation as a vital public service than the environmental movement and host of federal assistance programs. We have been given a powerful mandate to show the value of urban parks compared to other public services. The park and recreation movement can flourish by using this opportunity to develop a new constituency for urban parks that reflect the diverse populations of urban America.

The situation suggests this agenda: (1) asking the right questions before we seek answers, (2) re-examining the fundamental justification for providing leisure opportunities, (3) developing effective methods of recreation, planning, design and management, (4) applying these experimentally in demonstration areas, and (5) critically evaluating the process and products of this effort. The situation also suggests: (1) treating the causes of problems instead of the effects, (2) sorting out means from ends in the context of public policy, (3) calling problems by their real instead of their reverse labels, (4) humility instead of arrogance in relating to taxpayers, and (5) a dimension of serious thought and bold action uncommon in this field.[9]

This agenda will not be easy, but it is worth the effort if we believe public parks and recreation can make a significant contribution to the quality of urban life and environment. If we do not believe this is possible, it may be time to shift this responsibility to the private sector and accept the consequences or blessings of our action or indifference.

A PROFESSIONAL MANDATE

The personal challenge is to understand the dimensions of change or the future and accept a profession that may be more conditioned by world events and the media than tradition or reason. It is time to be bold and visionary instead of fatalistic. There is much hope; we can begin coping with change by: (1) discarding the romantic myths and conventional wisdom that pervade this field, and (2) turning the changing values, technology, and lifestyle of society into an advantage for this field that has so long stood for human and environmental values. It is time to ask and answer these questions:

1. How can we finance and justify park and recreation systems in an era of limits?

2. How can we build political constituencies for parks and recreation now?

3. If we cannot finance or justify public parks and recreation or build effective political constituencies in the 1980's—what alternatives are possible?

4. How should the profession and each of us respond to these challenges? Can we act instead of react to crisis or do we even believe there is one?

5. Are we part of the problem or part of the solution in terms of our level of commitment to this profession, understanding of reality, and interest in the future?

We have a mandate few similar professions have faced: to cope with the present and invent the future in an era of limits. The task will not be easy, but it is worth it, if we believe in the values of parks and recreation. We may be witnessing the end of one social order and beginning another, for better or worse. There is little time left for debate. What we do in the next few years will determine the future course of public parks and recreation in this country.

The Park and Recreation Movement and urban parks need not "muddle toward frugality" or become "endangered species" unless we want to. This profession has the guts and brains to cope with change in an era of limits. The essence of the past and hope of the future will not be lost, if we can sense this opportunity and do something about it now.

There is every reason for hope and optimism, if we begin to realize the potentials of living with nature in an era of limits. Of all our resources, the most precious is human awareness. This awareness causes us to re-examine the purpose of life and ask what fulfillment really means. Urban parks, recreation and open-space offer society unique opportunities for this examination. They can provide the time, place and means by which people can achieve self-discovery that leads to self-respect and a better society.

REFERENCES

1. Schumacker, E. F., *Small Is Beautiful: Economics as if People Mattered*. New York: Harper and Row, 1973.
2. Reich, Charles A., *The Greening of America*. New York: Random House, 1970.
3. See: United States Department of Interior, Bureau of Outdoor Recreation. *Outdoor Recreation: A Legacy for America*. Washington, D.C.: United States Government Printing Office, 1973.
4. See for example: Kaplan, Max. *Leisure: Theory and Policy*. New York: John Wiley and Sons, 1975.
5. See for example: Michael, Donald N., *The Unprepared Society: Planning for a Precarious Future*. New York: Harper and Row, 1968.
6. Toffler, Alvin. *Future Shock*. New York: Random House, 1970.
7. Dunn, Diana R. and Gulbis, John M., "The Risk Revolution." *Parks and Recreation* (August, 1976), pp. 12-17.
8. Fluegelman, Andrew (Ed.). *The New Games Book*. San Francisco: Headlands Press, 1976.
9. Gold, Seymour. *Recreation Planning and Design*. New York: McGraw-Hill, 1980.

Chapter Eleven

The Prospects for Leisure in a Conserver Society

Irene M. Spry

Since Adam and Eve left the Garden of Eden human beings have dreamed of a life free from drudgery. In the last century in affluent western countries the burden of incessant toil has largely been lifted from human shoulders. When the Toronto typographers, who in 1872, had won the right to organize a union, struck for a nine-hour day, the employers would not even meet them to discuss the matter.[1] The work week in Canada, as in the United States, has contracted progressively since the turn of the century. Average hours in manufacturing had fallen from 59 a week in 1890 to just over 40 hours a week in 1960.[2] Unions have fought long and hard for an eight-hour day,[2] and today a seven-hour day is not uncommon. A five-day work week is normal and experiments are being made with a four- and even a three-day work week. Besides longer weekends, most Canadians have ten or more paid holidays a year with two weeks or more paid vacation time. Pension plans have made possible retirement at an earlier age and the young stay longer at school and university before entering the work force. Besides, the unemployed have unwanted free time on their hands.

Side by side with this increase in time-off from earning a living, there has been a reduction in the hours that must be spent on household chores. Washing machines and spin-dryers, mechanical ironers and electric and steam irons, vacuum cleaners and electric polishers, microwave ovens, juicers and blenders, kleenex and throw-away diapers – a whole array of devices offer possibilities of cutting down the time and effort that must be spent keeping homes and their inmates clean and tidy and providing meals. Eating out at the local branch of a fast food chain, or buying ready-cooked fried chicken, pizza, or Chinese dishes make possible a further escape from housework.

Whether there has been a proportionate increase in time that is free to be spent as individuals chose is by no means clear. Many put in far more hours earning a living than the average work week, especially those who are self-employed, while women who combine work outside the home with household duties commonly have little if any spare time. Hours spent commuting and waiting in line-ups at the supermarket cash register and the like also erode leisure time.[3]

Whether the trend to shorter income-earning hours and a reduction in the time that must be spent on household and personal maintenance will continue in the future is even more uncertain. If we are approaching limits to the growth of an energy-intensive way of life and as the price of electricity and gasoline goes up, we may find that we must go back to using more human effort and more time in industrial, agricultural, and commercial activities as well as at home. It may be, however, that new discoveries of fossil fuels and new technologies will, for a time at least, allow a still further expansion in free time. This would intensify the already critical problem of the role of leisure time in human happiness and of participation in the demands made by leisure time activities on material resources and on the environment.

THE DAILY ROUND OF ACTIVITIES

Nearly all Canadians spend at least some of their time watching television, while 15 per cent of us spend a massive 30 hours or more a week in front of our TV sets. Eighty-four out of every hundred of us spend some time listening to radio each week, and 45 per cent of us listen to records, tapes or casettes. No doubt many of us, as viewers and listeners, do other things at the same time as we look and listen. Sixty-one per cent of us read newspapers and magazines, but only some 16 per cent of us spend seven or more hours a week reading books as a leisure time occupation.[4]

A smaller proportion of Canadians go to the theatre, opera, ballet, concerts, but more than a third of us go to the movies. A similarly small proportion visit museums, art galleries and historic sites, but nearly a quarter of us spend at least some time attending sports events, some of us as regular spectators.

How many of us spend time wandering round the stores does not seem to be recorded, but this is undoubtedly one of the major diversions of the crowds that throng shopping malls and department stores, window shopping and "just looking." Eating out may be necessary at school or at work, it may be a quickie substitute for a meal at home, or it may be – and seems increasingly to be – a leisure activity, along with drinking.[5]

Travel and tourism, ranging from Sunday driving and holiday camping trips to tours to Europe, and escape to sunny climes by refugees from a harsh winter, are becoming more and more important in our affluent and increasingly leisured lives. Some two-thirds of all Canadians indulge in recreational driving,[6] while in 1978 we spent more than $4 billion in travel abroad.[7]

A different type of leisure time occupation involves arts, crafts, music and hobby activities. A quarter of all Canadians spend some time, effort and imagination each week on arts, crafts, and music, though the estimate is uncertain as it is difficult to draw the line between such activities as dress-making undertaken as a pleasing activity, for the fun of it, or as a necessary household chore. Twelve per cent of us spend some time on hobbies, but only half as many of us give fifteen hours or more a week to those hobbies.[8]

Substantially more than half of all Canadians spend at least a little while in sports and physical activities, a few in sports events and many of us in swimming (apparently the most common type of exercise right across Canada), jogging, hiking, and doing exercises, ice-skating, skiing, playing tennis and badminton or golf and other games and sports.[9]

Besides card games, chess, bingo and TV games, there are other ways of spending free time, entertaining and socializing, lazing in the sun, indulging in more sleep than is physiologically essential to maintain health and strength, or just sitting around, like the old lady in Vermont who said "Sometimes I sits and thinks and sometimes I just sits."

THE COST OF THE DAILY ROUND

Of all these varied ways of putting in leisure time, some entail very heavy demands on material and environmental resources. Travel means jet planes, the fuel they use, and the cloud cover they create; automobiles mean gasoline and smog. Television means cameras and kleig lights, congested air waves, production studios, elaborate transmitting and receiving equipment, including satellites and other apparatus of space technology. Movies mean cameras, sound recording equipment, filmstock, sets and costumes, cutting rooms, theatres and projection apparatus, to say nothing of the extravagances of the glamour industry. The record industry has similar requirements as does sport, both professional and amateur, organized as entertainment. International competitive sport has escalated jet set glamour and the kind of emulation that gave rise to Olympics extravaganzas. Even unassuming, personal participation in sport has become the *raison d'etre* for promoting sales of elaborate equipment and clothing, while the record industry and disco dancing have become multi-billion dollar businesses.

Underlying the expansion of the mass media – TV, radio, records, the press and periodicals – and their role in leisure time, is the proliferation of sales promotion and advertizing. Shopping as a pastime simply adds to the perpetual pressure to buy more, have more, and consume more.[10] Increasing leisure time has become a market to be exploited through the ruthless promotion of the idea that more and ever more elaborate possessions and expenditure will add immensely to the satisfaction that can be won from leisure time. Power boats and snowmobiles, ten-speed bicycles and fancy skis, stereo-phonic record players are becoming widespread items of household equipment, besides TV sets, radios, telephones and cars.[11] Emphasis is given increasingly to the apparatus used in leisure time activities. This is generally true of affluent societies. A recent publication, *Leisure Markets in Europe,* was announced with the statement that:

> Leisure goods and services absorb more than one fifth of total consumer spending in Europe. That makes leisure very big business.
>
> Leisure markets are expected to grow faster than all consumer spending in the 1980s' with an average growth for Europe as a whole of around 5% a year at constant prices.[12]

Should leisure time continue to expand in the future as it has expanded in the recent past, and should emphasis persist on leisure as big business, leisure time activities will undoubtedly play a part in the continued expansion of our mass consumption economy. Increasing spare time may well become the focus of intensified consumption and sales in the entertainment industry, the travel and tourist industry, and the sports equipment industry. Even jogging and cross-country skiing are now the target for sales of special clothing, special footwear, and special equipment.

Paradoxically, increasing leisure time creates a need for so much increased expenditure that it induces people to undertake more income-earning activity, moonlighting or mothers going out to work to procure the income to buy skates, skis, cameras and the like, or to pay the installments due on a color television set or a car, or even on the labor saving equipment that is designed to increase leisure time. The choice does not seem to be a choice between more consumption and more leisure time, but between more consumption for leisure time activities and more consumption of other sorts.

Does this mean that more and more leisure time will inevitably reinforce other pressures in the direction of continued economic growth? Does the novel expansion of substantial leisure time to an increasingly wide range of classes make the possibility of a conserver society increasingly difficult to achieve? Is the transition from an economic system based on a high rate of material growth to a slow-growth economy, or even a stable economy,[13] all the more unlikely by reason of the growing demands of the expanding leisure market? The answer depends on the forces which shape our preferences and choices as to how we spend our leisure time.

LESS COSTLY POSSIBILITIES

The TGIF ("Thank God It's Friday") view of the working week suggests that few of us get much satisfaction out of what we do to earn a living. In that case we must depend on what we do in our leisure time to give us a satisfying life. This raises the question whether modern conveyor-belt workers, whether in a factory or in an office, when they finish a shift – even a short shift – of mind deadening work have energy and initiative, enough resilience, to launch into any mind or muscle stretching activity, even though they may have time and to spare. Is there any impetus in their environment to stimulate them to creative effort? Do the mass media and the conversation of their associates suggest any possibilities other than seeking diversion and excitement from television, and spending more and consuming more? Ideas as to the good life absorbed from television programs and advertisements combined with conspicuous consumption to keep up with the Joneses mean continued, open-ended increases in consumption that bring very little satisfaction to the consumers.[14] Thorstein Veblen's *Theory of the Leisure Class* is as relevant today as it was when he wrote it in 1899. Contemporary economists, notably Fred Hirsch and William Leiss, have developed the same theme.[14] One-up-manship means bigger and faster cars, more lavish household furnishings and equipment, up-to-the-minute power boats and snowmobiles, as well as travel to more remote and unusual places than those which neighbors and work-mates have visited. Emulation in consumption satisfies no one and there is no limit to the burden which it imposes on scarce environmental and material resources.

There are, however, a few straws in what may be a wind of change. The popularity of jogging, of trail skiing, and of cycling suggests that simple activities, without a great elaboration of apparatus, are coming into their own. Yoga and meditation, similarly, make very little demand on material support systems. Gardening, crafts, carpentry, and all sorts of do-it-yourself activities, ranging from home dress-making to household repairs, may actually conserve material and environmental resources, since they combine recycling of materials with satisfaction of the instinct of workmanship. Leisure time pursuits should be undertaken, not in the hope of winning Oscars or Olympic gold medals, but for their own sake, because they are fun or interesting, or because they contribute to a cause that is considered to be useful or worthwhile. Participation in the work of public interest groups intent on achieving desirable social objectives is an example of an activity that can give great satisfaction while making few demands on material or environmental resources.

Would a shift to such low consumption leisure time occupations mean serious losses in leisure time satisfaction? The answer seems to be that there is wide scope for increased leisure time activities of a type that would not increase consumption expenditures and might actually decrease demands on the resources of the bio-sphere, while contributing more to human happiness than do many of today's high consumption activities and entertainments. More and more satisfying leisure need not mean more expenditure; it might well mean less.

The most obvious use of leisure time is to give respite from stress, rest and relaxation, "re-creation" in the literal sense of restoration of depleted energies. More important, in a world of mass production conformity and monotony, leisure gives people a chance to exercise their own initiative, to follow their own inclination, to "do their own thing" in their own way. It is an opportunity for personal choice and self-expression, for the development of individuality, for exploring and cultivating the full richness of human diversity. In leisure time people can exercise cramped and atrophied bodies; exercise and develop powers of intellect and imagination and of independence of thought and character. In their time off from work and necessary chores they may cultivate the taste and sensibility which will allow them to enjoy the beauties of nature, the glories of great art and architecture, the splendor of music, the bouquet of fine wines, or the nuances of *cordon bleu* cookery. They may themselves experience the joy of creative activities. It is on leisure time occupations that most of us have to depend for the stimulus and excitement that human nature needs for fulfilment, and to leisure time encounters that we must look for "laughter and the love of friends," for chances to meet satisfying sexual partners, and for the satisfaction of working with close colleagues to achieve a shared objective. In our leisure time we may do things that engage our abilities to the full capacity, we may contribute something of importance to the community of which we are part, so earning the social esteem and self-respect which can come only from lives that have some significance.

CONSUMPTION VERSUS SATISFACTION

Few of us are lucky enough to find in our working lives opportunities for all these varied satisfactions. Do we find them in our leisure time? Might we do so? How heavy would be the burden of such human fulfilment on the material and environmental resources of our space-ship planet?

Rest and relaxation

For rest and relaxation we need some degree of comfort, tranquility, agreeable surroundings, and unexacting diversion. Many people, whose living conditions do not provide these requisites, escape into the image world of television, a world in which they may effortlessly join the jet set in gracious living. It is not a world that gives relaxed contentment; rather it generates restless discontent. It is a world in which the importance of having more and more consumer goods is relentlessly driven home, a world in which the emphasis is constantly on the apparatus of living, not on the quality of life itself.

Initiative and individuality

Watching TV may open new worlds to the viewer, the world of ballet, of opera, or of wildlife in the unspoiled wilderness of the far north or the sweeping Pacific beaches or of Newfoundland's cliffs and bays, but the message of the medium is more commonly that a finer car is essential, or a shinier floor polish or a zestier beer to ensure a good life. The emphasis is persistently on *having* things – the things that every one else has – not on *doing* the things that interest you as a unique human being, nor on *being* that individual to the utmost limit of your powers. In the barrage of advertising, in the flood of thrillers and "sit coms" and "shows," is there any spark that would fire individual enthusiasm for striking out on some personal line of activity, for following some special interest?

Bodies and beer

TV programs certainly foster admiration of physical prowess. The hockey or football star, the Olympic gold medalist is idolized, but what has the Stanley Cup play-off to do with the ordinary citizens' need for a stimulus to exercise neglected bodies? Hockey Night in Canada and Saturday afternoon sports programs are more likely to promote passive viewing, beer in hand, than physical activity. It is true that an occasional "Participation" advertisement may exhort the viewer to keep fit by taking to some form of exercise, but the insistent model is that of a car-borne, candy and beer consuming way of life which is the antithesis of a way of life in which leisure is used to build bodily health and strength.

Despite the huge disparity between the number of Canadians who watch television and the number who engage at least occasionally in some exercise or sport, there does seem to be a new interest in getting fit and in keeping fit. More and more Canadians "run for their lives" when they take to jogging, but the figures for participation in skating, skiing, tennis, golf and other physical activities suggest that there is plenty of room for higher standards of activity.

Intellect and imagination

Some programs on television or radio provide food for thought and stimulate the mind and the imagination, evoking a creative response from viewers and listeners. For the most part, though, viewers and listeners are merely passive spectators or auditors, whose minds and imaginations are neither challenged nor stimulated by what they see and hear.

The much smaller number of people who go to live theatre, concerts, ballet and opera have more chance of a stimulating experience that requires an active contribution of thought and sensitive imagination. Visits to art galleries, museums, and historic sites also are likely to stimulate both mind and imagination. Continuing education plays its part in developing intellectual muscle and opening opportunities for creative experience, as may also be the case with some formal education. The activities of public interest groups and voluntary organizations, ranging form tenants' associations to Women's Institutes, stimulate thought and imagination, widen horizons, and offer opportunities for active experience.

Taste and beauty

Music on radio and television, ballet, and some dramatic performances present beautiful sounds and sights for those that have ears to hear and eyes to see. Some wilderness programs may allow city dwellers hemmed in by walls and concrete to experience in some small degree the delights of natural beauty. Sights and sounds which are lovely to some people, however, may give little pleasure or even be distasteful to others. Their enjoyment requires not only the time that must be spent in looking and listening, but, as well, time and experience are needed to cultivate the taste which will give the viewer or hearer the capacity to delight in them, just as an educated palate is necessary for enjoyment of subtle sauces and exquisite wines. Enjoyment of beauty involves a learning process that goes on through a lifetime of leisure experience. Only if a person seeking satisfaction can contribute sensitive awareness can the full possibilities of the enjoyment of beauty be realized.

Creative experience

The active enjoyment of beauty is a creative, not a passive experience. The creation of beauty may give a still richer satisfaction, the satisfaction attained by a quarter of all Canadians, who take part in some kind of art, craft or musical activity. Playing a musical instrument, singing in a choir, drawing or painting what they see in the world around them, fashioning a carving or a sculpture, expressing their insights and ideas in poetry or prose, taking part in a play, or, at a more practical level, making a lovely quilt or a handsome piece of furniture, growing a glorious garden, or baking a splendid cake, they need never be dull; there is always something exciting and rewarding waiting to be done. Such leisure time arts and crafts may give outlets for the instinct of workmanship if earning a living fails, as it often does, to satisfy this deep human need.

Stimulus and excitement

Jobs may be repetitive and deadening, so it is leisure activities that must fill yet another fundamental human need: the need for stimulation and excitement. We no longer face the daily challenge of escaping from sabre-toothed tigers or running buffalo. It is true that driving a car or merely crossing busy streets gives some spice of adventure to our lives, but many of us seek an escape from boredom in purchasing every novelty that comes on the market and acquiring a vast variety of consumer goods.[15] Such attempts to maintain an interest in life require continual expansion, as the need for stimulus grows as it is satisfied. Similarly, neither television violence nor entertainment-sport can perpetually arouse interest and excitement without novel features and intensification. The only way in which we can hope to achieve a crescendo of interest and excitement through a lifetime is in pursuing some unfolding interest, achieving new skills, discovering new creative possibilities, exploring new ideas and widening horizons, developing a more and more lively creative imagination. Arts, crafts, and musical activities can give such stimulation, such unflagging and developing interest; so can a variety of hobbies which lead the enthusiast on from one level of attainment to another, unendingly. In the last analysis it is not outside stimuli that can solve the problem of boredom; each individual must generate his or her own interest and excitement in life through activities that hold the possibility of progressive achievement, invention and discovery. Competition – the excitement of winning a game or watching one's team win a game – gives an ephemeral stimulus, but only creative activities and intellectual and imaginative development will sustain interest and excitement that time and use will not dim, but constantly intensify. The solution lies not in a multiplication of consumer goods, but in the development of human skills and non-material interests and activities.

Friendship and team-work

Some people are so fortunate as to earn their living working with colleagues who are friends, with whom they can co-operate whole-heartedly. For many, if not most of us, this rewarding experience is more likely to be attained in activities undertaken in time off work, perhaps in sport, or in voluntary work with church groups, a political party, or other public interest group, or in a choir, an orchestra or band, or in a dramatic group. We have very little information as yet on how much time and energy is spent in spare time team work in such shared endeavours. That contact with other people is important for most of us, we do know, since more than three quarters of us spend part of our leisure time visiting friends and relatives.[16] Apart from the cost of establishing and maintaining contact with fellow workers and friends, telephone service, postage, travel, and the like, and perhaps the consumption of food and drink that ordinarily takes place on social occasions, such sociability and cooperation does not seem to require any extensive material support. The potlatch type of formal entertainment may be necessary to ensure social esteem, but it probably contributes little otherwise to human happiness, except insofar as it is the occasion for agreeable indulgences.

Social esteem and self respect

Conspicuous leisure, conspicuous consumption, and rivalry in lavish entertainment have all played a part in patterns of spending and patterns of leisure time activities: they have all been important as evidence of social status. They have all contributed to the association of leisure and lavish spending. Perhaps, as the idea of a conserver society spreads, other criteria of social worth and social respect may begin to make headway against competitive consumption. Just as concern is growing for the quality of life that cannot be measured in Gross National Product figures, so may concern for human quality that is not demonstrated by lavish expenditures and an elaborate apparatus of leisurely enjoyment be growing. If ways can be found of gauging the character and caliber of what individuals and groups contribute to the community in creative stimulus, artistic achievement, constructive intelligence, and the assumption of social responsibility, there may be hope that, in the time in which people do what they like, what they like to do will prove to be what will earn them the respect and esteem of their community. Such esteem is an essential element of a good life; even more important is the individual's own sense of contributing something of significance. If what one does to earn a living seems trivial, this vital sense of significance must be won in leisure time pursuits that are considered to be important in themselves or in the social results that may be expected from them.

A recent estimate puts average expenditure on recreation in Canada at some ten per cent of total personal expenditure. If one adds to that expenditure by governments at all levels on recreational services and facilities, to say nothing of the share of the cost of public goods (highways, waterways, education, communication and transport systems and the like) that are put to recreational use, the total becomes one of considerable significance. In addition, some family expenditures that are classified as expenditures on clothing and shelter, household operation, furnishings and equipment, and travel and transportation are probably related to recreational activities. What happens to leisure time and to leisure expenditures will, therefore, have an important part to play in future trends in consumer expenditure. Increasing emphasis on leisure time as an opportunity for the enhancement of human quality and the enrichment of creative experience, rather than as an opportunity for the elaboration of entertainment and multiplication of apparatus, would reconcile a trend to more leisure and a need for less spending.

Conserving the Self and the Surroundings

Pierre Falcon composed his ballads without any equipment other than his mind, his voice, and his enthusiasm for the feats of his compatriots, "ces braves Bois-Brules." Shakespeare and his actors performed plays that have lasted through the centuries with little costuming and less scenery. They depended for success not on super-colossal spectacles but on splendor of language and perception of human problems. The winner of a recent contest (that elicited 10,000 entries) needed only a pen (or, perhaps, a typewriter) and some paper and a sensitive mind to produce her poem. One of the finest performances of *Hamlet* given in recent years was performed by amateurs in a chapel in off-hours with only one "prop," a bean bag, and one item of costume, a cloak made from a table cloth. An Inuit theatre group from Greenland, using masks and costumes but neither scenery nor stage, created a deeply moving theatrical experience. A single flower can give enjoyment more exquisite than a mass of bloom. A family can have as much fun playing scramble-demon with old packs of cards as it might get out of a sophisticated electronic game. Spillikins or tiddly-winks can give more scope to precision of eye and delicacy of touch – and at least as much excitement – as playing a "one-armed bandit." Watching a bird in the back yard can give more delight than an array of exotic creatures on the TV screen.

Leisure time activities, stressing human perception and creative imagination, and human thought and skill, put material accessories in their proper place as simply the instruments of human experience and human creativity. If this shift in emphasis is supplemented by a shift from stress on competition to cooperation, the pressure for ever more elaborate equipment would be still further reduced. Leisure occupations might play a significant part in movement towards a conserver society.

There will, of course, be enormous difficulties, difficulties in overcoming ingrained pecuniary canons of taste and tests of achievement; difficulties in breaking through barriers of lethargy to open up the excitements and rewards of do-it-yourself leisure activities to everybody; difficulties of dislocations in the business world and in the labor market; to say nothing of the unsolved problem of how to turn persistent unemployment into real leisure.

Perhaps the greatest difficulty of all, and one which is not just one of a transition from a high consumption to a high activity leisure life-style, is the twin problem of space and of natural beauty. More and more space will certainly be needed for any massive expansion in creative activities. At the receiving end, all you need for TV viewing is somewhere to sit and a TV set. To act a play, to sing in a choir or play in an orchestra, to paint or sculpt, you need suitable space, and a good deal of it. For outdoor recreation you need playing fields, ski-slopes and beaches, lakes and rivers. For camping, wild river canoeing, mountain climbing, or bird watching you need unspoiled wilderness. When these delights become a wider part of the leisure life of growing urban populations with increasing leisure time, and, especially, bigger blocks of leisure time, (three days at work, four days on the ski slopes), how can sufficient wilderness be made available to meet the demands that will be made on it? Here is a dilemma: Of all leisure time activities, experience of nature may be the most truly recreational, the most rewarding, and the most health-giving to mind and body. The need is evident but how can it be met?

Being and doing, not having; using only what is needed to realize human values, instead of consuming conspicuously; these are surely the keys to the future. They are alike the keys to preserving unspoiled wilderness, our cultural heritage, finite resources, and, above all, personal and collective sanity.

REFERENCES

1. Innis, H. A. and Betty Ratz. "Labour," *Encyclopedia of Canada, Vol. III.* W. Stewart Wallace (ed.), Toronto: University Associates of Canada, 1936.
2. Ostry, Sylvia and H. D. Woods. *Labour Policy and Labour Economics in Canada.* Toronto: Macmillan of Canada, 1962. pp. 335-336.
3. *Perspectives Canada II.* Ottawa: Statistics Canada (Catalogue No. 11-508, 1977). p. 133.
4. Kirsh, Carol, Brian Dixon and Michael Bond. *A Leisure Study-Canada 1972* and the up-date for 1975. Ottawa: Arts and Culture Branch, Department of the Secretary of State, 1973 and 1976; and *Perspectives Canada II, op. cit.,* Chapter 7; and Cultural Statistics - Recreational Activities, 1976. Ottawa: Statistics Canada (Catalogue No. 87-501).
5. Martin, William H. and Sandra Mason. *Leisure Markets in Europe.* London: Financial Times Business Publishing Division, 1978. They list "drinking alcohol" as a separate type of free time activity.
6. *Perspective Canada II, op. cit.,* Table 7.5.
7. *Travel Between Canada and Other Countries, October-December 1978.* Ottawa: Statistics Canada (Catalogue No. 66-001). p. 3.
8. Kirsch, et al., *op. cit.,* 1975 up-date.
9. *Recreational Activities, 1976, op. cit.,* p. 7.
10. Cordell, Arthur. "Bye Bye to Buy Buy," *Conserver Society Notes,* II:3 (Summer, 1977). pp. 5-18.
11. *Household Facilities and Equipment.* Ottawa: Statistics Canada (Catalogue No. 64-202).
12. Martin, *op. cit.*
13. See, for instance, Daley, Herman (ed.). *Toward A Steady State Economy.* San Francisco: W. H. Freeman and Company, 1973; and Stapenhurst, Frederic. "Some Implications of a Conserver Society," *Labour Gazette* (November, 1977). pp. 511-513.
14. See, for instance, Hirsch, Fred. *The Social Limits to Growth.* Cambridge, Mass.: Harvard University Press, 1976; and Leiss, William. *The Limits to Satisfaction.* Toronto: University of Toronto Press, 1976.
15. Scitovsky, Tibor. *The Joyless Economy.* Oxford: Oxford University Press, 1976.
16. *Recreational Activities, op. cit.* p. 68.

Chapter Twelve

So Long Frank Buck: Some Changes In the Ecology of Outdoor Recreation

E. Glen Carls

In the Nineteen Thirties and Forties, Frank Buck was better known by his nickname—Frank "Bring 'Em Back Alive" Buck. He came by this flamboyant and rather bizarre sobriquet by writing a book with that title recounting his exploits as an adventurer and worldwide collector of wild animals. That volume (published in 1930) and two others, *Wild Cargo* (1932) and *Fang and Claw* (1935), were later made into Hollywood motion pictures in which, according to a "Who's Who" write-up of the day, "the keen-eyed, pencil-mustached explorer himself appeared."

As a young man coming out of Texas, Buck was a phenomenon looking for a place to happen. At that time his prospects were less than bright but in the course of a varied career he discovered that he could make a fortune as a captor and purveyor of exotic wild animals. In that enterprise he was very successful and he dispensed a veritable ark of zoological specimens to collectors throughout Europe and North America. And, proving the theory that success breeds success, he made the further discovery that a bigger bundle could be made by transforming his self-proclaimed heroics into books and motion pictures.

Today the Frank Buck movies, and others of that era, are interesting and sometimes embarassing in their recollection of the life and times of a bygone period. We notice, of course, the relative crudity of cinematic and acting technique that somehow escaped our attention at the time. But more importantly we are confronted with a composite of social prejudices that were equally invisible. Viewing those films now, out of the context of the times, we are most sensitive to those things, some profound and others trivial, that have become sources of social dispute in the years since—racial attitudes, sex roles and mores, cigarette smoking, et cetera. Perhaps more than the others, the Frank Buck movies also portray a set of environmental values that have undergone a radical, though incomplete, evolution.

In retrospect, Frank Buck symbolizes an era of social confidence and environmental extravagance that reached a peak sometime in the 1960's and then began to recede. In 1943, Frank Buck was a genuine folk hero who had captured the imagination (and the pocketbook) of a whole generation; today it is likely that he would be vilified and harangued as a fortune-hunter, a huckster, and an environmental miscreant. He would be, that is, if he wasn't all but forgotten in the minutiae of history.

OUTDOOR RECREATION: A SITUATIONAL DEFINITION

When teaching introductory outdoor recreation courses at the university, it has been my practice to begin the first class with a simple word association exercise whereby each student reports his or her first impression of outdoor recreation. The procedure is easy to administer and effective in its outcome. Not only do the students begin to examine for themselves the many ramifications of outdoor recreation as a subject of professional study, they also produce, through their collective responses, a useful working definition of outdoor recreation.

From semester to semester, replies from the students are fairly uniform and predictable in content. The list includes a staple collection of outdoor places and environmental conditions, natural resources, activities, and related public institutions. In sum, their responses also constitute a surprisingly conservative view of what outdoor recreation is and is not. Never, for example, has anyone associated outdoor recreation with "driving for pleasure," although this particular activity has become a standard variable in surveys of outdoor recreation activity preferences. These more liberal (shall we say muddled?) definitions of outdoor recreation seem to derive from the sometimes overly eutrophic minds of bureaucrats, academics, and survey researchers.

There are, however, some interesting and unusual exceptions to the rule. Once, when asked for her idea of outdoor recreation, one female student, who had had considerable experience in wilderness backpacking and canoeing, replied, "TVP." "TVP," we discovered, stands for Textured Vegetable Protein, a meat substitute that looks suspiciously like some brands of dry pet food. Nonetheless, this particular case is significant, provacative and possibly prophetic.. Both the product, which represents an impact of technology on outdoor recreation, and the student's reply, which reflects a system of social values, provide a keyhole through which we might look at the status and future of outdoor recreation.

Has outdoor recreation changed? Looking back on the history of outdoor recreation in North America, it is difficult to identify problems, issues, or fundamental changes that can be hailed as new or exclusively modern. Our problems are generally recurring and people participate in the same essential activities in approximately the same outdoor places. To illustrate:

> The statisticians tell us that the modern tendency is alarmingly and increasingly toward the cities; that the country is being drained, while the cities are becoming congested. But it is at the same time evident that there is on the part of city folk a constantly countryward tendency. Nearly all who can afford it now have country homes, either temporary or permanent.[1]

This particular passage is taken from an 1899 editorial in *Century Magazine*. But the message is so remarkably modern, it could easily have been published in a recent edition of *Atlantic*.

Does this mean, then, that nothing has changed in outdoor recreation? The answer is definitely, "No." What it does suggest is that the changes that have occurred have been more a matter of magnitude and distribution than of kind. Indeed, the progress of outdoor recreation is better described as a ride on an outward curving spiral rather than a journey with neatly cornered turning points.

Developing this idea of change in outdoor recreation, we can profit from the thinking of E. A. Gutkind in his illuminating analysis of man's historical role in changing the world's environment. Taking a synoptic view of the man/environment relationship, Gutkind calls forth three main parameters of change, which he describes as follows:

> No transformation (by man) produces a static and lasting result. Hence our environment is at any moment of human history the product of a perennial revolution, of a continuous process of change. Man's adjustments to his environment are not a series of unrelated stages of development, each more or less accomplished and self-contained entities, but an organic and integrated chain of events. Thus permanency exists only in the uninterrupted *continuity* of change and in the dynamic relations among all aspects of human activities. In other words, permanency without synthesis is a delusion. To these two criteria a third has to be added: The growing scale of the transformations, expanding from small and individual to large and collective operations.[2]

In summary, (1) change is continuous, though dynamic, (2) it involves interrelationships among all human (and we might add environmental) processes, and (3) the magnitude of change is increasing. Of the three, this last item is most critical in its impact on human lifestyle and ecological well-being.

These ideas and their implications are relevant and generally applicable to all facets of the outdoor recreation mix. Taking Gutkind's view of the world into consideration, two particular aspects of change seem to be of special significance to outdoor recreation: (1) the evolution of social values and its effect on outdoor recreation systems and (2) the impact of compounding technology on recreation environments and patterns of recreation behavior. The combination of these describes the outdoor recreation situation today and in the future.

THE VULNERABILITY OF ATTITUDES

Over greater or lesser periods of time the values of people, as reflected in their attitudes, change in ways that are often trivial (e.g., elevator hemlines in the world of fashion) and sometimes profound (e.g., religious beliefs and doctrine). Outdoor recreation has frequently been the recipient and at times the protagonist of these attitudinal oscillations. Sport hunting is a case-in-point.

I have just re-read one of the more recent public debates between the advocates and adversaries (there seem to be no ambivalent middle-of-the-roaders) of sport hunting as reported in *Harper's*.[3] The arguments are regretably, albeit predictably, jaded. A distillation of the rhetoric, hysteria, and mythology that emanate from opposing sides generally come down to this:

Against: Sport hunting is brutal, environmentally exploitive, and immoral.

For: Sport hunting is humane, centered on sound practices of conservation, and an individual right, both legally and morally.

Unfortunately, both sides miss the point. While the popular literature continues to spew forth a cloud of innuendos and half-truths, the scientific literature is quite unambiguous about the role and outcome of hunting in the physical and social evolution of humankind.

Sport hunting, like all of the traditional activities of outdoor recreation (i.e., backpacking, sport fishing, canoeing, cross country skiing, etc.), is derived from the everyday occupations of prehistoric, primitive, and pioneer people. Aside from certain technological improvements in equipment and methods, the only essential difference between the original form of the activity and its recreational counterpart is the individual's motivation for participation, and even that difference is not as neatly cleaved as might be expected.

The weight of ethnological research shows that all of the essential common factors that constitute *Homo sapiens* were evolved in the 99 percent of human existence that predated the development of agriculture, i.e., during the economic era of hunting and gathering. Moreover, the hunting regimen exerted certain selective pressures on protohominids that led to the social and biological beings of modern humankind. As noted by Washburn and Lancaster, "In a very real sense our intellect, interests, and basic social life—all are evolutionary products of the success of the hunting adaptation."[4]

Washburn and Lancaster, in their provocative paper titled "The Evolution of Hunting," made an even more telling point regarding hunting behavior: "Men enjoy hunting and killing, and these activities are continued as sports even when they are no longer economically necessary."[5] The operative word here is *enjoy*. This one essential point—that hunting and killing are enjoyable—is almost always omitted from the sport hunting debate. Both sides tacitly deny the pleasure of hunting just as we have for so long denied the pleasures of sex.

In North America, as in the other parts of the world, the traits and skills of the hunter, whether his objective is economic or recreational, have long been valued by both native people and pioneer immigrants to this continent. Until the turn of the century, and thereafter for two or three decades, sport hunting was an accepted, though not universally valued, outdoor recreation activity. But the harbingers of change were becoming evident even then.

In 1907, John Burroughs, who was known in his day as the "Hudson River Naturalist," wrote of the conflict that he experienced between his public image as a "preservationist" and his own personal interest in hunting. The occasion was a western hunting expedition organized and led by Teddy Roosevelt. Because of his reputation as a paragon of environmental beneficence, Burroughs lamented the fact that it was *assumed* he would not participate in the actual hunt, even though that was not necessarily his choice.[6] In some quarters, especially the more densely settled East, the tide of opinion had already turned.

Today, the existing and growing aversion to sport hunting has little to do with the activity itself or the genetic hunter that is in all of us. It does reflect a fundamental shift in the society in which we live. In a relatively short period of time, we have gone from a frontier, to an agrarian, to an industrial, and now a cybernetic society. Along the way, we have become detached from the substance and processes of the natural environment; the aboriginal skills that were once our cultural inheritance have atrophied into uselessness. As John Bleibtreu writes in *The Parable of the Beast*: "This scrim of culture has blurred our perception of the natural *umwelt*;[7] this blurring loss of contact is symbolized by a lack of knowledge of how to do certain things, such as make a fire without matches. But the real loss is far more extensive. We have lost whole areas of experience."[8]

The shifts that we observe in social values and attitudes toward hunting and certain other aspects of outdoor recreation are not so much transcendental as transitional. For sport hunting, the overall change has been a negative skew in popularity resulting in a hostility toward the practices and practitioners of that activity. That sport *fishing*, which embraces the same essential objectives and values, hasn't been subject to the same sense of outrage is one of the vagaries of social psychology.

While sport hunting has been one of the more obvious and most strongly maligned activities to face the vicissitudes of social change, outdoor recreation has been affected in other ways that are perhaps even more profound. There has been, for example, an astonishing transformation in attitudes toward wilderness.[9] The progressive domestication and/or degradation of the landscape has been a two-sided cultural coin. On one side it has caused, or at least contributed to, the reaction to sport hunting; on the other side it has produced an affection for wilderness and certain outdoor recreation activities (e.g., wilderness backpacking and canoeing) that is unprecedented in the history of humankind.

Apparently, the well-known total increase in the number of people who participate in wilderness recreation activities (e.g., backpacking, canoeing, mountain climbing, etc.) does not reflect, however, a general increase in the *percentage* of the population that participates. A recent national survey of Canadians indicates, for example, that only 7.2 percent of the population took overnight wilderness backpacking trips and only 3.7 percent took overnight wilderness canoe trips. Wilderness, like public art galleries, opera houses, and museums, has obviously become a cultural/environmental amenity to be valued though not necessarily used.

In overview, these are some of the basic social changes to which outdoor recreation systems and personnel must adjust. They are usually slow to evolve and easily overlooked in the bustle of day-to-day and fiscal operations. And that is precisely the reason why students who aspire to become outdoor recreation planners, resource managers, administrators, or educators require a liberal, as well as a professional, education. The welter of user days, cost-benefit ratios, and user attitudes with which we bombard our policies and decisions are vulnerable to short term change and subject to misinterpretation in the long term without a broader social scale against which they can be weighed.

THE IMPACT OF TECHNOLOGY

Anyone who has taken an extended wilderness trip, using primitive methods of travel, will have experienced the kind of technological time regression that takes place in adapting to a non-mechanical way of life. At some point in the adjustment process, one begins to respond to the stimuli of wind, slope, and river current rather than stop lights, RPMs, and mid-hour television commercials. Then, returning to the "civilized" world, the process is reversed in a kind of rapid historical recapitulation of technological development.

In the book, *Understanding Media: The Extensions of Man*, Marshall McLuhan makes an especially salient point regarding the influence of technology on our lives: "During the mechanical ages we had extended our bodies in space. Today, after more than a century of electric technology, we have extended our central nervous system itself in a global embrace, abolishing both space and time as far as our planet is concerned."[10] In short, technology and its by-products are ubiquitous. For some people the direct effect of technological development on outdoor recreation is a boon—freeze-dried food, lightweight camping gear, helicopter skiing, et cetera. For others the technological anachronism of outdoor recreation is the important thing, i.e., getting away from it all.

Perhaps the greater impact of technology has been on outdoor landscapes and resources. I recall camping one summer on the up-stream point of a Moose River island in northern Ontario. In front of the camp, there was a shallow wash of water flowing across a gravel bar. The curious thing was that this little "stream" periodically flooded and dried up. The cause of this phenomenon was the regular release of impounded waters on the Groundhog River, a tributary of the Moose.

While the effect of the dam and reservoir on our camp was largely esthetic, others who had canoed the Groundhog itself reported more concrete effects. Upstream from the dam the reservoir created canoeing conditions more akin to lakes than wild rivers; downstream white-water rapids became boulder fields during periods of low water and shoreline camps were sometimes left high and dry. In short, the technological manipulation of resources can change the very nature of the outdoor recreation experience.

In medicine, there is a particular category of illness known as iatrogenic disease. These are, literally, diseases caused by doctors, usually through the misapplication of medication. Probably the most well-known example of an iatrogenic disease was the congenital deformity of children whose mothers were treated with the drug Thalidomide during pregnancy. In much the same way, most of our environmental problems, including those associated with outdoor recreation, are derived from the unanticipated and dibilitating effect of mismanaged technology. Consider, for example, the case of the Great Lakes.

The Great Lakes ecosystem is a collage of interconnected energy flows and nutrient cycles that has been little understood and much abused in the past. The combination of industrial and domestic dumping of wastes and the run-off from agricultural lands have poisoned the lakes with a variety of toxic substances (e.g., DDT, PCBs, Mirex, Asbestos fibers, etc.) and lake waters artifically enriched by the uncontrolled addition of nutrients (e.g., untreated sewage, chemical fertilizers, phosphate detergents, etc.). Now consider, briefly, the compounding effect of these miscalculations on sport fishing on one of the Great Lakes–Lake Ontario.

Historically, Lake Ontario has supported a productive fishery for both sport and commercial uses. Although a variety of species have been popular with anglers, the premier sport fish was the lake trout. It was popular, that is, until the lake trout population was decimated by the parasitic Sea Lamprey. Although the lamprey was known in Lake Ontario for several decades, their numbers were limited by a variety of natural controls until the St. Lawrence Seaway was opened some 20 years ago. In addition, the lamprey was introduced to Lake Erie (first reported in 1921) via the Welland Canal and finally became a spawning resident in the upper lakes by the late 1940's.

In an effort to control the lamprey in the Great Lakes, weirs and later electrical barriers were erected on tributary streams to capture and kill lamprey larvae as they migrated downstream from tributary spawning waters. The lamprey's wide distribution and the task of monitoring hundreds of spawning streams made the task almost impossible. In 1956, however, a toxic chemical specific to the lamprey larvae (i.e., 3-trifluormethyl-4-mitrophenol, better known as TMF) was discovered and adopted for general use in 1958.

The success of this new eradication program both in Canada and the United States permitted a second phase of the Lake Ontario sport fishery rehabilitation to begin. Following the example of fish stocking programs in Lake Michigan, certain non-native species of fish, primarily the Pacific salmon and rainbow trout, were introduced into Lake Ontario waters. These predatory fish filled an ecological gap once occupied by the lake trout, and by the middle of the 1970s they were growing and proliferating at a remarkable rate. The expectations for a rejuvenated sport fishery were dealt another blow, however, when high concentrations of the pesticide Mirex were discovered in the tissues of these and other fish. As a result, the stocking program was sharply curtailed, and anglers were warned against eating large amounts of their catch.

While this brief description of the Great Lakes ecosystem and some associated environmental problems has been brutally simplified, it illustrates the compounding folly that typifies so many attempts at environmental control and manipulation. Part of the problem stems from the genuine complexity and interrelatedness of ecological systems. For example, the increased acidification of lake waters that plagues some areas of Canada and the northern states is caused by the burning of fossil fuels in major industrial areas hundreds of miles away. But the larger part of the problem in nearly all cases comes from the premature and/or excessive application of innovative technology.

The impact of humankind on the environment is multiplied many times over by the use of our technological appendages. The impact on outdoor recreation systems is both internal and external. Obviously, the environmental impact on outdoor resources is compounded as user transportation progresses from bare feet to Vibram soles to horses to trail bikes to four wheel drive vehicles to paved roadways. These and similar situations are within the purview and responsibilities of the recreation resource manager. Resource based recreation areas are also open ecological systems, however, they are part of and depend on larger ecological systems over which the manager usually has no direct control.

The need, obviously, is for an ecosystems approach not only to recreation resource management but to environmental management in general. The Great Lakes, as we have seen, must be managed as a total ecosystem, including associated land and atmospheric resources. Within this larger ecological system, outdoor recreation operates as a functional and dependent subsystem. As far as recreation resource planners and managers are concerned, the need is for more skill and greater sophistication in working with *ecological* systems rather than simple recreation systems.

AN OUTDOOR RECREATION PROLOGUE

One question that we have not yet considered is whether or not outdoor recreation is a necessary, vital element in our individual social lives. The answer, of course, is that it is not. Desirable, perhaps, but not necessary. Any number of futuristic scenarios could be formulated in which outdoor recreation would no longer be a matter of opportunity or choice.

The more important question is what kind of world do we want to live in. While the question is somewhat academic, it is highly relevant in a world where we can initiate changes that are not only rapid but also potentially catastrophic. One study, sponsored by the National Academy of Sciences and the National Research Council, concludes that:

> The quality of life, which we equate with flexibility of choices and freedom of action, is threatened by the demands of an expanding economy and population. This happens in three principle ways: (1) through the restrictive and harmful effects of pollution; (2) through the increasing frequency and complexity of unconstructive but unavoidable human contacts; and (3) through the necessary increase of regulatory measures–all in consequences of increasing use of and competition for resources, space, recreation, transportation, housing and even educational facilities.[11]

There are, then, at least two aspects of human life in which we share a common concern. If it is a matter of simple survival, as is the case in some parts of the world, then outdoor recreation will receive short measure in the ordering of social and environmental priorities. If, on the other hand, we are talking about the quality of life in a society that is not stressed to the edge of subsistence, then outdoor recreation is a viable, perhaps necessary, element in the free choice of leisure opportunities.

Realistically, the choice is not a matter of having outdoor recreation or not having it but the form that it will take in the more tightly constrained social, environmental, and economic system that is certain to follow a growing population and greater competition for resources. Like our problems, the basic decisions that will be made in the future are not unlike the decisions that have confronted us in the past. There are, however, some notable shifts in the priorities that affect public decision-making. And because change tends to occur more rapidly now than in the past, the need to conclude a decision is often more compelling. The challenge is to use our skill, knowledge, good taste, and common sense in avoiding the wrong decisions.

REFERENCES

1. "Outdoor." *The Century Magazine*. Vol. LVIII, No. 2 (June) 1899. p. 321.
2. Gutkind, E. A. "Our World From the Air: Conflict and Adaptation." Vol. I of *Man's Role in Changing the Face of the Earth.* Thomas, William L., Jr. (Ed.) 2 vols. Chicago: University of Chicago Press, 1956. p. 2.
3. "Letters: Man and Beast." *Harper's*. Vol. 257, No. 1540 (September) 1978. pp. 4-6.
4. Washburn, Sherward L., and Lancaster, C. S. "The Evolution of Hunting." In: *Man and the Hunter*. Lee, Richard B. and DeVore, Irven (Eds.) Chicago: Aldine Publishing Company, 1968. p. 293.

5. *Ibid.*, p. 229.
6. Burroughs, John. *Camping and Tramping with Roosevelt*. Boston: Houghton Mifflin, 1907.
7. The term *umwelt* was coined by German zoologists to describe the world as *perceived* by an animal as opposed to the true, objective environment that surrounds it.
8. Bleibtreu, John N. *The Parable of the Beast*. New York: Collier Books, 1969, pp. 6-7.
9. See, for example: Nash, Roderick. *Wilderness and the American Mind*. New Haven: Yale University Press, 1967, and Shepard, Paul. *Man in the Landscape: A Historic View of the Esthetics of Nature*. New York: Ballantine Books, 1967.
10. McLuhan, Marshall. *Understanding Media: The Extensions of Man*. New York: New American Library, 1964. p. 19.
11. Committee on Resources and Man. *Resources and Man*. San Francisco: W.H. Freeman, 1969, p. 3.

Chapter Thirteen

Planning For Leisure in a Pluralistic Society

Geoffrey Godbey

Leisure, in the sense of being free of the struggle for existence, is the oldest dream of mankind. To exist on one's own terms, to pass time in voluntary, pleasurable ways has been the ultimate transition hoped for by individuals in many cultures and the ultimate test of the few who partially achieved these conditions.

The situations which constrain leisure and those which shape it have varied historically among cultures. These different life situations, in large part, have been responsible for differing conceptualizations of leisure; different notions of what is meant to be free.

DETERMINANTS OF LEISURE

This chapter will examine some factors of our own society which are believed to be of great importance in shaping our potential for leisure, both at an individual and group level. Rather than defining leisure, a definition will be implied from examining its determinants. Particular attention will be given to implication for organized leisure services.

Work

Quantitatively, a higher percentage of the population now works for pay compared to the 1940's, because of both more female and more teenage employment. Additionally, a greater percentage of our population desires to work in some capacity. This trend, combined with rapid changes in the kinds of work available in our society and the educational requirements for such work, has brought about a break-up of the "linear life cycle" in which one received full-time formal education for one period of life, then pursued one career throughout his working life, and then retired.[1] Today, people starting second and third careers in midstream, taking an early retirement, returning to education in their middle-age, or switching from homemaking to part or full-time employment are redefining traditional patterns of work.

The content of our work has also shifted so that more people are involved in the production of services than the production of goods, and service occupations are devourers of time because service workers tend to be less efficient, live performance and personal contact are involved and capital cannot be substituted for labor. Thus, it is not surprising that the average workweek for the full-time employee has remained relatively constant since World War II.

The increases in leisure which are occurring are due to increases in large blocks of time such as vacations and holidays. There is evidence that workers prefer that any future increases in leisure come in large blocks rather than slight decreases in the total workweek. Three current trends constrain opportunities for us to increase our leisure: inflation, an aging population, and the energy crisis. As inflation continues, many people must work longer hours or have less material welfare. While some people will choose to do without, many will choose to work longer hours.

Increased leisure will additionally be constrained by the age characteristics of our population. While today one retired worker on social security is supported by almost five workers, that ratio may shrink to one to three or even one to two within the next hundred years. Rather than take the severe tax bite, retirees, teenagers, and housewives are likely to enter the job market, forcing wages down further.

While there is every reason to believe that alternative fuel sources will be found to solve the energy crisis, the transition period from fossil fuels will involve some temporary scarcities. These scarcities will further increase the cost of virtually all material things since the cost of making them and transporting them to the marketplace will be increased.

While these situations may help correct the overemphasis upon material things in our society, they will hardly contribute to increasing leisure in the short term.

Basic Values

When planners try to plan for leisure in our society, their focus must be on the total human experience. Vast changes have occurred in our techniques and meaning of work and there is increased unwillingness in much of the western world to accept the concept of fate.

In the last 300 years within the western world there has been increasingly less economic constraint on human behavior and yet an increasing inability of man to develop a meaningful reintegration with the rest of the living world. Our increased social and economic freedoms have been purchased at the cost of isolation and alienation from those systems which allow this world to survive and function. Our notion of

God and theology have become increasingly vague yet people still long for the simple faith and answers of former times. Our machines have shown us the uninhabited heavens while parting the angelless clouds. At the same time, another part of our collective mind begins to see what we could do to become God by controlling nature. We can unlock knowledge by which we can live like a logical extension of the Earth. With such aspirations, it is perhaps natural that what we do or what we achieve is dominant over what we are. Our ascribed statuses: gender, race, age, religion, etc. are used less and less to convey who we are to other people. Instead, we become virtual composites of what we do, and it is doing something that keeps us from being nothing.

The rush to experience, particularly among those with high levels of education and income in advanced industrial societies, has led to "time deepening."[2] Time deepening occurs when the individual seeks to undertake more activity than can be accommodated with existing economic and educational resources. In other words, the more activities people undertake, the more they desire to undertake. Time deepening has three primary consequences for planners: (1) people do more and more activities in less and less time, e.g., eat lunch in ten minutes or get strenuous exercise in less than an hour with a game of racquetball; (2) people increasingly have the desire and ability to do more than one thing at the same time, e.g., to watch television while eating dinner or to listen to music while talking with a friend and reading the newspaper; and (3) people increasingly have the desire and ability to deal with more precise units of time, e.g., to schedule meetings at 10:36 a.m. rather than 10:30 or know within fifteen minutes how long a 300 mile drive will take. Time deepening is caused by and in turn facilitates experientialism, and it means that most of us approach both leisure and work activities within the same set of values and attitudes. These values and attitudes reflect our seriousness, rationality, hurried pace and lack of playfulness. They also reflect our doubt as to whether we belong in this world.

Democracy

Leisure has always been closely interwoven with political belief and shaped by political systems. The systems by which humans exercise power directly influences the quantity and quality of our leisure experience. The original notion of leisure, born in the Golden Age of Greece, was directly shaped by a political system in which only a minority of its residents enjoyed citizenship. Participation in the decision-making process was mandatory. The ideal of cultivation of self was more fully realized through the existence of an extensive slave system which freed the citizen from mundane work.

Unlike that of the ancient Greeks, our own democracy has been built around two key ideas: individual freedom and equality under the law. Over one hundred years ago de Tocqueville observed:

> "When men living in a democractic state of society are enlightened, they readily discover that they are not confined and fixed by any limits which constrain them to take up with their present fortune. They all, therefore, conceive the idea of increasing it – if they are free, they will attempt it; but all do not succeed in the same manner."[3]

Thus, differences in well being were closely linked to one's personal efforts, to one's ability to compete, to one's level of aspiration, need or greed. Among those things early Americans pursued competitively was "happiness." Today happiness can be pursued by the acquisition of experiences as well as the acquisition of things. The struggle for the acquisition of material goods is more successfully undertaken by most people and the pursuit of happiness is today more a matter of individual self-expression than instrumental activities.

The combination of individual freedom of choice, voluntary action and technological capitalism have emphasized maximizing profit and production divorced from identified need. These have combined to change our notion of what is "voluntary" or "freely chosen." Since leisure is usually thought of as freely-chosen activity, this change of notion is important. "Voluntary" formerly meant a choice from among many alternatives which was freely and agreeably made by the individual, not externally constrained. Choice meant foregoing several attractive alternatives in order to gain the most satisfying one. In short, pleasure involved sacrifice.

People today are more nearly able to avoid sacrifice, seeking instead to experience all choices, do it all, see it all, and do it and see it now. In the 1977 Nationwide Outdoor Recreation Survey (undertaken by the U.S. Heritage Conservation and Recreation Service), respondents listed "time" more frequently than anything else as a factor limiting their participation in outdoor recreation.[4] Not money, or transportation, or crowding or health problems, but time. This could be taken as a statement of our system's success. Imagine a former generation saying that the main limitation on their leisure was neither capital nor technology but merely enough time to use them. In *How Americans Use Time* Robinson found that one of four American adults said they *always* felt rushed.[5] This rush to experience, in one sense, indicates people have more democracy to do more and more chosen activities.

The lack of willingness to sacrifice one desirable activity in order to undertake another, however, suggests a new way of attempting to deal with our mortality: to deal with our greatest enemy, time, by doing more and more within a given period of time. Democracy has always dealt in finite terms, allowing us to choose either A or B. For a democratic government to work, people must be able to choose and accept, for example, either a clean environment or reduced taxes, either better health care for the aged or an alternative use of funds such as space exploration, either a president or prime minister with one set of beliefs (and faults) or another. Democracy involves sacrificing that which is potentially good for that which is potentially better. When we are no longer willing or capable of doing that or no longer allowed to, democracy will no longer function and we will enslave ourselves for one more eutopian dream of life without limitation.

Cultural Pluralism

Our cultural pluralism also shapes our leisure behavior and values. The many ethnic, religious and political minorities who maintain their identify rather than completely assimilating further the process of pluralism. The United States has historically represented a model of cultural pluralism due not only to its historic ties with Britain, Europe, Spain and Africa, but also due to immigration policies which continued the immigration of new groups. Canada has also experienced a more pluralistic culture during the last few decades as immigrants from Europe, Asia, the Caribbean Islands and the United States transform the country from one which was dominated by the French and English to a multicultural nation.

The effects of cultural pluralism on the leisure behavior of a post-industrial society are illustrated in the following table. The table attempts to identify the features of cultural pluralism in a mass culture which moves toward having even more things in common, primarily due to the pervasiveness of the mass media. Mass culture has been defined as:

> "Elements of culture that develop in a large, heterogenous society as a result of common exposure to and experience of the mass media. . .The emergence of mass culture is a part of the process of the development of common unifying cultural values and attitudes in the new and vast population of modern national social units."[6]

Cultural pluralism emphasizes the role of leisure as anything the individual chooses to do for pleasure. The limits of such behavior are defined only by laws, with activity representing an expression of personal interest or "lifestyle" rather than one's culture. The social pressure resulting from fads and created leisure needs stimulates further innovation and a speeding up of the consumption of leisure experience.

Leisure in Singular and Plural Cultural Societies

	Plural Culture Society	Single Culture Society
Concept	Leisure is anything the individual chooses to do which he finds pleasurable. Leisure is unlimited. An end in itself.	Leisure is a set of identifiable experiences which the individual is taught to enjoy. Leisure is limited. A means to an end.
Variation in Behavior	Range of acceptable behavior wide.	Range of acceptable behavior narrow.
Standards to Judge Behavior	Laws set limits. No universally accepted mores by which to judge leisure behavior.	Mores and folkways set limits of behavior. Universal standards for leisure based upon perceived cultural necessity.
Role	Individual and sub-cultural identity linked to leisure behavior.	National identity linked to leisure behavior.
Role Problems	Difficult to judge leisure ethically. Dispute over leisure values. Lack of meaning	Lack of experimentation or alternatives. Persecution of that which is foreign. Easy to use leisure as a means of social control.
Government's Role	Identification of recreation needs difficult. May provide only selected kinds of services or serve certain sub-cultures or groups disproportionately.	Identification of recreation needs easy. May provide services which provide as a common denominator.
Commercial Organization's Role	Commercial sector has more diverse opportunities. Can cater to individual or sub-culture's tastes. Easier to create needs.	Commercial sector has more limited opportunities. More difficult to create needs or cater to individual or sub-culture's tastes.
Mass Media's Role	Limited in its ability to reflect culture. Diversion and entertainment function.	Less limited in its ability to reflect culture. Transmission of culture function.

One solution to the accompanying uncertainty over what is worth doing is to do nothing, but a more prevalent reaction is to try to do or experience everything.

Self-Consciousness

Social psychologists claim that consciousness of self is what distinguishes us from other animals. Self-awareness is necessary and worthwhile for humans, but only within limits. Perhaps no society has been more self-conscious than our own. Our physical selves are seen instantly by cameras, we see ourselves dancing on our mirrored dancefloors or on the moon, and we receive advice concerning how to change ourselves for the better from a myriad of sources. We see and adjust ourselves daily in test scores, in beauty contests, in TV instant replays, in tape recordings, in factor analyses, in insurance company predictions and equations concerning our death, in newspapers, in sociograms, and, of course, in advertising. Advertising teaches us to be self-conscious. Am I succeeding? Am I having fun? Reaching for all the gusto? Am I in command?

Heightened self-consciousness shapes our leisure. It may limit our playfulness. Play is outside ordinary life, limited in time and space, and surrounded by an air of mystery. Self-consciousness allows us to dismiss mystery, to take the element of surprise out of ordinary life. We may actually take leisure counselors seriously, shy away from singing in public or reciting limericks to strangers, seek to rig our competition in advance or analyze why we like music. Thus, while leisure and play allow us to "get lost" in what we are doing, it becomes increasingly hard to get lost. Our heightened self-consciousness undoubtedly prevents us from doing some things in our leisure which would surprise or harm us. Additionally, it may make it more difficult to have fun. Fun, as Huizenga pointed out, is an irreducible category.[7] You cannot successfully analyze fun and break it down into component parts, although a number of social scientists are now trying. When you try too hard to analyze fun, it disappears.

Post-Industrial Capitalism

Daniel Bell has characterized post-industrial society not so much by the absence of certain traditional forms of material scarcities such as food and shelter, but by the development of new forms of scarcity.[8] Such new costs or scarcities include the cost of information, the cost of coordination, and the cost of time.

Information is mandatory in our society, and the rate at which we are bombarded with information increases daily. Every new social or political movement seeks to "educate the people." Thus, consumer activists want to provide more and more accurate information to the consumer to insure logical choice. This movement's success, however, is predicated upon individuals digesting large amounts of information, processing decisions, not unlike a computer. To buy the best tennis racquet requires extensive data not only concerning comparative price, but also on durability, flexibility of head, throat, and shaft; weight and weight distribution; head shape; size of "sweet spot"; racquet head torque; vibration; stringing pattern; grip composition; string type; string composition; and so forth. Such an approach assures that the individual pays for the racquet not only with money, but with his time, energy, and added complexity to his life. Here the consumer movement becomes an apology for materialism, not usually questioning the need for products, just instructing the potential buyer on how best to choose among alternatives.

Similarly, our society is characterized by new costs of coordination. A more complex society means more interdependence and as our ability to interfere or do harm to each other increases, planning and regulating our society becomes more important and more complex. The necessity of interacting with increasing numbers of people and a greater number of social situations involves more travel. Such coordination is not just the prerogative of elites, but necessary for everyone to minimize the possibility of killing ourselves with our own cars, chemicals or radioactive wastes.

Both the need for information and coordination help create a third scarcity – time: the ultimate scarcity for those who wish to consume and experience at an historically unprecedented rate. Those who wish to achieve or conquer in such fashion have a problem which is, in many ways, a luxury to have: not enough time to do all the things they want to do.

The desire to experience all things pleasurable, to be needed and involved in as many sets of human experience as possible is, in many respects, the ultimate greed. Two things must be said about this greed for experience. First, it springs directly from the processes and mentality of economic capitalism, where competition for goods and the production process is divorced from need. It is natural that this progression has taken place. Much as the capitalist accumulates and invests money, we can see that the investment of time by individuals in diverse, pleasurable activity is a capitalist form of self-actualization: a competition with time as the scarce resource to find out who we are by literally recreating ourselves experientially.

Capitalism also sowed the seeds of experientialism by saturating us with unneeded material objects. As the ability of our economic system continually to create needs for new material products begins to find limits, these needs are transferred to leisure experiences. People are sold the experience of gambling, traveling through Europe, viewing other people's sexual activities, going down a wild river on a raft, learning tennis from a Zen Buddhist perspective, changing personal relationships through a multitude of therapies, making wine, and any other experience they will buy. What is produced is a wanderlust, not for other places but for other lives.

THE EMERGING LEISURE SERVICE PROFESSION

The industrial revolutions were responsible for an increasing collectivization of work, concentration of power and the increasing organization of many aspects of our lives. The recreation and park movements in both the United States and Canada have historically represented an attempt to counter the negative effects of industrialization: the growth of urban areas without provision for children's play, the decreased contact of people with the natural environment, and the insidiousness of commercial recreation. Thus, it was a movement to reform, and reform takes organization. Yet a classic negative consequence was inevitable: in order to fight for their beliefs, those in the recreation and park movements were often forced to adopt the tactics and mentality of the system which produced the situations they were fighting to correct. To counter those who wished to plan, acquire and develop land for financial profit, parks people have had to maneuver in the same political arena with similar tactics to plan, acquire and develop land for the purpose of leisure. Rather than preserving leisure as it had been in pre-industrial society, it became more organized, more specialized, more scheduled in accordance with the demands of mass production, more influenced by consumerism and the increasing ability of the economy to produce "things" to play with, more fadlike, and so forth.

The movements for public recreation and parks, then, were not centered on freedom of leisure expression but with improved opportunity for participation in several forms of activity, such as outdoor recreation, sports and supervised play which were believed to be superior to the alternatives provided by the urban environment. The movement's founders were missionaries, seeking to convert people to forms of leisure expression they believed to be superior. Informed, rational choice, they believed, would lead people to the activities they advocated. The problems they fought against were real: children left with only the dangerous streets for playgrounds, men and women in the grim factories cut off from nature, the lack of recreation resources among the poor, and urbanites badly in need of exercise.

As these movements became institutionalized, recreation and parks became separate, then a combined function of local government. Both world wars, the depression, and the urban riots of the 1960's all served to heighten the growth of such agencies. Growth has brought a corresponding push for professionalization of employees, including specialized higher education curricula, attempts at certification of practitioners, professional societies and a specialized literature. Such professionalization has tended to minimize the advocacy role of most practitioners, and led to a posture where the recreation and park (leisure service) professional seeks to assume a role of only passively reacting to recreation need or demand, serving all people "equally" and reacting to rather than initiating societal change.

At the same time this professionalization is taking place, there is evidence that the growth of leisure service agencies in the public sector has largely halted or even been reversed, after a decade of growth.[9] This trend appears to be most pronounced at the local level, where the bulk of such services take place. Responding to such constraints will require new ways of proceeding, some of which may not be in keeping with "professionalism."

PLANNING FUTURE LEISURE SERVICES

How can the emerging leisure service profession respond to these complex situations? While the question is complicated, leisure planners will not have to invent things for people to do. They should provide a mechanism to encourage people to do things which are necessary for society but unfunded. In concert with the emerging deurbanization or atomization of our society, public leisure service planners must abandon the large scale planning mentality which has ignored the quality of neighborhood life and substituted standardization, formality, efficiency and bigness. The leisure service professional is no longer viewed as a public servant, but as a bureaucrat lacking respect for variation in life style and particularly leisure life style. Public leisure services, in short, must reflect rather than create culture.

Each of the previously outlined situations call for some redefinition of leisure services. With regard to work trends, for example, as a higher percentage of our population becomes involved in part-time employment, as the linear life cycle of education, single career and retirement ends, and as leisure or non-work time becomes available in large blocks of time, the purposes or satisfactions from leisure activity may have less to do with refreshment or diversion from work and more to do with activity which is considered worthwhile or satisfying on its own merits. Relations between work and leisure may become far less systematic. The common work leisure cycle may become increasingly differentiated. For the leisure planner, services can no longer be confined to a few common periods of time such as weekday evenings, weekend holidays, and summer vacations.

While the relation of leisure services to work may in some ways be diminished, the impact of continuing inflation will be such that leisure service agencies will have to sponsor more activities which provide a useful end product as well as the pleasure of doing them. Gardening, cooking, crafts with useful end products such as furniture reupholstering will all increase in popularity as will voluntary activities which provide a useful end product for the community and a worthwhile experience for the participant.

The rush to experience in our society which has brought about time deepening, and the attendant diminished spirituality must be countered by the provision of leisure experiences which require commitment, sacrifice and a progression of skills. Timelessness, simplicity, joy and celebration are leisure values which must be promoted in such activities if leisure planners are to actually serve as advocates of leisure. Public leisure service, in short, should be concerned not only with "the pursuit of happiness" but also with "insuring domestic tranquility." Remember those phrases?

Our pluralistic culture makes it difficult for leisure service agencies to "create" culture. Rather, they must reflect the many cultures around them. This cannot be done without intensifying efforts to involve citizens in decision-making using a diversity of formats. This is not to say that the agency should be culturally neutral, having no values other than those interjected by various public lobbies and pressure groups. Rather, the agency cannot afford to be ignorant of public opinion and diversity of opinion among sub-cultures. Maintaining cultural pluralism requires that a delicate balance be maintained between ignoring differences in culture to the extent that those within specific sub-cultures are either alienated or surrender their identity and recognizing such differences to the extent that members of society have little in common. Leisure service agencies must seek this balance.

Our heightened self-consciousness may indicate a greater need for opportunities for individuals to lose themselves in play and in service to others. While facilitating service to others may mean serving as a clearinghouse for voluntary action, promoting play will require much effort including redesigning many physical environments so as to encourage it.

In the future many unconventional types of property will be valued for their potential as a leisure resource. Cemeteries, for instance, are already undergoing a transformation from a burial place to one in which people may play. A spokesman for the archdiocese of Chicago said, "The trend is clear. Cemeteries will increasingly have more than one use. They have to. It's just good citizenship. In many areas the cemetery is about the last open green space left."[10] Churches, schools, museums, shopping centers, and private organizations are increasingly providing recreation and leisure services, and leisure service planners must be aware of them in the planning process.

Streets also have a leisure potential which planners must seek to recognize, particularly in the urban areas. The Chief of Comprehensive Planning of Baltimore City Department of Planning recently pointed out that the conversion of streets into public play areas sometimes appears to be an ideal solution but in doing so the system of space management that exists is disrupted.[11] Since many urban residents, however, center theii leisure activity around the sidewalk and street in front of their houses, he suggests the following:

> "Sidewalks should be widened, traffic lanes should be reduced and traffic speed cut down by using such devices as bumps in the road bed. Suitable space should be provided for sitting, playing games, congregating around activity nodes such as bookmobile stops, places for vendors of fruit, fish, vegetables, ice cream. These spaces should be suitably paved, well lighted, equipped with mailboxes, telephone booths, trash containers. They should have trees or some other shading devices."[12]

Additionally, he suggests the demolition of old buildings in such areas, that windows be introduced into any standing blind walls, that playground equipment should *not* be introduced but that street furniture should be provided so that it can serve a recreation function. Steps should be wide enough for comfortable sitting and playing step ball, fire hydrants should be made suitable for leap frog, paving surfaces should be useable by residents, adjoining residents should be encouraged to exercise surveillance over neighborhood playgrounds. Undertaking such steps would represent a revolution in thinking on the part of leisure service planners because it would be, in effect, creating a new leisure environment, rather than dropping a few pieces of playground equipment into a decaying environment and then expressing surprise when such equipment is not used or misused.

In all these undertakings, leisure services must help us to be humble; take ourselves less seriously. Help us attain a new tranquility which can come only with the sense of wholeness, the holiness, of this world.

Those leisure services which are of greatest benefit to our world and for which we must plan will be those which help us see why it makes sense to celebrate this world and our very lives.

REFERENCES

1. See, for instance, Best, Fred, Bosserman, Phillip and Stern, Barry. *Changing Values Toward Material Wealth and Leisure in the United States,* Washington, D.C.: NEW, January, 1976.
2. See, for instance, Scheuch, Erwin, "The Time Budget Interview." In: Alexander Szalai, ed., *The Use of Time – Daily Activities of Urban and Suburban Populations.* The Hague, Netherlands, 1972. p. 77.
3. de Tocqueville, Alexis. *Democracy in America.* New York: Mentor Books, 1956. p. 161.
4. Piney, John, Godbey, Geoffrey and Robinson, John, *A Survey of Outdoor Recreation in America – Summary.* Washington, D.C.: Heritage, Conservation and Recreation Service, 1979.
5. Robinson, John, *Leisure and Our Changing Use of Time,* College of HPER Colloquium, The Pennsylvania State University, University Park, Pennsylvania. (November 13) 1976.
6. Theodorson, George A. and Achilles G. *Modern Dictionary of Sociology,* New York: Thomas Y. Crowell, 1969. p. 246.
7. Huizinga, Johan. *Homo Ludens: A Study of the Play Element in Culture.* Boston: The Beacon Press, 1950.
8. Bell, Daniel, "The End of Scarcity." *Saturday Review of the Society,* (May) 1973. pp. 49-52.
9. See, for instance, Kraus, Richard. *Urban Parks and Recreation: Challenge of the 1970's.* New York: Community Council of Greater New York, 1972.
10. "Cemetaries Opening Gates for Recreation." *The New York Times,* (December 10,) 1972. pp. 1, 76.
11. Brower, S.N. and Williamson, P., "Outdoor Recreation as a Function of the Urban Housing Environment," *Environment and Behavior,* (September) 1974. pp. 342-3.
12. *Ibid.,* p. 343.

Chapter Fourteen

Lifestyles and Lifecycles: A Recreation Programming Approach

H. Douglas Sessoms

If we look critically at the activities and services offered by most recreation and park systems, we will find they are not too different from those provided a half a century ago. In many ways, the recreation and park service continues to do what it has done in the past: scheduling certain types of activities for specific age groups and operating and maintaining areas and facilities. Has the public and the recreation profession "agreed" upon the role of the organized recreation movement – what we do is what we are expected to do – or is programming an open issue?

Most of our professional literature on programming and the delivery of recreation services deals with the what and how (content and technique), not with the why (conceptual basis) of our services. Little is said about the assumptions we make about human behavior and the role recreation experiences play in each stage of life. We focus largely on the activities of children, the importance of diversionary activity, the values of sports and physical fitness, and the necessity of providing spaces for recreation.

If our role in meeting critical leisure needs of the public is limited, it is because of the weakness of the conceptual basis for the services and activities we provide. If our programs are static, consist largely of the same kinds of activities and attract primarily the same individuals, it is because of our program concepts; our understandings of behavior. Activities are like the tip of the iceberg: they are what we see. The real determinants of the program are undetected. The invisible aspects of the program iceberg are our concepts and assumptions about our services – who we serve, how we serve them, and what we serve them. To a large extent, recreators have accepted our approach to program conceptualization and content as an act of faith, rarely questioning the basis upon which we make program decisions. Occasionally, rumbles are heard as to the validity of our program offerings, techniques and methods, but little serious effort has been given to the study of programming. For the most part, those in therapeutic recreation services, those who are interested in the phenomenon of activity analysis, have been the profession's most vocal critics of the program status quo.

To understand and deal with this phenomenon, we need to look at our historical origins and earlier program assumptions, a process which should aid us in identifying the concepts needed to guide future programming strategies and approaches.

HISTORICAL PRECEDENTS

To a large degree, the organized park and recreation movement evolved out of society's need in the late 19th century to socialize its youth, particularly the children of immigrants, into an urban way of life.[1] Recreation settings and activities were viewed as means to an end – the development of character and the instilling of the "American way of life." It was generally assumed, as reflected in the writings of Lee, Gulick, Curtis and others, that there were inherent values in recreation and play activities. Play was deemed as a natural process and, through the playing of "proper games," children grew and developed into socially useful adults. They assumed the values of society and became "law-abiding citizens." The misuse of leisure and/or the pursuit of "sinful" activities was felt to bring about social and personal problems.

Since many of the early activity leaders were teachers, it was not surprising that recreation programs took on a school-like quality. Activities were scheduled in much the same way as teachers scheduled academic subjects. This was especially true at camp or on the playground. The sequence of activities offered each day reflected a logical functionalism. The more energetic sports programs were scheduled for the early and mid-morning hours or in the late afternoon. Story telling and arts and crafts, the more sedentary activities, were programmed in the middle of the day during the periods of intense heat. Children were moved from one activity to another according to a time schedule. There was little choice in all of this. It was assumed by those in positions of responsibility that they knew more about the consequence of participation than did the participants. Since the participants, urban children, had limited opportunity for alternative play activities, and since the efficiency of the activity approach did maximize the utilization of limited play spaces, the organized recreation movement accepted this approach as sound and appropriate. Activities were highly structured, functionally scheduled, and closely supervised.

As is often the case, approaches that are found to be functional for one period of time become institutionalized and are continued even though the rationale for their original function no longer exists. When this occurs, the institutions develop rationalizations for their continuence rather than discarding them. It is much easier to justify why something is being done than it is to discontinue the "proven practice" and begin anew. This has happened with the organized recreation movement. We have continued to use the highly structured approach designed for the playgrounds even though the social and physical environment of our world was changing. Society's ability to control the environment through the use of artificial lights and air-conditioning negated the rationale for many of our traditional schedules and program emphases (activities) for children but it did not radically alter our approach.

To justify our program structures, two popular rationales for what we did developed. They were couched in the "need" theories developed by psychologists and sociologists in the mid 1930's and early 1940's. They have had tremendous impact on present day thinking and functioning.

The first approach held that recreation programs should provide the needed balance between active and passive forms of expression. Since it was assumed that most workers and children were passive in their daily routines of factory or school work, participation in vigorous sport should be encouraged. Artistic and other more passive forms of physical expression were to be promoted for those who expended considerable labor in the performance of their daily work. However, since most organized recreation agencies programmed primarily for children, few agencies assumed any responsibility for promoting cultural programs. This void was partially filled by the establishment of community theaters and allied art centers, services administratively separate from recreation and parks, thereby limiting the focus of recreation and park agencies. It seemed recreators were supposed to be concerned with youth, sports, and diversionary activities, not with the arts or adult interests.

An activity typology based primarily on the major focus of the activity was developed. It was assumed by its advocates that all activities could be grouped under one of four major headings: physical, emotional, cultural, and social. Furthermore, it was believed that a balanced recreation program should include activities from each of these four types since it was unrealistic to expect any one activity to meet all four "needs." How could participation in tennis, a physical activity, provide cerebral and social expression? Likewise, how could a cultural activity such as dance accommodate ones physical and intellectual needs? No recognition of the complexity of an activity or experience was apparent; those who supported this approach were only concerned with the major structure of the activity. The simplicity of the approach allowed for its immediate implementation. Programmers could quickly categorize their activities and events and could readily report if they had achieved complete coverage of activities from the four program groupings.

The second major approach to the classifying of activities was similar to one just described. It focused on the form the activity took. Activities were viewed as being either sports and games, nature and outings, dance, music, dramatics, social literary, and arts and crafts. Activities could be placed in any one of these eight types according to the activity's structure or the setting in which the activity occurred. Proponents of this approach acknowledged the potential of any activity to meet various needs such as physical, emotional, cultural and social expression. However, they assumed that the "complete individual" should participate in activities from each of these categories in much the same way that nutrition experts assume each meal should contain foods from each of the seven major food groups. Some writers have coined this classification and program approach as the "balanced diet" approach to recreation services.

According to the supporters of this theory, the benefits derived from any one activity were not as important as the need to participate in a wide range of activities. Although not stated, one of the underlying assumptions of this theory was that balanced growth and development (a socialization ideal) could only occur when individuals experienced and participated in a wide range of activities. Specialization or concentration on one activity or activity group would result in inadequate development – a narrow personality. Though this approach was more holistic than the other – accepting that multiple satisfactions could be derived from one activity – it was no more humanistic. It too ignored the theory which holds that leisure expressions are an extension of personality. The focus was on the activity, not the individual. Scheduling was still more important than were the motives, interests, and judgements of the participant.

For the most part the recreation professionals advocating these classification systems were very value-oriented. They believed certain activities were inherently more valuable than were other activities. They even went so far as to develop hierarchies of activities based upon their perceptions of the ability of each activity to meet specific needs and add to the quality of the individual and the experience. J. B. Nash was one of the leading proponents of this hierarchical approach.[2] Nash valued creative expression and thought participation in physical activity was of greater value than viewing sports competition, which he called "Spectatoritis." He discounted the emotional and psychological involvement one can experience as a spectator since, according to him, sitting required little or no physical involvement. To Nash and those who subscribed to the "activity" school of thought, physical activity was a highly desired form of recreation expression. Their influence on recreation programming was significant; their philosophy reinforced the importance of sports as a major program component. Furthermore, their view of the role of the recreation agency further reinforced the public's perception of recreation and sports as synonymous activities.

The late Charles K. Brightbill was an advocate of the balanced diet approach. He strongly urged public recreation departments to provide "cafeterias of activity and services" so individual freedom of choice could be promoted. Brightbill felt recreators should not impose their values on the participant but should encourage participants to develop a wide range of expression so they could "choose" their activities. He held freedom of choice was essential to leisure; the more knowledgeable the individual, the more skills he possessed, the greater range of choices he had. The provision of facilities, the offering of instructional programs, the scheduling of activities and events – all of these were important in assuring the public a wide range of opportunities for expression. He felt agencies should offer activities from each of the eight activity groups and should encourage participants to develop skills which would allow them to participate in as many of the activity groups as possible.[3]

These views of programming dominated the thinking of park and recreation professionals during the middle decades of the 20th century. They might have continued to be the dominant view of the profession had it not been for the emergence of outdoor recreation interests in the late 1950's and the merging of the park and recreation movement into a single profession in 1965. The amalgamation of parks and recreation into one single administrative unit had tremendous impact on the recreation programming philosophy. Interest in selecting activities according to their major form or dominant focus gave way to concerns for the resource in which people engaged in their preferred leisure activities. The critical program issue became one of determining which activities were appropriate for which environments. Interest in the classification of activities or the proper sequencing of activities on a playground or community building faded as recreation and park professionals turned their attention to the carrying capacity and design of recreation spaces. New classification systems such as the one developed by the Bureau of Outdoor Recreation (now the Heritage Conservation and Recreation Service) became the yardstick for measuring program balance. Questions, such as "does the park and recreation system have adequate balance of recreation spaces for each of the six BOR* categories?", replaced the older one of "does the recreation agency offer activities from each of the eight activity families?"

Concomitant with the merging of park and recreation programs into one administrative unit was the public's general rejection of having their free time expressions highly structured. Their dependency upon public recreation and park services to provide them and their children with leisure opportunities declined although their interest in recreation increased. In response to these changes the leisure service delivery system grew in complexity as commercial and private recreation interests developed their constituencies. The role of recreation and park agencies was impacted by the development of these "new" elements of the leisure service delivery system. To compete, public playground and community building programs became more flexible. For the most part, only the instructional classes and athletic contests continued to adhere to the traditional fixed time schedules. All of this happened at about the same time as the civil rights movement, the "war on poverty," the student movement and the anti-Vietnam war protests. New patterns of life were emerging. New approaches for the provision of services were expected. America was entering the post-industrial age, urging its government officials to humanize all of its delivery systems.

RECENT EVENTS

In response to these changes, the 1970's were characterized by the development of the humanistic program approach to the provision of recreation and park services. David Gray, Sy Greben, and James Murphy were among the leading advocates of this cause. According to them, the recreation interests and behaviors of the public cannot be programmed independently of the public's need for other services. In order to reduce the impact of bureaucracies and the arbitrariness of administrative edicts, a holistic approach must be established. Recreation activities and services must be consistent with the lifestyle and the resources of the people involved. No single program approach or planning design can possibly meet the needs of a highly diverse population with its many ethnic and cultural sub-groups. Thus, a new philosophy of programming, one which would deal with diversity, had to be developed.

*The Bureau of Outdoor Recreation classification system is based upon expected behavior patterns and physical resource characteristics. The six BOR classes are: I–High Density Recreation Area; II–General Outdoor Recreation Areas; III–Natural Environment Areas; IV–Unique Natural Areas; V–Primitive Areas; and VI–Historic and Cultural Sites.

At the same time Americans were reacting to governmental bureaucracies and political and social unrest, their lives were being impacted by two other major forces of social change. One was economic; the other demographic. Declining sources of cheap energy, coupled with inflationary and recessionary patterns, altered the recreational habits of millions. People were less able to travel long distances to recreation areas and less willing to expend the same percentage of their income for recreational pursuits. As a result, in the summer of 1979, scores of commercial recreation enterprises, particularly those in tourist areas, experienced severe financial losses. Many went bankrupt. On the other hand, municipal and county recreation agencies reported increased participation; there seemed to be no loss of interest in recreation pursuits, only a change in the form of the pursuits and the places in which they occurred.

The demographic changes were equally dramatic. Rather than being a nation of youth (the average age of the U. S. citizen in 1966 was 25 years) America was becoming a society of adults. Demographers project that the median age in the United States in 1984 will be 35 years. Less than a third of the population will be under 21. Services and programs geared primarily for children and youth will, for the first time in this century, become programs of the minority. Those approaches and philosophies developed by the profession in response to the need to socialize the young are being found to be inappropriate and inadequate when applied to adults. New explanations and theories of programming and new structures for delivering services will have to emerge if recreation services are to remain vital.

Successful recreation and park agencies have found that their approach to services must be multi-dimensional if they are to serve more than one segment of the population, and, since they depend upon the financial and political support of various elements of the community, they *must* serve more than one segment. A variety of lifestyle and age groups must be accommodated, each in its own way and each in its own time. The concepts of lifestyle and life stages developed by the social gerontologists of the 1970's may serve as a conceptual framework for future provision of recreation services. The notion of life stages (also referred to as life cycles) encourages recreators to take a longitudinal view of leisure behaviors while the concept of lifestyles focuses attention on the experiential and qualitative aspects of behavior. Both stimulate a holistic and integrated view of man and his behavior.

As stated previously, the park and recreation movement has been largely concerned with the activities of youth and children. Children were perceived to "need" organized play and although there were variations in the play patterns of different groups according to their social class and residence (urban - rural), the general pattern was much the same. Young boys were expected to participate in athletics; adolescent girls were to be majorettes, cheerleaders and good dancers; etc. Racial and sexual stereotypes abounded. The offered activities both reflected and shaped the values and expectations of society. Service approaches for adults were similar. Recreation departments were expected to provide facilities where adults could play their favorite sport. Those who happened not to engage in these so-called recreation activities, were not likely to find the recreation system very responsive to their needs. The latter point is a key one. Recreation and park departments tend to program only those activities and services which are "acceptable" to the large society. Youth, exhibiting lifestyle patterns contrary to the accepted mode, have been discouraged from participating in many of our programs or, if they did, were expected to give up their "offensive" style. After all, park and recreation agencies were established to aid in the socialization process, not to accommodate those who deviated from the norm.

In general society has been very optimistic about its ability to shape and modify the behavior of youth. It assumes that the child and adolescent are immature and therefore need direction; adults are presumed to be socialized and are thus able to function on their own to organize their own associations and groups.

But the social gerontologist and developmental psychologist now tell us adults, too, need socialization throughout life. The need to adapt to new roles and statuses is ever present. Each life stage requires adaptation. Thus, there is a potential role for recreation and park agencies in the ongoing socialization of adults. It is, therefore, imperative for the profession to develop program strategies which allow it to work with all segments of the population, adults as well as children. The concepts of lifestyle and life stage are fundamental to those strategies.

LIFE STYLE DEFINED

The term *lifestyle* has become popular in recent years. Prior to the counter-culture movement in the mid 1960's it was a nice sociological term, used only in the classroom. Now it is viewed as an essential concept for planning and expediting various human delivery services, recreation included. In many instances, it is a misused term, a popular catch-all phrase used to explain the significance of behaviors which we do not understand or with which we are not familiar.

Essentially, lifestyle is a mode of expression. When sociologists speak of lifestyles they are really describing the behaviors and attitudes that characterize one's existence. It is the way one lives. An individual's behaviors are determined by the unique configuration of social values and personal experiences which influence behavior and cause him or her to identify with those who also share those behaviors. The outward manifestation of one's lifestyle includes such items as dress, speech patterns, language, activity selection, living arrangements, etc. Most sociologists agree that there is an integrated core of activities associated with each dominant lifestyle. Lifestyle behaviors result from the interaction of the means by which we fulfill our needs (personality development) and the experiences we have which reinforce those behaviors (our socialization). Those who share a similar lifestyle tend to form sub-groups which constantly reinforce individual choices and set the behavioral priorities. These patterns are reinforced by the skills and self-concept which one develops in order to express and benefit from the chosen lifestyle. All of life's experiences are influenced by these learnings, attitudes and personality expressions.

Generally speaking, there is also a dominant force at the center of one's lifestyle. For example, drugs dictate the behavior and social relationships of the drug user. Likewise, dress and appearance dominate the thinking and behavior of those "into" fashion. For the avid camper, camping and camping concerns shape his or her associations and actions. The books and magazines read, the friends chosen and the priorities set are determined by the central focus of the lifestyle. In a leisure oriented society, specific recreation activities tend to set lifestyle patterns. Other lifestyles may center around religion, politics, social relationships or some other potentially all-consuming activity.

Lifestyles are dynamic; one may exhibit various lifestyles during a lifetime. Some lifestyles, such as those of college students, are characteristic of specific life stages while others, such as those associated with religion may cut across many age groups. Even within a dominant lifestyle, such as that of a college student, there are sub-lifestyles. The lifestyle of the fraternity/sorority member and that of the athlete may be similar since they share a common student orientation experience but may be quite different in their own way. Each has the potential of becoming the all-consuming activity.

LIFE SPAN AND LIFE STAGE DEFINED

The concept of life span implies that life is a series of connected stages (life stages), each influencing one another but each being distinctive.

Each life stage is characterized by a unique configuration of roles and dominant activities which seem to be related to biological and/or psychological (developmental) changes. Developmental psychologists have spent considerable time and energy in explaining the progression of life stages, particularly those of youth. Less work has been done on young adults, adults and the elderly. According to psychologists, there seem to be well-defined developmental patterns which we all go through. There also seems to be a predetermined mechanism for triggering change as we age.

Each stage of life is characterized by certain "expected" behaviors. Consequently, as one moves from one life stage to the next, role modifications occur; new role sets emerge as we respond to both our own and society's perception of what is proper at any given stage. What may be an engrossing recreation activity at one stage of life may be dropped or only tolerated in a later stage. There seems to be a physiological and psychological readiness for specific roles and the activities which characterize those roles. The question is one of what triggers or initiates shifts in roles. Are these changes biological in origin or do they result from social expectation and experiences or a combination of these?

We are all quick to offer explanations for our observed behavior. When we see an eighteen year old fraternizing with a member of the opposite sex, we say "that's what adolescents do." We expect teenagers to interact with members of the opposite sex, and they do. Is it because of the development of their biological sexuality or is it a socially expected behavior of eighteen year olds? More likely it is a combination of both. If we see the same kind of behavior among members of the opposite sex when both participants are married and not with their spouse, we describe the fraternizing in other terms. We may talk about philandering. On the other hand, if this behavior occurs publicly, say in an office party or at a class reunion, it may be dismissed as regression or be rationalized by saying "they've had too much to drink." These perceptions have great significance for recreation and park programmers since we, too, are "victims" of the propensity to stereotype. In our haste to help an individual adapt to a new life stage, we may actually discourage participation in some activity which he/she enjoys but which seems to be related to a previous life stage. Similarly, we may encourage and even force participants into new activities assuming they are the proper involvements for that stage of life.

There are certain roles such as parenthood, which do occur in a specific life stage which tend to dominate that phase of life. In the case of parenthood, the triggering mechanism is biological; in the case of recently married young adults, the role shift may be culturally determined. The move from one life stage to the next appears to be developmental rather than hierarchical. No one stage is more or less than another, only different.

LIFELONG INTERESTS

Our expectations of what we should do in a specific stage of life are conditioned by the attitudes and values of the larger society. The specific forms by which these expectations are manifested are determined by the values of those who share our lifestyle. We tend to do only those things which are socially approved by those we respect. It is unrealistic for recreation and park professionals to expect those whose lifestyle is centered in literary and antiquity interests to join in recreation programs designed for the sports enthusiast. Likewise, it is unrealistic to think recreation and park departments will be effective in attracting to their programs members of a given neighborhood, say, where there are strong ethnic influences if those person's friends dislike the recreation program offerings and leadership. The same holds true for those in specific life stages. We live in a very age oriented society where we see activities begun or discontinued according to one's life stage.

I remember when our youngest son finished the sixth grade and was promoted to the seventh. During the spring he played dodge ball daily as did most of the older elementary school children. It was the activity of the sixth grader. Four months later, when he entered junior high, he lost interest in dodge ball; junior high students did not play it. His personality and biological self had not changed to any great extent in that four month period but his perception of the role of a junior high student – a new life stage for him – and the activities they pursued prevented him from playing dodge ball, even though he dearly loved it. Occasionally he would "fall off the wagon" and would play with some of the neighborhood elementary school children who still thought of it as a good sport, but he did not let his junior high friends know of his transgressions. His behavior reinforced what we know to be an operational fact; what we do at any stage of life depends more upon what our peers do and their perceptions than does the activity skills we have learned. Social expectations and social pressures can be powerful forces available to recreation programmers when they are sensitive to the role played by life stages and lifestyles.

Childhood experiences are important primarily as antecedent conditions in the selection of our lifestyle expressions. To illustrate the point, consider the promotion of lifetime sports and the athletic pursuits of children. For many recreators, being physically active is a highly desirable way of life. But not everyone is interested in being physically active, at least not in the sense of playing sports and games. To them, to be physically active may mean hiking or working in the garden. Sports are not a part of their priority system even though physical fitness may be an essential element of their lifestyle. To assume that everyone should participate in sports because sports is a major form of keeping fit is to ignore the realities of a population with diverse lifestyles.

It is hypothesized that the adult lifestyle which has sports as a part of it could have been predicted by earlier activity behavior of its members. In other words, children who play sports and get positive reinforcement from it generally continue to participate in sports as adults and select friends who also engage in them. The motivation is not necessarily for physical fitness; sports is an integral part of their reward system. Their earlier behavior did not determine their later recreation interests and experiences, only forecast it. The selective process was already in operation. For those who are not inclined toward physical activity or who are physical but not sports oriented, introducing them to sporting contests or suggesting that they should play sports rather than hike or play the piano is like washing dirty clothes without soap; it accomplishes little. This is true for both youth and adults.

There also appears to be a readiness for participation in specific activities and that readiness is tied to one's life stage and lifestyle. For ghetto children, basketball seems to be an important activity. To suggest to these children that they should be playing tennis or golf because they can continue these in their adult years makes little sense to them. The reinforcers are not there. In fact, it is difficult to convince most eleven year olds they should be learning the skills and activities they will enjoy in the future when their present social environment says they should be playing team sports. The same holds true when introducing music appreciation or teaching someone to play an instrument. What the child wants to play and hear is what his peers want to play and hear. At best we can develop an individual's sensitivity or receptiveness to participation in the so-called "lifetime activities" when they reach the appropriate stage in life to enjoy them. Whether they do engage in them as adults depends upon a host of variables over which we have little control. Recognition of this fact should not deter professional program planners from introducing new activities to their constituents but it does demand a more careful reading of how those experiences are introduced and what the expected results may be.

Our lifestyle and stage of life serve as our antennae. We only pick up those vibrations which are in tune with our receiving units. Our psychological readiness is directly related to our life stage and our willingness to participate is a function of our lifestyle. True, without exposure to a variety of activities there would be no knowledge of what might be acceptable and therefore little diversity in lifestyles. However, exposure does not determine choice; it only makes choice possible.

In her work on development and perspectives of aging, Bernice Neugarten vividly described and documented the life selecting process.

> Life is essentially a two-stage phenomenon in which the first stage is devoted to the development of abilities, skills, and mechanisms for dealing with the world and with one's self. It is an expansive stage. The second stage or phase of life involves the reorganization and evaluation of behaviors. Changes in the quality of social interaction and a growing concern for the inner life are its major components. The maintaining of one's self and one's interests becomes paramount.[4]

The first stage is quantitative; the second, qualitative. Youth is characterized by growth, will, exploration and expansion as a part of the growing process. Learning requires a wide range of experiences; from them, a variety of lifestyles evolve. This is an important understanding for those who see leisure education and leisure counseling as responsibilities of the park and recreation professional. They need to know the origin of various lifestyles and the relationship of those behaviors to specific life stages.

The adult stage of life is characterized by selectivity. Having experienced the expansiveness of youth, adults tend to sort out activities and channel their energies. These characteristics are typical in the mature state where one seeks to maintain and stabilize preferred behaviors rather than continue to be as explorative. Of course, exploration occurs in all stages of life as does maintenance behavior; it's really a matter of degree.

The number of activities in which we engage during our leisure is somewhat reflective of our life stage. During the expansive years we participate in a greater variety and number of activities. As we age, we modify this pattern. For those who participate in sports, who like to be physically active, substitution occurs but the emphasis on physical activity remains. For example, baseball and basketball may give way to slow pitch softball and golf. For others, life is an integrated process with satisfactions being derived from a variety of expression.

Some behaviors are measured by our more conventional recreation activity inventory schedules. As youth, they probably did not play many of the playground games, choosing other activities as their means of satisfaction. The services of recreation departments probably were rarely used. As adults, they continued to "tune out" the offerings of the recreation agencies; they appear not to be a part of our constituency. Also, they seem to engage in fewer activities but the number of activities engaged in is not directly related to the quality of involvement. The more complex the activity, the more absorbing it is in terms of lifestyle development, the less need there is for diversity of activity in order to "meet needs." To the dog fancier, raising and showing canines is "all there is." It provides social interaction, a sense of purpose and achievement, travel, new experiences – all the elements of a satisfying recreation lifestyle. Finally, some people are passive/dependent, always relying on others to tell them what to do or to entertain them. They probably have been this way all of their lives; television and some of our organized recreation programs may actually encourage this type of dependency.

Most recreation and park professionals would argue vehemently that their program approaches do not encourage dependency. After all, dependency is contrary to our notions of freedom, and freedom is essential to recreative experience. Recreators like to believe in their ability to move people to self-directed behaviors. If this goal is achieved, however, the likelihood of the participant returning to the recreation professional for direction and, even support his interest, may be minimized. The recreator is in the same position as is the teacher. If he does his job well, he may be no longer needed; his client now knows how to learn, how to process experiences, how to problem-solve, and, hopefully, how to have a more meaningful and satisfying life. Fortunately for recreators, fostering independence and autonomy are not incompatible with our mission. As individuals develop these qualities, their needs for services continues, but the type of services required may change. Park and recreation programs must be able to respond to those changes.

Recreators must also overcome the fallacious belief that people only recreate when they go to recreation centers. Only a small percentage of one's free-time is spent in a designated "recreation" area or participating in a recreation "activity." It is unrealistic to think that those who do not come to organized recreation and park facilities or to programs sponsored by recreation and park departments are recreationally illiterate or not engaging in satisfying experiences. Self-directed adults frequently reject the services of recreators when they perceive these approaches as inappropriate to their life stage or lifestyle. We, therefore, need to make sure that our concept of growth and development is broadly based, that our approach to services takes on a longitudinal dimension, and that we accommodate diversity of those who march to the beat of different drummers.

THEORY OF CONTINUITY/DISCONTINUITY

Besides the work on life stages and life cycles, there are additional research findings from gerontology which have meaning to recreators. Among those studies are those related to the theory of continuity which suggests a technique for predicting future behaviors. The theory holds that if the activities of youth are known, a person's general patterns throughout life can be predicted. People tend to continue in the same general mode throughout their lives although there are patterns of discontinuity. The discontinuity concept states that when a lifestyle pattern changes as a result of an accident, a crisis, or some other unexpected event, the person involved generally reacquires an interest and a lifestyle he has known in the past but discontinued as a result of his concentration on those activities which were more consistent with the lifestyle he was developing. For example, the theory of continuity would say that those interested in the out-of-doors will pursue activities related to that dominant interest and lifestyle throughout each stage of life. If, however, something prevented the individual from participating in those activities, he/she would drop back to an earlier stage of interest and pursue an activity, say crafts, which had been enjoyed but had been discontinued.

The theory of continuity assumes an integrated and holistic approach, an evolutionary process, which moves people from one stage of life to the next with no radical departure from their previous activity patterns. The implications of the theories of continuity and discontinuity for therapeutic recreation are enormous. If the theories are valid, they suggest to therapeutic recreation specialists that they should determine the past preferences and behaviors of a client to see if there might be a discontinued set of activities or lifestyles which could be re-established. This is a current strategy of those working with alcoholics and drug addicts. What were the leisure behaviors dropped when alcohol or drugs became the dominant time consumer? Could they be reacquired? Which would be more expedient – the development of new skills and essential interests or the resumption of a discontinued activity pattern? Would it be easier for the client to develop a new set of relationships to support new interests or should the reinforcers come from earlier associations?

For those patients who do not need to modify their current life behaviors, the theory of continuity has relevance. Activities should be selected which are consistent with one's lifestyle and stage. They should be an extension of the present behavior and in the direction in which the personality (life stage/lifestyle) is developing.

Recent research findings suggest that the activity level of childhood directly influences the adult activity level and that there is a direct relationship between one's social class and one's lifestyle. Yoesting and Burkhead[5] reported the first observation; Havighurst and Feigenbaum contributed the second finding.[6] Both observations support the theory of continuity. They say nothing about the "healthiness" of high activity participation, only that our previous experiences are correlated with our present activity patterns and that one's social class and expected role configurations are more involved with what one does than with the satisfaction derived from the activity *per se*. In fact, the number of activities engaged in (high activity patterns) is not necessarily correlated with satisfaction. It is the quality, not the number of experiences, which determine satisfaction. Being highly active, both in terms of the variety of activities engaged in and the amount of physical exertion required, is not a prerequisite for a satisfying leisure lifestyle.

Finally, the fear of failure seems to be a major determinant in the continuation of previous activity patterns. Loofts reported that the fear of failure is a major problem in adult socialization.[7] With experience, "historical time" is developed; one comes to know the results of failure. To avoid it, we continue those patterns we know. Possibly this is why life span patterns are so predictable for a given individual. The lifestyle remains the same, being comprised of experiences which are understood and which provide satisfaction. We adapt to the expected role patterns of each stage, fearing to deviate from the expected since we know the potential consequence of failure.

IMPLICATIONS FOR PROGRAMMING

The implications of the concepts of lifestyle, life stages, continuity/discontinuity, holism and adult socialization are critical to the future programming efforts of park and recreation professionals. They are useful concepts in developing leisure counseling strategies, in selecting approaches and activities for a constituency which is growing older, for broadening our professional sphere of influence and acceptance, and for the maintenance of the vitality of the park and recreation movement. The content of our delivery system as well as the means by which we offer services and programs should reflect our understanding of concepts, which take into account the interactions between various psychological, sociological, and physiological factors. If the park and recreation profession chooses only one mode of programming or plans only for one lifestyle and/or life stage, its appeal and impact will be limited and its public support minimal.

There are a variety of program actions the profession can take to assure broad public support and valid programs. The usefulness of the concepts described in this paper to recreation programmers does not require a rejection of previous explanations for recreative behavior. Earlier classification systems and explanations of recreation activity are still useful, although somewhat simplistic. The more contemporary explanations acknowledge the interactional dynamics of behavior which were ignored in our earlier attempts to explain the need for activity and our justification of the programs we offered. Contemporary life requires a multi-faceted approach to recreation programming.

The first step necessary in the implementation of this action is the recognition of the target groups to be served. Different lifestyles and different life stages require different programs and program approaches. For some segments of the population, the scheduling of activities and events and the supervising of recreation experiences is suggested. This may be the most appropriate approach for the young, the inexperienced and the socially dependent. It may be totally unacceptable for the mature or the self-reliant. For them, another approach is indicated.

The provision of recreation spaces – areas and facilities – is a program approach in its own way. Providing places where people can go to enjoy themselves in self-directed activity may be all that's required for some individuals and groups. Occasionally, these areas must be reserved for specific activities and events, such as athletic contests, in order to accommodate large numbers of participants.

A third program approach involves the amassing and dissemination of information and knowledge about activities and services offered. This approach embraces the concepts of leisure counseling and leisure consulting, including the offering of technical assistance. When recreation and park professionals share their knowledge about the recreation opportunities and processes available in the community, regardless of who sponsors or offers them, or influences behavior through leisure counseling and consulting, they are providing a program service. They are aiding the citizenry to engage in meaningful recreation experiences just as much as they do when they provide facilities or supervise activity. Some constituents only want or need this level of service. Once they know what is available (leisure information) or how to prepare their equipment (technical assistance) or what are the costs involved in developing different hobbies upon retirement (leisure counseling), they can act accordingly. Adults are certainly more likely to seek out leisure counseling services than are youth; the same may be said about those who ask for technical assistance services. They want the recreation and park agency to respond to their request for aid rather than their being dependent upon the department's schedule and activity offerings for some of their recreation experiences.

The fourth and final program thrust involves learning. Interpretive services, activity instruction, and skill development classes are examples of educational program efforts. Like the information approach, the end result of this element of programming is the freeing of the participant, making him/her more knowledgeable and self-reliant about his/her leisure. Although appropriate for all lifestyles and life stages, the means by which instruction and learning occur should vary. Certain methods are more appropriate for specific lifestyles than they are for others; then, too, certain techniques are more appropriate for those in one life stage than they are for those in another stage.

The more diversified the populations served, the more diverse the program approach and program structure must be. If the recreation and park movement is to develop its own body of knowledge and maintain its viability as a profession, it must integrate contemporary theories of sociology and developmental psychology into its methods and techniques of programming. The organized park and recreation profession exists to provide a service so that people might have more meaningful leisure expression. To measure against this objective, recreation and park professionals must recognize the diversity of interests, lifestyles, and age groups (life stages) of its citizenry and program accordingly.

REFERENCES

1. Cheek, Neil H., Jr. and William R. Burch, Jr. *The Social Organization of Leisure in Human Society*. New York: Harper and Row, 1976, 283 pp.
2. Nash, Jay B. *Philosophy of Recreation and Leisure*. St. Louis: The C. V. Mosby Company, 1953, 222 pp.
3. Brighthill, Charles K. *Man and Leisure*. Englewood Cliff, N.J.: Prentice-Hall, 1961, 292 pp.
4. Neugarten, Bernice L. "Developmental Perspective," *Reading in Gerontology* by V. M. Brantl and St. M. R. Brown. St. Louis: The C. V. Mosby Company, 1973, p. 33.
5. Yoesting, Dean R. and Burkhead, Dan L. "Significance of Childhood Recreation Experience on Adult Leisure Behavior: An Exploratory Analysis." *Journal of Leisure Research*, Vol. 5, No. 1, 1973, pp. 25-36.
6. Havighurst, R. J. and Feigenbaum, K. "Leisure and Life Style," *American Journal of Sociology*, Vol. 64, 1959, pp. 396-404.
7. Loofts, William R. "Socialization in a Life-Span Perspective: White Elephants, Worms and Will-O-the-Wisps." *The Gerontologist*, Vol. 13, No. 4, 1973. pp. 488-496.

Chapter Fifteen

An Enabling Approach to Leisure Service Delivery

James F. Murphy

> "Give a man a fish, as the saying goes, and you are helping him a little bit for a very short while; teach him the art of fishing and he can help himself all his life. On a higher level: supply him with fishing tackle; this will cost you a good deal of money and the result remains doubtful; but even if fruitful, the man's continuing livelihood will still be dependent upon you for replacements. But teach him to make his own fishing tackle and you have helped him to become not only self-supporting, but also self-reliant and independent."[1]

The delivery of community recreation and leisure services is characterized by sameness. Managers and workers in leisure service agencies have been chiefly concerned about the organization as an end and the mass packaging of activities for clients as a means. Conformity has defined for recreation and leisure service organizations the rules of play and procedures for the planning of areas and facilities. Deviance from the norm, spontaneity and innovation are often questioned, even suppressed. This method of leisure service programming and planning, reflected in the direct service approach, grossly limits human endeavor, particularly for the participant.

We have come to a point in our development as a community service in which decisions must be made regarding our service approach during the last two decades of the twentieth century. A dilemma persists which requires us to discard existing programming models which tend to support a consumption-pleasure ethic (characteristic of a continued growth society scenario) at the expense of an ecological/holistic ethos (characteristic of a steady-state society scenario) and advocacy of simpler, interdependent life styles.

At the *core* of the dilemma of which path to pursue is the often misguided, unintentional, bankrupt philosophical and operational perspective of the recreation and park movement—discretionary time. Despite each new unfolding of our understanding of human behavior as it relates to leisure, we continue to support a network based on a discretionary time concept and therefore a perspective which is couched in a linear, industrial rhythm of life.

Discretionary time is that portion of time which remains when work and the basic requirements for existence have been satisfied. Leisure is discretionary or unobligated time, a concept which parallels the economic concept of discretionary money. Time falls into three classes: time for existence (sleeping, eating, meeting biological requirements); time for subsistence (working at one's job); and leisure (time remaining after the basic necessities of life and work requirements have been accomplished).

The glorification of work owing principally to the Industrial Revolution led to the separation of work and leisure, and an emphasis on economically productive functions as the most significant aspects of life, with the eventual relegation of leisure to the status of "spare time." When viewing leisure as discretionary time or free time one must recognize the description is based on the leisure experience being determined by and set apart from work. This frequently accepted conceptualization of leisure, serving as the premise upon which the formal organization of recreation and leisure service agencies operate, is misleading and erroneous in organizational design. This single-factor concept, based on the premise that one's occupation stemming from the organization of work, has become accepted as the primary determining element of all other aspects of one's everyday life, including leisure.

This perspective, however, has meaning for fewer and fewer people. It ignores the disabled, women, non-white racial minorities, older persons and individuals who don't work at all. Contributing to the dilemma of the leisure service programmer is that social organization in contemporary North America is increasingly representative of diverse, flexible, cyclical, and holistic life rhythms.

Our field has attempted to fit in with society's prescriptions for what is considered normal, appropriate behavior. Leisure becomes defined in this process as "happiness adjustment protocol." People are encouraged, guided, and even controlled in their pursuits of enjoyable self-expressive behavior off the job. What has developed is a "leisure myopia" which has led to institutional racism, sexism, ageism, and handicappism within society. The recreation and park movement serves largely as the fulcrum, albeit perhaps unintentionally, providing the necessary leverage for this behavior to be promoted. Utilizing a discretionary time perspective as the only philosophical basis for leisure service programming is nearsighted. It serves only to keep people where they are; it perpetuates the myth of an industrial rhythm of life; it limits the development of human potential and reduces the prospects for a high standard for quality of life, two important goals of leisure service agencies.

SHIFT IN LEISURE IDEOLOGY

The gradual shift in values, life styles and tastes among people is resulting in the requests for a leisure ideology and management system to embrace them. The leisure service administrator today finds that previous professional training, educational preparation and successful service delivery methods and programs may no longer be effective in meeting the current expectations of leisure consumers.

Leisure service administrators must continually strike a balance between achieving practical accomplishment with theoretical analysis. This delicate combination of management demands that the administrator who is bombarded by community constituents, government regulatory agencies, consumer rights forces, and the exploding research and information environment of the university setting, must develop a "workable" theoretical framework from which to operate on a daily basis. The administrator must seek to blend all of the responsibilities of planning, organizing, staffing, directing, and controlling involved in management within the context of the continually changing framework of human values and relationships in community life. *All* leisure service practitioners must have meaningful guidelines to direct their own lives and to facilitate opportunities for others. These guidelines must be founded on a sound philosophical premise. By embracing philosophy the administrator is better able to appraise existing knowledge, beliefs and human relations and is more likely to evolve a systematic and coherent plan of life in general and provide more astute professional focus in order to determine what is important and significant.

Much of the knowledge base, values and beliefs which guided the recreation movement in general and the development of agency approaches to serving people's leisure experiences specifically, have essentially been characterized by a *continued growth* oriented society. A continued growth society has been represented by the system goals which have dominated the industrial era (e.g., material progress, individualism, freedom of enterprise, few constraints on capital accumulation, social responsibility mainly the concern of government rather than other institutions). These larger goals have been approached through a set of fundamental subgoals (e.g., efficiency, productivity, material wealth, continued growth of production, consumption and technological and manipulative power).

Industrializing goods and services has resulted in the creation of an insatiable consumer demand. Some people have argued that the continuation of this type of society will counteract human ends, represented by the demand for enriching work roles, resource conservation environmental enhancement and equitable sharing of the world's resources. One other possible scenario for the future, a *steady-state* society, which would result in a movement toward "voluntary simplicity" characterized by lowered material consumption, increased emphasis on community, inner exploration, relationship to nature and meaningful work, appears to be the most viable alternative for the future. This latter approach, while projecting seemingly worthwhile images on human relationships and community life, nonetheless serves as a threat to most current social institutions and is deemed untenable by many recreation and leisure service organizations.

A continued growth society, while leading to run-away inflation, high unemployment, environmental imbalances, and a consumption-convenience way of life representative of a growing number of people, has made available leisure resources and opportunities and led to an accepted profession of leisure services. However, with a constantly changing and dynamic society, the social fabric of community life reflective of a continued growth state has become depersonalized and fragmented for many and various forms of human association, rituals and ceremony have broken down altogether. Community life, representative of work, family and leisure, are inseparable components of living and essential ingredients to human life. Leisure involves social interaction, celebration, mastery and self-expression. These are *not* segmented aspects of living; they are a part of life. However, because of the influences of industrialization and technology which have severed family ties by freeing individuals to express their life styles independently of others and divided and weaned craftsmanship from work, there is an increasing need for recreation and leisure service administrators to work toward the improvement of the quality of life by rejecting discretionary time as the only leisure concept and assisting in the unification of the fragmented parts of community life by adopting a more holistic/ecological leisure conceptualization as a philosophy of service delivery.

The steady-state scenario seeks to reconcile growth in human terms with a high quality of life. It suggests at least three ethics to the leisure service administrator to consider when evolving a service delivery plan: 1) an *ecological ethic*, which recognizes the limited nature of resources, sees Homo sapien as an integral part of the natural world, hence inseparable from its governing processes and laws. The ecological ethic fosters a sense of the total community and responsibility for the fate of the planet, and relates self-interest to the interests of fellow human beings and future generations; 2) a *self-realization* ethic, which asserts the proper end of all individual experience is the further development of the emergent self of human species. The appropriate function of *all* social institutions is to create an environment which will foster that process. The self-realization ethic would push society toward the restructuring of social institutions to satisfy the individual's need to full participation in society. As corollaries to this ethic, self-determination of individuals and minority groups should be fostered, and social decision-making should be decentralized; and 3) an *holistic ethic*, which sees meaning and satisfaction in both work and leisure. The freedom, relationships and satisfactions that develop and express our humanity cannot be allocated to either work or leisure. Rather, each may be designed and developed to maximize the realization of the fullest human values.

Altogether, these three ethics—one emphasizing the total community of homo sapien-in-nature and oneness of the human race, another the placing of the highest value on the development of selfhood and finally the latter expressive of an integration of life through the human ordering of both work and leisure in a unified life space—encourage both cooperation and desirable individual achievement and opportunity for a fusion of life roles.

HUMAN DEVELOPMENT AND LEISURE

Since the early 1970's the Recreation and Park Movement in North America has been marked by a growing concern for the individual and qualitative improvement of community life. The progression toward a humanistic, ecological based human service field suggests that the Recreation and Park Movement is beginning to recognize and increasingly manifest an enabler or community catalyst approach to service delivery in an effort to optimize human growth potential and mobilize a sense of community throughout neighborhoods in cities and towns. Social change has been most readily evident by shifts in program orientation, the adoption of a broadened and more flexible service perspective, altered role models of professional staff, new career areas, and shifting emphasis in university curricula. An important catalyst within the recreation and park movement that helped accelerate the reexamination of its direction was the Gray-Greben position paper, "Redefining Leisure: An Action Plan for the Recreation and Park Movement," presented at the National Congress for Recreation and Parks in Washington, D.C., in 1973. A series of workshops, forums, and action plans followed as a result of the recognition that the "activity" centered service delivery approach that had guided the movement for over 50 years was no longer a useful and relevant operational model of service. It was argued that the end of a recreation experience was not activity, that it was merely a means to satisfy a full range of needs– the goal of recreation experience, they stated, was human development.

This perspective is important given the technological thrust of North America and the growing recognition that there are several life paths, each of which may lead to productive, enriching lives for people. Recreation and leisure service agencies increasingly have come to recognize that there is a diversity of human values and that efforts should be made to allow for divergent life style patterns of behavior.

The current human development phase is also characterized as ecologically based, in which recreation and leisure service agencies are concerned with interrelationships among people in their physical and social environments and the ways these relationships contribute or hinder their ability to realize their human potential. This new humanistic strategy of programming is seen as a more active approach to human service in an effort to satisfy total human needs, ranging from physical and social to self-esteem and self-actualization, and minimize barriers to participation in community life before they occur. Leisure service agencies have as much responsibility to provide worthwhile leisure opportunities for people as they do assisting community agencies prevent unhealthy or restrictive situations which hinder individuals from realizing outlets for self-expression.

LEISURE SERVICE DELIVERY CONTINUUM

The concept of leisure service delivery within a humanistic framework implies two general goals: 1) making available through an event or series of experiences, opportunities for human expression which enable a person to grow in dignity and self-worth and develop to the fullest of one's capacity; 2) removal of barriers which impede or prohibit participation because of social, physical, racial or sexist discrimination. Traditional service delivery models have tended to recognize a singular approach to meeting people's leisure needs. A direct service approach, dominated by a centralized agency is the predominant model. Typically, the agency takes exclusive responsibility for planning and organizing programs, scheduling areas and facilities, and developing organizational priorities.

Figure 1
Leisure Service Delivery System–Approaches to Program Delivery

------Direct ---------------------------- Broker ------------------------------ Enabler----------
Service (Information and Referral) Community Catalyst

Direct Service	Broker (Information and Referral)	Enabler Community Catalyst

In effect, the recreation and leisure agency preassembles the essential program ingredients (e.g., leadership, materials, facilities, etc.) to create a number of immediate, ready-made participation opportunities. The participants' basic task is to pick and choose, "cafeteria style," from an array of opportunities made available to them. For the most part, then, participation opportunities are prescribed by the agency's professional staff. When utilizing this programming process, the agency assumes total responsibility for decisions made. The participant is provided "expert" opinion and guidance and the result is the public's consumption of a ready-made product.

An intermediary approach, the broker role, involves the recreation worker acting as a liaison, a large part of the total activity being devoted to putting people in touch with community resources they need but are either not aware of or cannot locate. When utilizing this approach leisure service personnel must be aware of all of the potential human service agencies and facilities which may assist in providing opportunities for participants to meet needs not otherwise fulfilled by a single agency. This approach encourages collective action on the part of community agencies.

In the future, recreation and leisure service personnel will need to give careful consideration to an enabling process in order to extend the leisure service delivery continuum to include a spectrum of programming which will account for a wider diversity of human expression. This process recognizes two important considerations: 1) no one agency, relying on its own resources, can possibly meet all the leisure needs of a community and 2) individuals can effectively describe their leisure needs and interests. In this process the recreator acts as a catalyst and serves as a link between participant groups and all the leisure opportunity resources available to them. In such a process, public involvement at all levels is *critical* to developing viable program services or helping the participant function effectively in society. Recreators become community figures. The "chain-link fence" mentality Dr. David Gray has warned us against, and characteristic of the direct service provider approach, must not become a general pattern of leisure service delivery. Such a facility oriented perspective results in recreation personnel being responsible not for the development of people, but for the management of people, the management of a center, referral service or activity dissemination operation, or with supervision of grounds or computer print-out sheets.

NEEDED GOALS AND PROCESSES

In more specific terms, the goals of an enabling leisure service approach which is oriented to facilitating participant independence while fostering community interdependence, are:

1. to develop the community member's capacity to solve his or her own problems. This might mean establishing advisory boards or recreation councils made up of a cross-section of community residents. These councils might survey existing conditions and then recommend ways to improve current conditions;
2. to make use of outside human services and resources. The leisure service agency must be knowledgeable about and initiate comprehensive planning and coordination of existing social services. There is an increasing emphasis on incorporating an interdisciplinary approach—synergistic programming—a process of combining the resources of more than one agency to produce leisure service which could not be carried out successfully by one agency acting alone;
3. to recognize and meet community needs. A needs assessment process and plan should be developed by each agency to correctly measure the extent of service delivery needs, gaps, and areas of duplication;
4. to view leisure services as an holistic entity and community problems as an outgrowth of the total environment. In order for an individual to realize self-fulfillment, other basic needs (e.g., physical and safety needs) must be fulfilled. This will require leisure service personnel to serve as community catalysts to assume several roles interchangeably.

In the enabling process, participants in leisure service offerings must be responsible for their own change. Brill suggests that one of the basic tenets of the philosophical foundation of human services is that "fundamental change must come from within"[2] but that an outside force can facilitate it. The worker acts as a catalyst to set in motion the conditions and forces that help lead to change. The catalyst approach is illustrated by Brill in the following structure of the worker's activities:

"1. Engagement—involving oneself in the situation, establishing communication, and formulating preliminary hypotheses for the problem.

2. Assessment—appraising the situation on the basis of data—facts, feelings, persons, circumstances.

3. Definition of the problem—formulating the need.

4. Setting of goals—the end toward which the effort is to be directed.

5. Selection of alternative methods and an initial mode of interven-

tion—looking at all the possible ways of tackling the problem and selecting the most propitious one.

6. Establishment of a contract—agreeing on a definition of the roles and responsibilities of the participants.
7. Action leading toward the desired goal—the work that is necessary.
8. Evaluation—weighing the outcome of action in terms of success or failure.
9. Continuation or termination of ongoing contact based on repetition of this process."[3]

The central premise of Brill's "scientific method" of working with people is that people have a need and a right to be involved in decisions on matters that concern them.

Figure 2
The Ongoing Process of the Community Catalyst

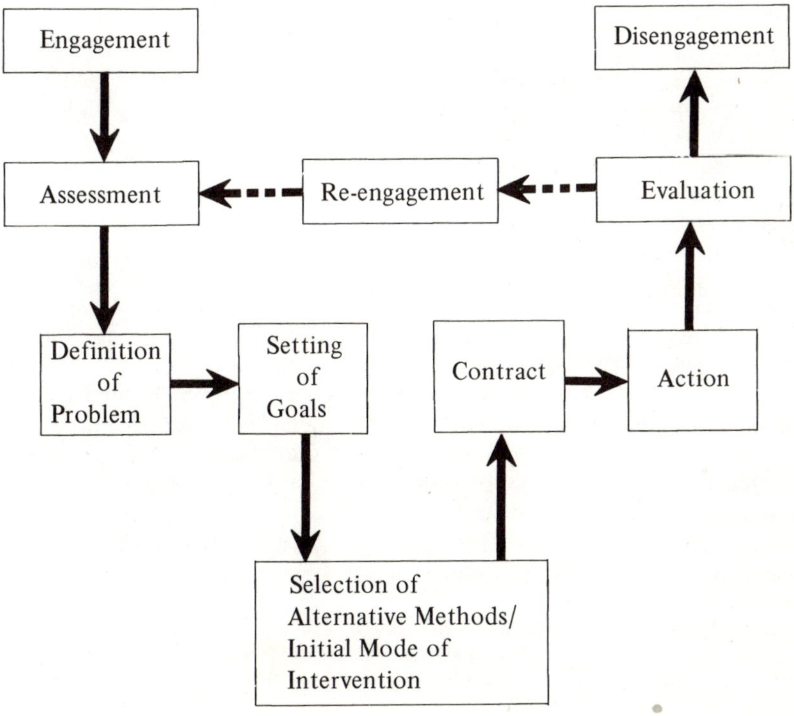

AGENCIES WHICH ENABLE SELF-RELIANCE AND INDEPENDENCE

Some examples of self-help organizations in which catalysts are enabling individuals and groups to move toward independence include the following:

1. *Take a Giant Step (TAGS).* A group of visually impaired individuals ranging in age from six to over 21 share a common interest in learning to deal with their complete or partial loss of sight. The goal of TAGS is for members to learn to be independent. This is achieved by participants who learn to cook, clean house, write checks, and count money as well as roller skate, have parties and go on hikes. They engage in social and educational programs both as a self-contained group and with non-visually impaired groups. In the latter instance they assume responsibility for their own affairs. The program enables people to develop the skills to do different things than they do in their home or school environment.

2. *Self-Determination.* This organization has developed as an alliance of individuals and groups who recognize the need to develop supportive communities. The goal is to build a statewide network (in California) of people who are exploring the day-to-day realities of living and politicking a positive vision of society and are interested in ongoing efforts at personal and social change. This is accomplished through a self-determined framework centered around three functions: 1) promoting an awareness that there is an intimate connection between personal values and political acts; 2) developing the tools essential to improving our personal effectiveness and our political environment; and 3) generating a personally supportive, localized network to initiate and sustain efforts at personal and political-social change.

   The approach of Self-Determination applies to the leisure service field in that by facilitating individuals to become connecting points of a network, each person gains the opportunity for helping and being helped. The network provides an empowering structure to improve the relationships with everything and everyone around us. This is an effort to confront powerlessness and disenchantment head-on, by fostering community "core groups" and wider network affiliation for the purpose of mutual personal support and a shared commitment in public things.

   Some of the specific programs pursued by Self-Determination potentially applicable to leisure service agencies incorporating a catalyst approach are:

   a) networking: an effort to confront powerlessness and disenchantment by developing community "core groups."

b) resource exchange system: a method of continuous intersecting of exchange information, ideas, talent, experience, programs and support between those with specific knowledge and experience and people or groups seeking knowledge or experience.

c) quarterly journal: a publication by and for members and the general public which discusses alternatives in life-styles, institutions and politics.

d) public dialogue program: the organization fosters a continuing exchange with those seeking public office or exercising formal authority at every decision-making setting or level of government.

e) personal/political skills workshop: this provides local communities with personal growth opportunities and interactions with political skills and processes.

3. *Parents Without Partners, Inc.* An organization serving the needs of widowed, divorced, separated or never married persons who are raising children alone through a support system and network for single parents who often find themselves isolated from society. They provide discussion programs, professional speakers, study newsletters and international publications. The basic effort of the organization is to help an individual reshape his/her life to meet the unpredictable conditions of single-parenthood, and become self-determining community members. The existence of such an organization points out that so many of the existing social institutions tend to cater only to the more traditional two-parent nuclear family concept when developing and offering programs and services.

4. *National Self-Help Clearinghouse.* This national information and referral clearinghouse organization serves to provide resources to those seeking help. It is estimated that there are over five million people (in the United States alone) who are members of several hundred types of self-help groups (like those described above). It is suggested that the increasing popularity of such groups represent a growing anti-professional mood and dissatisfaction on the part of the public with traditional governmental services (as witnessed at the close of the 1970's with the passage of Proposition 13 in California which set limits on local government). The existence of such an information and referral organization to serve as a broker for people seeking to become more self-reliant and less dependent on direct service agencies which do not meet their needs, appears to be providing a new direction in human service delivery program structure. This development seems to be paving the way for more self-help organizations which are oriented to providing people a greater

measure of autonomy in running their own lives within a community support network.

The goals of enablers of leisure expression in any leisure setting should focus on facilitating the growth potential of individuals and eliminating barriers which restrict human expression. Preserving a dependent relationship with a participant, although an inadvertent or unconscious process, still results in an individual requiring the agency's decision-making bureaucratic staff to make "choices" for him or her and thereby restrict growth potential. Certainly, enablers have a similar responsibility to not only point out areas where community members need to address aspects of service which reduce full participation in day-to-day living, but they similarly must assist the public to assume responsibility for their actions and behavior as it intersects with others. All professional recreators must come to understand that an important role should be to ensure that the civil and human rights of all individuals are not unjustly restricted from leisure expression and that people have full and complete accessibility in order to realize their leisure needs.

FACILITATING THE "GOOD LIFE"

We are approaching the time when the "good life" can no longer be defined solely in terms of increasing material wealth and of consumption of leisure activities which deplete energy and non-renewable resources. Considering the extent to which the notion of continual growth in material affluence permeates our personal and social values, life-styles, and institutions, the transition to a steady-state society could (and does) cause serious problems as well as create unprecedented opportunities. Already many communities in California, who felt the impact of serious revenue reductions following the Proposition 13 enactment, have had to redesign their whole delivery systems, revenue procedures, jobs which were duplicated in various departments, and in general become more self-sustaining and less wasteful units.

The key to a successful conversion from the discretionary time, "activity" leisure philosophical program delivery model to a holistic/ecological/humanistic philosophical model will necessitate administrators, educators, and practitioners to decide (as everyone living in society) what type of society they feel leisure services should support and reflect. It is apparent that an important role for recreation and leisure service personnel in the future would be to recognize the personal and societal conditions that would facilitate and encourage self-generated, non-consumptive, spontaneous leisure and make this a viable alternative to leisure activities dependent upon material goods and energy and the continual use of leisure agency personnel, time and resources. This potential role involves the consideration of two separate but complementary issues: 1) how to develop an individual's capabilities for self-generated leisure; 2) how to design the relevant environments, facilities and resources to be compatible with these leisure activities and experiences.

The growing self- and social-consciousness with respect to the governance of public and private bureaucracies has led to the need on the part of human service agencies to facilitate more participation in this governance by the people being served. There is an increasing recognition that a more flexible and pluralistic philosophical perspective is needed to fit with the requirements of a qualitatively oriented civilization, one which emphasizes relationships and experiences rather than things and possessions. We have tended to identify our private concerns regarding our relationships, work and leisure as stemming from personal deficiencies and not societal problems. We tend to remain isolated and attempt to solve these problems on our own. This may involve taking growth-centered therapy programs to enable us to be better equipped to "cope" with life. Certainly there are benefits from such courses or experiences but there is a need to take personal problems and relate them to larger institutional structures and work with other people in a community support network (refer to Self-Determination, an organization which is dedicated to fostering self-reliance and community interdependence) to overcome root causes for alientation, anxiety, depression, boredom and dissatisfaction that are endemic within institutions. The traditional approach to most leisure service program models (direct service approach) involves principally a personal (isolated) experience. We need to create a sense of community, where self-generated skills can be practiced and shared with others.

SUMMARY

We have reached an era—the second hundred years of organized recreation in North America—where individuals comprising various age groups, social class, gender, occupational groups, or stage of human development, must be granted the opportunity to participate in activities of their own choosing and treated impartially, without regard to discriminatory class divisions, sex role stereotyping or other arbitrary forms of social or physical restrictions. Additionally, there is a paramount need for recreation and leisure service agencies to recognize the fragile state of the ecosystem and better perceive the direct relationship between leisure expression and the quality of life.

The evaluation of the enabling service delivery approach–which extends the leisure service delivery system to be more encompassing of diverse individual needs–is primarily a response to the desire by people for engagement in self-help processes in the community context and elimination of dependency creating direct service leadership methods. The enabling concept of program delivery serves both as a process and political strategy. The dominant facility dependent, direct service delivery method is ecologically unsound, fragments the recreation experience from the rest of a person's total development and results in the agencies "fitting people in" to predetermined behavior patterns based on archaic roles no longer functional or acceptable.

Since the first Earth Day held on April 22, 1970, the environmental impact on decisions made on our growth patterns, including housing, production and manufacturing, waste disposal, transportation, nuclear energy, and recreation has steadily increased. We have all learned about the interrelated life support system that exists on earth and the dangers of unrestricted growth. The recreation professional in the years ahead will become a more viable part of the community to the extent he or she participates as a team member with others in a mutual approach, facilitating life enhancement for everyone. Recreators cannot continue to arbitrarily encourage some forms of human expression (particularly those which result in the consumption and waste of non-renewable resources) while denying others without understanding the environmental impact and worth of such decisions.

If the recreation and park movement is to be oriented toward the fulfillment of human needs and concerned about the development of people and not just the provision of "things to do" or activities to "fill up people's free time," we must become more responsive to total community needs and problems and utilize a multi-service approach and extend the service delivery continuum to serve the whole person. By acting as an enabler, recreators become stewards of an individual's right of leisure expression and responsibility for understanding the impact and relationship of one's decisions in the community as a whole.

REFERENCES

1. Schumacher, E. F. *Small is Beautiful.* London: Spere Books Ltd., 1974. p. 165.
2. Brill, Naomi. *Working With People: The Helping Process.* Philadelphia: J.B. Lippincott Company, 1973. p. 71.
3. *Ibid.*, p. 72.

Chapter Sixteen

Of Godots and Goodbars: On Waiting and Looking For Change

Thomas L. Goodale

An often repeated short dialogue may be a useful beginning. It's a brief exchange between a native and a missionary.

> Native: "If I didn't know about God and sin, would I go to hell?"
> Missionary: "If you didn't know. . .well, no you wouldn't go to hell."
> Native: "Then why are you telling me these things?"

There is little doubt, anymore, that during the closing decades of this century we will experience change; perhaps as rapid, pervasive, and dramatic as at any time in our history. And there is no doubt about which shoulders the burden of change rests upon, ". . .the cutting edge of social change works at the level of the individual. Social change is change in an aggregate of individuals."[1] For a number of reasons, those working in the field of recreation, especially those employed by government at the municipal level, will be "front and center" through these decades of change and will bear their share and more of the burden.

WE SHOULD CHANGE

First, even in a welfare state, the direct provision of recreation services is a peripheral rather than a central task of government. That does not, in any sense, diminish the importance of recreation or the legitimacy of government involvement. Rather, the nature of government involvement is at issue, as is the nature of recreation. The provision of recreation services through a large and complex organizational and institutional framework may, in fact, be antithetical to the nature of recreation; blocking rather than opening paths to the goals we espouse. This fundamental problem has been addressed by philosophers and utopians – Plato and Mill, Bellamy and Orwell for example – of every age. Bertrand Russell summarized it well more than 60 years ago:

> The problem which faces the modern world is the combination of individual initiative with the increase in the scope and size of organizations. Unless it is solved, individuals will grow less and less full of

> life and vigor, more and more passively submissive to conditions imposed upon them. A society composed of such individuals cannot be progressive or add much to the world's stock of mental and spiritual possessions.[2]

WE MUST CHANGE

The second major reason why recreationists will be shouldering the burden of change is that most of the indicators of the decline (failure, demise, crisis, bankruptcy, etc.) of the present institutional order point to problems to which the recreation movement has always addressed itself. Perhaps the problems would have been worse if the recreation movement had not been concerned about them. And certainly recreation can't be faulted for the world's ills. Still, the problems remain, and remain the concern of recreationists in particular. Among indicators of failure, and consequently the need for dramatic change are, according to one of America's leading futurists, Willis Harman:

> decreased sense of community;
> increased sense of alienation and purposelessness;
> increased frequency of personal disorders and mental illness;
> increased rate of violent crime;
> increased frequency and severity of social disruptions;
> increased use of police to control behavior;
> increased public acceptance of hedonistic behavior (particularly sexual), of symbols of degradation, and of lax public morality;
> increased interest in non-institutionalized religious practices (e.g. cults, rituals, secret practices);
> signs of specific and conscious anxiety about the future;
> in some cases, economic inflation.[3]

As has frequently been noted, recreationists have been trying diligently, through organizations and institutions, to forestall or resolve these problems and the recreation movement has been drawn along in the development of a vast, public, social service system during the past several decades. But the problems remain; some suggest that we have made conditions worse through our well intended efforts to make them better. More and better of the same, we now recognize, will not help. What is required is different; not re-doubling our efforts or even reform. What is required is change.

New genres of literature have emerged in the past several years; notably the literature of crisis and transformation. We have, it seems, a population crisis, a food crisis, an economic crisis, an energy crisis, an urban crisis, a government crisis, and an environmental crisis. At the root of all this is said to be a crisis in values. Much recent literature has been devoted to discussions of "old" and "new" values, transforming values, and shifting from these values to those. But another genre of literature has emerged which suggests a crisis related to but perhaps even deeper than the crisis of values. It is a crisis, variously, of spirit, hope, courage, or will evident in the writings of Fromm, Tillich, May, and many others. Unless that crisis is solved, none of the others can be. And without intending "gloom and doom," Alexander Solzhenitsyn, in his widely debated 1978 commencement address at Harvard University, noted that, historically, the loss of spirit marked the beginning of the end.

The difference between a crisis of values and a crisis of spirit, hope, will or courage is important in another respect. The former exists at the social, organizational, institutional level; the latter exists at the individual level. As Kristol writes:

> "A crisis in values is something that happens *out there.* It is something you can cope with through rational manipulation of institutions, of beliefs, of ideas. A spiritual crisis is something that happens to *you* – deep down – and that you have to cope with. Therefore the phrase crisis in values can mislead by emphasizing what is essentially a technological approach to a problem that is not technological; this technological approach asks; how do we look at society; how do we manipulate it; how do we shape it in such a way that we don't have a crisis in values? I don't think that's the way. Real spiritual crises are resolved not by social science but by mysterious cultural processes which somehow reach inside every human being."[4]

Thus the indicators of widespread, systematic failures and the need for change relate particularly, but of course not exclusively, to the recreation field and the burden of change it must bear. And if the most fundamental crisis is not environment or population, or even values, but spirit and hope and courage and will, then the burden rests on the shoulders of individual recreationists and not on our agencies, organizations, or institutions.

Perhaps a brief, practical illustration will clarify the point and show the cutting edge in operation. A few months ago I had the opportunity to converse at length with about 35 recreationists employed in two Ontario municipalities. The informal interviews ranged into the future, dealing with goals, values, aspirations and the like for the society, their respective agencies and themselves. Materialistic and consumptive values and aspirations came under attack many times, and there seemed a longing for a conserver society and simpler and more authentic lifestyles. It was often mentioned, too, although with an air of chagrin, resignation or sometimes anger and frustration, that for the past three or four years, salary increases had been about six percent – significantly below annual increases in the cost-of-living – consequently they were falling further and further behind. Can it be that materialism is an "out there" notion while falling behind in salary is something that reaches deep down?

WE WILL CHANGE

The third reason why the burden of change rests heavily on the field of recreation, on individual recreationists, and particularly on those working in municipal government agencies is that our social-political-economic situation is already bringing about change. Slow growth is the underlying characteristic of our situation now and for the forseeable future. Slow growth in population, especially the decline in birthrate to below replacement levels in North America and other "advanced" nations, is one element of this situation. The reshaping of age distribution from a pyramid to a diamond has consequences more far reaching than a shift from mainly child and youth oriented recreation services to serving adults and seniors more than previously. The impact on schools, teachers, local taxes, transfers of funds from other governments for education and other consequences is just one, albeit highly visible, example. Slow population growth also contributes to the present and foreseeable future situation of slow economic growth.

Inflation alone results in a smaller economy and at the present time the annual rate of inflation in the U.S. and Canada is about ten percent. Stagflation has recently entered our vocabularies to cover an economic period characterized by high rates of inflation and unemployment, both at the same time. In a global village, every nation's economy is shaped by international economic forces; the cartel of the major oil producing nations and the increasing industrial capacity of developing nations, among them. Slow growth, and perhaps eventually no growth – material growth at least – is the major force already reshaping our present situation and certain to shape our future.

The consequences of these changes in the economy and in the age distribution of the population are already being felt by many. Some examples are widely recognized; affecting the world of work, families, and government, and they apply to recreationists as individuals as well as employees. Work: increased competition for jobs; less job mobility; slower advancement for younger employees; increased frustration with conservative managers and administrators at the top; those with several years in a position "locked in" or "priced out" of other positions; unemployment and underemployment. Families: more two-income families in order to acquire today's standard necessities and modest amenities; more children and teen-agers on their own much of the time; pinched "discretionary" income forcing harder choices; more marital stress related to finances and to child rearing; alternative "family" groupings. Government: increasingly costly government sponsored social welfare programs for children and teens, the unemployed, and the growing number of retired and elderly persons; larger and costlier programs to combat alcoholism and other social problems; higher taxes when there is already widespread public concern with the size and cost of government in relation to its perceived efficiency and effectiveness.

The dilemma confronting government – increasing demands for government sponsored programs and services on one hand, and increasing concern about the present size and cost of government on the other – is a difficult one. "Proposition 13," a phrase understood everywhere in North America and in overseas places as well, had, as one significant consequence, a serious demoralizing effect on the public service in California.[5] Low morale among government employees at all levels seems a universal problem.

The impact of increased demand and increased disenchantment about the size and cost of government is felt most, but not exclusively of course, at the local government level, despite the fact that most people believe the efficiency and effectiveness of local government is greater than that at federal, or state or provincial levels. Diseconomies of scale alone warrant that belief. That the impact is felt most by local government is related to accessibility and familiarity and also to the tax structure. The bulk of local taxes is raised through the property tax, an annual visible bite taken after other taxes (income, sales, etc.) have already been paid. In a sense, property taxes are paid out of "after tax" dollars. Despite the fact that only a small proportion of an individual's or family's total tax burden is for municipal purposes, the impact of taxpayers discontent is felt first, and most, at the local government level.

After two or three decades of successfully competing for local tax dollars and good treatment in the hands of local taxpayers and politicians, "leisure service" expenditures have declined as a proportion of municipal government spending during the past decade or so.[6] It appears, too, that personnel expenditures, while still taking the lion's share, are decreasing as a proportion of leisure service spending. A review of budgets for six cities in Ontario for the years 1974 and 1978 revealed that while the combined budget increases totaled nearly $8,000,000, only 30 new, full-time positions were added. (If the average salary was $14,000, this accounts for only 5 percent of the total increase. Without detailed data, one can still safely guess that the increases must be due to inflation – energy costs and current capital expenditures – and probably debt service, both important budget items after salaries and wages).

What seems clear from all this is that we have created a large and complex array of public agencies and have "institutionalized" recreation as part of the total government social service system. It also seems clear that the recreation institution, if not the whole social service structure, cannot be sustained and we are caught having created demands and expectations that probably can't be met. This point has been argued by many, but perhaps none more cogently than Geoffrey Vickers:

> If our world is to survive for another generation in any form which we today should regard as worth striving for, I have no doubt that for everyone, what we expect of ourselves and each other will have to go up and that for most of us in the western world what we expect of the system will have to go down.[7]

WE ESPOUSE CHANGE

The fourth reason recreation and recreationists must bear the burden of change is that for many years now, we have professed to want change. We even prided ourselves on being "change agents." And we have experienced in recent years a period of critical self-analysis, and either evolution or devolution to a philosophy suggesting quite different service modes than those characterized by direct provision of programs and facilities, telling our constituents about ourselves and encouraging them to participate with us.

Like Bertrand Russell, we want people to grow more full of life and vigor; we want to promote individual initiative. Is that not what we mean when we speak of learning, growth, development, positive health, self-actualization? Like Irving Kristol, we are concerned about what happens inside individuals, deep down. Is that not what we mean when we speak of individuation and holism, of qualitative dimensions and experiential qualities and therefore our subjective and intuitive selves? Like Geoffrey Vickers, we want people to rely more on themselves and each other rather than on the institutional complex of leisure services. Is that not what we mean when we speak of citizen participation and involvement and community development, and of self-sufficiency and self-determination? These and so many other voices are not singing a dirge; they're singing our song. That it may sound like a dirge merely illustrates that change is difficult, and sometimes threatening and abrasive. It may mean, too, that recreation is not institutionalized but recreationists are.

The roles and functions we have defined for ourselves during the past several years, and thus a service mode different from programmer and provider are widely accepted, at least among recreationists. So we have come to describe ourselves as educators, advocates, facilitators, enablers, catalysts, animators, encouragers, and developers. Still, this is more the idea than the practice.

WITHOUT GODOT OR GOODBAR

Godot, in the form of organizational or institutional change, is not likely to appear. What we get is reorganization. Petronius Arbiter, in the year 210 B.C., noted: "I was to learn late in life that we tend to meet any new situation by reorganizing; and what a wonderful method it can be for creating the illusion of progress while producing confusion, inefficiency, and demoralization." Creative organizations, we have found, tend to be characterized by small size and autonomy.[8] Neither of these conditions obtain in most municipal recreation agencies, and only size may be characteristic of others. Organizational development, however widely touted, may be beyond us. As Donald Michael has noted, this requires years of effort and a champion at the top who can control the organization's resources and boundaries; requirements not found in government. Further:

> The personal and interpersonal skills and flexibilities needed to cope with the emotional and intellectual burdens of the changeover and the operating situation far exceed those that most people seem to possess, and certainly exceed those that organizations, particularly public agencies, reward.[9]

Chris Arygris carries the argument further in discussing "Some Limits on Rational Man Organization Theory." He notes a process by which individuals become passive, lose a sense of being an origin or cause, deny or suppress their own self-actualizing needs, and rationalize being passive and controlled by taking it as a measure of loyalty and maturity.[10] Warren Bennis, in exploring reasons why leaders can't lead, notes that all of us conspire in submersing ourselves in routine and formulates Bennis' Law (joining Parkinson and so many others) stating that routine work drives out important work. He, too, notes that change may be possible for small groups given enough truth and trust.[11] In most large organizations, accounting to and informing everyone else about virtually everything one does has become a major task and a major source of succumbing to routine. Whatever arguments support this routine, still it is a symptom of generalized lack of trust.

Organizational change, like social change, results from change in an aggregate of individuals. Waiting for change is a non-exercise in futility; in the meantime an organizational climate conducive to change may deteriorate as incompatible demands from the outside are felt more and more. Too, the gap between the idea and the practice widens. Similarly, Mr. Goodbar, in the form of answers to questions or solutions to problems, may not be found no matter how harried our search. At issue is the nature of change, organizations, leadership and the like. Without that understanding, we might as well keep working on blue-ribbon task forces, which, Bennis argues, insures the status quo as "their reports get better and better while the problems get worse and worse."[12]

Organizations, anymore, are beleaguered by attempts to provide answers and solve problems. Technique after technique is adopted and soon discarded. Barely was the Management by Objectives technique understood before Management by Results replaced it. After struggling with Program Performance Budgeting Systems, we are now struggling with Zero-Based Budgeting. We have sharpened and flattened pyramids changing steps in the hierarchy and span of control, and developed matrices and ad hocracies. Even if all these techniques contributed enough to off-set the drain from other efforts required in adopting them, the major effect seems still to be on organizational efficiency – an internal, system criteria – rather than on effectiveness – an external, service criteria. Organizational change does not appear to result from technical remedies for internal problems. The cutting edge of change is at the individual level.

SOME OBSTACLES

If the emerging philosophy of recreation service and the emerging social and economic forces point us in the same direction, then smooth and orderly change, and a smooth transition to a new service mode for the future should be expected. But the reality is that each of us resists change; each of us being products of our past; each of us better able to respond to yesterday's situation than tomorrow's. Understanding and managing change as a personal process is a requirement for all of us and there is a rich and growing literature to help meet it.[13] Along with obstacles to change which face everyone, recreationists have others, in addition to those noted or alluded to above, to overcome. A few are noted that seem sufficiently general as to apply to many.

1. Lack of union strength or professional status may result in some anxiety and insecurity. Difficulties in identifying specific and special competencies (a problem now being addressed in several quarters) adds to the problem.
2. Direct provision of programs and services is visible, tangible proof of a service being rendered. The roles attendant on the emerging philosophy – enabling, facilitating, and the like – are much less visible. There is some risk in foregoing visibility, since credit tends to be contingent upon it.
3. The development of successful programs, even if only measured quantitatively, is not always easy. There is an investment and some satisfaction of the need to be needed. The emotional task of letting go is difficult.
4. Recreationists do much simply because it's easier; that is, more efficient. Effectiveness may sometimes require a recreationist to do nothing, a task difficult enough in itself, and exacerbated by presure from those who appreciate no objective except efficiency.
5. Success as providers, and the resulting dependency of the public on direct services, will be a source of stress and friction.
6. While recreationists are intent on enabling growth, learning, self-determination, development, involvement and the like, increasing stress on members of the public may mean that their primary objective in a recreational pursuit is simply escape.
7. Roles have been identified, however ill-defined, but less progress has been made in identifying goals and objectives and even less in establishing criteria by which to judge the success of the new service mode suggested by philosophy and identified roles.

The last obstacle listed is one which recreationists, as a group, can address so some fairly specific goals and objectives are suggested, not for adoption but for discussion and debate. While the goals and objectives relate to recreation service rather than individual change, they can only be achieved when the aggregate of individuals in their respective agencies, change. Some uncertainty, stress, risk, and failure will likely accompany change since the amount and pace of change is hardly uniform, and since organizations and institutions are not conducive to it. In this process we cannot expect much from our institutions. What we expect of ourselves and each other will have to go up.

SOME ASSUMPTIONS

By way of a summary and to re-set the context in which the suggestions are cast, six assumptions about our present and foreseeable future situation are noted.

1. It is assumed that the foreseeable future will be characterized by a slow growing and smaller economy: slow growing as population growth slows and at some point stabilizes; smaller as a result of inflation, resource shortages and limits and the like.
2. It is assumed that the pressures of increasing demands for service and increasing concern about the size, cost and inefficiency of government will be felt first, and most, at the local government level.
3. It is assumed that what we expect of our institutions must go down and what we expect of ourselves and each other must go up.
4. It is assumed that the cutting edge of change is at the individual level. Institutions and organizations are not going to collapse, as some suggest, nor are they likely to change rapidly or markedly. Social change is the result of change in an aggregate of individuals.
5. It is assumed that there is already much individual stress in the society and that there will be much more. The reconstruction of viable, convivial institutions in family, neighborhood, and community groups and among colleagues will be essential if people are to have the necessary base of support from which to foster and manage change.
6. Finally, the fundamental assumption underlying all of this is that individuals and groups are fully capable, with support as needed, of generating most of their own recreational opportunities, including most of what is now provided by governments. The hesitancy and reluctance born of paternal dependence, thus far agreeable to both the people and the government, is perhaps the overriding obstacle to change consistent with our professed beliefs and contemporary situation.

If the assumptions are not acceptable, then the suggestions certainly won't be because many will be difficult to accept in any situation. Each suggestion leads to many others, some of which may be even more difficult to accept. To suggest, for example, decreased budgets and personnel complements in the public sector is a direct challenge to our thinking about manpower, college and university enrollments and curricula, and a host of related matters.

SOME TASKS

Some objectives and criteria for the new service mode might be:

1. A smaller role for government: reduced program expenditures by government with no reduction in participation; reduction of total man hours of employment in the public sector; wholesale reduction in the number of rules, regulations, policies, and laws.
2. More assistance to others: redistribution of government resources to community groups via grants; sharing space, office supplies and equipment, technical administrative support, and the like; "no strings" support of voluntary, non-profit agencies; more incentives and more cooperation with the private sector.
3. Greater community identity and autonomy: decentralization of decision making authority throughout staff and back to community groups; indices of shifts of power away from government; reemphasis on smaller, decentralized, and community controlled facilities.
4. More public (versus special interest group) service: increased emphasis on geographic community rather than communities of interest; increased shares of resources for the general public rather than special interests; increased integration of age and interest groups.
5. Less structure and rigidity: reduced "red tape" and faster response time; increased flexibility in scheduling; fewer leagues, teams, and classes; increased spontaneous activities and events.
6. More efficiency and (hopefully) effectiveness: improved coordination of current and comprehensive community information for all programs, resources, social services and government affairs; increased coordination of all community programs, facilities and resources; increased use of all facilities in place; reduced debt service and current capital expense.
7. Less political alienation and social anomie: increased political sophistication and participation in the political process; decreased brutal, sensate, and escapist activity; reduced vandalism, alcoholism, and other indices of social malaise.
8. Increased individual assumption of responsibility: growth in volunteer services; increased neighborly sharing and self help; increased family activity; reintegration of the young and old in meaningful community service roles.

MOVING ON

Essential next steps include refining and consolidating appropriate objectives; redefining or "operationalizing" statements into measurable terms; identifying indicators by which progress or its lack can be observed; establishing baseline information. Another critical next step is to educate elected and appointed officials and the public about our situation, philosophy and assumptions about the next decade or so, and thus the efficacy of a different service mode and the objectives being pursued. Again, the service will become lower profile, if not invisible. Too, there is much evidence that the public is happy with the status quo based on direct provision of programs, facilities and services.[14] And if Lasch is correct in his depiction of a narcissistic culture,[15] these steps are very long ones and they're uphill all the way.

None of this will come about by "Waiting for Godot" or "Looking for Mr. Goodbar." Every individual recreationist is responsible for change. There are no easy or universal answers to our questions or solutions to our problems. The circumstances of every municipality are different. The circumstances, mandates, and resources of every agency are different. Problems and opportunities in one area do not exist in another; an appropriate strategy here would be inappropriate there. If the burden of change finally rests on the shoulders of each individual, then the ubiquitous question of how can only be determined by each individual according to his or her own lights, abilities and limits.

We began with a dialogue and end with one since the question of how we get from where we are to where we would like to go reminds one of the exchange between a tourist and a New York City cab driver.

Tourist: "How do I get to Carnegie Hall?"
Cab driver: "Practice, my friend, practice."

REFERENCES

1. Pizer, Stuart and Travers, Jerry. *Psychology and Social Change.* New York: McGraw-Hill, 1975. p. 11.
2. Russell, Bertrand. "Individual Liberty and Public Control." In Desaulniers, Louise (Ed.), *119 Years of The Atlantic.* The Atlantic Monthly Company, 1977. p. 272.
3. Harman, Willis. "The Coming Transformation." *The Futurist,* 11:2, (April, 1977). p. 107. That these are recreation's tasks see Weiner, Myron E., "A Systems Approach to Leisure Services." In Lutzin, Disney G. and Storey, Edward H. (Eds.), *Managing Municipal Leisure Services.* Washington, D.C.: International City Management Association, 1973. p. 7.

4. Kristol, Irving. "Values in Contemporary Society." *Working Paper of the Rockefeller Foundation,* (March, 1974). p. 7.
5. From a conversation with Dr. David Gray, Vice President for Administration and Staff Development, California State University at Long Beach, January, 1979.
6. Crompton, John L. and Van Doren, Carlton S.. "Changes in the Financial Status of Leisure Services in Thirty Major U.S. Cities, 1964-1974." *Journal of Leisure Research,* 10:1, (1978). pp. 37-46. This is also the case in Ontario cities according to data compiled by James Maxwell for presentation to a meeting of the Ontario Municipal Recreation Association, March, 1979.
7. Vickers, Geoffrey. *Making Institutions Work.* New York: John Wiley and Sons, 1973. p. 15.
8. Steiner, Gary (Ed.). *The Creative Organization.* Chicago: University of Chicago Press. 1965.
9. Michael, Donald. "On the Social Psychology of Organizational Resistances to Long Range Planning." *I.E.E.E. Journal,* SCM2:5, (November, 1972). p. 583.
10. Argyris, Chris. "Some Limits on Rational Man Organization Theory." *Public Administrative Review,* 33:3 (May-June, 1973), pp. 253-267.
11. Bennis, Warren. *The Unconscious Conspiracy: Why Leaders Can't Lead.* New York: Amacom (A Division of the American Management Association), 1976. p. 161-186. As to succumbing to routine, see especially Mintzberg, Henry. *The Nature of Managerial Work.* New York: Harper and Row, 1973.
12. Bennis, *Op. Cit.*, p. 33.
13. See Pizer and Travis, *Op. Cit.* and Adams, John, et. al. *Transition: Understanding and Managing Personal Change.* London: Martin Robertson and Company, 1976.
14. Goodale, Thomas and Witt, Peter A.. "Goals for Municipal Recreation in Ontario." *Recreation Research Review.* (forthcoming).
15. Lasch, Christopher. *The Culture of Narcissism: American Life in an Age of Diminishing Expectations.* New York: W.W. Norton and Company, 1978.

SECTION THREE

Rethinking Professionalization: A Word of Caution

Introduction

Thomas L. Goodale and Peter A. Witt

The first two sections of this book deal with a) the need to clarify the conceptual basis of our field in order to improve our understanding of the phenomena (recreation, leisure, play, etc.) we are dealing with and b) the kinds of service provision changes that are necessary if we are to make the park and recreation movement more responsive to the needs of citizens in the 80's and beyond. The six articles in this section deal with a variety of issues concerning growing professionalization within the park and recreation movement. For example: Lord, Hutchison and VanDerbeck (17) question the way leadership is conceptualized and practiced in our field. Throsteinson (20) and Witt (21) deal with the struggle by recreation personnel to gain professional status, while Reynolds (18) and Witt (19) describe the potential conflict between the way we are attempting to lead and the actual or perceived needs of citizens for direction, guidance and assistance.

Lord, Hutchison and VanDerbeck (17) challenge us to carefully examine the impact of professional practice on the needs and goals of consumers. Witt (21) critically analyzes whose interests (professionals' and/or consumers') are served by burgeoning efforts to establish recreation as a profession and Reynolds (18) challenges us to examine whether our professional efforts lead to too much social control over citizen expectations and values. Together, they ask us to examine whether we inappropriately blame individuals for lack of motivation where in fact inadequate service provision may be equally at fault. They also ask us to determine whether we inadvertantly disable individuals via too narrowly defined professional responsibilities, buckpassing, or misguided benevolence.

The articles in this section present issues that are too often ignored by those who argue for the necessity of recreation workers achieving professional status. In an age where it is not clear whether professionalism implies service or survival, Witt (21), for example, raises significant questions that must be dealt with before the recreation and park movement rushes head long into acquiring the trappings of professionalism such as accreditation, certification, registration, licensing, and a code of ethics. In essence, the authors in this section are more concerned with the impact of professionals on people's lives than with the criteria for being a professional.

Woven through the articles are a series of dilemmas which face any aspiring profession. One series deals with the thin line distinguishing between attempts at helping versus influencing or leading versus directing. Another series deals with means for preserving the delicate balance between independence and dependence of action or intrinsic and extrinsic motivation. In the rush to achieve status and authority, Lord, Hutchison and Van Derbeck (17) ask whether the recreation and park movement has failed to consider whether professionalization is consistent with meeting the needs of the people we intend to serve.

Indeed, as Reynolds (18) and Witt (19) note, it is not clear whether the people we serve are considered clients, recipients, or consumers. Although just labels, each designation has broad implications for determining the source of control, motivation, evaluation, and mandate for services.

Another theme that is touched on by a number of the authors is the growing uneasy feeling, or perhaps even a malaise, among many professionals that all is not right. Our public self increasingly seeks status, recognition, and security; our private self wonders whether we are really fulfilling the kind of dream for the recreation and park movement that Duncan (22) saw many of our founding leaders as having. In a field dominated by civil service workers, and given the dilemmas and contradictions that daily haunt our decisions and practices, there is a tendency to ask too few questions. The conspiracy of silence thus threatens to become a pattern of "benign neglect." It is not clear whether the recreation movement as it has emerged in the latter half of this century has the philosophic foundation or creative instincts to get beyond muddling through the difficult issues that lie ahead.

Given the problems formed by rising consumerism (partly in response to rising professionalism) emerging institutionalization and bureaucraticization of services, and a growing sense of mistrust (or perhaps disinterest) in collective attempts at meeting individual problems, recreation and park workers face a profound challenge to their *raison d'etre* and mission. Professionalism has become a distinct force in society having the power to influence almost every aspect of our daily lives. Thus, Witt (21) and Lord, Hutchison andVan Derbeck (17) ask about whose interests are really being served by those who seek professional status.

Witt's article (21), as well as others, has strong implications for the way workers are socialized into the recreation field via education and training processes. What is the best path to be followed by universities and colleges in their quest to educate or train (is there a difference?) the leaders of tomorrow? How will we help future leaders to balance their personal concerns for status and prestige with the needs of citizens for services and opportunities? What type of individuals are attracted to career opportunities in the recreation and parks field?

Together the chapters in this section offer a voice of concern and caution. While being supportive of efforts to improve the quality of services being provided, they reflect the strong need to carefully examine the inter-relationship between consumer and practitioner needs as well as the impact of professional actions on the needs, goals and aspirations of consumers. While supporting the need to improve the quality of services provided and the degree of accountability of those providing services, the authors also call for careful consideration of both the positive and negative consequences of increasing professionalization as a means for achieving these ends.

TLG
PAW

Chapter Seventeen

Narrowing the Options: The Power of Professionalism in Daily Life and Leisure

John Lord, Peggy Hutchison, and Fred VanDerbeck

Choice, risk, and involvement are vital elements in growth and development and human experience. In our society, however, adults have become less playful and more security-oriented. Many of our institutions are dominant and unresponsive, making it difficult for people to feel a sense of purpose and control in their daily lives. To regain a willingness to risk and change, we need to increase the options in our lives, beginning at the personal level and moving to community and social system levels. So it is necessary to examine the inter-relationships between our creative, playful selves and the system of professional dominance which narrows our options. It is timely to analyze this process in the field of leisure services because of the current thrust toward certification, standardization and professionalization. An exploration of the power of professionalism in daily life and leisure will help us to clarify the relevant issues and to come to an understanding of our role in creating more options for ourselves and our communities.

NEGATING PLAY THROUGH PROFESSIONALISM

Professionals often destroy or exclude play and playfulness by disregarding and institutionalizing the central elements of play. Spontaneity and exploration are obliterated by a preoccupation with teaching and structure. Internal motivation is weakened by imposing rewards and external controls. We become dependent upon professionals, rather than relying on ourselves and our community of friends.

We have become serious about ourselves and our work, unable to be playful, and unable to recognize opportunities for play. Most of us probably smile when we observe children laughing, sharing, creating, and exploring at play. But do we smile only because we fondly remember how important play was to us? In other words, is children's play an external event to us, rather than something in which we feel comfortable joining?[1]

Perhaps some of us wonder why we have lost our ability to play and self-generate. One possibility is that professions which dominate our lives lower people's trust in themselves to generate energy, ideas, and alternatives. Our lives are permeated by services which create dependency on the part of both the client and the professional. Dependency for the client means that the capacity for self-development is narrowed to the choices offered by the experts in a particular field. Dependency for the professional means that his or her actions become nearly synonymous with the professions need to help and to create needs.

Play is also negated or destroyed by control and fragmentation, two characteristics of professionalism. Both these elements have had an impact on children by the time they are six years old. Children at school soon learn that play is relatively unimportant and that the only valuable knowledge is formal knowledge which is acquired primarily from professionals. It is in this sense that professionals and institutions control the lives of children and adults. As several researchers and social critics have emphasized, children's sport and recreation programs reflect the dominant social values, as indicated by competition, leader-directed activity and exclusion.[2,3]

Beliefs which permit professionalism to dominate and control our lives lead people to separate their work and play. This kind of fragmentation makes it difficult for people to have meaning and understanding in an increasingly complex world. Many people with whom we have spoken see their lives as routine and unconnected. The way we separate our lives into units for leisure, work, family, and sleep are disabling, particularly as recreation and leisure become residual events in our lives. Play is no longer a space for exploration and learning but becomes a space, like work, for the accomplishment of narrowly defined tasks. The negation of play by professionalism, then, is a serious paradox for recreationists, since play and professionalism have become fundamentally antithetical practices.

THE GROWTH OF PROFESSIONALISM

Two important historical periods have been identified with the rise of professionalism in western culture. The first took place in the middle of the last century with the development of cities and a corresponding rise in commerce. From these influences, a middle class emerged which resulted in increased inequalities of wealth distribution.[4] The idea of individual career patterns and upward mobility, in contrast to community sharing as a way of meeting human needs, became important. This historical perspective remains relevant today since most professionals continue to support inequality and social hierarchies. Consider how human service workers at the direct programming level are devalued, both in terms of social status and financial remuneration.

The second period associated with the rise of professionalism was the middle part of this century when professions became more dominant in people's lives by acquiring authority and control.[5] This period was in contrast to earlier times when professionals had a more benevolent role. For example, a medical practitioner made home visits, diagnosed sickness, and recommended a variety of prepared and home remedies. In contrast, the medical profession today controls health-related matters and provides impersonal service.[6] It has been suggested that medical practices themselves stimulate further problems by focusing on illness rather than health and prevention.[7] Doctoring today is thus an industry, not a service. A second example concerns recreationists who, in the past, cooperated with citizens' groups in order to provide a variety of formal and informal leisure opportunities for the community. Again, this is in sharp contrast to many current recreation professionals who feel they need to institutionalize our leisure and organize our time. Have you ever tried to go skating in a municipal rink more than once or twice a week? Schedules, leagues, and narrow age groupings for organized sport dominate most hours of the day and night.

THE MAKING OF A PROFESSIONAL

Professionalism is a way of thinking and acting, which reinforces fragmentation and control, rather than unity and change. It is a way of surrendering to the few, the power which should belong to people in general.

In our society the professional occupies a privileged position. S/he did not get there because of innate individual characteristics, but rather because of our particular societal organization. However, the power of the person who is a professional is also dependent upon the willingness of that person to conform to the standards created by his/her profession.[8] Professionals view themselves as owners of their area of expertise and as custodians who have the right and responsibility to control access to that occupation. The definition of a profession, then, is largely determined by:

> the professional's authority to define a person, as client, to determine that person's need, and to hand that person a prescription which defines this new social role.[9]

Thus, this relationship of mutual dependency creates a social distance between the client and professional and reinforces the idea that one needs a service which is best provided by an expert. In essence, this is a *political* relationship, since it legitimizes the professional in the role of policy and decision-maker for the client. Rather than fostering a sense of shared responsibility for the problem, the professional behaves in ways which are designed to maintain awe of and respect for the profession.

Our daily lives are a source of constant confrontation with such professional enhancement. Haven't we all had the experience of waiting in line at an agency office and hearing a person introduce himself or herself as a Doctor, Attorney, or Professor. Is this done as a means of identification or is it a professional claim to be placed ahead of the people waiting in line? Perhaps it would be useful for all of us to try an experiment to test the reality of this system. Introduce yourself, either in person or on the telephone, using your usual name one time, and a professional designation another time. See if the tone of voice, the demeanor of the person to whom you are talking or the quality of service changes. For even more impact, try slurring your words or add a foreign accent and see if the response is any different.

This way of acting is acquired during a period of training in which the professional acquires a certain self-concept which gives legitimacy to these actions in her or his mind. This training consists of absorbing a particular way of thinking about oneself and one's society which emphasizes success over support and nurturing. We are taught to get to know people according to their accomplishments rather than for their human characteristics. Upon meeting someone, we are most often concerned about their status (assembly line worker, housewife, vice-president), rather than the possibility of a shared relationship or learning experience. Contacts such as these tend to reify and depersonalize human relations. This superficial way of interrelating becomes dominant in everyday interactions. It would require a very different way of thinking about ourselves and our society, for us to become more humanly, and less technically, concerned about our fellow persons.

Those of us in professions know very well the narrow, procedural training we received. We can remember the emphasis on technical solutions to social problems and moral dilemmas. Jeffry Galper reflects upon the process of professional training.

> Students, for example, are encouraged to think analytically, but not to connect the material before them to the major emotional dynamics in their lives. Similarly, the survival needs of many workers dictate that they not feel, in any profound way, the emotional poverty of their work situations. . .To encourage people to deny and compartmentalize their emotions, therefore, serves to maintain a public myth about the acceptability of the social order, since it encourages the belief that the pain people experience is idiosyncratic. [In addition] this serves to isolate the professional from the fullest awareness of the amount of pain that exists in the society and the relative powerlessness of the professional to deal with it.[10]

Certification is an attempt to ensure that professionals will acquire their profession's view of what's best for people. Unfortunately, both the client and professional too easily conform to expectations each has of the other and therefore both maintain the status quo. This established hierarchical form is generally restrictive and constraining to human development and human relationships.

UNDERLYING IDEOLOGIES

It is helpful to reflect on the dominant ideologies and values in our society which create and support this professionalized training. One underlying ideology emerges from the examination of worker alienation as technological changes are introduced into the workplace. The story of the worker moving from crafts person to baby sitter is symbolic of this situation.[11] Technology tends to dominate the workplace, thus allowing a system of cost effectiveness to emerge, which devalues human beings. Purpose and meaning give way to narrow productivity measures and work and leisure are subordinated to specialized, industrial functions. When this occurs, it is difficult for individuals and society to feel a sense of control over their own lives. Professions and others have responded to this dilemma by interpreting social problems from a narrow perspective. Using this ideology of rationalization, professionals often focus upon facts, objective data, and procedures as a way of explaining social problems, rather than trying to understand the political-economic and human issues underlying a problem.[12] Unconsciously then, rationalization has become a way of explaining and resolving daily life issues.[13]

To what extent do recreationists accept the rationalization of leisure by assuming that play is what you do away from work? Does professional education for recreationists reflect the strong conservative bias which seems to dominate professions in general? Examining the leading books in a field is one interesting way to dicipher these questions. Our reading of the recreation literature suggests a consistent theme, which focuses upon the present and future growth of leisure and recreation as a result of technology. Some textbooks on leisure services argue that diversion and escape from a highly complex industrial society are central to the growth of mass leisure.[14] Many recommendations for organized recreation emerge from this assumption. Based upon this material, one clearly gets the impression that social, political, and economic systems are accepted unquestioningly. When purpose for recreation is gained from technological and social forces, however, recreation services controlled by professionals remain distant from people's daily lives.

Recreationists educated in such a narrow focus will continue to promote recreation as a means of coping with or avoiding oppressive and alienated work. Our leisure, however, is hardly more fulfilling than our work. Workers currently employed in unsatisfying jobs know that the "frustration and tension of the job are not easily left at the plant gate."[15] It is in this sense that recreationists often use leisure as a way of placating people. For example, disabled people are offered recreation programs but not jobs, often with thc rationalization, unlike normal expectations, that they are fortunate *not* to be working, and that free time should be used more constructively. As a second example, recreation focuses upon activity, skills, procedures, participation, and programs. It seldom, if ever, emphasizes self and community development, women's groups, workers' study groups, political, theatre, or participant-directed activities.

In a similar manner, a second ideology known as positivism, attempts to objectify the world in order to control events and persons.

> The positivist refuses to be introspective. His concern is to get on with the task of explaining, without considering what he is doing . . . The political failure of positivist thought, as related to its intellectual failure, is its acceptance of the status quo. There is no questioning of the established order, just as there is no examination of scientific assumptions. . . The positivist takes for granted the dominant ideology that emphasizes bureaucratic rationality, modern technology, centralized authority, and scientific control.[16]

Thus, both the positivist and rationalist way of knowing and organizing the world presuppose the existence of objective knowledge and decision-making, processes which devalue subjectivity in order to maintain control. This approach legitimizes technique at the expense of human interrelationships.[17] The contrast illustrated by the chart below, adapted from Harold Hodges Jr., clarifies the socialization process which occurs as young people become professionalized.[18]

THE CHILD	THE PROFESSIONAL
spontaneous, unrestrained,	self-restrained, inhibited,
risk-taking, adventuresome, change seeking	cautious, fearful of unfamiliar, security-oriented, stability seeking
intuitive, affective	logical, cognitive
open-minded	closed-minded
innovative, exploratory	conventional, custom-bound
at ease with chaos, complexity, disorder, mystery	fearful of the unstructured, undefined

The socialization process outlined above by Hodges makes it possible for the dominant ideologies of rationalization and positivism to be maintained and strengthened. In our view, these dominant values represent social processes which create daily life situations which avoid the real problems, support hierarchical relationships, and view people as commodities. Professionalism and the professional reflect the power of this socialization process.

PROFESSIONAL DOMINANCE OF HUMAN SERVICES

In recent years there has been a rapid expansion in social, medical, and human services. Jeffry Galper, in a penetrating critique of social services in America, views current social services as a logical extension of capitalism.[19] Galper presents a great deal of data to support the viewpoint that social services allow the dominant ideology and commodity relationships discussed earlier to be maintained. Obviously, this approach will dismay many liberals who see welfare, homes for the elderly, and minimum wage laws as progressive and humane practices. In reality, however, many of these are band-aid arrangements which delay the implementation of fundamental changes in social services and political-economic structures. The myriad of existing human services which are constantly increasing to respond to yet another need is society's way of approving professionalism. In this sense, the human service industry serves as professionalism's stamp of approval.

Professionalism in human services is maintained by a belief in a political and value system which is supportive of competition as natural process, people as commodities, and hierarchies as the logical means of organization in people's lives. Thus, recreation departments teach primarily competitive values, slot people into programs, and force individuals and consumer groups to compete for artifically scarce resources. The cruel paradox of this value system, is that individuals are often blamed for problems which are, instead, created by this unjust system. For example, in one community, a fitness program for senior citizens was run on Sundays from five to six-thirty. When few attended, the recreation department blamed the seniors for being poorly motivated.

Four practices help to maintain and institutionalize professionalism in human services.[20]

Narrow Focus

Professions develop a narrow frame of reference by focusing upon one aspect of a client or a problem. Such specialization narrows the range of solutions which are considered possible. In fact, real problems are often avoided and any solutions apply more to the symptom than to the cause of the problem. For medicine this means that a headache is viewed as the problem, and thus, treatment is aimed at eliminating the headache. Deeper perspectives beyond the germ theory are neither sought nor welcomed. It is only very recently, for example, that some physicians have hesitated before applying chemo or radiation therapy to cancerous cells and have encouraged the patient to participate in making choices about his/her own treatments. In developing a broader frame of reference, medical doctors would spend less time on cure or surgery and more time on prevention and self-care. For recreation, many problems and the solutions tend to revolve around the issue of activity. We struggle to determine how to get and keep people active, but seldom do an analysis of meaning and purpose in people's lives.

Professional Detachment

Professions emphasize that their members should not become emotionally involved with their clients. It is ironic that many so-called "helping professions" train people and deliver services based upon these values. By "helping," we have come to mean doing something for someone without involvement. To *not* be neutral is to be involved and might mean cultivating a sense of wholeness. This includes playfulness, empathy, and support for enabling others to view their own oppression collectively and the facilitation of alternative courses of action. This issue creates a dilemma for the recreationist. To be professionalized means the recreationist loses a certain degree of involvement and playfulness. Once these vital personal ingredients are lost, recreation becomes another commodity, another marketplace item to be packaged and sold. Thus, recreationists need to be deeply reflective about the growing professionalism in their field. Godbey is one of the few recreation professionals to express concern at the growing professionalization of recreation. He wonders whether:

> the recreation and parks movement, in seeking professional status, has moved toward an inappropriate model to bring about its initial ideals, such as restoring a sense of community through recreation, provision to the poor, and increased recreational self-sufficiency for citizens. . . (professionalism) may increasingly alienate the practitioner from the social reform ethic and "grass roots" approach to community involvement.[21]

We must ask ourselves whether increased professionalization in the field of recreation will lead to further degradation of play values which are inherent in the minds and spirits of children, but which have lost their impact and meaning for most adults.

Professionalized Service Ethic

Professionals develop an ethic of service based upon their standards and expectations. Lack of cooperative efforts between the professional and client ensures that this process continues. For example, games are not adjusted for *mutual* participation when disabled individuals, health-impaired persons, or children wish to take part. The standard of performance continues to be the professional sports player. Some recreationists would segregate participants of unequal capabilities rather than change the rules to permit the inclusion of all persons. This is another illustration of the permeation of the competitive ethic in our society. For many participants socialized in this society, the game would lose its meaning if the rules were changed. Thus, service to others is most often seen as the service *needed by the client*, in order to adjust him/herself to the requirements of the existing structure of power in any society.

Impartial Service Delivery

Human service providers generally claim impartiality in terms of the allocation of their services. Race, creed, and sex, for example, are said to be irrelevant factors in distribution of resources. In practice, however, people start at very different levels when seeking services, and thus require different degrees of support. As Galper puts it:

> To guarantee equality of opportunity without assuring equality in the places from which people start to compete is to assure that equal opportunity will mean unequal outcomes.[22]

Impartiality becomes an ethic reinforcing the status quo, since the system of professionalism is set up to maintain the distance between professionals and non-professionals. In order to show how this is part of our social-economic lives, we need to examine the unequal basis from which people begin. First, we recommend the study of income distribution and poverty in North America.[23] Second, despite improvements in recent years, there is evidence that women and minority groups with equal training compared to white males earn considerably less on entry into the labor market.[24] Third, consider the claim many community recreationists make that their services are equally available to all citizens. In reality, few recreation facilities are physically accessible to all persons, costs are often prohibitive, and opportunities for particular age groups are lacking.

In our view, then, professionalism reflects a strong conservative bias in human services. Professional control serves to dampen personal and collective action and to encourage dependence on professional remedies. The human service and leisure industries support this dependence by serving as a link in the institutionalization of professionalism. The diagram on the following page summarizes the relationships among the components which serve to institutionalize and perhaps to change professionalism.

WHY THE TRUST YET THE QUESTIONING?

In a society where professionalism has become dominant, people continue to have tremendous trust in the process of professionalism.

> It is one of the maddening facts of our time that people believe themselves incapable of dealing with the most ordinary human conflicts without the aid of a 'specialist.'[25]

Professionalism engenders trust because it penetrates and controls most aspects of our lives. Three of the ways in which professionalism affects people and gains trust follow.

FIGURE ONE – INSTITUTIONALIZING PROFESSIONALISM

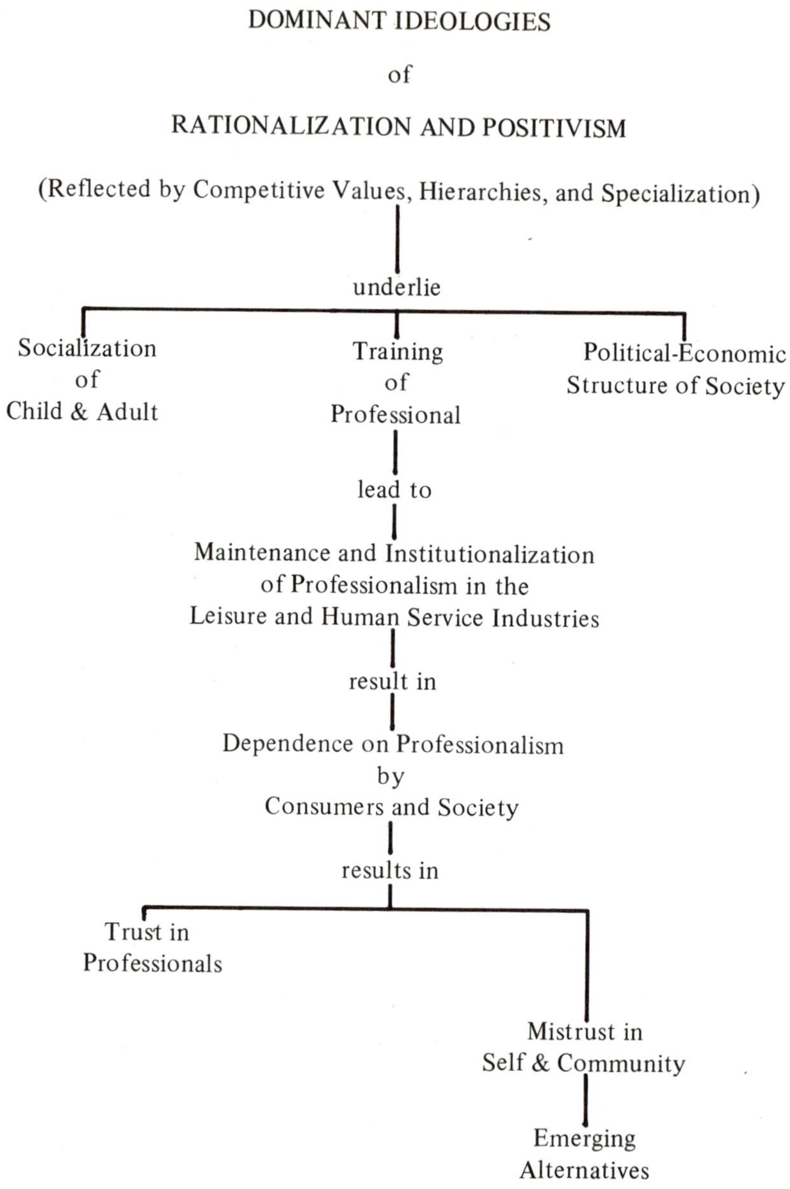

First, the institutionalization of professionalism has resulted in a trust of institutions rather than community, and a trust in professionalism instead of self and others. We have been taught to believe that institutions have something that we need. For example, knowledge is of value only when given by an expert; therefore, learning must occur at school. Thus, it has become difficult for people to self-generate or put trust in oneself for learning the essential nuances of our day. Similarly, we believe we can't play without a recreationist, get better without a doctor, or gain rights without a lawyer.

Second, the trust in professionalism should not be so surprising, when one considers how professional power is subtly and effectively enshrined in our common speech. In an excellent book by one of the few persons to examine the relationship between power and helping language, Murray Edelman wrote:

> Consider a common usage that staff, clients, and the general public all accept as descriptive of a purely professional process: the term 'therapy'. In the journals, textbooks, and talk of the helping professions, the term is repeatedly used as a suffix or qualifier. Mental patients do not hold dances; they have dance therapy. If they play volleyball, that is recreation therapy. If they engage in a group discussion, that is group therapy.[26]

In other words, the professional's relationship to the client is based upon controlling the other's context by defining the possibilities for the client in professionally advantageous ways. By calling a relationship or an activity therapy, an immediate power hierarchy is established which makes it difficult for the devalued client to develop any self-help skills except those sanctioned by the professional. The client comes to rely on a professional for cues which will indicate the appropriateness of behavior and thoughts. Linguistic support for this situation is emphasized in professional jargon: solitary confinement is called a quiet room; an attempted escape is referred to as attempted elopement; and compulsory personal revelations at group meetings are defined as "benefiting from peer confrontation."[27] There is implicit power in these new terms and clients readily respond to the professional's orders.

Third, public policy is shaped, to a large extent, by our dependence upon, and trust in, professionals. An example occurred during National Health Week in Canada, when the former Minister of Health and Welfare was discussing health problems. He emphasized that:

> ". . .of all the problems we face, motivation of Canadians has to be singled out as the crucial one which will ultimately decide whether our strategy will be a success or failure. . .public education therefore cannot be overemphasized. Although education alone has had only

> limited success in the past, there are exciting new approaches to be explored by scientists, psychologists, professional educators, social workers, and all professional workers."[28]

Professional intervention is thus seen as necessary for overcoming people's needs which have been described as deficient. By seeing the problem within the citizen, a fertile climate for professional dominance is maintained. Individualizing the problem leads to blaming the victim, when the root causes of health and leisure problems are much deeper. Examples of causes include: the dominance of professions and corporations in dictating our needs; political-economic priorities which devalue certain citizens; loss of citizen control of schools, the work place, and the community. In addition, institutionalization and loss of personal power result in persons being viewed as clients rather than developing human beings.

It is understandable why professionals are able to acquire so much trust and control in our society. Our ideals of trust and love are contradicted by the reality of a society which is essentially based upon mistrust. Fragmented demands of our time and space further lead us to question the potential usefulness and practicality of concepts of wholeness and unity. Forced to respond in a fragmented way to specialized demands, we lose our own sense of integration and trust in our environment acquired through out early playful years and begin to feel encapsulated and alone with our own list of problems. When acting alone, we become the only integrators of our experience and our perception of ourselves becomes as fragmented as the world in which we live. We get caught in a vicious cycle of believing ourselves to be fragmented, and thus share with others in fragmented ways. It is at this point that we become most susceptible to the influence of professionalism.

Despite this professional encapsulation of our lives, or possibly because of it, cracks are appearing in the dominant trust of professionalism. In our view, two major thrusts account for this questioning. First, citizens and their families who have been systematically devalued by the society have often had the courage to speak out about the oppressive nature of professionalism. For example, a young couple gives birth to a baby who is mentally retarded. They oppose the overwhelming advice of physicians and social workers to have their baby institutionalized. Such people are tired of professionalism and all its trappings, its bureaucracy, and its inequality. The result is a growing advocacy effort by parents, disabled persons, and their friends directed toward changing the human service industry.

A second attack on professions has come from social critics who see professionalism as avoiding the root causes of problems. In fact, some critics point out that professionalism contributes to our problems, rather than resolving them. For example, John McKnight asks:

> Why are we putting so much resource into medicine while our health is not improving?
>
> Why are we putting so much resource into education and our children seem to be learning less?
>
> Why are we putting so much resource into criminal justice systems and society seems less just and less secure?
>
> Why are we putting so much resource into mental health systems and we seem to have more mental illness?[29]

While many citizens are beginning to echo these concerns in their daily life experiences and dialogue, it is interesting to note the response of professionals to the growing criticism of professionalism. Some appear shocked and claim that any wrong-doings or problems in the profession are rare and must be the result of incompetent individuals. If one pushes the critique further, the professional may ask: "are you in this field?" This defense, which assumes that one must be certified in a field in order to understand and criticize, squelches any attempt to critique professionalism on the basis of human values and system problems. These defenses serve as excuses which function to limit the creation of new options.

BROADENING THE OPTIONS

Developing alternatives to professionalism means broadening the options which people believe they can create to transform our society and daily lives. We suggest three broad approaches which we believe can have an impact on daily life and leisure. We also trust that readers can generage more specific alternatives and applications which are appropriate to their contexts.

New Vision

Creating serious alternatives to professionalism involves developing a vision of a different kind of society. As Margaret Mead once said:

> Periods of social disorganization invite correction in two directions, one an order imposed by force. . .the other a radical transformation of society that relies on the creation in individuals of a spirit of deep dedication to new social goals.[30]

A new vision would involve new social goals which enable *all* individuals to develop to their fullest capacities. Social reconstruction would entail a deep concern for the quality of life of every citizen. Society would no longer be based on the principle that the individual is respected only insofar as s/he is profitable.[31] We need to acknowledge that we have a very crucial identity as persons separate from our role in economic and institutional life. Valuing people as developing human beings would mean new goals and new priorities for human and leisure services. For example, elderly people, disabled persons, minority group individuals, and native people would no longer be systematically devalued. We would link the oppression of these groups to our own lives. Professional practices would cease to assume that people's needs are best resolved by psychological and specialist answers. Recreationists would ensure strong consumer input and control in planning services. And quality of the leisure experience would take precedent over the quality of services. Cooperation and collective understandings become central to these values. Too often, our sense of self is tied directly to our individual, professional goals. If we truly valued the potential of sharing with others, we would transform our work and leisure. Decision-making would become decentralized. Egalitarian relationships would replace professional domination and hierarchies. And leisure services would become a community and neighborhood project rather than a professional responsibility.

Changing Relationships

The professional-client relationship must change significantly. It must be viewed as an inter-relationship rather than a controlling relationship. In practice, professionals must not only share knowledge in a natural way, but struggle into the unknown with their clients through shared experiences and shared reflections. Barry Kaufman writes in a deeply human manner about his struggle with professionals in seeking effective approaches with his autistic son.[32] All professionals either had rigid prescriptions or responses which clearly indicated that nothing could be done. Finally, one professional was willing to explore the unknown and to converse with Kaufman about a range of options. It is in this sense that broadening the options means that professionals must be open to altering their theories in response to ongoing experiences in which alternative realities have been demonstrated. This also involves shared control over contexts rather than professional domination in relationships. Lack of consumer input into decision-making and planning in recreation makes it unlikely that recreation professionals either alter their perceptions or relinquish control through cooperative efforts with citizens.

Advocacy

Recreationists must serve as advocates for social change to ensure that professionalism does not dominate the field of recreation. Advocacy has generally had its roots in social movements for change. Many of these movements have been single-issue advocacy. While this is not unimportant, we also need advocacy which understands the interconnectedness of issues and which concerns itself with broad social change. The recreationist as an advocate can serve both these roles by working to deprofessionalize recreation and to deindustrialize the leisure industry.

A deprofessionalized view of recreation restores community and play as central to the recreation movement. Advocates will cooperate with others to identify barriers to community and play. They will infuse their jobs and their lives with a sense of community and a sense of playfulness. In practice, this will mean having a support group of deprofessionalized friends and colleagues who share the commitment to create a more just and humane society. It also entails being comfortable with negotiation and confrontation about the practical issues in everyday life. Creating links with community groups to ensure that consumers gain control of community resources is one example.

A strong advocacy movement in recreation might also begin to deindustrialize the leisure industry. First, this requires a fundamental critique of who controls our leisure needs. Corporate permeation of our lives through television and advertising creates expectations in which pursuit of material things is the major goal.[33] Second, most people in the leisure field unquestionably accept the notion that a technological society frees people for more leisure. As we have emphasized, however, failure to confront this notion contributes to the technological permeation of our lives. Instead, we need to take learnings gained away from the job and vice versa and fuse them into the work-place. Common phrases such as "be serious, this is business we are talking about" or "stop talking about the office, we are here to have fun" also need to be confronted. And participating in a shared, cooperative venture in a leisure setting raises consciousness about the possibility of such sharing in other environments.

Is it possible that bottom-up change, with cooperative efforts of recreation advocates and others, could change the leisure delivery system? The risk is worth it since the alternative is more professionalization and more recreation leaders imprisoned within their allegories and loyalities to the organization and the profession. Fortunately, alternatives are emerging in people's lives which involve cooperation, shared knowledge, and a different set of social goals. Change is fundamental to this search and struggle. It challenges us to reemphasize collectivity, self-worth, advocacy, and responsibility in social affairs. As Richard Bach states in *Illusions*, change is perfection; the sea and the sky are changing every second, but they are always a perfect sea and sky![34] Can we find security in changing ourselves and our society?

REFERENCES

1. For a delightful, yet extremely important, analysis of children's potential to grow and develop through play and natural learning, see Pearce, Joseph Chilton. *Magical Child: Rediscovering Nature's Plan for Our Children*. New York: E. P. Dutton, 1977. esp. pp. 138-145.
2. Orlick, Terry. *Winning Through Cooperation: Competitive Insanity: Cooperative Alternatives*. Washington, D.C.: Hawkins and Associates, 1978.
3. Sage, George H. "American Values and Sport: Formation of a Bureaucratic Personality." *Leisure Today*, October, 1978. p. 10-11.
4. Bledstein, Burton J. *The Culture of Professionalism*. New York: W. W. Norton and Company, Inc., 1976. pp. 21-22.
5. Illich, Ivan. "Disabling Professions." In: Illich, Ivan, et.al. *Disabling Professions*. London: Marian Boyers, 1977. pp. 15-21.
6. Heidenheimer, Arnold, Heclo, Hugh, and Adams, Carolyn Teich. *Comparative Public Policy*. New York: St. Martin, 1975. p. 14.
7. Illich, Ivan. *Medical Nemisis*: *The Expropriation of Health*. New York: Bantam, 1977.
8. Smollet, Eleanor, "Schools and the Illusion of Choice: The Middle Class and the 'Open' Classroom." In: Martell, George (Ed.). *The Politics of the Canadian Public School* Toronto: James Lewis and Samuel, Publishers, 1974. pp. 92-102.
9. Illich. "Disabling. . ." *Op.Cit.* p. 50.
10. Galper, Jeffry. *The Politics of Social Services*. Englewood Cliffs, N.J.: Prentice-Hall, 1975. p. 95. Jeffry Galper's book continues to be the primary reference for those interested in a radical critique of social service delivery systems. Our four practices in systematizing professionalism follow his suggestions with adaptations.
11. Shaiken, Harley. "Craftsman into Baby Sitter." In: Illich, Ivan, et.al., *Disabling Professions*. London: Marian Boyars, 1977. p. 120.
12. Fay, Brian. *Social Theory and Political Practice*. London: George Allen and Unwin, 1975. p. 44.
13. For a valuable analysis of the rationalization of the conduct of life, see: Goldman, Robert and Wilson, John. "The Rationalization of Leisure." *Politics and Society*, 7: 2, (1977). pp. 127-156.
14. See, for example: Sessoms, H. Douglas, Meyers, Harold D. and Brightbill, Charles K. *Leisure Services Services: The Organized Recreation and Park System*. Englewood Cliffs, N.J.: Prentice-Hall, 1975. And Shivers, Jay S. *Principles and Practices of Recreational Service* New York: MacMillan Company, 1967.
15. Shaiken. *Op.Cit.* p. 122.
16. Quinney, Richard. *Critique of Legal Order*. Boston: Little, Brown and Company, 1974. pp. 2-4.

17. See especially two essays: "Technical Progress and the Social Life-World," and "Technology and Science as 'Ideology'." In Habermas, Jurgen. *Toward A Rational Society*. Boston: Beacon Press, 1970.
18. Hoedges, Harold M., Jr. "The Humanistic Intellegentsia." In Gella, Aleksander, (Ed.). *The Intellegentsia and the Intellectuals*. Beverly Hills, California: Sage Publications, 1976. pp. 157-158.
19. Galper. *Op.Cit.*
20. *Ibid.*, p. 91-98.
21. Godbey, Geoffrey. "The Professionalization of Recreation and Parks in the Public Sector: Implications for Social Development." *Society and Leisure*, 1: 2 (November, 1978). pp. 280-81.
22. Galper, *Op.Cit.* p. 98.
23. See, for example, Johnson, Leo A. *Poverty in Wealth*. Toronto: New Hogtown Press, 1977.
24. Baker, Sally and Levenson, Bernard. "Earnings Prospects of Black and White Working-Class Women." *Sociology of Work and Occupations*, 3: 2 (May, 1976). p. 123.
25. Henley, Nancy and Brown, Phil. "The Myth of Skill and the Class Nature of Professionalism." In: Radical Therapist/Rough Times Collective (Eds.). *The Radical Therapist*. Middlesex, England: Penguin Books, 1974. p. 61.
26. Edelman, Murray. *Political Language: Words That Succeed and Policies That Fail.* New York: Academic Press, 1977. p. 59-60.
27. *Ibid.*, p. 61.
28. Lalonde, Marc. Quoted in: *Halifax Mail Star*, (March 18, 1978). p. 2.
29. McKnight, John. "Professionalized Service and Disabling Help." In: Illich, Ivan, et.al. *Disabling Professions*. London: Marion Boyars, 1977. p. 75.
30. Mead, Margaret and Heyman, Ken. *World Enough*. Boston: Little, Brown and Company, 1975. p. 56.
31. deBeauvoir, Simone. "Old Age: End Product of a Faulty System." *Saturday Review*, (April 8, 1972). p. 42.
32. Kaufman, Barry Neil. *Son-Rise*. New York: Warrier Books, 1976.
33. Hamelink, Cees. *The Corporate Village*. Rome: IDOC International, 1977. p. 138.
34. Bach, Richard. *Illusions*. New York: Delacorte Press, 1977.

Chapter Eighteen

Leisure Services and Social Control

Ronald P. Reynolds

. . ."To submit to however wise a master planner is to surrender an illusion that may be the bedrock on which life flourishes"[1]

LEISURE, CONTROL AND THE GOOD SOCIETY

While those concerned with the study of "leisure" and/or the provision of leisure services have yet to reach a consensus regarding its exact substantive definition, there is general agreement that the element of choice or freedom from constraint is one essential aspect of the phenomenon.[2] Conversely, *control* or imposed external influences affecting the leisure participant may preclude the achievement of the desired leisure state. With the notion of personal freedom as an atmosphere engendered by the absence of external control, the ideal society for promoting leisure is one which allows and encourages the individual to exert maximum autonomy over his or her own lifestyle. Sites[3] describes such a set of social conditions:

> A good society then is a society which is structured by allowing optimum control possibilities to each person of his own life experiences within the framework of an identity which he has been free to work out, maintain, or change on his own terms, so long as he does not infringe upon the possibility of others doing the same thing.

There are increasing indications which suggest that North Americans may not count themselves members of the "good society" nor perceive that they have adequate control over their own life experiences, including leisure. Cult organizations, Equal Rights Amendment movements and taxpayer revolts represent divergent attempts to regain or insure personal control of one's own religious ideology, human rights and monetary resources. Concern for leisure autonomy also prevails in our society as individuals flock to leisure counselors seeking dispensation to enjoy their free time and business executives forsake established careers to hand-fashion boats and sail the world.

In the midst of increasing discontent with personal and leisure lifestyles in a highly unpredictable and inflationary society, members of the leisure service profession must address several critical questions relative to the notion of social control. To what extent has the field of leisure services contributed to the personal autonomy of the individual? What has been and what will be the response of the leisure service profession to threats upon individual control and freedom as we approach and leave behind 1984? Has our field in general functioned to maintain the status quo at the expense of the freedom of the individual? Are we subtly yet effectively selectively shaping and promoting subservient behaviors for our "clientele"?* In responding to those with special needs are our notions of therapy, as Angel[4] suggests, "obsolete, elitist, male-centered and obsessional, clinging to concepts often outmoded and rarely questioned?" Has recreational therapy today become a commodity? A means of Social Control?

THE INFLUENCE OF OUR "ROOTS"

As a profession, the Recreation and Parks field traces many of its historical ties to the discipline of social work as practiced in the early 1900's. Despite its eventual emergence from social work, the leisure service profession has retained and continues to model many practices exhibited by social workers who promote and perpetuate the social service system today. Recent critics of this system have charged that the social service delivery structure "fosters particular behavior patterns in clients both as a condition of usage and as a consequence of service,"[5] thus denying personal control and autonomy to individuals served by this system. Three such practices – economic responding, functionally specific professionalism, and "socio-psychologism" found in the social services also appear to permeate the field of leisure services. A brief examination of each concept reveals the potentially deleterious effect which adherence to these practices may have upon the type and quality of service provided by contemporary recreation and parks personnel. Also suggested are some future directions which leisure service providers might explore to insure the leisure autonomy of our "clients" in the 1980's and beyond.

---

* The term "client", when utilized, appears in quotes to symbolize the incongruous relationship those in the Recreation and Parks field have established with both disabled and non-disabled service recipients. As the basic methods and content of this interaction change over the next decades, it is hoped that leisure service professionals will develop alternative perceptions of individuals as "consumers" or "citizens."

ECONOMIC RESPONDING AND LEISURE SERVICES

A basic criticism of today's social service practices relates to the system's perception of the good society as one exhibiting an overriding commitment to economics and materialism which in turn causes the state to "view human needs as being primarily economic and serve the needs of private capital in many ways."[6] Competitive behavior is viewed as an inevitable part of the human condition and welfare programming is designed to prepare people to excel through practicing individualism and self aggrandizement. Work in turn is viewed as being a means to high levels of leisure consumption.

In several respects, the field of leisure services plays a major role in reinforcing a materialistic and competitive orientation to leisure thereby perpetuating a form of economic control on the recipients of its services. This practice is effected both through the *types* of activity offerings provided and the *method* in which participation in recreational experiences is structured. The largest proportion of content of our professional magazines is devoted to private and commercial enterprises proclaiming the necessity to install $100,000 fiberglass skateboard parks, purchase vanilla ice-cream bars "wrapped in attractive sports motif foil" for concessions or appropriate funds for peacocks as "exotic accents" for parks. This is symptomatic of our growing tendency to respond to the leisure needs of the public in an overly materialistic fashion.

Similarly, we frequently find ourselves in the uncomfortable position of denouncing the work ethic in our writings and teachings while continuing practices such as offering community recreational pursuits which stress activities requiring high initial monetary outlays, the purchase of expensive consumer goods, the consumption of fossil fuels and the construction of extravagant facilities. Practices such as these are particularly disconcerting in current times of high inflation when rising prices and decreased discretionary income mean increased work hours to purchase leisure goods and services. The dilemma is apparent – individuals are encouraged to utilize their leisure in a more personally satisfying manner but to work longer and consume more in the process.

When scarce time is found for leisure participation, an inordinate emphasis is placed upon individualistic competitive pursuits. Recreation program texts suggest a plethora of competitive events varying from sports and drama tournaments, sandcastle sculpturing contests and spelling bees to baking contests, shingleboat races, flower arranging contests and sidewalk chalk art competitions. Elitist sport for disabled and non-disabled athletes consumes a disproportionate amount of our human and physical resources while comparatively little energy is expended for developmental activity programs for the non-competitor at the grass roots level. Our largest single effort to promote activity for mentally retarded persons, the Special Olympics, is modeled after the highest echelon of competition, the Olympic Games.

Lest there be misunderstanding relating to competitive endeavors between and among the sexes and disabled persons, current texts provide the following advice concerning sport:

> . . .there is organized support for recognizing limitations, which says that a big bosom and throwing things are incompatible. Menstrual cramps don't contribute to record-making physical outlays. But then these are foreseeable handicaps, perhaps more psychological than physiologically restricting. A fat boy doesn't throw too well either, nor does a mentally or physically depressed male rise to great efforts in recreational activity.[7]

Sports medicine clinics continue to cater to a younger and younger clientele. As a recent article points out "For the anxious mother of a little league player or a mosquito, a sports injury is a nightmare which she must hope is never played out."

Programmatic interventions designed to rehabilitate disabled persons have also fallen prey to the paradox extant in the economically oriented philosophy of the mental health field which defines emotional well being as "the active pursuit of a career, the engagement in competition within the rules of the game, the focus on recreation (asceticism) and on purposeful activity in general (utilitarianism).[8] The current controversy over the inclusion of recreation services in sheltered workshop settings for mentally retarded people speaks to our confusion regarding the relationship between work and leisure in "therapeutic recreation" service.

FUNCTIONALLY SPECIFIC PROFESSIONALISM AND LEISURE SERVICES

According to critics of the current Social Service System, professionalism, characterized by functional specificity is a second critical issue threatening the autonomy and self control of its clients. Briefly, functional specificity may be defined as:

> the condition whereby professions are characterized by their development of technologies. As a result of the orientation clients and professionals are prevented and "protected" from forming relationships which transcend this orientation. As a consequence of this

ideology, the professional tends to concentrate on one facet of a client's life to the exclusion of other areas. In short, the person is viewed only in terms of their problem.[9]

Undesirable by-products of this orientation appear to be emotional indifference toward clients and faulty perceptions and practices relating to the delivery of service. The field of leisure services has in no way remained immune to the development of functionally specific professionalism or the undesirable consequences of this practice in removing control of personal leisure lifestyles from our "clients." As we move toward another decade of service, the following questions must be addressed: Have our technologies prevented us from forming meaningful relationships with colleagues in our own field, with others in related disciplines and with the individuals served by our profession? Does the leisure service field as a whole concentrate on certain facets of a "client's" life to the exclusion of other needs and interests? To what extent has our own "functional specificity" resulted in a loss of autonomy and control by the individual consumer? A brief examination of two current practices in our field – specialization of training and compartmentalization of services illustrate the extremes to which unchecked overspecialization may lead in the next decade.

FUNCTIONAL SPECIFICITY IN PROFESSIONAL PREPARATION

Specialization appears rampant in professional training in the field of leisure services. A cursory glance at our professional preparation institutions reveals that individual curriculums provide program options in "Public Recreation," "Commercial Recreation," "Resource Planning," "Church Recreation," "General Programming," "Private Recreation," "Turf Management," "Vocational Corrections," "Recreation for the Socially Deviant," "Agriculture Teaching," "Ranger-Enforcement," "Naturalist-Historian," "Social Service Agencies," "Recreation for Minorities," "Youth-Family Leadership," "Maintenance," "Industrial Recreation," "Volunteer Management," "Community Schools." Junior colleges specialize in the training of "technicians." Four year curriculums spawn graduates who aspire as "leaders," "supervisors" or "administrators." Competency based graduate education attempts to develop "Educators," "Researchers," "Master Administrators" or "Clinicians." The "Researcher - Practitioner" dichotomy controversy periodically rears its head in our professional writings and conferences illustrating the real or imagined rift between "providers of service" and "generators of new knowledge." "Special groups" personnel segregate themselves from "community recreators" in professional societies and universities. "Therapeutic Recreation Personnel" frequently see themselves as concerned exclusively with one particular "clientele" (visually impaired mentally retarded persons), setting (institutional, hospital or community), or media (art therapist, crafts specialist, physical activities instructor). The effects of this overspecialization on the autonomy and control of the individuals served by the leisure service profession can be profound. As Therapeutic Recreation Specialists and Community Recreators isolate themselves, those trained in "T.R." will lack a working knowledge of leisure service provision in the public sector and consequently will be unable to influence this system and act as advocates for their "clients." Similarly, those trained in "community recreation" will not be imbued with an awareness and understanding of the needs and abilities of disabled persons. The current rift between institutions and community based services will remain thus depriving disabled persons of the right to participate in generic services. While functional specificity reigns supreme, landscape architects and resource planners will continue to design aesthetically pleasing environments and facilities which are architectural nightmares to disabled persons. All leisure service providers lacking extra-disciplinary study in economics, political science, sociology and human development will continue to perpetuate economic control in leisure services as previously described.

COMPARTMENTALIZATION OF SERVICES

A second manifestation of functional specificity exhibited by those charged with the provision of leisure services concerns the fragmentation of leisure experiences offered to recipients of our program efforts. By limiting our attention to certain aspects of a "client's" life, we inadvertently assign and perpetuate stereotyped roles and sets of expectations on the basis of our preconceived notions of the characteristics of groups of individuals. Labeling, a commonly used technique to insure functional specificity in therapeutic recreation, controls peoples' lives and potential through:

> . . .categorical judgments about individuals' interests, skills, level of functioning and previous experience. This practice has the effect which I am sure we do not intend, of proving to others that persons with a particular illness are "within their category" "alike in all respects" and "distinctly different" from the "non ill, non-disabled, non special in all respects."[10]

Once this labeling process is complete, the removal of control from the disabled person is inevitable. The recreator provides "packaged programs" or activities based on the diagnostic label of the "client" which exist in a vacuum devoid of other skills, abilities or interests of the individual. Functional specificity prevails – mentally retarded people receive one regimen of activities, the aged another, and so on. Compartmentalization of activities also extends to the time frame in which leisure pursuits are scheduled. This condition is dramatically illustrated in the account of an ex-mental patient:

> It's a pretty dull existence in which everything you need is handed out in neat little packages – even the therapy – not when you need it most, but again at specific times.[11]

While the labels utilized by the "community recreator" are not as mystifying as those adroitly adopted by the "therapeutic recreator" they too have the effect of perpetuating social control through stereotyped responding to the leisure lifestyle needs of the general public. A cursory examination of commonly used municipal recreation labels identifying program offerings include: Boys, Girls, Men's Women's Adult, Child, Novice, Advanced, Intermediate, Teen, Handicapped, Special. "Women's" programs are still offered primarily during the day ignoring the fact that over 40% of married women are now gainfully employed. Children's activities are scheduled at times so as not to interfere with adult activities or disturb family cohesion. Program levels such as beginner, intermediate and advanced stratify ability levels and promote competition. Specialized instructors are relied upon to provide technical expertise rather than general assistance in planning a leisure lifestyle. Leisure counseling and education necessitating personal contact and familiarization with all aspects of the "client's" life remain low priorities of parks and recreation agencies. "Handicapped" programs insure that groups of individuals sharing only one common feature will congregate at a certain place at a certain time. Functional specificity again promotes social conformity and control in leisure services.

"SOCIO-PSYCHOLOGISM", LEISURE SERVICES AND SOCIAL CONTROL

A third factor threatening the personal control of "clients" served by the leisure service profession is the profession's adherence to the concept of "socio-psychologism." Briefly stated, socio-psychologism is the practice or philosophy of emphasizing or focusing on the problems which an individual has in his or her personal interactions with the social order, rather than exhibiting a concern for the underlying basic nature of the social order. In terms of the social services:

> If a diagnosis does not incorporate a concern for the way in which the whole society may be pathological and produce pathology in individuals as a normal condition of functioning, then the condition of pathology that is shared by all will be, paradoxically, the standard of behavior and existence toward which treatment is directed.[12]

The implications of the application of this orientation in the field of leisure services are obvious. If all existing values of society are embraced as a given, service efforts will center around the adaptation of the "client" to existing conditions, thereby exerting a form of social control. Our professional interventions tend to be "time limited" and "technological" and treat symptoms of discontent within the "client" rather than dealing with the fundamental environmental sources of the person's discomfort. The following points will illustrate the prevalence and effects of socio-psychologism in the field of leisure services.

Like the social services, leisure service providers seem most willing to interact with individuals who do not exhibit major differences in behavior and lifestyle. By selectively excluding persons who manifest significant deviations from commonly accepted norms, leisure service providers are spared the cognitive dissonance which would be engendered if the environment instead of the individual was viewed as being pathological. For example: an individual of lower socio-economic status is parolled to a community from a correctional facility. He or she is motivated to become involved in community recreation and leisure opportunities. After locating the recreation department, the individual finds the program offerings foreign to his/her previous experiences. Secondly, no one is available in the department to offer assistance in developing the skills necessary for participation or to suggest alternative forms of leisure pursuits. The "parolee" returns to his or her former lifestyle, the environment influencing this deviance remains unchanged, and the socio-psychological orientation triumphs.

When the recreation field is involved in providing services to devalued or disadvantaged people, it also frequently adopts a socio-psychological "time-limited," "technological" intervention. To illustrate – leisure programs and services to delinquent youths are frequently aimed at altering the "clients" beliefs, values, attitudes and actions without attempting to change the pathological environment which may be responsible for the behaviors of the person. By ignoring economic, familial, and social conditions, such interventions are doomed to failure. Partington graphically illustrates the results of adopting a strict socio-psychological approach to aiding disadvantaged individuals. Commenting on the failure of a wilderness project to engender measurable changes in delinquent youths, he laments:

> Perhaps the most crushing inference to be drawn from this project is that in retrospect it is seen to rest on a suspect assumption; namely, that troubled youth can be helped by making them think more like "normals"–to expect that they can influence outcomes in their own lives. Unfortunately, changing expectations without changing realities may arouse frustration and resentment. The WILD program, like most current therapeutic interventions, was not designed to change the actual reward structures in the schools and communities to which these participants returned. Moreover, no efforts were made to change their future probability of success through social–economic–political engineering to create broader potential occupational opportunities. Maybe the 86% of WILD participants who chose not to complete the four trip program understood this conceptual error.[13]

Our approaches to leisure counseling and education are also frequently colored by a socio-psychological and technological orientation. If an individual becomes motivated to seek assistance in his or her leisure planning, what is frequently offered is a value laden "choice" of activities to fill the individuals time. Usually these pursuits are predominently middle-class in nature and are "prescribed" without concern for altering the environment which has caused the basic dissatisfaction with the person's current leisure lifestyle. For example, a counselor might urge a person in a disadvantaged area to select an activity or series of activities limited by the existing resources in the community rather than working with the individual to secure new and better leisure resources in the individual's neighborhood. Additionally, many recreation departments fall victim to the socio-psychologism approach in their attempt to assume sole responsibility for the provision of leisure opportunities in communities. This role is undertaken in lieu of providing services not currently offered by other existing generic agencies and organizations *and* instead of lobbying for leisure environmental changes which would ultimately result in improved services to all community members. As a result of this orientation, energy is expended providing "patchwork" diversional programs which could be better used in analyzing what services are needed and (if so) what agencies could best provide these services.

Meanwhile the practices of the public sector of leisure services exhibit a subtle socio-psychological approach. The area of leisure services to and for "special populations" blatantly embraces this orientation. Even a casual review of past and current literature reveals numerous examples of technological approaches aimed at changing the person to fit the environment rather than dealing with the pathology of the external conditions impinging on the individual. The social control function which is attributed to recreational activities in many institutions (and community based programs) is ample testimony to the orientation. Obvious examples are the diversional and inappropriate activities offered in correctional settings and residences for mentally retarded people. The purpose of these activities is the distraction of the individual from their living conditions (in which they may have cause for rebellion) and the release of surplus energy which they may misdirect toward themselves or their keepers. In both instances, social control prevails.

In psychiatric settings, a more clandestine form of social control through recreation exists. Individuals have the following idea communicated to them in many subtle (and not so subtle) ways.

> Healthy people take part in recreation. You are currently unhealthy and therefore don't take part in recreation. Your participation in recreation will be taken as a sign of getting well. Therefore, if you want to get out of here, you had better participate!

Consequently, a great deal of stress is placed on participation in highly structured and controlled activities which are often inappropriate to time, age, and skill level of people. (Has anyone else observed "mentally ill" adults throwing bean bags in a day room at 9:00 AM?).

A more direct form of social control through socio-psychologism and technological intervention is evidenced by the persistent "prescription" of activities for disabled persons in institutional settings. This interventionist strategy by definition "precludes the voluntary aspect of recreational activity."[14] Ironically, this belief and practice may be the last remaining vestiges of choice, control and autonomy of the individual. Behavioral technology poses a similar threat to the personal freedom of the individual. Recent experimental investigations[15] in which participation in "client" preferred activities was made contingent upon participation in therapist "prescribed" activities raises some serious questions concerning our rationalization for mandatory activities and the degree to which individual choice (control) over participation must be respected in all leisure service settings.

RETURNING THE LOCUS OF CONTROL

With the previously outlined threats to client autonomy exposed, it is imperative that the field of leisure services develop new orientations and strategies resulting in more personally responsive, consumer-controlled leisure lifestyles. To meet this end, the following directions and practices are suggested:

1. *Future Recreators Must Encourage the Development of Leisure Lifestyles Which are Consistent With the Means and Therefore Under the Control of the "Client."* If the vicious circle of spiraling work and extended credit to meet high levels of leisure consumption is to be overcome, individuals must learn to locate, utilize and enjoy leisure opportunities which are geographically and economically accessible. As these words were written, a 1.2% per month cost of living increase, gasoline shortages and prices in excess of 83 cents per gallon were announced. Developments such as these will necessitate an increased use of leisure resources within home, community and neighborhood, in which the individual resides. Trips of 500 miles in aerodynamically inefficient vehicles obtaining 5 miles per gallon of gasoline (if available) to distant facilities will become untenable. Vest-pocket parks, home-centered family leisure participation and low-budget "new games" will prevail. Leisure interest finders may be re-designed to emphasize non-commercial leisure activities which do not reinforce or create materialistic "wants" for their users. The artificial work/leisure dichotomy may disappear from our therapeutic interventions as occupational and recreational "therapists" de-emphasize professional boundaries in favor of providing opportunities meeting the total lifestyle needs of the individual. "Vocational" and "avocational" counseling interventions will merge into client-centered educational experiences fostering an integrated rather than fragmented lifestyle in which work and leisure needs are complementary, realistically achieved, and under the control of the "client."

2. *Recreators Must De-emphasize Limited Technological Interventions in Favor of Developing a Fundamental Understanding of the Phenomenon of Leisure.* By departing from traditional, functionally specific educational training and professional placement, several changes in service delivery would take place, resulting in increases in "client" autonomy. First, by emphasizing the exploration of the underlying human needs and motivations relevant to the leisure experience, future service providers would be less likely to stress

traditional facility planning and the provision of stereotyped activities. As concepts such as "activity substitution" are substantiated, consumers will be provided with *choices* of several leisure pursuits within cognates of low-cost, readily available activities which satisfy a basic human leisure need. This practice will be in sharp contrast with current practices of offering a finite number of highly structured "programs."

Secondly, "client" leisure autonomy will be enhanced as professional recreators are encouraged to view individual's leisure and lives in total rather than as a series of compartmentalized activities. Those individuals involved in public and quasi-public agencies will take an interest in the consumer's leisure beyond the four walls of the agency. Activities within institutions will cease to be served up "in packages." Rather, opportunities for free play and social interaction of the "client's" own choosing will predominate. The role of the recreator must hence be shifted from that of a therapist or programmer to that of a facilitator.

3. *Recreators Must Recognize Participants as the Only Reliable Monitors of the Effectiveness of Their Services.* Contemporary leisure research[16] has tended to reaffirm early notions of leisure as being a state of mind or a personal perception of the individual engaged in a "leisure experience." Despite the growing recognition of leisure as being subjective (participant defined) rather than objective (second party defined), recreators continue to offer narrow, structured, time limited programs which ignore the subjective feelings of the "client." In seeking a solution to this situation, Ellis[17] admonishes recreators to "consult more with individuals regarding their leisure perceptions and reactions and abandon the orientation that any activity *we* provide for people is recreational." In the public sector, this may mean polling individuals as to *their* needs and wants and altering community centers from program facilities to places for consumer-centered leisure counseling and resource referral. In institutional settings, this orientation may involve the abandonment of the weekly activity schedule, the initiation of free choice of activity on the part of the "client" and the right to refuse recreational treatment. The "client" must in fact play the most significant part in the restoration of his or her own health if personal autonomy is to be insured.

4. *Recreators Must Engage in Reciprocal Relationships With "Clients" Which Stress the Development of Independent Leisure Skills.* A final step in insuring the personal leisure control of the individual involves a re-definition of our relationships with our "clients" in both public and "therapeutic" recreation settings. No longer must the recreator

be seen as the mentor or ultimate source of expertise in handing down or prescribing activities for the consumer. Rather, the "client" must be viewed as having the primary responsibility for the quality of his or her own leisure. This does not suggest that the recreator has a diminished role to play in achieving this end. It does however, suggest a fundamental change in our interventions with our "clients." Fifty-minute-hour, counselor oriented leisure counseling sessions stressing computerized activity matching must give way to more personal reflection on the part of the "client." Counselors and other personnel in municipal recreation and institutional facilities must "de-mystify" their techniques to the point where the "client" may understand and adopt these practices to his or her own betterment. In short, recreation personnel in general cannot afford to become priviledged and unaccountable at the expense of the freedom and control of the individuals they serve.

> When man creates his own meaning he takes possession of the world; when he does it recreatively with style and dignity, he stages the dream of human life as only it can be staged.[18]

Perhaps our greatest challenge of the next decades will be the creation of a climate of personal freedom in which this "dream" can be realized.

REFERENCES

1. Lefcourt, H. M.. "The Function of the Illusions of Control and Freedom." *American Psychologist,* (May, 1971). p. 425.
2. Neulinger, J.. *The Psychology of Leisure.* Springfield, Illinois: Charles C. Thomas, 1974.
3. Sites, P.. *Control: The Basis of Social Order.* New York: Dunnellen Co., 1973. p. 214.
4. Angel, J.. *The Radical Therapist.* New York: Ballantine Gooks, 1971. p. XV.
5. Galper, J.F.. *The Politics of Social Services.* New Jersey: Prentice Hall, 1975. p. 47.
6. Galper, *Ibid.,* p. 22.
7. Tillman, A.. *The Program Book for Recreation Professionals.* California: National Press Books, 1973. p. 63.
8. Galper, *Op. Cit.*, p. 54.
9. Galper, *Op. Cit.,* p. 92.
10. Meyer, L.. "A View of Therapeutic Recreation: Its Foundations, Objectives and Challenges." Paper presented at New England Therapeutic Recreation Society Meeting, Durham, New Hampshire, October, 1976, p. 15.
11. Angel, *Op. Cit.,* p. 50.
12. Galper, *Op. Cit.,* p. 123.
13. Partington, J.. "Project Wild: A Wilderness Learning Experience for High Delinquency Risk Youth." *Leisurability,* 4:2, (1977). p. 40.
14. Shivers, J.. "Why Not Recreational Therapy?" *Leisurability,* 4(4), (1977). p. 4.
15. Quilitch, H. R. and de Longchamps, G.. "Increasing Recreation Participation of Institutional Neuro-Psychiatric Residents." *Therapeutic Recreation Journal,* 8:2, (1974). pp. 56-60.
16. Shaw, S.. "The Problem of Leisure: A Comparison of Subjective and Objective Methods of Calculating Leisure for Males and Females." Unpublished Master's Thesis. Dalhousie University, Halifax, Nova Scotia, Canada, 1978.
17. Ellis, M. J.. "Some Leisure Studies – Review and Preview," Paper presented at the Allen V. Sapora Symposium on Leisure and Recreation. University of Illinois, Champaign, Illinois, May, 1977. p. 10.
18. Becker, E.. *The Structure of Evil.* New York: George Braziller Co., 1968. p. 213.

Chapter Nineteen

Buckpassing, Blaming or Benevolence: A Leisure Education /Leisure Counseling Perspective

Peter A. Witt

There are several professional stances that can be taken toward an individual in need of service. One can, for example, act with benevolence, attempting to "do good" relative to meeting the needs expressed. On the other hand a posture of "it's not my concern or within my professional domain" can be adopted. Or we can blame the one in need for their own misfortune and thus hold them responsible for extricating themselves from the causes and consequences of their own actions. As recreation and leisure services begin to move toward "enabling" and "facilitating" services, adopting a philosophic stance toward the cause, responsibility and remediation of problems of leisure functioning will become an increasingly important concern. Whether to act with benevolence, pass-the-buck or blame the victim will become an increasingly difficult moral and practical issue.

No where is this problem of focus more acute in the realm of recreation and leisure services than in the burgeoning attempts to conceptualize and initiate leisure counseling and leisure education services (LC/LE).[1] In general, theory and practice have tended to develop along the twin paths of the "helping relationship" and educational models. Remediation or learning has been largely assumed to be client, student or participant focused. School systems, recreation programs and counseling relationships have been seen as the locus for some kind of intervention. All of these developments have emerged within a general framework that has emphasized individuals learning to cope with problems or barriers that block leisure fulfillment.

While there is every reason to believe that the LC/LE movement will further crystalize its methods and broaden its base of support over the next few years, there are several issues which it must come to grips with if it is to make a lasting impact on peoples' leisure functioning. Of particular concern is the fact that to date most of the attention has been focused on helping *individuals* change or modify some combination of their values, attitudes, skills or knowledge re: leisure. Little attention has been directed toward dealing with systemic problems that support the work ethic, productivity, and societal definitions of usefulness as basic criteria for success, well being and meaning. The belief within LC/LE seems to be that individuals need to be educated or counseled to fit into society and its institutional structures. Little attention has been given, however, to changing the basic social, economic and political conditions within the society that affect an individual's ability to undertake personally meaningful leisure experiences. It is not clear whether "changing" individuals will have any significant impact on the values and attitudes expressed by the institutional structures of the society as a whole. It seems more likely that efforts to educate or counsel individuals will be significantly over-ridden by the basically conservative and slow nature of social change that will continue to support the status quo and a work ethic dominated definition of purpose, success and personal well-being.

While not suggesting that we abandon attempts to help individuals develop the tools necessary for a personally more meaningful leisure lifestyle, it is proposed that significant attention be directed toward reforming the social institutions that support the dominance of the work ethic (at least to the extent that it undermines leisure lifestyle). This stance does not necessarily imply a supplanting of work by leisure or the downgrading of attempts to create a society that meets the material needs of its populace. Rather, this position is aimed at helping to create a society that provides a climate conducive to leisure. While it is not being proposed that work be made obsolete, the work environment and its accompanying ethic of production, quantity and conformity does need to be humanized to make the possibilities of leisure more achievable and meaningful at the individual level. Significant attempts must also be made to make recreation environments more "hospitable" to human needs for play and leisure.

BLAMING THE VICTIM

Up to now, leisure education and leisure counseling have proceeded based on a "blame the victim" model. With this model we blame individuals as the source of their own problems and "justify inequality by finding defects in the victims of inequality."[2] Ryan goes on to explain that the stigma, defect or fatal difference (whether it be an inability to read, the failure to obtain or maintain employment, or the failure to achieve a personally satisfying leisure lifestyle)

> ". . .is still located *within* the victim, inside his skin. With such an elegant formulation, the humanitarian can have it both ways. He can, all at the same time, concentrate his charitable interest on the defects of the victim, condemn the vague social and environmental stresses that produced the defect (some time ago) and ignore the continuing effect of the victimizing forces (right now). It is a brilliant ideology for justifying a perverse form of social action designed to change, not society, as one might expect, but rather society's victims."[3]

Thus, Johnny can't read because Johnny is not smart enough to read and is poorly motivated as opposed to looking at factors such as poor teaching methods and inadequate reinforcement (perceived value to bother learning). In the case of leisure "problems" we tend to overemphasize the "defects" in an individual's values, attitudes, skills and knowledge regarding leisure without giving proper attention to the service provisions and reinforcements provided by the society which influence leisure choices and outcomes. Further, we fail to give proper weight to factors such as unequal distribution of income, social stratification, inequality of power, plus mechanization and urbanization as the source of significant portions of the "leisure problem" for many individuals.

Overcoming the "blame the victim" mentality of LC/LE requires that we pay more attention to why, for example, poor leisure habits arise in the first place; why individuals are unprepared for increased free time; why playfulness is considered only the perogative of children, and only then if its the work of the child in his quest to grow up to be a productive adult; and why competition versus cooperation, and physical versus artistic and intellectual activity, are the socially accepted and reinforced bases of leisure involvements. We blame victims who turn to spectatoritis and non-involvement through our tendency to overprogram and plan for people to the point where "many are almost incapable of creating their own satisfying activities or of finding lasting meaning in what they do."[4]

Orlick provides numerous examples of children, as they get older, dropping out of competitive, hierarchially based sports programs because these programs are not conducted at an appropriate skill and competitive level for their needs.[5] Of course, we can undo Orlick's evidence by "blaming" the drop-outs as being unmotivated and insufficently competitive. We may even rationalize that they've learned an important lesson in life by failing and being rejected. It is in this context that some have argued for the need for LC/LE to help dropouts deal with rejection and failure when a better system of opportunity and meeting their skill or interest level may be what's really required.

Preparing people to cope better with an unfit, dehumanizing and non-growth encouraging environment is only part of the answer. Rendering the environment more hospitable is the necessary correlate.[6] Lane goes even further by suggesting that we place too much emphasis on individuals as if they had personal power and choice and on human behavior as if it was primarily determined by enduring and consistent characteristics of the individual. "We perpetuate the cult of individualism by refusing to consider the existence of interrelated power structures as necessary if not sufficient variables in determining behavior."[7]

BLAMING THE ENVIRONMENT

In recent years several other authors have suggested more emphasis on a change (blame) the system versus change (blame) the individual approach in leisure services. Most have voiced their opposition to the medical model approach often adopted toward members of special populations. For example, Rusalum suggested what he called the ecological model as an alternative to the therapeutic model in therapeutic recreation. This model

> ". . .is built upon the belief that the overwhelming majority of disabled and disadvantaged persons do not need therapy. Despite their limitations and a denying society, they are relatively well-integrated, emotionally healthy persons struggling to survive in a given unrewarding, unhospitable environment. . . . For example, America's urban areas are polluted, crowded, unattractive, inconsiderate of people's needs for intimacy and warmth, poverty-stricken, inconvenient, dangerous, and most important from the vantage point of the exceptional individual, intolerant and inflexible in relation to extremes of human differences."[8]

The ecological approach would significantly "shift professional emphasis from the therapy of people to the therapy of environments."[9]

Thibault outlines three general approaches that can be taken to leisure education.[10] The first of these he labels the *traditional education* model. Under this model leisure activities are offered by service providers that are judged appropriate and good according to the dominant values of the society. Individuals are then informed via advertising of the availability of these opportunities and sensitized to the value of participating in them. The *psycho-education* model assumes that individuals lack self knowledge regarding leisure values and attitudes. A variety of individual and group counseling methods are used to help individuals develop personally appropriate values and attitudes. Finally, the *psycho-socio-education* model sees actual leisure involvement as a result of the interaction between economic, social and political influences of society and the individual's own will to actualize his needs, values, and attitudes. The aim of leisure education is to demystify the actions of these social forces thus enabling the individual to perceive and act differently relative to his leisure. This demystification is accomplished by working to reduce the pressure of the social forces impinging on leisure via strategies to change the dominant value and institutional systems within the society as well as influencing the individual's perceptions by offering social alternatives that make real choice possible. Thibault seems to favor this latter model as having the most potential for influencing the options available and resultant outcomes for leisure lifestyle.

Edginton and Compton also have taken a middle ground position in the system versus individual change controversy by arguing for more attention to consumerism and advocacy as essential service approaches for those working with special populations. Consumerism will help individuals develop "personal competency in making qualitative and quantitative judgments about goods and services received and consumed."[11] Advocacy involves efforts to improve the quality of goods and services rendered to consumers via roles such as planner, strategist, negotiator, lobbyist, or educator. Thus, the emphasis is on both enabling individuals to deal with their environment and bringing about significant environmental change to meet the needs of individuals.

To blame the victim or blame the environment is a controversial issue in a number of other helping professions as well. Of particular relevance is the controversy going on in both the psychology and the health fields. For example, Lewis and Lewis argue that a preventive or developmental approach to community mental health problems is more efficient than a remedial one.[12] The intent of prevention is "to anticipate future problems and move to prevent them by providing individuals or groups with needed skills or by creating changes in the environment so as to prevent the development of problems."[13] These authors do not argue against the validity of direct efforts to help people deal with the problems they confront in their lives. Rather they see the need for equal attention to changing the social surroundings that affect people's lives. To accomplish this Lewis and Lewis outline four programmatic approaches to intervention:

> "Extensive-experiential: programs that provide direct experiences available to the population as a whole.

Intensive-experiential: programs that provide special experiences to individuals or groups that need them.

Extensive-environmental: programs that attempt to make the entire community more responsive to the needs of all its members.

Intensive-environmental: programs that intervene actively in the environments of specific individuals or groups, so that their special needs can be met."[14]

Rappaport *et al.* suggest that we tend to place too much emphasis on problems, whether a victim or environment blaming model is adopted. As community psychologists they argue that services should emphasize building on "community strengths and aiding in the development of those, while leaving amelioration of deficits to physicians, clergyman social workers and clinicians."[15] The point of view may have a valuable parallel when trying to delineate the responsibility of recreation professionals to remove leisure deficits of individuals. Building on strengths via community development and enabling functions may be much closer to both the traditional roots and the training of most recreation professionals. Creating new avenues to desired goals and helping to transfer skills from areas of already existing competence via identification and utilization of community resources may be better avenues than attempts to repair weaknesses. In a sense this calls for emphasis on a "what are you good at" versus "what can I help you with" model.[16]

IMPLICATIONS AND FUTURE DIRECTIONS

The preceding ideas have a number of implications for the ways that the recreation and leisure services profession should conceptualize and deliver services aimed at dealing with people's leisure problems or deficits. Emphasis should change from trying to initiate person remediation and counseling approaches to strategies emphasizing consumerism, advocacy, environmental change and education, particularly in community settings. Because it's new and sounds "professional," jumping on the leisure counseling, "bandwagon" may appear to be a more attractive alternative than services aimed at redistributing opportunity, removing barriers to participation, and providing a humane environment in which people can make personally meaningful leisure choices. However, given the roots and basic expertise of the leisure service profession, our real mission lies in helping to reshape the opportunities available for leisure involvements, whether these be municipally, school or privately sponsored, as well as providing the supportive and skill training services that would facilitate participation.

In addition, the leisure services profession also has a vital role to play in educating itself, other professionals and citizens regarding a new outlook on the benefits and potential of leisure experiences. This education process should probably begin "at home" with the staff of existing recreation, park and leisure services. It is necessary that workers in these areas assess their own attitudes toward play, recreation, leisure and work. In the process, workers should analyze how their own biases and philosophies become a filter through which the problems and needs of others are viewed. As Freedom points out:

> "Embedded in the claims of each of the professions is a "paradigm," a taken-for-granted conception of what the issue is, and how it is solvable. Each tends to see the world in terms of its own characteristic conception of problems and solutions."[17]

The paradigm within recreation and park services has been based on seeing the essential problems as 1) *recreation*, i.e., involvement in activity that would prepare an individual to go back to work refreshed; 2) *idleness*, i.e., people need something to do to fill the time freed from work due to automation; 3) *catharsis and compensation*, i.e., helping people act out frustrations derived from dehumanizing work and living environments. In a sense we've avoided blaming ourselves for our service conceptualization and provision failures by passing judgment on participants. This paradigm has led to a system of park and recreation services which has generally served the interests of a society committed to the work ethic. In many cases the profession has been the hand maiden of a "bread and circuses," social control approach to serving the public good. The argument that what is currently being provided is what people want is to ignore the process by which people learn to want. The delivery system as a value giving, reinforcing and reflecting entity helps to shape and reinforce particular patterns of activity within the population.

Up to now, the profession has had a basically conservative focus. It has been largely a civil service profession, allied closely with the purposes of perserving status-quo governmental priorities and assumptions. These assumptions have led to a mainstream system of park and recreation opportunities that tend to reinforce existing values and keep people busy or entertained. The profession must do some serious soul-searching and self-evaluation if a revised set of assumptions and eventually services is to become a reality. The "bankruptcy" warnings of Grey and Grebin[18] and the need to adopt a more holistic and humanistic perspective, as suggested by Murphy,[19] must be seriously examined.

Perhaps Charles K. Brightbill best summarized the basis for a new paradigm when he stated:

> "If we are to educate for leisure, it will be necessary to change many of our basic values. It will be necessary for us to revise our ideas of what constitutes success in life. We shall have to think less of bank accounts, fur coats and estates to leave to our children and cherish more the wonders of nature, the arts, the zest of leisurely physiological release, as well as service to our fellow man. We shall have to want more time not to produce and consume more material goods, but rather, to live more of life."[20]

In addition to adjusting our own paradigm, the profession must also place substantially more emphasis on becoming a catalytic change agent in the society at large. The profession must become more active in the political and social development process to help foster a better understanding of leisure needs and barriers to leisure fulfillment. The profession must also help to foster a social, political and economic environment conducive to leisure fulfillment. This will require the profession to become an active force in promoting an awareness of leisure's potential among political leaders, school officials, the clergy, business leaders and social service workers; an awareness that goes beyond a work ethic definition of re-creation.

The profession must also help overcome the emphasis on competition (to the detriment of cooperation), busyness (to the detriment of involvement and meaning) and consumption (to the detriment of experience and quality). On a wider scale, this involvcs seeing the role of leisure in fostering personal autonomy and growth; building a foundation for personal expression and self-defined meaning. It builds on the potential of leisure to add to an individual's life rather than repair problems created by interaction with the work or urban environment. Thus, increased emphasis is placed upon prevention and building on strengths rather than remediation and overcoming weakensses.

REFERENCES

1. Epperson, Arlin, Witt, Peter A. and Hitzhusen, Gerald. *Leisure Counseling: An aspect of Leisure Education.* Springfield: Charles C. Thomas, 1977. Compton, David M. and Judith E. Goldstein (Editors). *Perspectives of Leisure Counseling.* Arlington: National Recreation and Park Association, 1977.
2. Ryan, William. *Blaming the Victim*. New York: Vintage Books, 1976. XIII.
3. Ryan, William. *Op.Cit.* pp. 7-8.
4. Czurles, Arthur. "Art Creativity vs Spectatoris." *Journal of Creative Behavior*. 10, 1976. p. 107.

5. Orlick, Terry. *Winning Through Cooperation: Competitive Insanity: Co-operative Alternatives.* Washington, D.C: Hawkins and Associates, 1977.
6. Witt, Peter A. "The Art's in a State." In: D. M. Compton and J. Goldstein (Editors). *Perspectives of Leisure Counseling.* Arlington: National Recreation and Park Association, 1977. pp. 1-8.
7. Lane, Mary Kay. "A Reconsideration of Context: Perspectives on Prediction-Mote in the Eye." *American Psychologist.* 32 (12), 1977. p. 1056.
8. Rusalem, Herbert. "An Alternative to the Therapeutic Model in Therapeutic Recreation." *Therapeutic Recreation Journal.* 7, 1973. p. 12.
9. Rusalem. *Ibid.* p. 15.
10. Thibault, Andre. *La Situation Professionnelle des Travailleurs en Loisirs du Quebec comme Determinant de la Possibilite Differentielle de l'Education au Loisir.* Thèse de Doctorat, Universite Laval, 1979.
11. Edginton, Christopher R. and David M. Compton. "Consumerism and Advocacy: A Conceptual Framework for Therapeutic Recreation." *Therapeutic Recreation Journal.* 9 (1) 1975. p. 27.
12. Lewis, Judith A. and Lewis, Michael D. *Community Counseling: A Human Services Approach.* New York: John Wiley Sons, Inc. 1977. p. 16.
13. Morrill, W. H., Oetting, E. R., Hurst, J. C. "Dimensions of Counselor Functioning." *The Personnel and Guidance Journal.* 52 (Feb.), 1974. p. 357.
14. Lewis and Lewis. *Op.Cit.*
15. Rappaport, J. *et al.* "Alternatives to Blaming the Victim or the Environment." *American Psychologist.* 30 (4), 1975. p. 526.
16. Rappaport, *et.al. Ibid.*
17. Friedson, Eliot. "Professions and the Occupational Principle." In: Friedson, Eliot (Ed.). *The Professions and Their Prospects.* Beverly Hills: Sage, 1973. p. 31.
18. Gray, David E. and Seymour Grebin. "Future Perspectives." *Parks and Recreation.* 9, 1974 (July). pp. 26-56.
19. Murphy, James F. *Recreation and Leisure Service: A Humanistic Approach.* Dubuque: W. C. Brown, Co. 1975.
20. Brightbill, Charles K. *Man and Leisure.* Englewood Cliffs, New Jersey: Prentice Hall, Inc. 1961. p. 193.

Chapter Twenty

Beyond Professionalism

William Thorsteinson

"All Professions are conspiracies against the laity"
George Bernard Shaw

Shaw is not alone in his mistrust of the professions but even with the mistrust there is a strong desire on the part of everyone to wear the mantle of professionalism. There is a dishwasher who appears on television and begins his pitch for a particular washing compound with the words, "Professionally speaking. . ." Then, on the same medium, there are young children busy selling one another toy real estate, while wearing a parent's yellow blazer and referring to themselves as "Your neighborhood professional." It is a clear case of everyone wanting to get into the act.

The question that this paper addresses is whether or not recreation practitioners want to or should join the pack pursuing this goal. There is no doubt that we are in the race toward professionalism and have been for some time. The idea that this quest may not be worth the effort has not been proposed until recently. Geoffrey Godbey, writing in *Society and Leisure,* cautions us that while there are many benefits, it would be foolish to proceed without realizing there are drawbacks as well.[1] Not only should close attention be paid to Godbey, but also it is quite likely that to continue towards professionalism would be to chase an anachronism.

The recreation field should abandon its present course toward establishing a profession in favor of the creation of a new model of relationship between the professional and society. This seems evident considering the definitions and characteristics of professions. When the practice of recreation is cast against these definitions and characteristics, it becomes evident that there are areas of congruence and incongruence. Advantages and disadvantages of the present thrust toward professional status also become evident, thus the case can be made for moving in a different direction. References throughout will be made to direct experience in the Province of Ontario. It is assumed that similar situations exist in the rest of Canada and possibly other parts of the world, but the readers can test this against their own experience and determine the validity of the argument.

WHAT IS A PROFESSION?

It is not difficult to find a definition of a professional. An endless variety appear in texts from many fields. The problem is to determine which are the essential elements. An easy trap to fall into would be to select that definition which best suits the realities of the occupational grouping under examination and the particular bias of the writer. The intention of this paper is to avoid this pitfall.

Perhaps the most thorough job of defining the term is done by Schein in his chapter "What is a Profession?" He lists ten basic criteria which are generally employed, all or in part, in the various definitions that appear.[2]

Using this list one could easily prove that the recreation practice is or is not a profession. Elements such as strong motivation, a service orientation and a prolonged period of education and training do exist for the recreation practitioner. But whether there is a specialized body of knowledge and skills has often been brought into question and this is a key to Schein's definition. Also he suggests a professional should deal directly with specific clients. The recreation practitioner tends to deal with client groups rather than clients. Thus, the matter of professionalism is left to opinion.

Greater light is cast on the problem by Wilbert E. Moore. He suggests that identifying a fixed definition that would apply to all occupational groups that define themselves as professions is an unrealistic task. Moore suggests a "scale of professionalism" such that occupations would possess degrees of professionalism.[3] Moore's scale would be based on certain of the items that Schein identified, particularly the full-time aspect, the idea of a calling, the existence of a professional organization, control over training and education, a service orientation and autonomy.[4] Thus, it is possible to include both the classic profession of the clergy and an emerging profession like recreation within the same definition.

If one argues from a conservative position then only those occupations at the upper end of the scale would qualify. The liberal position would be far more inclusive and would be favored by those from among the striving occupations like recreation. Another who offers the step process is Wilensky and his sequence is as follows:[5]

- Full-time activity of the task.
- Establishment of university training.
- National professional association.
- Redefinition of the core task, so as to give the "dirty work" over to subordinates.

- Conflict between the old timers and the new men who seek to upgrade the job.
- Competition between the new occupation and neighboring ones.
- Political agitation in order to gain legal protection.
- Code of ethics.

It is not difficult to see that the field of recreation has been through some of these steps and is involved in others. Furthermore, it is clear where it goes next if it is to continue along this sequence.

About the same time Wilensky was asking when professionalization was going to end, William Goode was attempting to provide the answer. In his article, "The Theoretical Limits of Professionalization,"[6] he suggests that some occupations will never become professions. He identifies as four classic professions, law, medicine, the clergy and university teaching, and goes on to indicate that while some occupations may approach these classics, others like school teachers, librarians and nurses, will never make it.[7] Some may think Goode to be unduly harsh, but none could doubt that he would include recreation on his list of futile strivers.

Borrowing from all the various contributions quoted above, a profession will be regarded as an occupational grouping which is consciously moving along a scale of increasing control over its own affairs with regard to the following factors:

- the entry of individuals into the field including the evidence of motivation and academic qualifications.
- the definition of the service to be rendered including the method of delivery (code of ethics).
- the monitoring of performance to ensure the quality of the service delivered.
- the accumulation of new knowledge and techniques to allow continued development of competence.

While these criteria may help identify the essence of a profession, at least for now, social dynamics are such as to require modifications over time. As Schein noted:

> . . .the basic definition of a profession is more than a matter of applying a number of complex criteria since the many settings within which professionals do their work are changing some of the very criteria by which their role was defined in the first place. To put this matter another way, as society is becoming more differentiated and complex, the work roles of professionals are becoming more varied and complex. This complexity generates forces toward differentiation of the professions into many more specialities, creates jurisdictional problems among professions and among special-

ities within professions, forces new definitions of the proper role of the professional and his responsibility to clients, and creates the need for more integrators to coordinate the efforts of different specialists.[8]

DOES RECREATION QUALIFY?

Before proceeding to any arguments about whether recreation should continue in pursuit of professionalism it would make sense to determine if it belongs in the race at all. If recreation presumes to a status for which it cannot qualify then this paper needs be quite short and the efforts totally futile. The fact is, that despite Goode's arbitrary dismissal of many occupational groupings, a number of them, recreation included, are well on the way and could achieve some degree of professional status. Certainly, there are major difficulties, which are often more easily seen in other groups. Nurses and teachers for example, have wavered between union status and full professionalism for many years.

Recreation has successfully defined itself as a full-time occupation. In virtually all its expressions; municipal, agency, therapeutic and so forth, full-time workers are the norm. At the same time, however, the field is quick to acknowledge the role and importance of the part-time worker and volunteer. At its Annual Meeting in 1975, the Ontario Recreation Society acknowledged the status of part-time workers by opening its membership to any recreationists working 26 hours or more per week.[9] To achieve the status of a profession as defined by most authorities, the field must be more firm than the O.R.S. in excluding part-time employees.

Many recreation practitioners see their service as a calling. In the vernacular, the field is often referred to as a movement, which indicates a sense of mission. The various national and regional professional organizations have developed ceremonies and rituals of inclusion which further emphasize the idea of special status. While less tangible than hours of work, it would seem that the attitude of many recreation practitioners would qualify on this criterion.

Another criterion by which recreation appears to qualify as a profession is that of education and training. There are numerous degree programs in Canada and throughout the world and the Province of Ontario, at least, has been certifying professionals for years. Practitioners are granted certificates on the basis of successful completion of either a university course (Type A certificate) or community college course (Type B certificate). On the basis of hiring certified personnel, grants are made to municipalities by the provincial government and thus the process of certification has tangible rewards for the municipality if not for the practitioners directly. What makes this process a bit tenuous is the ambivalence that exists in the field regarding the relative values of the degree programs at university and the two year diploma courses offered at the community college level. A resolute profession would have reinforced the university program and either condemned the college program as a threat to professionalism or directed it to the training of second level personnel such as technicians or clerical assistants.

As well, the process of certification has been a fragmented affair over the years. The YMCA, for example, certified its own professionals for many years. The Boys & Girls Clubs of Canada have been diligently working at their own certification process. The "A" and "B" certificates offered by the Province of Ontario have been aimed at the Municipal employee. The extensive study and design of a new process of certification in this province has resulted in the establishment of the College of Recreationists of Ontario. This body essentially is a vehicle to encourage continued professional development as opposed to certification, thus skirting the problem rather than resolving it.

In the matter of professional societies, recreation appears to be in the position of a generous donor being able to offer its surplus to other fields. Ontario has a dubious reputation in Canada, but it may not be alone in having a plethora of professional groups. A study conducted for the Ontario Recreation Society indicated the variety of professional bodies that exist in one single province of Canada. Twenty different organizations operate in the recreation field in Ontario.

But even if Ontario is regarded as unique, there is ample evidence that by this criteria recreation fails to qualify as a profession. There is no professional society at the national level in either the United States or Canada. What do exist are associations representing both layman and professionals: National Recreation and Parks Association in the United States and Canadian Parks and Recreation Association in Canada. In Canada, many of the provincial associations are also combinations of laymen and professionals. Very few professions, if any, advance in concert with the laymen.

To continue this train of thought, discussion of the relationship to clients and client groups would follow and the growing incidence of specialization would be examined, but there seems no need to proceed further. Perhaps with effort, the recreation field could be molded into a profession. The fact that it seems to work as hard at avoiding professionalism is of greater significance. An examination of ambivalent behavior, such as working cooperatively with laymen or avoiding a clear cut stance on certification, will help to set direction for future action.

WHY BECOME A PROFESSION?

The advantages of obtaining professional status are, perhaps, obvious. For the individual professional there is the status and respect accorded to the doctor or lawyer to serve as a stimulus. As well, there is the potential of increased rewards that result from a valued service which can be kept scarce. The control of both entrants and the number of graduates can ensure that such rewards are kept at a desired level by practitioners. At the same time, the quality of service rendered the public can be more readily increased.

From the point of view of society there are distinct advantages to clearly defined professional disciplines. The professional can be held accountable by his peers, and theoretically, the aforementioned quality of service can be maintained and improved. Further, the systematic and logically discreet collection of knowledge has inestimable value, especially over generations of time.

There are however, some negative aspects that must be noted. . . Professions are often accused of inhibiting the spread of knowledge. Moore puts it succinctly when he states:

> . . .What is of enduring importance is the homely truth that new knowledge or innovations in techniques and practice threaten the very basis upon which established professionals rest their claim to expert competence.[10]

Professionals are conservative and resistant to change and the folklore of modern man is replete with examples of the young Turks who defied the statesmen of their professions to bring about progress. Clearly related to this is the sense of secrecy that surrounds professional knowledge. The layman often feels suspicious because of the jealousy by which professions protect their members. The protection of knowledge, while at the same time expanding it and using it as a basis for public service, is a delicate task.

Another criticism of the professions is their tendency to elitism. In her discussion of the formation of the more mature professions, Gilb makes it clear that elitism was essential to development while at the same time sewing the seeds for later discontent, both within and without the profession.[11] This social distance which was characteristic of the professional is certainly out of step with today's world. Evidence that this is not only apparent to the classic professions but is influencing their present direction can be seen by the existence of such things as neighborhood legal or medical clinics. There are priests who frequent the pubs and doctors specializing in family practice. A recreation practitioner cannot afford to have his relationship to clients characterized by social distance. The existence of the various lay-professional groups indicates the desire to work together and negates smooth progress to professionalism.

The advantages to be gained by becoming a profession may be attractive, but the disadvantages are not only apparent but often strike at the basic values of the aspiring professional. As Goode puts it:

> The advantages of being accepted as a profession are obvious. However, few of even the privileged occupations can or will pay the costs of transforming themselves enough to become accepted.[12]

Recreationists, by their behavior, seem to be living evidence of this point.

WHAT ARE THE ALTERNATIVES?

If it is assumed that Goode is right, then all the efforts to establish recreation as a profession are futile. On the other hand, it could be argued that, while never achieving the position of medicine or law, recreation could edge upward on the scale of professionalism. But even if this were possible would the end result be a desirable one? The thesis of this paper is that efforts towards establishing a profession in the classic sense would be a waste of valuable time and energy.

To meet the criteria noted previously, it is apparent that the following action steps would be required in Canada in order to reach full professional status:

1. Develop a national professional society or change the C.P.R.A. orientation more strongly in the direction of professional concerns.

2. Exclude part-time workers and volunteers from professional societies at the national, provincial and local level.

3. Define the "core task" of a recreation practitioner and stress this to the exclusion of specializations.

4. Gain greater control over entry to college and university programs and over the curriculum of such programs.

5. Adopt a universal process of certification, inclusive of continued professional growth if desired.

6. Absorb or clearly exclude those closely related occupational groupings, e.g. community school workers.

7. Begin agitation toward the achievement of legal status.

Not only are recreationists unlikely to take such steps, there is very little motivation to do so. As Goode has implied, the end state might be desired, but not at the cost that these actions imply.

But what are the alternatives? Is it a lost cause that should simply be abandoned? Has all the effort made to date been worthless? As long as the classic model of professionalism is the goal the answer is "yes." However, it may be that this model has done its job and new models are in order. What recreation needs is such a new model.

There are trends which can be identified and point the way to future development. Continued efforts to increase the quality of leisure service and the competence of recreationists should be made in the light of these trends. At a future date the model will have sufficient form to be analysed and, no doubt, give way to even newer forms.

In the introduction to the book, *The New Professionals,* the editors suggest that there are three fundamental aspects of professionalism which are the focus of changes being made.[13] The new model for professionalism will arise from changes in: a) purpose; a move from self service of professionals to service to the total community, b) client control; opening the profession to influence and participation of clients and c) the credential system; allowing greater flexibility and more alternatives to the traditional education programs. There are developments in the field of recreation that relate to the changes that Gross and Osterman predicted.

The most obvious trend is the partnership concept between the recreationist and the layman or volunteer. The recreation practitioner's reluctance to shut out the volunteer may prevent the establishment of a traditional profession, but it does pave the way for a new, more effective method of operation. Thus, organizations such as C.P.R.A., N.R.P.A. and others should not be changed to reduce the role of the layman, but rather to strengthen it. The fact that there are often tensions and conflict between the professional and layman should not be regarded as a problem, but rather as an opportunity to use the conflict to reach a new understanding and increased quality of service. Instead of building the barriers to diminish overt conflict, methods should be developed to use creatively the conflict for growth.

Another manifestation of the growing partnership between the practitioner and the client can be found in the trend in municipal recreation to get out of direct program operation. While this is talked about more than acted upon, it is still a step in the right direction. It demands active client participation in the services delivered. The fear that it will strip the professional of his role is abated by the fact that a new role, that of "facilitator," is emerging. It means learning new skills and adapting to a different relationship, but then what does "being a professional" mean if not continuous learning and adaptation of basic skills.

Recently in the province of Ontario there has been concern expressed about the system of education of the young professional. Educators have been frustrated because the concern has not been made specific. In reality it cannot be because at this point the practitioner is not really clear about what the problem is, but he does know something is bothering him. He doesn't say the education system is wrong or ineffective, but he does say he isn't sure. In this discomfort with the present system are the roots of another trend.

The method of preparing professionals must change and this relates to the changes in credentialing referred to earlier. The establishment of programs of continuing professional education, such as the College of Recreationists of Ontario, is a clear manifestation of movement in this direction. Practitioners are saying that the idea of learning basic skills and knowledge at the undergraduate level and then spending a career putting this to work is an inadequate model today. Following a solid basic preparation, the professional must continue to learn throughout his career and the College attests to that belief. As yet the nature of preparatory learning has not been articulated, but it will be and it will fit the new developmental model. What is needed is the confidence to act and this will come from the realization that the recreation field is on the right track.

Still another trend that is disturbing to some, but is actually a progressive step, is increasing specialization. The report referred to earlier indicates the number of groups representing specific aspects of recreation service. There are municipal recreationists, aquatics personnel, arena managers, community school workers, outdoor educators, agency workers and so on. It would have been nice if all these spin offs had waited until the "core task" had been clearly defined. Now there are many variations, but variations of what? The trend to highlight though, is not specialization itself but the growing efforts to provide linkages between the specialties. The need for communication networks is clearly seen and is being dealt with. The structure and function of N.R.P.A., while often criticized is an attempt to deal with this reality. More forceful attempts must be made despite those who would oppose such efforts.

Closely related to this and perhaps of ever greater significance is the recognition of the need for related fields to work together. In some communities, social services and recreation have been combined into one department. Schein suggests that such relationships are not only convenient to the professional, but are most necessary if society hopes to deal with the complex problems that it faces.[14]

The field of recreation is faced with one of its greatest challenges in this regard. Some professions such as social work or teaching are more highly developed along the traditional scale and may look with disdain at cooperative efforts. It is recognized that one avenue of solution to the problems presented by declining school enrollment can be found in recreation programming.[15] Will the school system and the teachers' organizations turn to recreationists for help and advice. Will the recreationist speak up forcefully in regard to his profession's potential contribution?

At the same time there are occupational groupings not as far advanced as recreation and some of these are diligently working toward the traditional concept of certification. Those who work in the community school or community education movement are an example of this. In the light of what Gross and Osterman and Edgar Schein have to say this is certainly a retrogressive step, but it is a difficult one to resist. There is no doubt that there is a new order in the making. There are powerful forces which are set up in resistance to it, but it is too late to go back. The classic models of professionalism such as law and medicine cannot be attained by emergent professions. Therefore, bold steps must be taken to reach for a new model. As Schein says:

> Professionals will have to work not only with each other, but, . . . they will also have to learn how to work more collaboratively with client systems, particularly the ultimate clients or users of the services.[16]

Recreation is a field which is halfway along. It started with a conscious goal of the classic model, but was continually sidetracked by influences which were essentially unconscious and yet accurate in terms of future trends. It now becomes imperative for recreation to make these unconscious movements consciously and with a firm resolve to create something new which will root the noble values of traditional professionalism in the 20th century.

REFERENCES

1. Godbey, Geoffrey. "The Professionalization of Recreation and Parks in The Public Sector: Implications for Social Development." *Loisir et Société/Leisure and Society,* 1:2 (November, 1978). pp. 269-284.
2. Schein, Edgar H.. *Professional Education.* New York: McGraw-Hill Book Company, 1972. p. 8-9.
3. Moore, Wilbert E.. *The Professions: Roles and Rules.* New York: Russell Sage Foundation, 1970. p. 5.
4. *Ibid.,* pp. 6-22.
5. Wilensky, Harold. "The Professionalization of Everyone?" *American Journal of Sociology,* (September, 1964). pp. 142-146.
6. Goode, William J.. "The Theoretical Limits of Professionalization." In Etizioni, Amitai (Ed.). *The Semi-Professions and Their Organization.* Glencoe, Illinois: The Free Press, 1969.
7. *Ibid.,* p. 267.
8. Schein, *Op. Cit.,* p. 20.
9. See the Constitution and By-Laws of the Ontario Recreation Society.
10. Moore, *Op. Cit.,* p. 44.
11. Gilb, Corinne L.. *Hidden Hierarchies: The Professionals and Government.* New York: Harper and Row Publishers, 1966. pp. 28-32.
12. Goode, *Op. Cit.,* p. 269.
13. Gross, Ronald and Osterman, Paul. *The New Professionals.* New York: Simon and Schuster, 1972. pp. 9-30.
14. Schein, *Op. Cit.,* p. 34-36.
15. Sullivan, Keith. "Community Schools: A Solution to Declining Enrollment," *Working Paper Number Three of the Commission on Declining School Enrollment in Ontario.* Toronto: The Commission, 1978.
16. Schein, *Op. Cit.,* p. 37.

Chapter Twenty-One

Capturing the Service Market: Licensure, Certification, Accreditation

Peter A. Witt

Among the elements considered necessary to anoint a given occupation as a profession are: a) the establishment of a mechanism of self-regulation (certification) or governmental sanction (licensing) which insures that practitioners acquire a select body of theory, technical skills, and occupational values and b) the establishment of control by the profession over the educational processes and curricula (accreditation) through which individuals acquire the above body of knowledge and skills. These processes are deemed essential in order for a profession to gain the powers and privileges to which it deems itself entitled and to establish its credibility in the eyes of the public.

Interest in creating certification, licensing, and accreditation procedures in the recreation and park field is not new, with attempts at accreditation dating back to the 1930's[1] and certification to the 1950's.[2] However, beginning with the merger that resulted in the establishment of the National Recreation and Park Association (NRPA), efforts have intensified to create the accoutrements of a full-fledged profession. Since 1965 procedures have been worked out for certification/registration (1973) and accreditation (1975). Licensing of therapeutic recreation workers has begun in certain states as well.[3] These efforts have been generally hailed by those within the park and recreation field as tangible evidence of the growing acceptance of the legitimacy of the park and recreation movement and the viability of attempts to insure quality and high standards of service.

Acquiring professional status has become increasingly necessary as a means of establishing legitimacy, autonomy, and status for almost every type of work. For example, sanitation personnel and barbers have begun to label themselves as professionals and demand their adjudged fair share of status and privileges. Professional status is increasingly seen as the natural right of anyone who works for wages. Many of these efforts at acquiring professional status have more to do with protecting worker salaries and insuring job security than attempts to promote higher standards of service provision for consumers. In addition, professional status per se provides gratifying respectability. Often professions become more interested in protecting themselves from the encroachment of other professions rather than working to meet society's needs.

Limiting access to job opportunities by setting educational or experience standards and requiring an individual to gain education from an accredited institution and be certified or licensed as a condition of practice, while theoretically controlling the quality of service rendered, also effectively controls the service market. It may create a situation, for example, where salaries are artificially inflated because demand for workers outstrips the sanctioned supply and where quality of service is controlled by occupational standards as opposed to consumer criteria. Often this means that a profession and not consumers control the basis, rationale, and mechanics of service delivery. Professional control of entry, knowledge to be acquired, and standards of practice may give it undue autonomy and powers of self-regulation.

> As a result of acquiring this highly specialized knowledge, professions demand autonomy and independence for their actions. They demand immunity from the consequences which result from intervention (except by peer evaluation). In a sense, professions which are accorded [this status] are removed from the competitive marketplace. . . .Once an occupation is able to subordinate the consumers freedom of choice, it has monopolized services.[4]

THE PROCESS OF SOCIALIZATION

While professionalization has clear advantages for workers, it is necessary to ask if the granting of professional powers and privileges is of ultimate benefit to consumers or if the process of professionalization has debilitating consequences that may outweigh its presumed advantages. One of the potentially negative consequences of the accreditation/certification/licensure process is to establish a process of socialization that individuals must go through to gain the right to practice. Thus, individuals are selectively admitted to degree granting programs, educated with regard to a particular body of knowledge, taught accepted skills and techniques, and reinforced for absorbing a prescribed set of occupational values and attitudes.The more rigid the accreditation (what can be taught) and certification/licensure (what should be learned) processes, the more rigid will be this socialization process.

It has been observed in the literature dealing with a variety of professions that each profession tends to develop a paradigm based upon "a taken-for-granted conception of what the issue is, and how it is solvable. Each profession tends to see the world in terms of its own characteristic conception of problems and solutions. . ."[5] Thus, professions tend to become like social movements. "They recruit only certain types of persons, they develop highly elaborate ideologies and supra-individual values, they have their own mechanisms of socialization and they often attempt to proselytize and bring new members into the fold."[6] Implicit in these statements is the danger that the paradigm may cloud professionals' perceptions of consumers' problems and needs and thereby diminish the prospect of successful service delivery. Two major sources have been identified to account for the development of a professional paradigm: 1) the personality and other characteristics of individuals who self-select or are chosen to enter a particular profession; and 2) the training and socialization process that individuals go through prior to and during their professional careers. Both of these sources have the potential of developing filters or biases concerning the problems a particular profession chooses to address and the solutions adopted for dealing with the perceived problems.

Bishop, et. al.[7] found significant differences in selected personality traits and achievement measures between students in recreation and those in other university departments. Of particular interest was that recreation students were shown to be exceptionally high in extraversion when compared to students in other departments or to general population norms. Based on these results and on similar test results involving recreation students at four other universities, along with Eysenck's[8] theory of extraversion-introversion and its behavioral implications, Bishop observed that:

> Many recreation students (and in our judgment many recreation professionals) tend to be socially oriented and dependent, somewhat conventional, need fairly large amounts of temporal variation or change, tend to prefer action over thinking. . .All of these characteristics cannot be explained by extraversion. They do suggest a consistent recreology character or type, however, of which extraverted tendencies appear to be an important part.[9]

Added to Bishop's results are our own observations that recreation students tend to have a significant history of recreational involvements through which they developed the requisite skills to participate and the motivation for continued involvement. Many of these interests are in physical activities although recreation students currently seem to have more diversified interests than previously, when recreation was largely associated with physical education and a "jock" mentality. In addition, most students entering the recreation field have had significant contact with some form of recreation service agency through part-time work.

The socialization and training process that professionals are subjected to via educational experiences prior to entering the field and on an ongoing basis via inservice training and contact with fellow workers, exposure to a common group of books, magazines and other professional materials and so on, also has a significant impact on the development of a paradigm.[10] These experiences are usually endorsed by educators and practitioners alike as necessary to successful professional development and socialization.[11] There is a tendency to adopt a fairly consistent in-group philosophy of the need for recreation services, the benefits of participation and the best means of organizing recreational opportunities. Many of these perceptions will be "correct," i.e., they will prove useful in meeting needs as defined by consumers. However, in some cases professionals seem to develop a paradigm either for the rationale or the methods of offering services that differ dramatically from citizens' perceptions of what needs to be done. As Hughes notes, "Professions *profess*. They profess to know better than others the nature of certain matters, and to know better than their clients what ails them or their affairs."[12]

An individual's need to belong along with the tendency of the in-group to preserve itself via subtle pressure to conform to ideas and working practices, leads workers in most professional areas through an acculturation process wherein the social values, behavioral norms, and symbols of the occupational group are internalized.[13] In this way the philosophy and practices of a given profession are institutionalized and protected from erosion from outside influences. Most professions tend more toward the status quo being led by an old guard that depends heavily on tradition and years of "experience" rather than an ongoing process of questioning of assumptions and practices as a basis for future services. Of course, every profession also has its "black sheep" and its radicals, those who resist the acculturation process. They, in fact, play a valuable role by questioning underlying assumptions and providing a basis for innovation and change.

RISING CONSUMERISM

As a result of the socialization process, recreation professionals may develop and protect assumptions about consumer needs that do not match consumers' perceptions of their own needs. Thus, professionals may over- or under-estimate the extent to which particular barriers such as lack of time, money, or equipment, are problematic for consumers. For example, recreation professionals may see lack of motivation, inability to maintain commitments, or even lack of physical fitness, as problems of greater magnitude than they actually are. Such "conclusions" may be self-serving in that they can be used to justify the development of services to overcome professionally perceived barriers. Note that service professions need people who need the services. Another example of where professionals and consumers may differ is over how to define what is a "wholesome" leisure activity.

> Obviously, it can be viewed differently by the provider of park and recreation services and the consumer. Therefore, the critical question becomes this: who is to determine what is wholesome, the consumer or the professional? Should the profession impose its values upon the consumer or should the consumer exercise control over the profession. . .?[14]

It should be noted that professional "biases" may actually be based on facts or knowledge not available or ignored by consumers such as the relationship between fitness and health and the demonstrated low level of fitness in the populace. On the other hand, it could be argued that citizens are as fit as they want to be, are aware of the implications for health, and do not share the profession's concern with developing a fit society. Who is "right" raises numerous questions for professionals, such as whether to be proactive or reactive or adopt a leadership as compared to a followership posture. Who has the right to make decisions is another issue; professionals have the responsibility to do so. The basis upon which professionals make those decisions is at issue.

One result of the growth of professionalism and the tendency toward developing professional paradigms has been a corresponding emergence of consumerism. Consumerism involves an attempt to insure that the type, quantity, and quality of goods and services provided are in keeping with needs and standards as defined by the ultimate user as opposed to the supplier. As professionals have moved toward increasing autonomy and control, consumers have fought back by demanding greater involvement in all aspects of the planning and provision of needed goods and services. Thus, for example, the delivery of park and recreation services is being increasingly affected by the emerging awareness, sophistication, and competency of consumers. As consumer involvement in decision making processes affecting the delivery of services increases, a clearer understanding of the relationship between consumers and providers must be established.

One result of emerging consumerism is an increasing responsibility to clearly identify the source and validity of professional assumptions and practices. Constant attention needs to be given to sorting out whose interests are served by service provision efforts. Professionals need to avoid self-serving ideologies that preserve the status quo in the face of evidence of more applicable alternative paradigms. On the other hand, professionals should avoid seeking change simply because it avoids routine or appears progressive.

In addition, ways need to be found to overcome professionals' perceptions based on personal needs or orientations of the provider and to adopt outlooks that give more credence to consumer generated perceptions of needs, problems, and solutions. Ways need to be found to return control over service conceptualization and delivery to those whom the services are designed to benefit. This will help avoid the dependence that professionalism often entails. It will also help overcome the mentality that professionals' views take precedence because of the supposed advantage accruing to those who have studied in a given area or devoted their working lives to solving a particular problem or issue. We must overcome the mentality that the capacity for solving problems is narrowly distributed within the society, existing only in the realm of the profession.

Raising consumer expectations and worker obligations (and perhaps expectations) is another of the undesirable and potentially dangerous side effects of accreditation, certification, and licensure. These practices create an aura of knowledge and infallability which can often in turn lead to dependence and unfounded expectations of success. The medical and legal fields are replete with stories of clients who grow to expect too much from others rather than being taught how to do for themselves and practitioners who substitute titles and degrees for real expertise and competence.

TOWARD INCREASED COLLABORATION

In the final analysis what is needed is a renewed spirit of collaborating between professionals and consumers. While professionals may have specific interests in gaining a personal measure of status, authority, and autonomy, it should not be accomplished at the expense of consumer needs or rights. Expertise has its place but professionals need to recognize that they serve at the behest of consumers and not in opposition. The granting of special powers and privileges through processes such as accreditation, certification, and licensing should only be done to the extent that tangible benefits to consumers can be shown. In the case of the park and recreation field, we need to ascertain more clearly the unique knowledge or skills that recreation professionals possess that would justify certification or licensing or the unique roles played by park and recreation curricula that would justify accreditation.

Ultimately, recreation workers may be simply playing a game within a structure established by perceived necessity and reality. However, to confuse economics, job protection, and liability limitation concerns with actions which purport to protect the interests of consumers is misleading and potentially dangerous. Creating a union, while less glamorous, may be more appropriate.

REFERENCES

1. Shapiro, Ira G. "The Path to Accreditation." *Parks and Recreation*. 12(1), 1977. pp. 29-31+.
2. Sharpless, Joseph B. "Registration/Certification." *Parks and Recreation*. 9(8), 1974. pp. 26-28+.
3. Rubio, S., Kelsey, C. W., and Barnhart, T. "Licensure in Therapeutic Recreation." *Leisurability*. 3(2), 1976. pp. 27-30.
4. Edginton, Christopher R. "Consumerism and Professionalization." *Parks and Recreation*. 11(9), 1976. p. 42.
5. Friedson, Eliot. *The Professions and their Prospects*. Beverly Hills: Sage Publications, 1973. p. 31.
6. Denzin, N. K. "Pharmacy: Incomplete Socialization." *Social Forces*. 46(3), 1968. p. 376.
7. Bishop, Doyle W. *An Investigation of Some Temperament and Ability Differences Among Advanced Undergraduates of Selected Departments at the University of Ottawa*. Mimeo paper, 1979.
8. Eysenck, H. *The Bilogical Basis of Personality*. Springfield, Illinois: Charles C. Thomas, 1967.
9. Bishop, Doyle W. *Op.Cit*. p. 29-30.
10. Pavalko, P. M. *Sociology of Occupations and Professions*. Itasca, Illinois: Peacock, 1971.
11. McChesney, James C. *Professional Development and Involvement of Recreation and Park Students*. Unpublished Doctoral Dissertation. Indiana University, 1974.
12. Hughes, E. C. "Professions." *Daedalus*. 92, 1963. p. 67.
13. White, R. Clyde. "Social Workers in Society: Some Further Evidence." *Social Work Journal*. 34, 1953. pp. 161-164.
14. Edginton, Christopher R. *Op.Cit*. p. 84.

Chapter Twenty-Two
Back to Our Radical Roots

Mary Duncan

The most dangerous woman in America, a civil rights newspaper columnist, a man who started a playground at his own expense, a publicist who exposed filthy tenement conditions and advocates of socialism and leftist politics are frequently cited as being the founders or cornerstones of the park and recreation movement. Unfortunately, these facts are seldom stated in our recreation textbooks. One has to read biographies, autobiographies and other publications before these facts become evident.

Why haven't our textbooks dealt with the personalities, commitments, failures, and political views of our professional predecessors? Is it because the authors were not aware of it? Has there been an unspoken conspiracy to make our new profession more "respectable" by glossing over our founders' sometimes unsavory and controversial pasts?

In order to fill these voids in our literature, herewith is a brief foray into the lives of Frederick Law Olmsted, Jacob Riis, Jane Addams, Luther Gulick and Joseph Lee. In many ways there were the radical counterparts of Eldridge Cleaver, Jane Fonda, Caesar Chavez, Gloria Steinem and Ralph Nader. They continually fought city hall, organized labor strikes, marched in the streets, gave public speeches, and wrote award-winning articles deploring the living conditions of the poor. The issues and problems they faced were well defined: slavery, the aftermath of the Civil War, thousands of new immigrants, slums, child labor, disease, the suffrage movement, World War I, and a rapidly industrializing nation. America was striving to develop its abundant natural resources and was also emjoying a booming economy. The work ehtic and the free enterprise system flourished, thus creating a paradox of strong economic growth at the expense of human suffering and exploitation.

Our founders faced these issues. They were not meek and mild, easily intimidated or swayed by local politicians. They worked in, around, and with the political system. The political battles they fought gave them the skills needed in order to establish the park, playground and recreation services we enjoy today. With these thoughts in mind, let's look at their radical pasts. Perhaps it will provide some insights to the present, and hopefully provide a model for the future.

FREDERICK LAW OLMSTED (1882-1903)

Frederick Law Olmstead, a political columnist, writer, traveler, farmer, and landscape architect, was also an abolitionist who later became one of the designers of Central Park. His biographer, Elizabeth Stevenson, states that his early years laid the groundwork for his dedication to public service.

His childhood was unusual and set the course for his interest in landscape architecture. Even though his family were prominent merchants and lived in Hartford, Connecticut, Fred was allowed to roam free in the nearby woods. At the age of seven, he was sent to live with a series of ministers where his formal education vacillated between very good and very bad. He was not always happy, but learned to cope by escaping to the woods for solitude and adventure.[1] Later he visited England where he was impressed with her parks and wrote that in "democratic America there was nothing to be thought of as comparable with this People's Garden."[2]

Even though he was not a good student, writing his thoughts seemed a natural habit for him. This ability led the liberal editor of the New York Daily-Times to employ Olmsted to travel South and write his impressions about slavery. While Olmsted's columns were simple and unemotional, they vividly protrayed the brutalities, both physical and psychological, of a slave society. Writing in a letter to a friend he said, "I would take in a fugitive slave and shoot a man that was likely to get him." One of his columns was attributed to influencing Abraham Lincoln to emancipate the slaves.[3]

Prior to the Civil War, Olmsted, who had "tried being clerk, tried being sailor, and failed at farming," was determined to be the Superintendent of Central Park. He succeeded and immediately ran into opposition from Chief Engineer Egbert Viele. When Calvin Vaux's and Olmsted's plans for Central Park were later adopted, Viele charged them with stealing his plans. Viele had designed a drainage system for the park, and based on that was initially awarded a court settlement of $8,000.[4] But the jealousies between the men did not deter the progress of Central Park.

For a while, Olmsted resisted entering the Civil War. He considered Lincoln to be "lacking in firmness and dependent upon others for direction." Later he changed his mind and became Secretary of the Sanitary Commission, which dealt with the health needs of Northern soldiers.

Following the war, Olmsted designed numerous other private and public parks. Almost as if he were psychic, he recommended that San Francisco's Golden Gate Park be designed to act as "a barrier of protection to large districts. . .during great conflagrations." Although he didn't design Golden Gate Park, his suggestions were followed and during the fire that followed the 1906 earthquake, the park served as a firebreak and later was used to house thousands of homeless people.[5]

Both Vaux and Olmsted served as consultants to the New York City Park Department, but were fired in 1870 when the Tweed Ring took over New York City. In spite of the political setbacks, they were later reinstated and continued to guide the development of Central Park.

During these years, his wife Mary cared for their children and also advised him on professional matters. Partially because of this he was not upset by the Suffrage Movement. "If an occasional woman was found to be doing a man's work. . .he was not alarmed." He welcomed Elizabeth Bullard, of Bridgeport, Connecticut, into the "brotherhood" of landscape architects and recommended her for several jobs.[6]

Conservation and preservation were also Olmstead's concerns. He continued to fight for maintaining the natural scenery of such places as the Niagara Falls area and Yosemite.

The tumultuous years of Civil War, corrupt politicians, suffrage, and increasing urban problems did not deter the thousands of immigrants who flooded our shores. Among them was twenty-one year old Jacob Riis, a Danish citizen.

JACOB RIIS (1849-1941)

Jacob Riis was a troublemaker. Using his position as a police reporter, he expanded his beat to include dramatic stories about the horrors of slum conditions in New York City.

Stressing the theme of two Americas, he wrote that "slums were an evil cancer born of public neglect and nurtured by private greed."[7] His book, *How the Other Half Lives*, recommended tighter health laws, the prohibition of child labor and improvement of public schools.

Lectures, photo displays and articles facilitated his meeting influential people. Together they conducted tours of the tenements and pressured politicians to clean up the filth. Philosophically he wanted to solve the problems by going further than simple charity but stopped short of socialism. His biographer stated:

> "Riis's programs of social, economic, political and humanitarian reform aimed to beautify the environment and to reestablish the position of the home, the school, and the neighborhood in the lives of the poor. . .Riis wanted school buildings to be open in the evenings, on weekends, and during the summers for recreational, cultural and civic use."[8]

Highly critical of organized religion, he admonished the churches to wipe the soot from their windows and take up the gospel of service. Settlement houses to him were the best example of practical christianity.

Parks and playgrounds were high on his priority list of urban needs. He believed cities should provide parks for "the rest and recreation of the poor," rather than "for the pomp and parade of the wealthy."[9] Like other members of our movement, he wrote that creative play was necessary for teaching proper citizenship. As local politicians grew tired of his crusades, Riis resorted to other methods. One of his favorites was to send women to the mayor's office because "they could worm a playground or small park out of him."[10]

Jake's concern for parks and play areas was undoubtedly a result of his rural youth environment. Like Olmsted, he preferred rivers, hills or trees to the structured classroom. The son of a school master, he enjoyed high social status but on an austere family income. He once commented that his father "was the one link between the upper and lower strata in our town. . . . enjoying the most hearty respect of both."[11] In order to support fourteen children, the elderly Riis wrote columns for a local newspaper. It was as his father's young assistant that Jacob decided he wanted to be a newsreporter.

Distressed by the rejection of his sweetheart, Elisabeth, and the lack of work, he travelled by steamer to New York in 1870. From that time until 1877, he lived on the brink of poverty, hunger, loneliness and humiliation. Cheated by several employers, Riis finally turned to the Danish consul who gave him shelter, clothes and a job.

His social life revolved around the Lutheran Church where the young people played "particularly energetic kissing games" because the pastor despised dancing.[12] But he still longed for Elisabeth who was now engaged to another man in Denmark. Finally, after years of effort and taking classes at a business school, he secured a job as a reporter. From here he embarked on his career as a social reformer and, when established, was able to marry Elisabeth.

Throughout his life he struggled to bring the "two Americas" that he knew so well—one rich and the other poor—into harmony with one another. Believing in the integrity of neighborhoods, he emphasized community rehabilitation by the families, schools and churches rather than distant experts.

On these points, he and his friend Jane Addams concurred.

JANE ADDAMS (1860-1935)

Jane Addams is frequently lauded for having started a playground next to Hull House in Chicago. Photos of her depict a kindly woman chatting with children. Addams was also a "woman's libber" who helped organize labor unions for women garment workers, investigated child labor practice, established a day nursery for the children of working mothers and struggled to help women gain the right to vote. In spite of her personal wealth, she chose to work among the poor. Her clientele consisted of immigrant settlers, sweatshop toilers, unwed mothers, the hungry, sick and aged. Programs at Hull House encompassed a myriad of social, educational and recreational services.

As an ardent supporter of Theodore Roosevelt, she seconded his nomination for president under the now defunct leftist Progressive Party. Her endorsement of him waned when he became a "hawk" regarding World War I while she was an avowed pacifist. Along with several other women she organized the Women's Peace Party and organized a large peace demonstration in Washington. Later in 1931 she was awarded the Nobel Peace Prize for her efforts.[13]

Psychoanalysts could offer some insights into what motivated Jane Addams. She was the daughter of a wealthy man whom she adored, but his attention to her was diverted by her stepmother. Marriage probably did not seem appealing because her mother died in childbirth; her father's remarriage disrupted her emotional ties to him and her sister's marriage was marred by much bitterness and recrimination. Her personal relationships revolved around Mary Rozet Smith, who was a donor to Hull House and Jane's closest friend, confidante and companion. For many years they lived together and when apart exchanged what only can be described as love letters. Her biographer Daniel Levine wrote, "there can be no doubt that each of the women filled some of the emotional requirements a spouse might have filled had either married. Whether emotional intimacy ever led to physical intimacy no one can say. Probably the strong sexual inhibitions of the age and of both women prevented it."[14]

What really matters though is that she channeled her energies into projects like Hull House and into creating a more humanistic society. Other wealthy women might have succumbed to their tensions, and retreated to a pampered, self indulgent lifestyle. Jane Addams dealth with her world and in the process touched many lives including Joseph Lee, the father of the American playground movement.

JOSEPH LEE (1862-1937)

Joseph Lee and Jane Addams both served as officers in the Playground Association of America and he, like her, came from a wealthy, prominent family. While Lee would not be considered as radical as Riis or Addams, he continually fought to make recreation a viable part of American life. Appalled by the jailing of children for playing in the streets, he established, at his own expense, an experimental playground in Boston.

His Harvard education, law degree, European travel and happy childhood provided a solid foundation for pursuing his interests in youth, delinquency and family life. His book, *Constructive and Preventive Philantropy* stressed the importance of recreation in molding youth development. Another of his books, *Play and Education*, focused on the relationships between play, recreation and the social problems facing our cities.[15] Lee, philosophically, felt that recreation was an integral part of everyone's life, both adults and children. His definition of recreation included many aspects of leisure time activities such as visiting museums, use of school fields and parks as well as children romping on playgrounds. Recreation, to him, was one important factor in life which also had to be integrated with the educational, political, social, religious and economic realities of neighborhoods and cities. To use today's terminology, Lee advocated utilizing an holistic approach to recreation services. This approach was shared by Luther Gulick, a pragmatic man who identified needs in our society and then created organizations or programs to meet those needs.

LUTHER GULICK (1865-1918)

The dignified and moustached Luther Gulick was shoved into the swimming pool, along with several other officers of the newly created Playground Association of America. Graham Taylor, who wrote "Everybody Played," cited this as the high point of that organization's first Chicago convention in 1907.[16] This playful and spontaneous prank was indicative of Gulick, who was described by his son as a "great initiator, a vigorous man who was fun, jovial, very inventive, and an energetic outdoorsman. He derived his greatest satisfaction from working with youth-serving agencies and once established, moved on to other projects." Halsey goes on to recall that his father "had a great interest in the suffrage movement. He fought battles with the New York City School Board in order to incorporate girls into the physical education classes, and organized an elaborate girls folk dance festival at a time when dancing was considered immoral."[17]

Frustrated by the lack of recreational opportunities for his three daughters, Gulick and his wife started a camping program which later became the Camp Fire Girls. He was also instrumental in promoting the YMCA and designed the triangle which symbolizes that organization.

As the first president of the Playground Association of America, the forerunner of the National Recreation Association, and the National Recreation and Park Association, Gulick struggled along with Jane Addams, Jacob Riis, Joseph Lee, Henry S. Curtis and Howard Braucher to establish recreation services as a proper function of government. President Theodore Roosevelt, honorary president of the Playground Association of America, heartily supported their efforts.

Gulick's parents were medical missionaries in the South Seas. One can only guess at the influence this had on Gulick's sense of strong moral purpose and commitment to the recreation movement. In spite of his strict, biblically based religious childhood, he was an evolutionist, a man with world vision. Many of his thoughts and ideas are expressed in his book, *Philosophy of Play* and in his formal address at the Chicago Convention. Unlike many other people, Luther felt that play was an absolute necessity for the maintenance of democracy in an industrial society. He and Addams both espoused a new social ethic which stressed society's responsibility to recognize and solve social problems.[18] This differed significantly from the prevailing philosophy that problems were separate, and segmented and could be examined on an individual basis.

Gulick argued that this social ethic could only be learned by experience and in an atmosphere of considerable freedom. Playgrounds and sandpiles were where children learned about self-control, mutual rights and the awareness and importance of group effort.

As a professor at Massachusetts's Springfield College he taught this philosophy and continued until his sudden death to promote progressive camping, physical education and recreation programs.

SUMMARY

In many ways, Olmsted, Riis, Addams, Gulick and Lee represented the left wing of Theodore Roosevelts' Progressive Party. They advocated government support and regulation of parks and playgrounds while Riis and Addams in particular wanted government to also control nickelodeons, penny arcades and pool halls.

Many of the problems they faced have been solved only to create a fascinating paradox. Immigrants and foreign laborers are now actively discouraged from entering our country. Our efforts to industrialize were so successful that now, in the 80's, we face dramatic energy shortages. Children who were once exploited in the factories are now economically dependent on their parents until their late teens or early twenties.

The slavery issue has been resolved, but racial injustices still exist. Others feel that white people or Anglos are discriminated against and have filed reverse discrimination suits involving college admissions and employment opportunities. Antibiotics and modern sewage systems have irradicated most communicable diseases only to find that cancer and stress related diseases like heart attacks have taken their place. Government at all levels has recognized its role in providing park and recreation services for the people but a growing taxpayers' revolt now threatens some of those same services. Women have been able to vote for many years but are still struggling to pass the controversial Equal Rights Amendment which guarantees equal rights to everyone regardless of sex. High infant mortality rates have been replaced by abortion laws which allow women to control their own bodies. Even the traditional family concept has been broadened to include the alternative lifestyles of singles, couples without children, divorced people and gay or homosexual relationships.

It's difficult to second guess how our founders would have dealt with these issues. But based on their past records one can imagine Riis marching with the Mexican migrant farm workers; Addams leading the fight to ratify the Equal Rights Amendment and opposing the Vietnam War; Olmsted an active member of the Sierra Club and writing columns opposing nuclear reactors; and the commercialization of our state and federal parks; Lee financing adventure playgrounds with his own money and Gulick initiating recreation programs on rooftops, under freeways and continually lobbying with government officials for better recreation services.

Some people may question if these leaders were really radical. When looking at definitions of "radical" one finds the following explanations: "A person favoring drastic, political, economic or social reforms; advocates extreme change of the social structure."

It would be difficult to deny that there have been "drastic, political, economic and social reforms" since the early 1900's. Our founders were an integral part of those reforms. Now as we look to the future, what role will park and recreation professionals play in addressing today's issues?

REFERENCES

1. Stevenson, Elizabeth. *Park Maker: A Life of Frederick Law Olmsted.* New York: The MacMillan Company, 1977. p. 113.
2. *Ibid.*, P. 55.
3. *Ibid.*, p. 72, pp. 112-131.
4. *Ibid.*, p. 335.
5. *Ibid.*, p. 268.
6. *Ibid.*, p. 383.
7. Lane, James B. *Jacob A. Riis and The American City.* New York: Kennikat Press, 1974. p. 50.
8. *Ibid.*, p. 91.
9. *Ibid.*, p. 113.
10. *Ibid.*
11. Riis, Jacob A. *Making of an American*. New York: The MacMillian Company, 1904. p. 22.
12. *Ibid.*, pp. 14-16.
13. Levine, Daniel. *Jane Addams and the Liberal Tradition*. Madison, Wisconsin: State Historical Society of Wisconsin, 1971. p. 203.
14. *Ibid.*, p. 71.
15. Lee, Joseph. *Play and Education*. New York: The MacMillan Company, 1916.
16. Taylor, Graham R. "How They Played at Chicago." *Charities*, XVIII (August 3, 1907). pp. 471-480.
17. Gulick, Halsey. Personal interview with the author, May 1979.
18. Gulick, Luther H. "Play and Democracy." *Charities*, XVIII (August 3, 1907). pp. 481-486.

SECTION FOUR

Improving Research and Policy: Better Quality, Better Used

Introduction

Thomas L. Goodale and Peter A. Witt

The chapters in section four deal with the status of current attempts to develop research and policy for the field of recreation *and* the emerging directions that are necessary to improve research and policy development efforts to meet future needs. The seven chapters cover a variety of topics but running through them are several basic unifying themes.

One theme covered by Kelly (23), Lamb and Crompton (25), and Noe (24) concerns the need for different kinds of research strategies to emerge that will take better account of the qualitative and multi-dimensional nature of the recreation experience. There is an obvious link here to the definitional issues concerning the nature of the recreation and leisure experience raised in Section One of this book. The need to pay more attention to soft versus hard data and values versus facts also emerges. Kelly (23), for example, urges us to use methods and models that go beyond enumerating what activities are participated in (ex. surveys, time diaries) to methods that place a greater emphasis on how participation decisions are made and what satisfactions are gained. Lamb and Crompton (25) point out the difference between attendance (efficiency) and experiential (effectiveness) measures for determining the success of park and recreation services. They challenge us to consider whether we are ultimately in the quantity of participation or quality of experience business.

Another underlying theme is the necessity for more attention to be given to theory building and problem conceptualization in the field of recreation and leisure studies. Noe (24), for example, argues for improved conceptualization of the link between class, status, and recreational behavior. He proposes a paradigm aimed at developing a better explanation of *who* one chooses to participate with and *how* one chooses to participate. Zuzanek (26) explores the myth or reality of a cultural boom. His article provides an excellent example of how secondary analysis of existing data can be used to develop new understanding and build a viable body of knowledge upon which to base future action. Burton (29) points to the dependence of recreation research on practical problem solving oriented government contracts and grants. He explores the impact of funding sources that emphasize expediency, immediacy and applicability of outsomes versus the need for research aimed at developing a theory base and better conceptual understanding. The need to balance basic and applied to research is evident with the current balance tipped largely in favor of pragmatic problem solving. While this approach may meet government policy and political priorities it may not yield the theoretical knowledge base necessary for the development of a strong discipline.

Several of the papers deal directly with the need to develop recreation policy at both the local and national levels and the relationship between research outcomes and policy formulation. Both Shafer (28) and Westland (27) point to the need to develop more complete policy paradigms. Shafer, for example, argues for the need to base future decisions concerning man-environment relationships on a model of the "spaceship-earth" utilizing as components the variables of available resources, political decision making processes, and the dynamics of human interaction patterns. He examines the complex nature of variables that must be considered if we are to organize, control, and coordinate public and private recreation development to protect and improve those environmental features we value most for recreation.

Westland (27) deals with the conceptual, jurisdictional, and bureaucratic problems of establishing national "free-time" policies. He points to the need to know why we are establishing policies (to what end) and how we expect goals to be achieved. He argues for an integrated approach to policy development that places recreation in the overall context of human services, the arts, culture, and sports. Westland also notes that policy making is not an entirely rational process that can be totally entrusted to the bureaucratic system. Thus, its formulation requires the overall cooperation of the public, private, governmental, and professional groups.

In total, the authors in this section would seem to agree with Burton's (29) assessment that recreation research is in a state of "young adulthood." The same could be argued for policy formulation. Strong efforts are needed to re-direct and re-orient the focus and methods of both research and policy formulation to the exigencies of an uncertain future. The need to get beyond muddling through is evident. The ever-present gap in language, methods, and even intent between researchers, policy makers, implementers, and consumers still is unresolved. We talk of relevance for our efforts but fail to have agreement as to goals and expected outcomes. In a sense we have come full circle to the opening section of the book. Failure to agree on basic concepts plagues our ability to study phenomena and establish policies upon which to base our planning and implementation efforts.

Given the above problems it is not surprising that individual trust in group decision making and academic research has waned. Although emerging pluralism, bureaucratization, and sheer size of population dictate more centralization of government planning and decision making, there is an obvious shift toward local control over policy decisions. Correspondingly there is a shift toward trust of intuition, feelings and values over systematic reasoning and facts. The task of researchers and policy makers thus becomes one of convincing consumers that their efforts are of value in solving everyday felt needs and concerns. This will require researchers and policy makers to do a better job of balancing short and long run impacts of their efforts as well as being able to address problems in a language and framework that consumers are able to understand and willing to support. On the other hand consumers will have to do a better job of understanding the nature of the research/policy process and be more willing to forego short run private gains for longer run social ends. These challenges place a tremendous burden on individual goodwill, and the willingness to establish a system that values personal goals within an overall system of interdependence.

TLG
PAW

Chapter Twenty-Three

Leisure and Quality: Beyond the Quantitative Barrier in Research

John R. Kelly

Research does not exist in a separate world of its own. While there is a developmental process in cumulative "normal science" that may be disrupted or redirected by internal crises,[1] there are also factors outside the research act that influence its nature. In leisure research, a practical issue has had an impact on research. That issue is the formulation of decision criteria for providers of leisure resources, both public and commercial. Especially when financial and logistical support for research has been supplied by government agencies with specific missions of recreation resource provisions, research has been designed to meet their needs for resource allocation.

Partly in response to this practical aim, research in leisure has tended to be concentrated on quantitative studies of participation and the development of methods and formulas of prediction. The goal has generally been the eventual development of an econometric prediction model that can be computer-programmed and universally applied.

At the same time, a central intention of bureaucratic functionaries in any modern social or economic system is to achieve personal career stability. One rule of bureaucratic survival is to minimize risk by employing standard and accepted methods of administration, problem-solving, and decision-making. The dangers of being responsible for judgments can frequently be reduced by having what appear to be "hard" quantitative data to apply to a statistical set of decision criteria. Regardless of the implicit assumptions underlying the quantitative model, it gives the appearance of objectivity.

At the same time, there are also accepted premises and even theoretical models that shape research aims and designs. In leisure research, the "functional" or "systematic" model has been dominant.[2] This model has led to social research employing survey techniques that attempt to explain behavior with indicators of institutional roles and positions. Most often economic positions have been assumed to be determinative for such "secondary" behavior as leisure, community, political, and even family roles. In sociology, those studying leisure have not often been daring enough to employ non-standard theory or methods. Rather they have either explicitly accepted the dominant paradigm or have implicitly followed its conventions in what appeared to be a-theoretical designs.

Research, then, has two aims: the practical purpose of providing a useful basis for resource allocation and the scientific purpose of building coherent and explanatory theory about the phenomenon. Leisure research, shaped by public funding and by theoretical timidity, has for the most part adopted familiar methods to examine traditional questions. Most often, leisure sociologists have used the correlational analysis of survey data to investigate the determinative power of social position on leisure behavior.

This chapter is intended to be complementary to an earlier work published in *Current Sociology* analysing how conflict (Marxist) and interpretive (Weberian) theory have largely been neglected in developing contemporary leisure research strategies and methods.[2] The following analysis will concentrate on the methods themselves. Following a brief review of past quantitative approaches, mainly in North America, I will outline transitional methodologies that lead to a set of qualitative research models that may yield new and significant theory formulations. Finally, I will outline possibilities for a more inclusive research strategy in leisure studies. Surprisingly, the new strategy may have a greater potential to answer crucial practical questions than the old model.

RETROSPECT: QUANTITATIVE RESEARCH IN LEISURE

While government-funded research, especially in outdoor recreation in the United States, has frequently been labelled "mindless empiricism," it might be more appropriate to understand national and community surveys as the application of common methods based on unquestioned premises. When economists are presented with a research problem, they tend to think in terms of adapting an econometric equation. Social psychologists select a scale. Sociologists are most likely to develop a survey instrument that will be analysed with social positions and status as the independent variables correlated to social behavior.

Participation Surveys

The underlying theory for most leisure sociologists has been an institutional social system operating functionally with status-differentiated roles. The familiar method, now escalated in sophistication by packaged computer programs, has been correlational analysis of survey data. While such surveys have been commissioned in several countries, repetition has characterized efforts in the United States and Canada. Not only national outdoor recreation surveys beginning with the ORRRC effort in 1962, but a series of inconsistent follow-ups have worked over the model.[3]

Some alterations have been made as factors of regional resources, distance and attractiveness of sites, and variation in tastes have been suggested as significant.[4,5] Despite the lack of consistency in format, some indications of trends can be extrapolated from data that have not been mislaid or lost by the sponsoring agencies. Further, there have been countless state and community surveys combining participation questions with common demographic information.

To what extent has such research proven useful? Several indications of problems are evident: (1) Very few scientific or theory-building papers have been based on such data. (2) The use of such data in planning has been rendered suspect because of the determination of current participation rates by available opportunities. (3) There is little evidence that respondents will reliably behave in accordance with expressed interests and attitudes about future recreation. (4) The predictive capability of such models has proven to be quite low, accounting for 30 percent of the variance at most and more recently less than ten percent.[5]

Time-diary Studies

A second quantitative methodology has been employed in comparable ways in several nations and thus provided rare cross-cultural comparisons. The time-budget or time-diary method is perhaps the most purely quantitative in its approach. Subjects are instructed to report their activity, location, companions, and other such information through a day or week in brief time segments. The activity is then classified and generally reported as daily and weekly means by population aggregates.

Differences among countries[6] and in one population at different times,[7] while not fully explained by the data, can be compared with some reliability and provide an initial basis for analysis over time and space. One appeal of the method, along with such comparability, is that it is so purely quantitative. It seems to have no ideological or political connotations and carries an aura of "objectivity."

However, the reports themselves illustrate the limitations of the approach. By themselves, time-diary studies explain almost nothing.

Tables of average hours spent by aggregates on arbitrarily-classified activities give a general "time map" of the employment of clock time. However, to the map we must add our interpretation in order to account for the data. Some explanations are not difficult. Differences in proportions of automobile or television ownership account for major nonwork variation among national cultures. In the United States changes in family structure provide a partial explanation for decreases in average family-task engagement between 1965 and 1975.[7] However, those interpretations are from outside the data.

Further, from time-diaries we do not know such basic information as whether a person is walking for transportation, leisure, health, companionship, or some combination of reasons. Rather, it is assumed that the form of the activity tells us whether it is work or leisure, required or discretionary, valued or dreaded. Like a road map, time-diary research gives us a one-dimensional sketch of activity, but requires considerable supplement for us to even begin to understand what it all means. Such limitations are recognized by John Robinson[7] and many others who are attempting to adapt and enrich the method to begin to provide some explanation of findings from within the data.

The Issue of Appropriate Methodologies

The issue is really a simple one. Methodologies are servants, not rulers. Research methods are chosen only after the phenomenon to be investigated is given preliminary analysis and the aims of the research clearly delineated. Then, methods appropriate to the specific task are selected, modified, and integrated. The unused and even misplaced mountains of survey data on recreation in the United States are evidence enough that starting with a method, however safe and acceptable, rather than with the problem generally yields results of little value. When a theoretical model is implicitly and uncritically accepted or the method is adopted a-theoretically, the result tends to be a failure to explain anything important.

In the case of research on leisure, the accepted methods have been quantitative. They have stressed the statistical analysis of aggregated numbers. Whatever the implicit notions of "science" underlying this approach, the consequence has been a failure to develop satisfactory theory about leisure – even on the terms of the model.

Is it possible that the phenomenon itself – leisure – requires other modes of research? Or, are the survey and time-diary methods valid within their scope, but unable to cope with fundamental questions about leisure such as *how* decisions are made, what satisfactions are gained, and the effects of providing new or different resources? Current developments in leisure research and theory-building suggest that both the nature of leisure and critical practical problems are requiring different research strategies.

TRANSITIONAL METHODOLOGIES

A number of problems and anomalies in results of the survey and time-diary methods along with entrance into leisure research of scientists with somewhat different theoretical orientations has led to adaptations of the standard methodologies. Not only the failure to account for major proportions of variance in participation rates, but raising questions about the socialization process, differential satisfactions, and the relationship of leisure to other non-work roles and social spaces prompted a number of adapted strategies.

Space and Access

At the same time that sociologists were concentrating on social position, resource economists were attempting to develop predictive equations for the recreation use of new or expanded public and commercial resources. While a number of complications both in application and theory have kept the effort from reaching finality, at least two major determinative factors were consistently identified. They are distance from user population to the site and the attractiveness of the resource itself. Along with price, some measure of predispositions of potential users, competing resources, distance, and resource attractiveness have been included in all such models.[8,9]

As a consequence, sociologists also began to include some measure of access and attractiveness in a few research designs.[3] In one comparison of communities, variation in resources and differential access was a major explanatory factor in differences between communities.[10] In Canada, regional differences in outdoor recreation were found that were directly related to geographical and environmental factors.[4,11]

While sociologists have not entered the study of distance, access, and environmental factors in leisure with enthusiasm, their employment in program-oriented research requiring results of some predictive substance has helped break the rigid focus on social structure and stratification. The method employed has still been that of the social survey, but with new elements of environment introduced.

Immediate Communities and Socialization

Even when it was agreed that social status did identify some differences in leisure patterns, the process producing those differences was left to speculation. While socialization into leisure through institutions of the social system was assumed to take place in ways differentiated by social status, little had been done to examine just how persons inaugurated and continued particular kinds of leisure activity.

When such research was undertaken, the methods tended to be only adaptations of survey approaches. While personal interviews that could obtain some greater richness of data[12] as well as self-report survey instruments with items on the history of participation[13] were employed, the approaches tended to be rather superficial. Rather than following the history of a person's participation in a set of activities from childhood on, discrete items on childhood participation, context of introduction, and first participation were included. Some advance, however, has been made in relation to sport participation by obtaining more sequential data from youth and adult participants.[14]

Satisfactions and Decisions

Two approaches to the issue of leisure meanings or satisfactions were also being developed, for the most part after 1970. One was built on the work of Robert Havighurst[15] and employed sociological design. The second was more closely related to "need" theories in psychology[16] and began the use of scales adapted to leisure research. Both approaches recognized the necessity of dealing with the attitudes and definitions of leisure participants rather than only with behavior and social position.

The sociological strategies sought to place leisure in a context of institutional roles and investigate how they were interrelated. In the Havighurst study, a variety of methods were used to go beyond what middle-life adults were doing in non-work time to questions of association, styles, satisfactions, modes of participation, and the relation of psychological to social factors.[15] While results were too diffuse to have an impact on conventional research commensurate with their significance, the importance of elements other than social position and the richness of multiple methods and instruments was demonstrated.

This approach was adopted in the United States in efforts to delineate the relationship between leisure and other social role constraints and opportunities,[10,12] the social contexts of leisure decisions for youth,[17] and contexts of socialization.[18] For the most part, respondents were directly asked questions about leisure companionship, perceived constraints in decisions, relationship to work, and dominant satisfactions. In one research sequence from open-ended interview formats, a self-report instrument was developed that examined meanings, contexts, and satisfactions.[12]

At about the same time, social psychologists were beginning to apply their tools to the study of leisure satisfactions and attitudes, both in general and in relation to specific activities. Scales were developed in relation to outdoor recreation and environments,[19] self-concepts and clusters of perceived satisfactions among students,[20] and the identification of types of leisure satisfactions.[21] The value of scales that can be validated for reliability and validity and administered to a variety of populations has been combined with new statistical techniques of factor analysis, cluster analysis, and multi-dimensional scaling to suggest considerable promise. Such techniques are increasingly being employed with non-student populations. In February of 1978, a working conference was held at the University of Illinois in which many of those seeking to advance such methodologies compared their current research efforts and began to agree on common elements.

These transitional methodologies were an important expansion of the limited data of the traditional social survey. Issues raised in an earlier era[22] about social contexts, personal meanings, and environments were reopened. Leisure socialization was approached more as a process and leisure as a multi-faceted phenomenon. Nevertheless, the analysis was still for the most part quantitative, data were gathered in structured self-report formats, and the time frame was cross-sectional. Nevertheless, new issues were raised, new variables introduced, and more varied analytical techniques were employed. The possibilities of using quantitative methods to investigate questions of meaning and perception were being drawn into study of leisure.

NEW METHODS IN LEISURE RESEARCH

There are two sources of innovative research methods in contemporary leisure research, one external and the other internal. The external source is the persistence of two other theoretical paradigms in sociology that have consequences for research.[2] While conflict or neo-Marxist theory leads to several critical research issues for leisure, the paradigm with special affinity for the existential and social phenomenon of leisure is the "interpretive" or Weberian. This perspective stresses questions of meaning to social actors, the constructed and problematic nature of social structures and collectivities, and the processual character of interaction. It, therefore, appears to be peculiarly suited for the investigation of a phenomenon that is defined in terms of freedom, intrinsic and social meanings, and some possibility of distinction from the world of necessity and major consequences.[23]

The internal source is derived from the kinds of issues increasingly being raised in leisure research and theory-building. When leisure is understood as a complex and multi-dimensional set of behaviors and meanings that may change through the life course,[24] simpler strategies and designs as patently inadequate. If the same activity may have different meanings for the same person in different social contexts of life-course periods and different activities much the same meanings, then both the contexts and the meanings must be included in the research design. Restricting data to who does what and where seems to yield little that is explanatory from either a statistical or substantive perlatively to research with both depth and diversity not yet realized.

As a result, at least three standard "interpretive" methods have been added to the leisure research repertoire. While none of the three is intended either to supplant quantitative analysis or to provide the final word on leisure, each makes special contributions to leisure sciences.

Collaborative Interviews

Collaborative interviews are those in which the subjects do more than respond to questions and scales. Rather, they are engaged in the process of seeking understanding and encouraged to join in the interpretive and theory-building process. While there have been several inaugural uses of this approach in the study of leisure, the most thorough is that of Rhona and Robert Rapoport.[24] Taking the life-cycle framework and adding to it the developmental perspective of Erik Erikson and others, they have sought to understand the relationship of leisure to the changing roles and identities of persons in various periods of their life

The method includes open-ended questions, checking with others close to the collaborator, full explanation of the aims of the study, recording partial histories of past roles and relationships, and probing for explanations from the respondent. Other research has included methods such as meeting for the interview in past or current leisure environments, joint interviews with significant others, and "what if" projective techniques of using imagination and fantasy to seek meanings. While collaborative interviewing is directed toward research goals, the aim is to be inclusive rather than predetermine what is relevant. Further the subject is consulted when profiles are written and interpretations offered by the researchers.

Although collaborative interviewing has its dangers and limitations,[24] it has the strength of dealing with the perceived worlds of persons rather than a world structured externally by research aims and assumptions. Various means of cross-checking both data and interpretations are possible that minimize the impression-management process that is part of any interview.[26]

Participant Observation

Perhaps a more radical departure from traditional methods is one that has been employed in social research for decades but has remained on the fringes of mainline sociology. Participant observation has been a central part of community studies since the 1930's. There has been an acceptance of the orientation and insight provided by systematic, first-hand observations in examining community behavior and specific sites such as playgrounds and bars. Often the method is accepted as an exploratory tool that is to lead to different strategies. Sometimes it is combined with other methods in a "grounded" theory-building strategy.[27] In locations with clear boundaries, observation can even yield quantitative data. However, participant-observation data is more likely to be reported as interpreted by the observer.

In recent years, there have been initial uses of this method in research on outdoor recreation, especially at campgrounds[28,29] and on playgrounds.[30] In these cases the observation is dominant and participation in a selection of community events and enterprises may be used to assess leisure styles and obtain informally the interpretations of participants while they are engaged in the activity. In one comparative study, interview and observation methods are compared and found to be complementary but not entirely consistent.[10] Analysis of the kinds of leisure behavior and events that are most amenable to such an approach suggests that observation may lead to an emphasis on public styles and datable events while participation and interviews lead to a focus on similarities in orientations and behaviors.

When social interaction is viewed as a process of symbolic meaning and exchange, a negotiation of self-presentation and identity establishment and a problematic construction of social structures, then only research that can encompass and follow that process can deal with its nature. Participant observation or observant participation can yield data on how the process develops, how the situation is defined and redefined, and on the dialectical nature of the interaction. Recognizing that no two situations are identical, multiple observations – especially when systematically recorded, compared, and verified – can produce explanatory generalizations grounded in the social world under investigation.

Kinds of leisure with face-to-face interaction, essaying of identities, dealing with problematic outcomes, and temporary suspension of external role status and norms[31] may be best studied with a method that follows the complexities of the social process. Especially when the freedom and suspension of external realities turn the event into play,[32] participant observation possesses an openness that does not predetermine behavior classifications and salient variables. Bar behavior, card games, cocktail parties, beach and swimming pool interaction, the outdoor play of children, and camping are only a few of the leisure situations that have been examined through observation with results that have already enriched our understanding of social leisure. As long as considerable leisure consists of socializing[31] and just "fooling around," then one-time methods that freeze the process will be inadequate to explain the behavior and its meanings.

Projective Techniques

Just being introduced into leisure research are some of the projective techniques that have been more familiar to psychologists in the past. They have been given attention by those who seek a systematic and reliable way to investigate what leisure activities, events, associations, and locales mean to persons in relation to their self-definitions, anticipations for the future, and personality characteristics.

One method relies on fantasy. Drawings, unresolved situations, or other stimuli are introduced to initiate an imaginative construction of behavior, attitudes, and interactions by the subject.[33] Such techniques have several advantages over more structured approaches. They do not close off possible responses through predetermination of categories or limit the scope of information to past behavior. Projective techniques seem to open the possibility of probing into the future. If leisure is defined in terms of freedom and even directed toward self-actualization and fulfillment, then research that deals with the past limitations of opportunities, prior socialization, and social expectations fails to introduce the free and existential element in leisure.

Most often such projective techniques will be employed in conjunction with various instruments that assess personality characteristics, value structures, and motivational orientations. Past concentration on social and economic factors in leisure has led to neglect of a central possibility for leisure understanding – that there are elements internal to social actors that are a part of their decision-making. Investigating social position and socialization history does not exhaust the personal elements in our thinking, feeling, initiating, responding, and deciding. Leisure research, to recognize the freedom element in leisure, must include methods that tap the existential as well as the social.

THE PROBLEM OF SYSTEMATIC ANALYSIS

Of course, there are problems with qualitative research. Beyond the quantitative barrier is a world with many uncertainties as well as possibilities. Perhaps the major problem is in the systematic comparative analysis of data. It is, in the jargon, the problem of reliability.

One response is to bypass the issue. If social interaction is understood as a process, then no two events, situations, or exchanges would be expected to be just alike. Outside the laboratory, neither conditions nor individuals can be controlled, replicated, or guaranteed consistent. Rather, social research seeks to extract the consistencies from human behavior with the aim of developing explanations for regular behavior and common conditions. What is surprising from one perspective is that behavior is as consistent as it is, that for the most part we can enter new situations with some assurance that we know how interaction will develop and what will be expected of us. Therefore, consistencies in the process may be identified and even predicted in terms of statistical probabilities.

But how do we compare data from a number of life histories, a series of collaborative interviews, community studies with participant observation, or imaginative constructions based on projective stimuli? A number of strategies of comparison, theory-building, theoretical sampling, evaluation, and case-study presentations have been developed and tested for many different kinds of social interaction.[25,26,34] One means of presentation often found useful in summarizing data and analyzing the interrelationships of the various elements in the social process is the writing of "profiles." When the varieties of types of situations, groups, communities, social actors, or role definitions are distinguished, a profile of each significant type can be presented in a way that introduces critical factors in their processual development. Thus, the "over time" nature of social interaction is not lost in the attempt to measure the quantitative effects of variables as though they were simultaneous.

In some cases, such qualitative analysis in profiles and typologies may become the basis for a sophisticated quantitative design. However, in other cases, a quantitative study can provide a beginning that leads to processual research in some depth. A survey may give something of the "lay of the land" as in aerial photography which then needs to be followed up on the ground. Social explanation in this Weberian rather than structural mode consists of more than concomitant variation of statistical aggregates.

VALUES OF QUALITATIVE RESEARCH

The foremost value of the qualitative study of leisure is that leisure is studied with methods that correspond to its nature. If leisure is defined as a qualitative experience rather than designated time or activities[23,35,36] then data that omits meaning, satisfaction, social definitions, and other elements of the quality of the experience may deal only with indices and contexts rather than with leisure itself. If leisure is an experienced process rather than a category of behavior, then research should examine the nature of the experience over time. Collaborative interviews, life histories that focus on particular relationships or transitions, observations, participation analysis, and projective techniques along with some of the adapted methodologies examine leisure rather than some arbitrarily designated behavior.

However, there are other values as well:

(1) Qualitative research "brings people back in" to the study of leisure. Knowing that so much of the meaning of leisure is in the definition of the actors, they are dealt with as thinking, feeling, deciding, experiencing, and changing beings. They are not simply digits in a computer printout.

(2) The presentation of qualitative data and analysis is understandable by those who are not technically proficient in quantitative analysis. A profile, case history, set of quotations from interviews, or grounded typology may gain the attention and comprehension of providers, planners, advisors, political decision-makers, and others who need to understand the implications of their decisions.

(3) A model that can encompass changes and continuities over time provides a scope of explanation far richer and more inclusive than one that must place a single number on every element in the analysis. The process of life, including leisure, is more like a story than a diagram.

(4) Qualitative designs allow for the introduction of new elements into the explanation that were not anticipated by the scientist. Not only the diversity but the complexity of human experience suggests that significant factors in leisure may be found *in* the research rather than identified prior to the investigation.

(5) So much leisure is a face-to-face interaction process with the interchange of symbols and gestures, negotiation of meanings, and slow or abrupt alterations of reference that explanation requires observing, assessing, and analyzing the total event. After all, one of the appeals of much social leisure is that it is problematic and unpredictable in outcomes; it has elements of play, games, and the suspension of rules and roles.[31]

(6) Perhaps most important, such research can begin to identify the satisfactions sought and found in various leisure events and settings in relation to social identification. The relationship between movement through the life cycle and changes in leisure interests suggests that providers can, in time, respond to the needs of their service populations by designing programs based on the meanings and priorities of the potential users. Planning may be based on need and potential interest rather than on participation rates shaped by current opportunities and provisions.

LEISURE RESEARCH IN THE FUTURE

Leisure is not so fully researched that it is appropriate to focus too narrowly on a few issues or concentrate on only one or two methodologies. Each method outlined here – traditional quantitative, adapted transitional, and qualitative – has peculiar values. Each does some things well and is most useful in relation to particular issues. Further, leisure is such a multi-dimensional phenomenon that each approach has the potential of furthering our understanding of some dimension.

However, one problem is that methodological models have been prematurely limited. Correlational analysis of survey data and time-diary studies have so dominated the field that "research" has often been identified with quantitative designs. The preference for studying leisure in natural settings or from household-based data rather than experimental laboratory studies has narrowed design to survey and structured self-reports. The unanswered questions, unresolved issues, and unsatisfactory performance of most research even by its own predictive criteria has led to a few attempts to adapt or expand such methods.

The argument here is that theory-building in the sense of substantive explanation requires the inclusion and acceptance of a number of qualitative methods. Further, the nature of leisure as experience calls for such research. Research strategies are not just a matter of familiarity, convenience, personal bias, or even professional acceptance. Developing a research strategy means beginning with the nature of the phenomenon and the particular aims of the research. There is no single method that can begin to encompass, much less exhaust, a complex phenomenon such as leisure.

Quantitative research has certain values related to replication, statistical analysis, comparative data bases, standardization, size and representativeness of samples, compactness of presentation, and inclusion of a wide range of variables. It is often useful for both exploration and confirmation.

Qualitative research has values related to depth, the definitions and perceptions of social factors, unobtrusiveness of some designs, inclusion of subjects in the research and discovery process, openness, analysis of process and history, personal and event histories, examination of decision elements and processes, and richness of presentation. Further, it has a special affinity to modern definitions of leisure that stress the quality and meaning of the experience to the participant.

At least for the next decade or so, some emphasis on such qualitative approaches would seem appropriate. If there has been a strong tilt toward the traditional quantitative methods for the past two decades, then some compensatory strategies would seem in order. Such emphasis should not eliminate the use of surveys, time diaries, and other cross-sectional methods when they are clearly appropriate. However, it is time that those doing leisure research admit to their repertoire those methods especially suited to study freedom, satisfaction, interaction, and personal development – the central elements in leisure.

REFERENCES

1. Kuhn, T. *The Structure of Scientific Revolutions,* 2nd edition. Chicago: University of Chicago Press, 1970.
2. Kelly, J. Sociological Perspectives and Leisure Research. *Current Sociology,* (22), 1974. pp. 128-158.
3. Cichetti, C. "A Review of the Empirical Analyses that have been based upon the National Recreation Surveys." *Journal of Leisure Research,* (4), 1972. pp. 90-107.
4. Zuzanek, J. "Social Differences in Leisure Behavior: Measurement and Interpretation." *Leisure Sciences,* (1), 1978. pp. 271-293.
5. Kelly, J. "Outdoor Recreation Participation: A Comparative Analysis." *Leisure Sciences* (4:1), 1980.
6. Szalai, A. *The Use of Time: Daily Activities of Urban and Suburban Populations in Twelve Countries.* The Hague: Mouton, 1972.
7. Robinson, J. *Changes in Americans' Use of Time: 1965-1975.* Cleveland: Communications Research Center, Cleveland State University, 1972.
8. Knetsch, J. *Outdoor Recreation and Water Resources Planning.* Water Resources Monograph, No. 3. Washington, D.C.: American Geophysical Union, 1974.
9. Krutilla, J. and Fisher, A. *The Economics of Natural Environments.* Baltimore: The Johns Hopkins University Press, 1975.
10. Kelly, J. "Leisure Styles and Choices in Three Environments." *Pacific Sociological Review,* (21), 1978. pp. 187-207.
11. Beaman, J., Kim, Y. and Smith, S. The Effects of Recreation Supply on Participation. *Leisure Sciences,* (2), 1979. pp. 71-87.
12. Kelly, J. Situational and Social Factors in Leisure Decisions. *Pacific Sociological Review,* (21), 1978. pp. 313-330.

13. Yoesting, D. and D. Burkhead. "Significance of Childhood Recreation Experience on Adult Leisure Behavior." *Journal of Leisure Research,* (5), 1973. pp. 25-36.
14. Spreitzer, E. and Snyder, E. "Socialization into Sport: An Exploratory Path Analysis." *Research Quarterly,* (47), 1976. pp. 238-245.
15. Havighurst, R. The Leisure Activities of the Middle Aged. *American Journal of Sociology,* (63), 1957. pp. 152-162.
16. Maslow, A. *Motivation and Personality.* New York: Harper and Row, 1964.
17. Noe, F. and Elifson, K. "The Pleasures of Youth: Parental and Peer Compliance Toward Discretional Time." Paper at the American Sociological Association, Chicago, 1975.
18. Kelly, J. Leisure Socialization: Replication and Extension. *Journal of Leisure Research,* (9), 1977. pp. 121-132.
19. Driver, B. "Quantification of Outdoor Recreationist's Preferences." In: van der Smissen, B., Compiler, Penn State HPER Series, No. 11. (N.D.).
20. Tinsley, H., et al. "Leisure Activities and Need Satisfaction." *Journal of Leisure Research,* (9), 1977. pp. 110-120.
21. McKechnie, G. "The Psychological Structure of Leisure: Past Behavior." *Journal of Leisure Research,* (6), 1974. pp. 27-45.
22. Lundberg, G. et al. *Leisure: A Suburban Study.* New York: Columbia University Press, 1934.
23. Kelly, J. *Leisure.* Englewood Cliffs, New Jersey: Prentice Hall, 1980.
24. Rapoport, R. and R. N. *Leisure and the Family Life Cycle.* London: Routledge, 1975.
25. Denzin, N. *The Research Act: A Theoretical Introduction to Sociological Methods.* 2nd edition. New York: McGraw-Hill, 1978.
26. Webb, E., et al. *Unobtrusive Measures: Nonreactive Research in the Social Sciences.* Chicago: Rand McNally, 1966.
27. Glaser, B. and Strauss, A. *The Discovery of Grounded Theory.* Chicago: Aldine, 1967.
28. Burch, W. "The Play World of Camping: Research into the Social Meaning of Outdoor Recreation." *American Journal of Sociology,* (70), 1965. pp. 604-612.
29. Campbell, F. "Participant Observation in Outdoor Recreation." *Journal of Leisure Research,* (2), 1970. pp. 226-236.
30. Lever, J. Sex Differences in the Complexity of Children's Play and Games. *American Sociological Review,* (43), 1975. pp. 471-483.
31. Simmel, G. "Sociability" Chapter 3 in K. Wolff, ed. *The Sociology of George Simmel.* New York: Free Press, 1955.
32. Bateson, G. "A Theory of Play and Fantasy." *Psychiatric Research Reports,* (2), American Psychiatric Association, 1955. pp. 39-51.
33. Nunnally, J. *Introduction to Psychological Measurement.* New York: McGraw Hill, 1970.
34. Schatzman, L. and Strauss, A. *Field Research: Strategies for a Natural Sociology.* Englewood Cliffs, New Jersey: Prentice Hall, 1973.
35. Murphy, J. *Concepts of Leisure: Philosophical Implications.* Englewood Cliffs, New Jersey: Prentice Hall, 1974.
36. Neulinger, J. *The Psychology of Leisure.* Springfield, IL: Thomas, 1974.

Chapter Twenty-Four

Qualitative Determinants of Recreation Opportunities

Francis P. Noe

Different types of recreation activities and activity patterns have often been shown to be correlated with a particular status level or with socio-economic class. Research into possible explanations of that relationship has resulted in unrefined, simplistic models easily tested by merely counting status or class quantities (income, education, or occupation) and then relating these quantities to frequencies of recreational participation measured by day, week, month or year. Theory has tended to ignore questions relating to class control, diffusion, sharing, and domination of an activity as explanations of different participation rates in particular activities. Many simply follow Veblen's diffusion theory on upper class stylizing of recreation or accept a Marxist model of class dominance as a guide to explaining recreation participation patterns. Unfortunately, neither of these formulations goes far enough in identifying the properties of inequality inherent in the organization of recreation except in terms of wealth or property.

Models of social stratification based upon class distinctions or status hierarchies are two possibilities that have been applied but not systematically tested with regard to explaining participation in recreational activities. Analysis of social behavior relating uniformity to either a class division model or a status hierarchy model suggests that " responses to societal issues tend to be structured along class divisions, but differences in individual life styles are more often distributed along a status continuum."[1] But delineating which model better divides recreation into plateau levels or what conditions might lead to overlapping on a continuum remains unresolved to date. In this chapter a model is described which uses both status and class distinctions for predicting recreational behavior. The status model, refers to a continuum assuming a graded hierarchy of occupational prestige. The class model emphasizes bounded divisions based upon a composite of income, education, and occupation. The two models may affect recreation behavior differently in that a class model suggests normative standards which control the selection process for group association (or who you play with for fun) while a status model suggests normative standards which control the actual role performance (or how you play at having fun). In considering either model, "it is impossible to say that any given society is strictly class or status oriented since this orientation is a function of the type of behavior."[2] When evaluating recreational behavior, some normative principles may be explained part of the time by class and other times by status distinctions.

Although social class and status correlates are recognized as producing predictable recreational differences, little meaningful elaboration has been given to why class, status, and recreation behavior should necessarily be related. In speculating about such differences, a theory is proposed which recognizes that in an equalitarian and utilitarian society, largely industrial and urban situated, notions of class and status inequality are antithetical to cultural beliefs. Because recreation is considered nonserious, trivial, expendable and, when under the guise of the protestant ethic, less than important, it may in fact preserve and give rise to class and status distinctions. In this way, recreation could provide a vehicle for instituting traditions, customs, and rituals that differentiate among the various organized strata of individuals.

Inequality of position is not easy to accept in a society which professes to be equalitarian. In the face of equalitarian pressure in society, any stressing of economic and political parity causes many groups to retreat behind a wall of secrecy. Attaining privacy was always a sign of privilege among the upper classes; less ostentatious signs provide a lower profile and less visible target for disenfranchised groups. No one can say for sure, but individuals appear unwilling to publicly divulge their symbols of identity. Consequently, "Class differences in styles of life have not disappeared but have become somewhat more subtle than they used to be."[3] A social illusion is created to hide the trend toward "a pattern of gross equality and subtle inequality."[4] It appears that a trend toward the blurring of recreational life sytles has taken place, though evidence for this trend is not yet conclusive. Being obscure and discrete does not detract from the fact that recreational patterns actually may be indicative of class position and merit status reward.

NORMATIVE PRINCIPLES

Because we are inescapably confronted with a mixing of class and status forces, a set of normative principles may help explain the stratification of recreation (See Table 1). A paradigm is presented and organized by both status and class categories which may affect both membership affiliation and participation in recreation. A class model is involved in the selection process of admitting members to a group whereas a status model is based on ability in performing a given recreational activity. A discussion of each of the dimensions of the paradigm follows, by describing the normative properties associated with status or class.

TABLE 1

PARADIGM OF CLASS-STATUS RECREATION DISTINCTIONS
(A Tentative Listing)

Principles of Organization Differentiating Access to *Social Affiliation* For A Recreational Life Style

	Upper and Lower Class Levels		Middle Class Levels
Class Model and Group Identity	Exclusive	–	Inclusive
	Private	–	Open
	Traditional	–	Popular

Principles of Organization Differentiating Levels of *Social Affiliation* For A Recreational Life Style

	Upper and Lower Status Levels		Middle Status Levels
Status Model and Role Performance	Serious	–	Easy
	Subtle	–	Obvious
	Identification	–	Massification

NORMS OF ORGANIZATION FOR SOCIAL AFFILIATION

The *exclusivity* of organized leisure recognizes that individuals are selective with whom they recreate, while being *inclusive* implies class members do not use many formal rules of recruitment. Part of the selection process occurs when individuals organize themselves into compatible class affiliated groupings. For example, the relationship between social class and voluntary associations has been well documented showing affiliation and participation patterns related to class. Membership association is related to the organization of recreation activities and includes even informal patterns of sociability. What is included or excluded in friendships between the classes relates to a range of activities and how the classes allow them to develop in prescribed situations.[5] In one case, the lower class members of an Andalusion town limited participation in a local festival to the extent that the upper class (senoritos) "not only ignore the holiday, but they make a point of abandoning the town altogether while 'carnival' is being observed."[6] Exclusivity of situations or an activity, not just membership, is also a consideration in developing a class model of recreation participation. Moreover, the products of a class may also be restricted and not distributed through the wider channels of mass communication. For example, high class culture "serves a small public that prides itself on exclusiveness"[7] and its products are not intended for distribution by the mass media. Sometimes the factors of exclusive product and membership operate together to provide a recreational experience of limited appeal and restricted group participation.

Participating in an activity and knowing that others are not involved is an important function of belonging to a group. It provides a standard by which members can define their social position. "Because people in these membership groups share values and build similar norms of spending behavior, membership groups are reference groups in which the life styles of members are said to resemble each other more than they resemble those of the population at large."[8] A group associated life style may directly affect an individual's sense of relative worth or perceived inequality and give support to a class consciousness. A final note on the idea of exclusivity stratum formation has been given by Eisenstadt who concluded that:

> "the development and upholding of such styles of life necessarily contain a very strong element of inclusiveness - exclusiveness, of inclusion of some people and of the concomitant exclusion of other social categories or groups. But such exclusiveness connotes a certain type of relationship with them basically a certain type of unconditional yet complimentary relation with them."[9]

Exclusivity is not tangential, but very much immeshed in deriving class identity through memberships which organize discretionary time.

The degree of *privacy* or *openness* is a second characteristic in a class model. Studies of norms on privacy have been done among different social classes. "Mostly privacy is associated with behaviors which are potentially highly variable (e.g. sexual or the volume at which one listens to music, etc.), but the norms of a particular class may put a limit on this variability by stipulating which of its possible forms are or are not acceptable."[10] The idea of exclusivity and its attendant relationship to privacy might provide a basis for staging an activity performance along class lines. For example, privacy has been shown to

> "positively limit the power of others in two ways. It limits the power of others to interrupt or interfere with the individual during activities which he wishes to pursue on his own, like reading or writing, and it limits the power of others to exert normative pressures with respect to certain private individual acts, thereby allowing potential nonconformity in relation to behavior."[11]

The private opportunity to allow oneself more freedom and autonomy with regard to social norms is possible, but obviously controlled where situations are class related. Usually, individuals can let themselves go and have a good time but within class limits. If certain "private behavior" was performed in a larger social context, the individual may be severely sanctioned. The norm of privacy or exclusivity in denying people access to a group has led to public acts of deviance. In surfing behavior, for example, conspicuous displays by outsiders in the surfing community constitute devious acts.[12] Marginal individuals ostensibly unable to achieve recognition and status within a class of surfers engage in exhibitionism to garner attention to themselves. These outsiders perform and display for the outside public in defiance of the internal norm of privacy.

Whether activities are *traditional* or *popular* is another important distinction. *Traditional* recreation practices contain barriers stressing form over content such that the rituals take precedence. Rituals not only set groups apart but control some part of society's time schedule. Parties, banquets, festivals and celebrations are often routinely planned within a framework of a social strata. A gala may signal the end of the tennis or golf season only to open the door to skiing and a new round of socializing. The annual and seasonal scheduling of activities with accompanying festivities may be more marked and pronounced within one strata than another. "Ritual carries collective information (the analogy with restricted codes) and thus reaffirms the collective reality of group life."[13] The "jet set," for example, requires "a performance of an extravagant and exuberant nature; it requires a decadent performance,"[14] i.e., the symbolic acquiring of goods and services not for a practical purpose but for the social prestige. By controlling information and situations, jet setters manage to stage their own magical mystery tour. The staging of extravagance immortalizes the participants in feats of extraordinary human endeavor far different from the reaches of mortal men. Recreational styles of life are described in the pseudo ritual displays of the jet set, the sober activity of corporate entrepreneurs and the rusticity of country gentlemen pictured in Wellingtons.[15] Although the upper classes give the appearance of fashioning many such rites, the lower classes have fashioned their own share. The "bowling banquet" and "stag picnic" are annual affairs that reunite many working class members with their peers around crap games, jokes and beer. Moreover, deviations from such traditional activities have been observed where people who play outside of their status are said to be "putting on the dog." The degree to which members of a class are "playing at something" might indicate anticipatory status, mobility, or status inconsistency.

NORMS OF ORGANIZATION FOR SOCIAL PARTICIPATION

The property of *seriousness* deals with the level of commitment an individual associates with recreational participation. Recreation contains elements of fun and frivolity, but also skills, practicality, and fulfillment. The degree of seriousness attached to participants' actions is often associated with membership in prestige ranked clubs and voluntary associations. The serious intricacies of many activities are learned through social interaction. Specialized vocabularies are formed and phrases of comprehension are communicated through word of mouth in the socialization of the potential member participant. Engaging in highly complex activities that require learning and preparation is often sufficient for discouraging outside participation. The upper social economic groups may be drawn more heavily into organizations requiring cognitive skills, especially as evident in art and involved gaming activity, than the lower classes among whom motor skills may be important.

As seriousness interjects itself into recreational behavior, the possibility for status differentiation increases. In examining the sport of autocrossing, for example, performance criteria differentiate prestige levels and rewards among its participants. Members of various auto clubs are accorded higher prestige based upon their mechanical and driving abilities.[16] Participation is directed not by work related attributes like occupation, education, and income but by driving abilities and finishing positions which strongly influence prestige rank. By being categorized by skill level, individuals become more serious about their activities. They learn skills, acquire more information, and train and strain to perform at a higher competitive level in order to achieve status. Particular recreational activities may be pursued and dominated by a particular status group and organized exclusively to promote a higher level of seriousness rather than allow a skill-free level of participation.

A second distinguishing characteristic is the degree to which behavior is subtle or obvious. *Subtlety* refers to the process of conducting recreational activities in such a manner that everything is not fully comprehensible by an outside observer. The idea, not unlike secrecy, implies that organized participation takes place outside the arena of public acclaim and scrutiny. For the upper strata, pleasure and pursuit of recreation involve learning discreet but unusual avocations that blend easily with the education and wealth of that strata. Patronage and support of the fine arts boasts many followers from the elite upper classes. Certain activities like gambling are pursued outside of the public glare due not only to legal constraints, but also to preclude the possibility of "opening up" a game to newcomers who may be more skilled. Concealing an activity from public scrutiny, or masking its appearance as a highly obscured enterprise helps insure a subtle image. Most avant newspaper narratives testify to the social transactions of the elite set, just as labor tradepapers and church newsletters do for their members. The masking process is achieved by manipulating symbols. Some symbols are material while others are semantic; together they weave a tapestry of meaning that one not privy to the inner circle will fail to understand. Material symbols that construct the physical part of a social setting are manipulated to create a definite impression. "In most organizations, distinctive signs, sometimes intentionally provided by the organization, sometimes covertly invented and promoted by the members, serve to identify the classes."[17]

Maintaining subtlety may require an even greater use of continually changing specialized equipment and gadgets. The more institutionalized forms of recreation possess many levels of meaning that specify objectives, channels of achievement, standardized regulations, and sanctions. Further, institutionalized symbols and their application to recreation vary by strata. Upper class observers of a Spanish Carnival referred to a celebration as "gross, ugly, and common."[18] Revelings, dress and interaction between the participants were overtly expressive, thereby mocking sexual, religious and political values. The results of this symbolic display served to reinforce group solidarity among the working class element.

The use of symbols in recreation activities may increase status and promote inequality according to the subtleties involved. For example, semantic symbols can build a mystique. The cultic language of a skydiver who refers to the "whole turkey," or the surfer making reference to the "charge," or a jazz instrumentalist speaking of the "it" use symbols which are intended to set them apart. In the flow of descriptive language, symbols expressive of something unique and special are interspersed in the dialogue and presented to the outsider as indicative of a separate life style. A discreet, nondirective use of symbols in recreation is yet another source for maintaining status. The degree of subtlety imparts a reward of speciality which reinforces the process of differentiation.

Identification, a third distinguishing characteristic, is established through both personal and social encourters. An important source of self-identification in a "fun situation" is that "fellowship with an elect who has a mystique not shared with outsiders."[19] We already know that club memberships and socializing with fellow workers is positively associated with social class levels. Personal identity may also be masked to facilitate engagement in opulent displays of status. The competition among Krewes over Mardi Gras in the city of New Orleans allows the member to identify with nationally known personalities who participate on the floats. The cost associated with being king or queen and the attending costs of the "costumes and throws" hide the individual members who, in their concealment, reinforce their prestige and importance within the community. Carnival "reinforces the boundaries of the group"[20] and serves to provide the participant with "social honor." Less formal social gatherings of friends, relatives or social groups like the Cook Island drinking groups "were places" where the culturally old and the socially new met, and for the individual a place of discovery to establish or redefine personal identity."[21] Conversations between group members symbolically tied individuals to a past, present and future and helped establish a place in the hierarchy. Identification with a leisure activity may bring personal status while massification in the faceless crowd may bring little personal reward.

IMPLICATIONS

After reviewing studies of class, status, and recreation, the evidence points to more fruitful organizational schemas than simply correlating class or status to recreational behavior. Efforts in the future must therefore reach beyond our present understanding to questions concerning the organization of recreation involvements and its role in determining class and status. The properties identified in this chapter provide a context that have theoretical implications for studying the process of class and status formation in determining recreational choices and their consequences.

Previous research has usually taken the position that recreational activities are stratified by differential opportunities based on income, occupation, or education. Investigators have considered recreational activity and participatory involvement as a response to an already existing system of social differentiation in society. In evaluating recreational activities from an organizational perspective, there is the possibility that in fact recreation molds social class and status distinctions among individuals, rather than the reverse – or in addition to it. Given the utilitarian, egalitarian ethic of modern industrial society in which there is greater pressure toward standardizing and leveling of man's wealth, education, and occupational distinctions, recreational pursuits may be one of the least offensive means of maintaining class and status differences. Conflicts over inequality of education and lack of opportunities for income and wealth have embroiled many industrialized nations, producing very serious social turmoil. There seems to be less resentment over cultural inequality than over income, occupation, residence, or education. If we accept this condition, then it is also possible that recreation contributes to the formation of social distinctions based on class or status. Information and knowledge about that process would be important for understanding the basic social processes of society.

The older Outdoor Recreation Resources Review Commission and State Comprehensive Outdoor Recreation Plan models that utilize straight forward socioeconomic status models in relationship to rates of participation have frequently been a part of the quantitative approach to the study of recreation in the last two decades. The order of relationship presumes that the socioeconomic status variables affect leisure or recreational participation when in fact recreational choice and participation may be the precipitate of class and status distinctions. More importantly, it is difficult to change the socioeconomic status of individuals either through political acts or through planned social programs. While class and status information may show that a particular strata in society participates in a certain activity, it is important to know the manner in which that activity is organized to provide the individual with rewards or status. Socioeconomic indicators are not subject to change or manipulation by managers or program directors the same way that organizational norms can be manipulated.

Institutionalization of recreation in modern industrial society has not occurred to any great extent except in certain areas of the arts and sports. But beyond that narrow form of institutionalization a great deal of freedom and voluntarism still persist. A practitioner who can take advantage of normative principles that provide rewards and reinforce the social background of an individual can better insure that his programs and activities are more successful in the community. Activities that do not provide class or status rewards may be less desirable and utilized by members of the community. By manipulating normative properties, we may create situations of greater social integration, consolidation and demand by select social classes and status groups. Instead of simply promoting, for example, a skills inventory for learning a sport, it may be equally important to organize symbols of distinction, provide medals, cups, and awards and establish traditions on an annual basis which enable individuals to participate in clearly defined frameworks. Norms for insuring ritualized behavior, traditional activities and ceremonies, and utilization of specific symbols both verbal and material may be more significant to the organization of an activity than the actual learning of skills and performance. Team and individual sports, art and music skills, and hobbies lend themselves particularly well to this kind of manipulation.

The principles tentatively defined may lend themselves to providing positive status rewards and class distinctions that will serve to motivate individuals to participate more fully in recreational options. This model is unlike the models of the past two decades that placed all the burden and all the social emphasis upon already established institutions found in education, the organization of wealth, and commercial/industrial organization. If this model has any value, it should be more adaptable to pragmatic application in the organization and institutionalization of leisure and recreation.

REFERENCES

1. Reeve, Vanneman and Pampel, Fred C.. "The American Perception of Class and Status." *American Sociological Review,* 42, (June, 1977). p. 424.
2. *Ibid.,* p. 435.
3. Barber, Bernard. "Social Stratification Structure and Trends of Social Mobility in Western Society." In Parsons, Talcott (Ed.). *American Sociology.* Basic Books, 1969. p. 191.
4. *Ibid.,* p. 192.
5. Graham, Allan. "Class Variation in Friendship Patterns." *The British Journal of Sociology.* 28, (September, 1977). pp. 390-1.
6. Gilmore, David. "Carnival in Fuenmayor: Class Conflict and Social Cohesion in an Andalusion Town." *Journal of Anthropological Research,* 31, (Winter, 1975). p. 325.

7. *Ibid.*, p. 336.
8. Fisk, George. *Leisure Spending Behavior.* Philadelphia: University of Pennsylvania Press, 1963.
9. Eisenstadt, S.N.. "Prestige, Participation and Strata Formation." In Jackson, J.A. (Ed.). *Social Stratification.* London: Cambridge University Press, 1968. pp. 62-103.
10. Kelvin, Peter. "Social-Psychological Examination of Privacy." *The British Journal of Social and Clinical Psychology,* 12, (September, 1973). p. 257.
11. *Ibid.*, p. 258.
12. Irwin, John. "Surfing." *Urban Life and Culture,* 2, (July, 1973). p. 154.
13. Bergesen, James. "Review Essay: Rituals, Symbols, and Society – Explicating the Mechanisms of the Moral Order." *American Journal of Sociology,* 83, (Jan. 1978). p. 1019.
14. Buiks, Peter. "The Decadent Performance of the Jet Set." *Mens en Maatschappij,* 50:4, (1975). p. 399.
15. Giddens, Anthony. "The Rich." *New Society,* 38, (October, 1976). pp. 63-66.
16. Aveni, Adrian. "Alternative Stratification Systems: The Case of Interpersonal Respect among Leisure Participants." *Sociological Quarterly,* 17, (Winter, 1976). p. 58.
17. Anderson, G., *et.al.*. "Status Classes in Organizations." *Administrative Science Quarterly,* 11 (September, 1966).
18. Klapp, Orrin E.. *Collective Search for Identity.* New York: Holt, Rinehart and Winston, 1969. p. 187.
19. *Ibid.*, p. 195.
20. Seneviratne, H.L.. "Aristocrats and Rituals in Contemporary Ceylon." *Journal of Asian and African Studies,* 11, (Jan.-Apr., 1976). p. 98.
21. Lemert, Edwin. "Koni, Kona, Kava." *Journal of Studies on Alcohol,* 37:5, (1976). pp. 568-575.

Chapter Twenty-Five

Qualitative Measures of Program Success

Charles W. Lamb and John R. Crompton

> We really aren't talking about how many people pass across a park, but we are talking about such things as who had a better day because they saw the planting of azaleas on the way to work, or the wild-flowers in bloom in a meadow, or the squirrel climbing that tree in an undisturbed area, or the handicapped child that learned to swim, and in later years saved somebody's life, or the senior citizen that learned a new handicraft. You cannot put a value figure on these experiences and attendance figures have nothing at all to do with it.[1]

The authors of this paper are concerned that, despite frequent utterances professing the need to be concerned about the quality of individuals' recreation experiences, we continue to use only quantitative measures to evaluate the success of recreation and park services. Theobold[2], in a review of the literature, identified nineteen measures which have been proposed by a variety of authors for evaluating recreation and park services. Out of these nineteen measures only one addressed the perceived recreation satisfaction of citizens.

We do not mean to imply that the recreation and park field has not made progress in the area of evaluation. The early efforts at evaluation tended to focus more on inputs such as the number of acres of land, number of facilities, size of the budget, or range of programs provided. Now, at least, most agencies focus their evaluation efforts upon outputs. However, it is contended in this chapter that too much emphasis is currently placed on evaluating a program's output in terms of the *efficiency* with which it is delivered and insufficient attention is given to evaluating the *effectiveness* of a program's impact on clients. Efficiency is usually measured in quantitative terms based upon the number of people who participate in, or use, a recreation and park program, or the cost efficiency of servicing those people. Although measures of efficiency are necessary management tools, when used *alone* to evaluate the success of a program, they may be misleading. In addition, we contend that quantitative efficiency measures are of secondary importance and that primary attention should be given to measuring client satisfaction.

There are at least two good reasons why an agency's primary evaluation focus should be upon client satisfaction. First, many agencies have traditionally defined their purpose or objectives in such terms as: to enrich the quality of life; promote physical, mental, social and emotional development; and contribute to the self-fulfillment of all citizens in the community. Hence, it would seem that appropriate measures of an agency's success should address how well it used its resources to achieve such psychological benefits rather than how many people used its programs or services.

As Weiss has pointed out, evaluation has a utilitarian purpose, it is not a pie in the sky phrase conjured up by some academic.[3] Its function is to provide evidence of the outcomes of programs so that managers can make wise decisions about those programs in the future. To the extent that a program is achieving its goals, evaluative evidence supports continuation, expansion and increased allocation of resources. But if evaluation discloses that a program is not achieving its goals then it should be modified, cut back or shut down.

The pressures for evaluation are increasing. Federal programs now demand evaluation of program outcomes and require that a proportion of operating funds be budgeted to determine program effectiveness. At the local level the tax revolt has put increasing pressures on recreation and park agencies to prove their legitimacy in order to justify continued community support. The justification efforts of agencies have focused almost exclusively upon efficiency measures based upon the number of people served. These types of evaluation measures appear to represent the present state of the art in this field.

In the first part of this paper we review the use of attendance as a measure of evaluating a service's success. This is a frequently used criterion in the field. We discuss the rationale for using it and point out pragmatic and conceptual weaknesses in its use. We go on to distinguish between efficiency and effectiveness and argue that the reason the wrong primary criterion (quantity participating rather than quality of participation) is frequently used for evaluation is because we fail to correctly answer the quation "What business are we in?" If this question is answered correctly, the objectives of the program will become clear and appropriate evaluative measures will be implemented. Finally, in the latter part of the paper we suggest measures for evaluating client satisfaction.

RATIONALE FOR THE USE OF ATTENDANCE AS A CRITERION OF SUCCESS

Traditionally, the most frequently used criterion for measuring the success of recreation and park programs has been attendance. In many cases, particularly in state or regional park systems, the use of this measure of success has led to financial resources being allocated on the basis of attendance. In other words, those parks or programs which have had the largest attendance in the past often receive the largest budget allocations in the future. Alternatively, those programs that have not demonstrated their success in terms of attendance (including new programs) have received relatively small budget allocations.

The popular use of attendance figures as the criterion for evaluating the success of recreation and park programs and services can be attributed to a number of factors. First, the method is intuitively appealing. Given a linited amount of funds to allocate among various programs or services, it seems reasonable to allocate the most money to those programs or services that are in greatest demand. Not only do these programs or services reach the largest number of people, but frequently they also have the lowest cost per participant.

A second reason for using attendance to evaluate success is that it is ostensibly politically appealing. It appears to adhere to the maxim of the greatest good for the greatest number of people. Hence, it is likely to be non-controversial. An important corollary to this strategy is the belief that more participants mean more supporting votes for the program from both legislators and their constituents.

Another justification for using numbers through the door is the simplicity and apparent objectivity of the approach. Often instead of using absolute attendance figures for evaluating the relative merit of programs, a ratio of attendance to costs is derived. This gives the cost per client served and may be used to determine which programs and services are most cost efficient. This approach seemingly eliminates any bias for or against particular individuals, groups or programs.

A fourth often stated reason for basing budget allocation on past attendance is the absence of alternative decision-making criteria. We use attendance because "it is not possible to measure the smile on a child's face." Attendance data are readily available, inexpensive to collect, and, hence, their use is expedient. Although some managers recognize that attendance is not an ideal criterion for evaluation, they continue to use this approach because they are unaware of any better way to measure success and allocate resources. Many also use attendance figures because they believe that this is the only basis for justifying their budget requests that will be acceptable to their superiors.

SHORTCOMINGS OF USING ATTENDANCE FOR EVALUATION

An obvious pragmatic limitation of using attendance to measure success concerns the difficulty of securing accurate data. If one knows the next year's budget allocation, or a supervisor's assessment of one's success, will be based upon this year's attendance, there is a strong incentive to produce large attendance figures any way possible. For example, if turnstiles are used to monitor the number of persons entering a facility, it is a relatively simple task for employees to inflate attendance data by spinning the turnstile. This possibility also exists when traffic counters are used. Employees may inflate attendance figures by running their vehicles over the traffic counters as often as they like. In cases where electronic or mechanical devices are not used to monitor attendance, program managers or other employees often have considerable discretion in determining attendance. A playground supervisor may count casual walkers through the playground as facility users if he or she thinks this will aid promotion prospects or next year's budget request. Securing accurate attendance data is particularly difficult at programs or facilities for which no admission price is charged. If a price is charged, then receipts can be used to cross-check attendance records and the data are likely to be more accurate.

In addition to this pragmatic limitation, there are a number of conceptual weaknesses in using attendance to measure success. If resources are assigned to programs on the basis of participation, then *funding allocations may sometimes be the result of success rather than a cause of success.* Almost any program can be made to generate the attendance necessary to classify it as a success, given enough resources. For example, free admission or increased promotion would probably encourage more attendance. If admisson is already free then paying people as an incentive to attend or providing them with free transportation would probably have the same effect. Following this same line of reasoning, a program with low attendance may be considered relatively unsuccessful because it has never had the level of financial support necessary to make it successful. If the program continues to have minimal financial support it may remain unsuccessful for the same reason.

The use of attendance to measure success ignores the fact that some programs or services are designed to appeal to smaller, yet equally important, client groups. For example, the potential market for a particular senior citizens' program may be smaller than the potential market for a youth oriented program. If a particular senior citizens' program attracted 100 participants which accounted for 80 percent of those capable of participating in the program and a youth oriented program attracted 300 participants which accounted for 10 percent of those capable of participating in the program, would the youth program be deemed three times as successful as the senior citizen program? Should it be funded at three times the level of the senior citizens program? If programs are funded proportionate to attendance there is little incentive for recreation and park agencies to deliver services to smaller client groups. However, in some cases, this may be the most important justification for a recreation agency's existence. The welfare or public benefits accruing from serving smaller client groups may be much greater than the public benefits accruing from serving larger segments whose wants may more easily be met by other leisure services suppliers or other types of services.

And what about new programs? If resources are allocated based upon past participation levels, how is the funding level for a new program to be determined? It is possible that established programs no longer need the same level of financial support. These resources might be better used to launch new programs or to resussitate programs that have previously received only modest support. Some new programs or services may require relatively more resources in order to become established, and some older programs may require relatively fewer resources. It takes time for new programs or services to become established and build up demand. They also usually require a substantial allocation of resources if they are to be successfully launched. Attendance may simply be an indicator of a program's stage in its life cycle. Higher attendance figures for one program over another may not indicate the superiority of the former. They may simply be a reflection of the length of time that the program has been offered.

Clearly, some programs require a larger per participant expenditure than others. Programs requiring a small instructor-to-participant ratio or requiring special supplies, equipment, or facilities obviously are more costly per participant than programs requiring little supervision, supplies, equipment, or facilities. The attendance criterion, or the attendance/cost ratio criterion, often depict such programs as being inferior. Similarly, some programs have limited ecological and/or social carrying capacity. The use of an absolute attendance criterion as the measure of success ignores this. Because these programs have a lower carrying capacity it does not follow that they are inherently inferior. Indeed, to increase the numbers participating in such programs may destroy the experience sought by their participants. Furthermore, increased participation may lead to the decay, destruction, or imbalance of the recreation facility.

Some argue that quantity of participation is synonymous with a satisfactory experience since participants would not indulge in return visits or encourage their friends to participate if their experience had not been satisfactory. However, this ignores the possibility that there may be no substitutable alternatives. For example, if the public recreation and park agency owns the only swimming pool in town, on a 95 degree day in the summer a large attendance is likely no matter how poorly it is operated. People will participate even though the experience may be considered less than optimally satisfying. Hence, numbers per se are not only incompatible with client satisfaction but are also likely to lead to erroneous conclusions if the numbers are interpreted as being synonymous with satisfaction. *Client satisfaction may result in large attendances, but large attendances are not necessarily indications that a service is providing high levels of client satisfaction.*

We noted earlier that advocates of the attendance criterion frequently equate increased attendance with increased support. This may be an erroneous assumption. Servicing a large number of people may be incompatible with having a well satisfied clientele. Frequently, large attendance or participation levels are obtained because the program is geared to appeal to the largest number of people within a community. Such a strategy suggests that relatively few participants will be well satisfied because compromises in the nature of the service have to be made in order to accommodate everybody. When the agency's budget comes up for review, it may be argued that the support of a relatively small number of highly committed people may be more desirable than a larger number of marginally satisfied people who will not miss the service sufficiently to fight for its retention in the budget. Politically, larger numbers are not necessarily transferrable into increased support.

These shortcomings of using attendance as the criterion to measure the success or failure of particular programs suggests that it is an inadequate criterion used on its own. We do not advocate that attendance should be ignored. Attendance may be a useful measure of efficiency, but we argue that efficiency should be a secondary concern to effectiveness. There are times when it is useful to use attendance numbers for the purpose of gaining support from the public or from politicians who feel that there constituents understand, and are sympathetic, only to efficiency, and do not recognize the weaknesses identified in the previous paragraphs.

If attendance figures are used for the purpose of gaining support, the recreation and park manager should be aware of their limitations. For example, major theme park operators use attendance figures for public relations purposes because large numbers generate good publicity. However, these operators are aware of the limited usefulness of these data for measuring their success. For their own internal measure of customer satisfaction, theme park operators give a simple, one page questionnaire to a sample of 50 to 100 guests in the park each day, seeking to identify their level of satisfaction. These are used as the primary internal evaluation tool. They serve as a way to continually improve the services offered so people will continue to attend and persuade their friends to visit the park. *In the commercial sector, level of customer satisfaction is seen as the necessary prerequisite to sustained sales volume based upon repeat business.*

EFFECTIVENESS – NOT EFFICIENCY – SHOULD BE THE PRIME CRITERION

The first step to improved evaluation is to develop greater conceptual clarity about what recreation and park services are intended to accomplish. The use of attendance or attendance/cost ratios for evaluation reflects a concern for *efficiency.* Efficiency is concerned with the amount of effort, expense, or waste involved in delivering a service. Budgetary constraints have forced recreation and park managers to increasingly direct their attention to this criterion. This is important but it should only be the second concern. Prime concern should be with *effectiveness.* Effectiveness is concerned with the impact or end result of the service on the clientele. Assessment of effectiveness focuses upon the extent to which goals are fulfilled. That is, effectiveness indicates how well the service succeeded in fulfilling the purpose for which it was established.

It is essential that a program's goals be established in a form that will permit evaluation. Unfortunately, some agencies use very generalized goal statements for a program which are not possible to evaluate. Assuming that the intended benefits of a program are specified at the outset, the first question to ask in evaluating the success of a program is, "Does the program facilitate the benefits which it was intended to deliver to clients?" Only when this question has been addressed is it appropriate to assess efficiency and ask, "Is the program being delivered in the least costly way?"

Efficiency deals with cost per participant and is a work measurement designed to gauge if the program is doing things better or worse. Effectiveness, on the other hand, attempts to ascertain whether the program, through its stated objectives, is doing the right things in the optimal manner.[4] Efficiency is input-output oriented, effectiveness is client oriented. The essence of this distinction was stated by Gray and Greben in the following terms:

> We should have discovered long ago the nature of the business we are in, but we have not. Only now are we beginning to rethink what recreation is. In the emerging view it is not activities, or facilities, or programs that are central, it is what happens to people.

They go on to state:

> We must evaluate everything we do in human terms. The critical questions are not "How many were there?" or "Who won?" The critical question is, "What happened to Jose, Mary, Sam and Joan in this experience?" . . . we must reorient our approach to services, to think not only in terms of activities and programs, but also in terms of human experience.[5]

If we reject the use of efficiency criteria as the sole means for evaluating performance and allocating resources, we need to propose methods of evaluating effectiveness.

ESTABLISHING THE RIGHT OBJECTIVES

Before an evaluation of the effectiveness of a program can be undertaken, there has to be a clear understanding of the impact that the program is intended to have on clients. That is, what are the objectives of the program? Appropriate objectives emerge in response to the question "What Business Are We In?" Often we lack clear vision as to the nature of our business. Our concern should not be limited to delivering programs or providing services. Rather our primary focus should be upon the end results which those programs facilitate. *People engage in leisure activities with the expectation of receiving benefits. Programs have no value; only their benefits have value to client groups. A program is simply a means to an end.* Benefits, or ends sought include such things as social interaction, prestige, excitement, security, relaxation, fantasy, or simply happiness.

If an agency defines its business, and consequently its objectives, in terms of specific programs, it is likely that it will measure its success in terms of the level of efficiency in offering those programs, rather than in terms of their effectiveness in facilitating anticipated client benefits. Instead of specific programs, the starting point should be identification of the benefits which client groups seek. Agency objectives should be stated in terms of these benefits. Specific programs and services designed to meet these wants can then be selected. Program performance can be assessed in terms of the extent to which it meets these wants.

Because benefits are qualitative rather than quantitative, it does not mean that program objectives cannot be written and subsequently evaluated. Failure to establish objectives leaves an agency in the uncomfortable position of the Cheshire Cat telling Alice that as long as she didn't care where she was headed, any direction she took would be acceptable! If objectives are specified and written in terms of benefits or what happens to people, then an effective evaluation measure must address these phenomena.

EVALUATING EFFECTIVENESS

Evaluating performance and allocating resources can be predicated on three propositions. These are:

1. the objective of recreation and park agencies is to satisfy client group wants;
2. by translating client group wants into benefits sought, the agency defines its objectives in terms of benefits; and
3. programs and services are the means to achieve ends, and not themselves ends.

If the agency accepts these propositions, it naturally follows that agency objectives will be stated in terms of the *specific* benefits it intends to provide selected client groups. Also, subordinates will establish objectives in terms of benefits provided and not in terms of programs or attendance figures. After this task has been completed, superiors and subordinates are in a position to assess existing programs and services according to the extent to which they contribute to the achievement of the specified objectives. They are also in a position to determine what changes are needed in existing programs, what new programs and services should be offered, and the various resources that are needed to achieve desired outcomes.

What measures are available for assessing the extent to which an existing program successfully facilitates the client benefits intended? It has been suggested that there are four approaches that can be used to directly measure client satisfaction.[6] These are (1) unsolicited client response; (2) observation; (3) client group surveys; and (4) saliency measurement.

The unsolicited client response technique is the least rigorous of the four. This technique simply entails establishing a mechanism to allow clients to comment on the quality of a program if they so desire.

Suggestion or comment boxes are a commonly used example of this approach. This approach has two important limitations. First, it is possible to generalize either positive or negative comments to the overall client groups, since the views of those taking the opportunity to comment may be very different from those who do not take the opportunity to comment. Second, the absence of a large number of complaints cannot be interpreted as demonstrating a high degree of satisfaction because many people are not prepared to take the effort to comment. In general, unsolicited responses do not provide a valid measurement of a program's effectiveness.

The observation approach represents an attempt to be a little more representative by directly observing and interacting with clients. A director may visit a park, swimming pool or recreation program and talk to participants about their likes, dislikes and suggestions. This technique has the advantage of allowing the manager to seek information from whomever he or she chooses, but again there is no guarantee that these people are representative of all potential clients.

Client group surveys are a useful method for assessing wants and measuring performances. They can be used to identify which client groups desire which benefits and to identify the size of respective client groups. This enables management to define the nature and size of particular markets, and also to determine minimum as opposed to maximum participation levels required for a program to be viable.

More important, surveys can be used to assess the performance of particular programs and services. As we noted previously, this is a procedure commonly used by commercial leisure operators for internal evaluation purposes. If we have established our objectives in terms of the benefits we intend to provide to our clientele we should be willing and able to measure our performance in terms of users' (and perhaps nonusers') evaluations of the extent to which they received specific benefits from our programs. If major theme park operators (and other private sector firms) are able to get their visitors to take a few moments to express their satisfactions and dissatisfactions, it should be no trouble for public agencies to gain this type of cooperation.

A final method of measuring clients' satisfaction entails assessing the relative saliency or importance of specific benefits sought. The difference between this method and the survey method previously discussed is that when measuring saliency a client is asked two questions instead of one regarding each topic about which information is desired. The first question asks the client to evaluate each of the benefits which the agency has anticipated may accrue from a particular program on a scale (1 to 7 for example) ranging from extremely favorable to extremely unfavorable. However, this information alone is of limited value for it gives no indication of the relative importance which clients attach to each of the particular benefits which the program facilitates. For example, if the following two scale items are among those used to measure the sociability and prestige facilitated by a program, both may receive a score of 4 on a 7 point scale (neither favorable nor unfavorable).

	extremely unfavorable	very unfavorable	slightly unfavorable	neither unfavorable nor favorable	slightly favorable	very favorable	extremely favorable
Opportunity to interact with others in this program is:	1	2	3	4	5	6	7
Discussion generated among my friends by my participation in this program is:	1	2	3	4	5	6	7

However, sociability may be a very important benefit to participants in the program, while prestige may be of very little importance to them. For this reason, the second question is included. This seeks to identify the salient or important benefit attributes sought by clients from a program, for it is these which are most likely to determine whether or not clients will continue to participate.

	extremely unimportant	very unimportant	slightly unimportant	neither unimportant nor important	slightly important	very important	extremely important
Opportunity to interact with others in this program is:	1	2	3	4	5	6	7
Discussion generated among my friends by my participation in this program is:	1	2	3	4	5	6	7

Hence, if clients rate the sociability and prestige benefits 7 and 2 respectively on this importance dimension, then the score of 4 on the first question may be considered perfectly adequate for the prestige benefit for prestige is considered very unimportant (a score of 2) on the second question. Thus, it is of little concern that the program is not facilitating this benefit particularly well. In contrast, sociability is rated extremely important (a score of 7) so it should be of great concern to the agency that the program scores only a 4 on the first question, for it suggests the program is not successfully facilitating this extremely important benefit. Unless the program is restructured in some way to increase its potential for encouraging interaction with others, client support is likely to diminish.

CONCLUSION

We are not advocating that the key to success is maximizing client group satisfaction. This is an unrealistic expectation given limited resources. Furthermore, since all public agencies must satisfy many client groups, it is often necessary to reduce the satisfaction levels of some client groups in order to increase those of other groups. The goal should be to provide acceptable levels of satisfaction to clients within the constraints imposed by the agency's resource base. This goal can best be achieved by periodically monitoring the benefit expectations and satisfaction of clients.

By focusing our attention on the extent to which client wants are satisfied we can, as Gray and Greben suggest, begin thinking about recreation in terms of human experience instead of activities and programs. We can also begin thinking about successful performance in qualitative instead of quantitative terms.

REFERENCES

1. Anonymous – Submitted to one of the authors in a term paper some years ago. The student's name was mislaid with the passage of time, but the vivid nature of the imagery remained.
2. Theobold, William F.. *Evaluation of Recreation and Park Programs.* New York: John Wiley, 1979. pp. 84-89.
3. Weiss, Carol H.. "Alternative Models of Program Evaluation." *Social Work,* (November, 1974). p. 675.
4. Zabezensky, M.. *Performance Accountability in Human Service Activities.* Indianapolis, Indiana: Board of Fundamental Education, 1974. p. 18.

5. Gray, David E., and Greben, S.. "Future Perspectives," Paper presented at the National Recreation and Parks Association Congress, October, 1973.
6. Adapted from Kotler, Philip. *Marketing for Non-Profit Organizations.* Englewood Cliffs, New Jersey: Prentice-Hall, 1975. p. 153.

Chapter Twenty-Six

Cultural Boom: Myth and Reality

Jiri Zuzanek

During the last decade or two we have been told on several occasions that a cultural explosion or cultural boom has taken place in North America. In the late 1950's and early 1960's several authors heralded the spectacular growth of the art audiences and cultural consumption in the United States. White wrote of the "cultural richness" at hand which no previous age could have given to the Americans.[1] Toffler, in his book *The Culture Consumers,* stated that:

> "Millions of Americans as consumers and participants, hundreds of thousands as members and volunteer workers, are putting a little bit of their lives not merely into a search of aesthetic satisfaction, but into building and leading the institution's need to produce and distribute culture in America."[2]

More recently, a similar enthusiasm was voiced by the authors of *Americans and the Arts.*[3] The American arts public was compared in this study to a sleeping giant. The rates of participation in performing and visual arts have been estimated as being greater than those in spectator sports. Putting this all into typical journalistic jargon, the *U.S. News & World Report* in an article entitled, "The Culture Boom," wrote: "All across the nation, the theatre, ballet, opera, and museums have become smash hits – topping even old favorites such as baseball. It's part of an insatiable market for culture that is transforming America."[4]

However, not everyone shares this enthusiasm, Baumol and Bowen, in *Performing Arts: The Economic Dilemma,*[5] noted that: (a) Only a rather small and scarcely increasing proportion of the population participates in the arts with any regularity. The size of the United States arts audience (theatre, symphony, opera, art galleries) was estimated by these two authors in the mid-1960's at 2.5 to 3 million persons, i.e. approximately 2-2.5 percent of the U.S. adult population; (b) Per capita expenditure for art admissions measured in constant dollars and as the proportion of disposable income have increased little during the period from 1929 to 1963, and most of the heralded increase in cultural spending could be attributed to the double effect of natural population growth and inflation; (c) The operating expenditures of art organizations have risen at a faster rate than in other services and faster than earned revenues, widening the so-called "income gap" and making arts increasingly dependent on governmental support and private subsidies.

Concern with the small population base of the arts and their growing dependence on public money collected from the users and non-users alike has become particularly strong in the recent years of slow economic growth.

In this chapter some of the dilemmas of financing culture and the arts in modern societies are addressed. The chapter will: (1) examine trends in cultural participation and cultural spending in the last two decades; (2) comment on recent trends in the so-called "income gap" of the art organizations; (3) discuss the dilemmas which these trends present to the politicians and social researchers; (4) argue in favor of a normative and structural rather than utilitarian and atomistic approach toward problems of cultural development.

LEISURE TRENDS AND CULTURAL PARTICIPATION

Many forecasts of the so-called "cultural boom" rest on the assumption that growing amounts of leisure time in industrial societies will result in a more intensive participation of the population in cultural activities.[6] This assumption is, however, only partially supported by the available empirical evidence. Except for the self-reporting statistics of various cultural organizations, the reliability of which has been often questioned,[7] we have no strong evidence that the amounts of time spent in attending and consuming the arts have increased much during the past decade.

According to Robinson,[8] who studied changing distribution of time in the United States, out of 35 hours of free time per week that the average American had at his disposal in 1965-1966, less than 0.1 hour was spent in theatre, opera and symphony attendance. Slightly more but still less than 0.1 hour was reported in the production of art, sculpture, painting, and writing, and an additional 0.1 hour was reported in practicing music, dance, and singing. By 1975 the total amount of leisure time had increased to more than 38 hours, but most of this gain was used for watching TV while the amounts of time spent in cultural and artistic activities remained virtually unchanged or perhaps even declined.

The rates of cultural and artistic participation apparently also did not change much in the last decades. In 1957, when asked about their "yesterday" leisure activities, three percent of Americans named moviegoing, 18 percent reading books, and one percent attending theatre, opera, or a concert. When a rather similar question was asked eight years later in 1965, the percentage for moviegoing was two percent, for reading of books, seven percent, and for attending theatre and museums, less than one percent. According to a survey of art audiences conducted in 1974 by the Ford Foundation, the percentage of those who attended a movie more than once a week was two percent, while less than one percent of respondents attended theatre, ballet or concerts.[9]

In a 1973 survey, *Americans and the Arts,* respondents of this survey were asked whether they attend cultural events more frequently or less frequently today than they did five years ago. Forty-four percent responded that they attended about the same amount, 20 percent reported that they attended more, and 33 percent that they attended less.[10]

Summarizing some of the above findings, we may say that in spite of the growth of the total amounts of leisure time during the last decade, this increase has been translated mostly into mass media consumption and had little effect on the amounts of time spent in attending the arts. As stated by Robinson, disappointingly to those expecting a more activist leisure constituency, while some upward shift in organizational participation and recreation could be established, theatre, concert and museum going and other "high culture" activities gained little.[11]

TRENDS IN THE DISTRIBUTION OF DISPOSABLE INCOME AND CULTURAL EXPENDITURES

Another major assumption on which most of the theories of the "cultural boom" rest is that the growing affluence of industrial societies, and the growing population's disposable personal income result in a greater share of income and personal consumer expenditures being spent for leisure goods and services, and for culture. This position has been taken, for example, by Toffler who connected his hopes of the cultural explosion with the emergence of the so-called "comfort class," i.e. a growing segment of the population characterized by both higher incomes and larger amounts of free time. The theoretical reasoning for this position was first formulated in the 19th century. According to the so-called Engel's Law, as the personal income grows, its share spent for such essentials as food and shelter declines while the proportion of income spent on non-essentials, including leisure and culture, increases.

Although some authors may find Engel's distinction between essentials and non-essentials somewhat simplistic by today's standards, both cross-sectional and historical comparisons suggest that larger amounts or faster growth of disposable income result in larger spending for leisure, recreation and culture both in absolute and relative terms.

According to the 1972 Canadian survey of urban family expenditure, families in the $25,000+ income bracket spent $941 annually on recreation (including culture) as compared with $395 spent by all families in Canada, i.e., 2.4 times more. The difference in expenditure for culture (measured as admissions to theatre, opera and concerts) between the more affluent groups and the average population was even steeper, i.e., 4.1 times more for the $25,000+ group as compared to the Canadian average.[12]

Historical statistics on United States and Canadian consumer expenditure also document rather convincingly that periods characterized by vigorous economic performance and rapid growth of personal disposable income, such as the 1960's for example, are characterized by a faster than average growth of recreation and cultural expenditure, while in the periods of slow growth, recession or depression expenditure on recreation and culture grows at a below average rate, or declines. During the years of the Great Depression for example, i.e. between 1929 and 1934, expenditure on recreation and culture declined by 28 percent while the disposable personal income declined during this same period by only 19 percent. Cultural expenditure may have been even more sensitive to changes in disposable income. Expenditure on theatre, opera and concert admissions fell by more than 50 percent during the period of 1929-1934.[13]

In view of the above mentioned facts, it is no surprise that, as the recession of the early 1970's made its inroads into North America's economy, the population's expenditure on recreation and culture started falling behind the growth of disposable income. It may even have stopped growing in absolute per capita terms. The average expenditure per family on admissions to plays, concerts and museums in Canada was $6.9 per annum in 1972 and it declined to $6.4 (in constant dollars) in 1974.[14]

Summarizing trends in personal consumption of and expenditure on culture, we may conclude that:

1. There is a direct relationship between the size of personal disposable income and the share of it spent for recreation and culture. Periods characterized by buoyant economic development see a larger share of the population's total disposable income being spent on recreation and culture;

2. In view of the present predictions of slow economic growth one cannot expect in the immediate future substantial increases in personal expenditure on recreation and culture;

3. Paradoxically as it may seem, since historically in North America greater amounts of leisure time were often a by-product of the job shortage rather than of social design or personal desire, we may find that the 1970's will be characterized both by increasing amounts of leisure time and by lower spending on leisure and culture. As some observers have noted, with more leisure on their hands and fewer dollars to spend on it, people may increase participation in such cheap leisure activities as watching TV, working around the house, etc., rather than attending cultural events;

4. Although in most instances there is a direct relationship between the amounts of disposable income and the proportion of it spent on recreation and culture, there may be some exceptions to this rule. Historical statistics from the early 1930's suggest that in the first years of the depression, the decline of recreational expenditure may have been slower than the decline of the total disposable income. Perhaps there was a short period of readjustment when people were living according to their past standards, using up savings in their more readily available free time. A similar psychological lag may have accounted for a short-lived increase in recreational expenditure in the early 1970's, but this hardly applied to cultural spending.

It is difficult to explain the different patterns of recreational and cultural spending. One possible explanation is that recreation spending consists mostly of commodity expenditures, which generally grow faster, while cultural expenditures are almost entirely service expenditures (admission fees).

TRENDS IN THE "INCOME GAP"

Baumol and Bowen[15] have suggested in their analysis of the performing arts that the operating costs of art organizations have been growing at a faster rate than their earned revenues because of the specific operating requirements of artistic organizations which cannot be easily adapted to the economies of scale. Skilled labor required in the performing and other arts becomes more expensive than other services which can be readily mechanized. How much has this trend affected developments since 1966?

We have two interesting sets of data which throw some light on this problem.

According to a survey of 29 large performing arts organizations conducted by Canada Council in 1973, the earned revenues of Canadian performing art organizations increased by almost 88 percent in current dollars between 1967 and 1972. However, the operating expenses rose faster. They doubled moving from $12,008,000 in 1967 to $24,091,000 in 1972. The earned revenue covered 53 percent of all operating costs in 1967. This proportion dropped to 51 percent in 1968 and levelled out at 50 percent in 1971 and 1972.[16]

The situation is not much different in the United States. According to a survey of 166 performing art organizations conducted in 1971 by the Ford Foundation, at the end of the 1970-71 season operating costs of the organizations under survey absorbed $138 million. Of these, $76 million or 55 percent were recovered through earned revenue. The size of the income gap as a proportion of operating costs has increased significantly between 1965-1966 and 1970-1971. The income gap of live theatres, for example, increased from 28 percent of the operating costs in 1965-1966 to 34 percent in 1970-1971. The symphony orchestras' income gap has risen during this same period from 37 percent to 49 percent, and opera companies' from 42 percent to 43 percent. Only in the case of ballet and modern dance has the income gap increased absolutely but not as a proportion of total operating costs.[17]

One should probably agree with Baumol and Bowen that "the economic pressures which beset the arts are not temporary – they are chronic and. . . any group which undertakes to support the arts can expect no respite."[18]

This, of course, represents a rather challenging dilemma for the politicians and social planners. In a society ruled solely by the principles of laissez faire economics, the financing of the arts has not been a major concern for parties other than the artist, his audience, and perhaps the patron and the dealer. Today, when a growing proportion of the cost of the arts has come to be paid from public funds, the problem of financing the arts has become a common concern. In the United States in 1970-1971 the governmental grants and grants from national foundations covered 26 percent of the income gap. This figure has rapidly risen since. In Canada governmental support from various levels amounted in 1971-1972 to more than 75 percent of the income gap of the large performing organizations. Instead of a direct producer-client relationship which existed in the past, the demand for the arts is delegated in part to public authorities which dispose of the tax money in accordance with a rather unclearly perceived ranking of social and cultural priorities. As a result, the so-called democratization of culture, according to Girard, often ends in "subsidizing the privileged from public funds obtained by taxing the whole population – including the underprivileged."[19]

If this is the case, how can the politicians justify their increasing expenditure on the arts, particularly when the economic slowdown makes public money scarce? As in so many other instances the politicians turned for advice and arguments to the social scientists. And, as usual, the social scientists turned out to be less than unanimous in their opinions. Let us therefore direct our attention now to the positions that social researchers have taken vis-a-vis the economic dilemmas of the arts.

SOCIAL SCIENTISTS AND THE ARTS: BETWEEN POPULISM AND WISHFUL-THINKING

Simplifying the whole issue considerably, we can say that social scientists dealing with the problems of cultural development and economics of culture tended to polarize into two camps, which, in the absence of better terms, I should call populists and wishful sympathizers.

Although authors belonging to the populist camp vary greatly in their suggestions on how to improve the cultural scene, most of them hold the view that traditional performing and visual arts are elitist in nature, that a lower emphasis should be put by the governments on supporting art organizations which require large financial subsidies, that greater attention should be paid to the amateur arts, community development, spontaneous creativity, etc. In Canada, for example, representatives of this position advocate greater decentralization and regionalization of cultural subsidies, encouragement of ethnic and subcultural initiatives (multiculturalism), support of various youth and local initiatives. Under pressure from these groups and as a part of its job-creating program, the Canadian government has, in recent years, launched programs which included support for non-organized and non-professional artistic and creative activities.

The populist position is based on the assumption that so-called high culture is just an expression of a minority taste and that it has no more right to financial support than any other taste or subculture. H. Gans summarized this position:

> "The choice of taste culture is a function of the class and educational level of the person. . .Consequently, it would be unfair to expect or demand that people of lower educational levels or incomes

choose high culture. Rather, I would argue, every person should be expected to choose the taste culture that accords with his educational and class status, and, conversely, every taste culture should be considered as having *equal worth* in relation to the people who choose it, simply because all people are of equal worth. . ."[20]

This position, unfortunately, confines each audience to its own taste culture, and, in essence, denies active interaction between the arts and the audience. Art is interpreted primarily as a status symbol, not an instrument of human development. Culture and the arts are viewed as a manifestation of limited group or class interests rather than as a part of a long and universal process of the unveiling of human sensitivity and an instrument of human self-actualization, which both affirm and challenge existing social realities.

At this point, however, I would like to turn my attention from the populist scepticism about the arts to, perhaps, a more familiar scene of academic and governmental social research which "sides" with the arts.

This latter type of research, in contrast to the populist one, suggests that the audience for the arts is considerably larger than we normally believe, that there is a potential demand for the arts among the public, and that additional money would help the arts to enlarge its audience significantly. The problem with this research is that in its attempt to help the arts, it often oversteps the boundaries of realistic analysis and enters the realm of wishful thinking. De Grazia's words on "myth" apply to it quite well. "A myth," de Grazia writes, "is not a lie. It is something almost everyone wants to believe. In believing it he sometimes embraces a cold figure too warmly."[21]

The most widespread practice of the wishful-thinking researcher as far as we can tell is a conscious or unconscious manipulation with factually accurate empirical data. When we read Baumol and Bowen's statement that 2.5 to 3 million people in the United States participate in the arts, and when we compare this statement with a claim made by the survey *Americans and the Arts* that "Forty-nine percent of the American public, or 71.3 million people have gone in 1973 to see things like art shows, museums, historical houses, or antique, craft, and furniture shows,"[22] we may think that we are reading about two different countries. In fact, however, both sets of data are probably reasonably accurate, albeit psychologically deceptive. Baumol and Bowen speak of the more or less regular audience of the arts, a group of people for whom the arts are an important part of their lives. In doing this they probably underestimate the size of the "irregular" or potential audience. The 1973 survey of Americans, on the other hand, lumps together regular and accidental attendance at professional and amateur performances with going to craft and furniture shows (does going to a furniture store count?), without making the reader aware of the true meaning of the inflated figures.

Similar misinterpretation of data is often achieved by using a different measurement scale or time referent. When the Opinion Research Corporation asked Americans in 1957 about their participation *yesterday* in leisure activities, less than one percent reported attendance at a theatre, opera, or concert. When Gallup Poll asked in 1963 how many Americans participated in these same activities during the last *seven days* the percentage went up to seven percent. When the Canadian Leisure Study 1972 recorded participation in theatre and concert going for the last *three months* the percentages had risen to 10 percent, and in 1975, when participation in culture was reported for the last *12 months,* the figure had increased again to 13 percent. Needless to say, all these figures may refer to an unchanged reality and are mostly a product of measurement. However, used by journalists and politicians, they may produce either a picture of a miniscule elite living off the public money, or of a reasonably large army of connoisseurs deserving public understanding and support. I may add that inflating figures of art participation by prolonging the time referent has become an increasingly common practice in applied art research.

Another way of legitimizing expenditures for the arts is to use projective (hypothetical) questions to discover the so-called potential or latent needs of the population. Mennell some time ago rightly criticized this approach and suggested that asking people about what they would like to do in their leisure time without spelling clearly what time or money commitment is involved "is tantamount to offering people free goods."[23] People under such circumstances often express desires and needs which have little bearing on their actual behavior and produce misleading, although well-intentioned, information.

I would like to use here only one illustration of such practice. In the survey already quoted, *Americans and the Arts,*[24] respondents were asked, among other things, whether they would be willing to pay an additional $50 a year in taxes if this money were used to maintain and operate cultural facilities such as theatres, concert halls and art exhibitions. Considering that the whole survey aimed at the study of cultural participation this was a highly biased question in the first place. However, this was not the end of it. If the respondent resisted the seduction of cheap generosity, there was a follow-up question prepared for him, "And how about a tax rise of $25 to pay for such facilities, would you be willing to pay that much, or not?" (You'd better be!). Finally, to make any escape impossible, the respondent was offered a "bargain" which he could hardly refuse, i.e. only a $5 raise in taxes. Should one be surprised that, in spite of the actual stagnation of cultural expenditures of which we talked earlier, 64 percent of U.S. respondents expressed a willingness to pay $5 or more in taxes to support the arts.

The final product of wishful research which I would like to comment upon here is known as the so-called "multiplier effect." According to this concept, the arts not only serve their consumers, but also contribute to the local economy by creating new jobs. They bring business into the community. (Theatre goers were observed going to restaurants or bars after performances and spending money there, etc.)

Using a "multiplier effect" of 3.5, presumably derived from some other studies, a Vancouver report on the arts claimed that $2 million invested into the city's arts produced a total income of more than $8 million. This is, of course, an example of tautological thinking, and multiple counting. If the same logic were extended to other public services then public transportation could probably claim a contribution to the local economy equal to the income of the workers which it carries to work. On the other hand, the factories could probably as "legitimately" claim the revenues of public transportation (if any) as their contribution, since without the jobs where would the workers go? The problem, of course, is that with all these multiplier effects the city still can easily go bankrupt. The concept of the "multiplier effect" has been widely used in tourist industries, where it makes sense, because we are dealing with transfusion of money and job opportunities from one area to another. In the case of the arts (with the possible exception of such places as Stratford or Niagara-on-the-Lake), we are, however, usually reallocating resources within a given community, transferring taxes from other areas, or simply double counting.

The number of similar examples could be expanded, but those few which have already been quoted will allow us to make some generalizations about the socio-economic research of the arts.

CONCLUSIONS

Paradoxically as it may seem, the shortcomings of populism and wishful thinking stem from the same root. In broad sociological terms, the common denominator of these two approaches is a utilitarian and atomistic view of culture. The culture's value and worth are defined as a sum of individual uses and gratifications of its members. Although Bentham's classical utilitarianism has been subject to profound sociological criticism through the 19th century (among its critics we may find such diverse figures as Marx, Weber, Durkheim, Cooley, and others), it somehow managed to survive in the studies of mass communications ("uses and gratification" studies) and cultural development.

Populism in its scepticism toward the arts and wishful liberalism in their defense both appeal to the same ultimate judge, i.e. the number of consumers, rather than to culture's contribution to society's viability and social change.

In Canada, for example, decentralization and regionalization of culture undoubtedly benefit local initiatives. Allocation of more government funds for amateur activities may increase the population base of cultural activities. However, a certain degree of centralization of talent is essential in Canada if the country wants to preserve and further develop its cultural identify. As important as the widely spread grass roots are, arts for their flouishment also need a supportive milieu of a concentrated artistic community.

In a very broad sense the arts represent not only a commodity or a resource of personal gratification, but also an important component of the spiritual fabric of the society, and an agent of social change. Perhaps, they serve as a pole, which cannot be reached by all at once, but which preserves the balance of tension and strife in the society and its culture.

I would like to conclude by suggesting that the issues of cultural development and the economics of culture should be viewed both from the point of view of the socio-cultural needs of society and from the perspective of the individual's self-realization. If we will respect this two-fold relationship, we may not need to deny the arts their support in spite of the smaller size of their audiences compared with sports audiences, nor will we be forced to create well-intentioned myths to legitimize generous support for the arts. It is my belief that such an approach will benefit both the arts and the social scientists.

REFERENCES

1. White, D.M.. "Mass Culture in America: Another Point of View." In *Mass Culture: The Popular Arts in America.* Rosenberg, B. and White, D.M. (Eds.). Glencoe, Illinois: The Free Press, 1957. p. 17.
2. Toffler, Alvin. *The Culture Consumers: Art and Affluence in America.* Baltimore: Penguin Books, 1964. p. 31.
3. *Americans and the Arts: A Survey of Public Opinion.* New York: National Research Council of the Arts, 1975.
4. "Culture Boom (The)." *U.S. News and World Report,* (August 8, 1977).

5. Baumol, W. J. and Bowen, W. G.. *Performing Arts – The Economic Dilemma.* New York: The Twentieth Century Fund, 1966.
6. See Kaplan, Max. *Leisure in America: A Social Inquiry.* New York: John Wiley and Sons, 1960; Dumazedier, J.. *Toward a Society of Leisure.* London: Collier MacMillan, 1967.
7. Ennis, P. H.. "The Definition and Measurement of Leisure." In Sheldon, E. and Moore, W. (Eds.). *Indicators of Social Change.* New York: Russell Sage Foundation, 1968.
8. Robinson, J.. *Changes in Americans' Use of Time: 1965-1975.* Communication Research Center of the Cleveland State University, 1976.
9. *Financing of the Performing Arts (The),* Vol. I-II. New York: The Ford Foundation, 1974.
10. *Americans and the Arts, Op. Cit.*, p. 77.
11. Robinson, J. "Culture and Leisure in Transition." Paper presented to the Canadian Conference on Social Research and Cultural Policy, Waterloo, Ontario, April, 1977. p. 14.
12. *Leisure Study (A) – Canada 1972.* Ottawa: Department of the Secretary of State, 1973.
13. *The National Income and Product Accounts of the United States, 1924-1972.* pp. 22-23, 90-91, 327.
14. *Urban Family Expenditures, 1962-1974.* Ottawa: Statistics Canada, 1975.
15. Baumol and Bowen, *Op. Cit.*
16. Sullivan, M.. *The Group of Twenty-Nine.* Ottawa: The Canada Council, 1973, p. 68.
17. *Financing of the Performing Arts, Op. Cit.*, p. 90.
18. Baumol and Bowen, *Op. Cit.*, p. 10.
19. Girard, A.. *Cultural Development: Experience and Policies.* Paris: UNESCO, 1972. p. 50.
20. Gans, H.. "The Politics of Culture in America: A Sociological Analysis." In McQuail, O.. *Sociology of Mass Communications.* Baltimore: Penguin Books, 1972. p. 384.
21. DeGrazia, S.. *Of Time, Work and Leisure.* New York: The Twentieth Century Fund, 1962.
22. *Americans and the Arts. Op. Cit.*
23. Mennell, S. J.. "Cultural Needs and Municipal Initiative." *Social and Economic Administration,* 10:2 (Summer, 1976).

Chapter Twenty-Seven

The Development of National Free Time Policies

Cor Westland

With the increasing importance of free time in our society, and the growing number of agencies offering opportunities to occupy that time, the concern about the cohesiveness of the ensuing delivery system causes many people to demand the development of national policies in this area.

POLICY OPTIONS

In attempting to react to these demands, governments have the choice from three basic philosophies.

1. They can look at the free time phenomenon from an integrative perspective and develop "umbrella" type policies, covering all offerings in a comprehensive fashion. This approach results in one overall "free time," "leisure" or "human services" policy, providing one set of basic principles and procedures from which the policies affecting the various activity areas flow.
2. They can deal with the issue in a sectorial manner and treat each aspect in a separate policy. This approach produces individual cultural, sport, tourism, continuing education, recreation and other policies.
3. They can decide that the nature of the issue does not lend itself to the development of specific policies and let events take their course; in other words, the policy decision can be not to have a policy.

Before discussing the various policy options, however, a few points must be made on policy formulation in general. Although politicians, pressure groups and other segments of the political system play important roles in the policy making process, the bureaucratic agencies are the central elements. It is important to keep this fact in mind, because, as a result of this, policies often suffer from the bureaucratic tendency to consider policy making as nothing more than one of the many aspects of public administration.

It is essential that all actors in the process realize that policy making is seldom a rational, intellectual process aimed at reaching clearly defined goals, but that policies normally are the result of complex and often arduous interplay between all economic, social, cultural and political forces of a given socio-political environment.

The values and beliefs extant in this environment provide the basic philosophies by which policy makers must be guided; the specific details are the result of difficult and often time consuming analysis of the frequently conflicting interests and objectives of the many elements involved.

Finally, Anthony King, who defines policy as "a consciously chosen course of action directed towards some end,"[1] distinguishes policies from what he calls "quasi-policies," a term he uses to describe "situations in which governments may have a wide variety of actions, past and present, within a given policy area, without necessarily having adopted consciously an overall set of goals."[2]

When applying the foregoing general statements and especially King's definition to the free time area, a few basic prerequisites emerge which are essential for policy development.

1. Especially in an area characterized by many quasi-policies, the development of policies must be preceded by substantial conceptual agreement on what it is we are talking about. For instance, there must be a concensus on what recreation is and what constitutes a recreation program. Further, the programs and actions that fall within each of the chosen categories of recreation must be clearly identified. Some integorizing is required for such a broad policy field. Unless this is achieved it does not make sense to talk about policy development because, if the dialogue depends on "the eyes of the beholder" understandings, then all discussion about coordination and cooperation will be futile and lead to a never ending series of conflicts, making the development of effective overall policies impossible.
2. The "end" must be defined as clearly as possible. Although we are dealing with broad goal definitions, attempts must be made to avoid meaningless generalizations and vague statements; policies should be formulated in such a way that a series of measurable objectives can be developed with reasonable ease.
3. "A consciously chosen course of action" implies not only that the policy gives some indication of "how" the goal is to be achieved, but also who is to achieve it. In other words, the various mechanisms to be used ought to be indicated, including a fairly clear statement

on the financial implications for the various actors. Provisions for effective coordination, consultation and cooperation are required and also matters of jurisdiction and the respective areas of responsibility need to be clearly defined.

4. Where coordinating mechanisms are developed, the policy must clearly indicate what is meant by coordination. It must make clear "who" coordinates "what," but especially "how." This means that the coordinator not only must be clearly identified, but must also be given the authority required to effectively accomplish this task.

THE INTEGRATED APPROACH

Some of the apparent advantages of this philosophy are:

1. The reciprocal influence among the various supply elements are recognized; an increase in theatre attendance, for instance, may be related to a decline in weekend and vacation travel and a sudden upswing in crosscountry skiing may effect cinema attendance. Judging the effectiveness of a given program in isolation is extremely difficult, especially in an area in which subjective value orientations play such an important role.

   In addition, this policy approach demonstrates a "holistic" philosophy, underlining the fact that "man" cannot be subdivided into "physical man," "intellectual man" and "spiritual man." It recognizes the fact that it is impossible to "pigeonhole" recreation, just as it is impossible to pigeonhole health, education or welfare.

2. The answer to a number of questions are of importance to all supply elements and influence all. For instance, the relationship of free time - work time, the influence of education, income, work and other variables on the choice of an activity, the trends in the availability of free time, expected economic developments, energy prospects and many more are inextricably related.

3. Integrated treatment of all offerings avoids many of the conceptional and definitional problems. This is an especially sensitive issue in North America where the recreation concept, largely derived from playground activities, has expanded over the years to include aspects of culture, tourism, adult education and much more. Since this has been mainly an extension advocated and promoted by those employed in the recreation field, it has received little or no positive response from those who feel threatened by what they often feel as attempts to take over and unjustified infringing upon their territory. Consequently we spend many hours "defining" concepts but, since most of this is done in an unilateral fashion, the final decisions still depend mainly on vested interests.

This is, indeed, primarily a North American problem. Most European countries are not faced with it in the same degree, partly because they look at free time in a more comprehensive way and also because, for them, recreation has a different meaning. For instance, in the Netherlands people talk about "Vrije tijds besteding," which can be translated as "Free time use," and whenever they talk about recreation in that context they think almost exclusively of outdoor recreation and sport, activities that can be identified relatively easily. In the German speaking countries the noun "Freizeit" or "Free time" is used, denoting not only a specific period of time, but increasingly also its content. Norway includes all free time activities in its concepts of culture; Sweden singles out cultural activities. France and the French speaking countries have in "le loisir" a potentially comprehensive concept with, as component elements, "loisirs socioculturels," "loisirs touritiques," "loisirs sportifs" and so on.

However, one must not get the impression that the European countries do not struggle with conceptual issues. Professor P. Thoenes, moderator of a recently held congress of the Stichting Recreatie in the Netherlands, probably touched on the major problem when he said, "It has struck me how much discussion at this Congress has been devoted to the old words and concepts; the new words have not yet emerged in our language. . . .We are still stuck with the old image of recreation. . . .If free time moves from the periphery to the center, that concept and the recreation notion will have to be reviewed. . . .We must begin to think in other terms. . . .If recreation is going to direct itself to the wider context many people will feel this as a loss of identity."[3]

4. A comprehensive approach is the most effective way to achieve a balanced program. Recent Canadian history provides evidence of the difficulties created when comprehensiveness is lacking. It has proven to be virtually impossible to strike a reasonable balance between, for instance, public expenditures on cultural activities and those related to sport development, as these programs are governed by different departments and separate budgets. The sectorial approach harbors the danger of the individual sectors becoming the end, rather than the means to an end. Again, the development in the cultural, but more specifically the sport sphere, has shown ample evidence of that danger.

5. A comprehensive policy can more easily be responsive to changes in societal conditions such as energy, mobility, and changes in the workweek. Especially in a society in which rapid change is a permanent feature, a comprehensive approach makes it easier to change emphasis in the overall policy if and when circumstances require it. Governments can put more weight on the development of activities close to the urban centers and reduce its support to tourism for

example, should energy problems and overall value change make this necessary.

6. Finally, it appears that a comprehensive approach is more in line with the thinking of the general public. The distinctions policy makers and professionals try to make between culture, tourism, recreation and others have little significance for the consumer. People go to the theatre, play sports and travel because that is what they want to do, and very few ask themselves whether this is a cultural, sport or tourist activity. Their main interest is that the opportunity be available when they want it.

THE SECTORIAL APPROACH

Advocates of the sectorial approach might point to several advantages:

1. The existing policies are already so tangled and fragmented that it would be virtually impossible to untangle or integrate them. The only practical endeavor, therefore, would be to refine the process as it exists, to develop separate policies in the various areas, to make sure that all are based on the same philosophic principles, and that effective mechanisms for cooperation and coordination be developed and implemented.

2. One of the major problems of a comprehensive approach is to determine what, and who, comes under the umbrella. This is especially so in a country like Canada, where free time does not refer to content (as in Germany, for example), and where, therefore, free time activities are less clearly identified. It would be very difficult to determine where Canada's National Capital Commission would fit or its Central Mortgage and Housing Corporation.

3. Each sector has its own specific problems requiring specific solutions. Comprehensive policies risk attempting to standardize for the sake of efficiency, losing in the process much of that which makes the component parts specific.

4. The various composing elements of an overall policy are for the most part still in the developmental stage and there is still a need to deepen and strengthen the knowledge of the various areas before an effective, comprehensive system can be developed.

5. Finally, there is the argument that one must go from the specific to the general in order to develop a proper perspective.

THE NO POLICY OPTION

Judged on the surface, the third option, not to develop policies at all, is highly unrealistic because it would either bring us back to Veblen's leisure class, with leisure as the privilege of the "idle rich" and therefore totally out of tune with government's role in modern society, or it would assume a utopian situation where all people have the resources and ability to make judicious choices for their free time behavior. Still, it can be argued that the development of either comprehensive or sectorial free time policies is not as essential as it is considered to be.

Policies may even be counterproductive, in that they might accentuate specialization and further fragmentation. Instead, we must work towards the development of leisure centered national *philosophies*, which must form the bases of all policies. Advocates of this option maintain that the ultimate objective ought to be the development of "quality of life," "lifestyle," or "human services" policies, providing an overall framework for all government action.

They point to arguments such as made by Bennett M. Berger, who noted:

> "The problem of leisure is difficult to treat intelligently because it lies in an area that is not amenable to our genius for organized solutions. . . If leisure is time free of merely instrumental obligations, it is not subject to the criteria of efficiency and hence is immune to the power of rationality and organization."[4]

POLICIES IN EUROPEAN COUNTRIES

How this problem is approached in a number of European countries may give us an interesting insight into the various models that have developed.

The Netherlands

The national ministry having primary responsibility is Culture, Recreation and Social Work. Its activities are restricted primarily to the provision of subsidies for the development of facilities. Culture is organizationally and operationally separated from Recreation and Social Work. Recreation is identified as outdoor recreation, protection of the natural environment, radio, television and press, and recreation sport. Youth, youth organizations and clubs fall under the jurisdiction of the sector "social development."[5]

Although the Netherlands is administratively divided into eleven provinces,[6] these have little or no political role, and, therefore, national grants are made directly to communities. Most communities have a section for "Youth, Sport and Recreation." Again, these are primarily administrative units, involved in the provision of grants. Therefore, Dutch communities do not have Recreation Directors in the North American sense although the public servants heading up the Youth, Sport and Recreation departments are increasingly selected from those with a sociology, sport or youth work background. They have no program responsibility; that is left to the many clubs. Clubs for practically every interest and activity imaginable develop and execute programs for their membership. This phenomenon is even more common in Europe than in North America. The clubs form the framework of all program activity, which implies that one who does not belong to a club is deprived from participating in certain activities.

This limiting factor is an issue of concern, and attempts are made to alleviate it. For instance, the Swedish clubs receive financial support, but with the proviso that their programs must be open to all. Furthermore, especially in a country like the Netherlands, which has a strong emphasis on the out-of-doors, the parks, beaches and lakes, being public property, are open to all. Policy development in the Netherlands is sectorial, although a special study group recently made a strong plea for the development of comprehensive policies, a plea which has surfaced from time to time in the past.[7]

Federal Republic of Germany

The coordinating agency at the federal level is the Ministry of Family, Youth and Health. The primary responsibility for the development of policies and facilities rests at the provincial (Land) and municipal level, where comparable political structures have been developed. Clubs, churches, trade unions and industries are extremely active in developing programs and offering activities.

It is probably still a reaction against a history of domination by a strong centralized and totalitarian regime that West Germany shows a reluctance against Government involvement in the affairs of its citizens, especially in the area of free time. The attitude appears to be: "as many organizations as necessary; as little organizing as possible."

For instance, the West German Sports Federation, of which practically the entire recreation movement is a part, is very careful to point to the absence of Government assistance. Also, the Trimm program, which is now in the process of staging massive "Spielfeste," finances all its activities from private contributions and donations.[8]

Although the emphasis for program development lies at the municipal level, the involvement of municipalities is still highly sectorial, and although the need for coordination of all these individual activities is increasingly felt, it is generally not considered necessary to develop study programs for those charged with this responsibility. The serious study of leisure and the development of professionals in the area are very recent phenomena; professional preparation is directed towards the development of "leisure educators" (Freizeitpadagogue).[9] Policy development is also still at a very basic level; the approach appears to be an integrated one.

Sweden

The Swedish example is almost the opposite of the West German one. Whereas in West Germany there is a strong emphasis on the individual and a down playing of structures, in Sweden there is a high level of organization and reliance on "Volksbewegungen" as the basic participation structure. The difference is one of political philosophy and development. The Swedish society is very much oriented toward the welfare state, toward a classless society in which the many organizations occupy a place between government and people. Up to 80% of the citizens between 12 and 25 years belong to some organization or another. The many youth organizations are considered key elements in the development of the Swedish democracy.[11] Leisure in Sweden is, other than a personal, also a socio-political issue. Sweden is probably the only western country where the educational objectives include the preparation for leisure. Here, too, one notes the emphasis on assistance programs at the municipal level; the federal and provincial governments can in no way influence the decisions taken at that level.

Virtually all Swedish municipalities have special leisure departments which coordinate all municipal services having an impact on free time opportunities. Policy development has been up to now, sectorial, with a clear distinction between leisure (freizeit) and culture, but with strong emphasis on cooperative planning.

Switzerland

Although the prime responsibility for the provision of facilities and opportunities. Policy development has been up to now sectorial, with Government has become increasingly involved. Examples include the "Federal Law on Area Planning" which has as purposes, "to preserve the uniqueness and beauty of the landscape and to ensure the continued existence of the recreation areas." The Federal Government is also developing a tourist concept for the whole of Switzerland.

The peculiar political relationships which exist in Switzerland, and which place specific emphasis on the municipalities as centers of decision making, result in the emphasis for the construction of local facilities. As virtually everywhere in Europe, the operation of programs is left to private clubs and individuals. Dr. A. Ledermann, Executive Director, Pro Juventute and President, European Leisure and Recreation Association, indicated that the Swiss see the role of Government as limited to the provision of space, money and facilities to which recently has been added the employment of "animateurs" to encourage broader participation.[10] Policy development has been sectorial, dealing with specific aspects of the overall free time area.

Norway

Norwegian policy is integrated; the concept of culture includes youth work, sport, and recreational pursuits. One of the basic aims of policy is to promote cultural democracy, to decentralize activities as well as decision making, to remove social barriers and to "build a society in which each individual may develop his talents and inclinations in an environment where he is free to make his choices on his own premises."[12] Emphasis is on amateur activities and on local club work.

At the present time all countries and practically all municipalities, have a cultural committee, appointed by their respective Councils. These are advisory agencies, with a few executive functions. The state authority is the Ministry for Church and Education. The Ministry receives advice from the Norwegian Cultural Council, the State Youth Council and the State Sport Council. The public sector, through the Ministry, supplies the major part of the finances for all free time programs. Leadership development in Norway seems to be more systematically undertaken than in most European countries, especially with the education of consultants in leisure and cultural work.

German Democratic Republic

When reading this short overview, one must realize that, in accordance with the Marxist anthropology, the development of the socialist image of man is the ultimate objective of the G.D.R. Based on this, man must, through work and leisure, develop into a socialist personality. The activities of the citizens' free time are part of the activities of the socialist policy; it must be planned and, whenever possible, executed collectively. As G. Bauermeister states, "in accordance with the collective social development, the utilization of free time must not be left to its own devices."[13]

The intent of policy is to integrate, as much as possible, the use of free time into the overall education and development process. Consequently, the goal of the free time policy in the G.D.R. is to prevent free time behavior which, from the party standpoint, is undesirable. The state attempts to achieve this purpose by: a) making free time behavior secondary to political plans; b) concentrating on free time activities for children and youth; and c) having people, wherever possible, spend their free time collectively. Free time policy in the G.D.R. is an integral part of social policy and essential for the existence of the system; it serves to increase productivity and facilitate adjustment to the norms of the party.[14]

THE SITUATION IN CANADA

Canada has opted for the sectorial approach. The national dialogue that has been rekindled by the Minister of State for Fitness and Amateur Sport with the publication of the discussion paper "Toward a National Policy on Fitness and Recreation" is an attempt to move in the direction of a national policy. The prospects for successful development of such a policy are difficult to assess as there are many hurdles that must be taken.

Some progress has been made in goal formulation. All levels of government seem to subscribe to a resolution issued at the conclusion of the First National Conference of Provincial Recreation Ministers in 1974, which states in part:

> "*Be it therefore resolved* that this conference accept the fact that recreation is a social service in the same way that health and education are considered as social services and that recreation's purpose should be: a) to assist individual and community development; b) to improve the quality of life; and c) to enhance social functioning."[15]

Also, on the contentious matter of jurisdiction, there appears to be some progress towards concensus. Everyone seems to agree with the notion that recreation is first and foremost a personal matter.[16] The Prime Minister of Canada wrote on July 12th, 1978, to the President of the Canadian Parks/Recreation Association:

> "I believe recreation services to be the domain of no single government jurisdiction. Recreation is a very personal activity which demands the same recognition, respect and encouragement as is afforded to all other basic social concerns. No one jurisdiction can fully provide for all the recreational services required by the citizen

and no jurisdiction can operate effectively without some impact on recreation."[17]

The Federal Minister for Fitness and Amateur Sport joined her provincial colleagues at the conclusion of an April 1978 meeting in a statement allocating special responsibility for national and international sport to the Federal Government and primary responsibility for recreation to the provinces.[18]

Furthermore, the Deputy Minister of the Saskatchewan Department of Culture and Youth wrote that recreation policy development is a "bottom-up process" and that:

> "the development process starts at the community level and that a national purpose of recreation be determined as a consequence of Canadian citizens' indicating what it is they want and expect in the way of recreation."[19]

Nova Scotia's submission of September 7th, 1978 to the Task Force on a proposed Federal Green Paper on Recreation added to this that: "the municipal recreation department is the primary agent in the public sector."[20]

These and many other statements indicate that Canada, in the jurisdictional area, is moving towards a position which is probably best expressed by the Council of Presidents of Recreation Association in Ontario:

> "The recreation delivery system should be designed to support and cherish the participant, operating at his or her own level. The individual Canadian is encouraged to plan and provide for him or herself, acting as his or her own leisure resource. All support services to that individual then operate under the residual principle, with the bulk of services provided by voluntary community groups, controlled directly by the same individual participant. Those services that cannot be provided by the individual and/or his or her community then become the responsibility of local agencies (both public and private); more specialized services forthcoming from regional and provincial governments, in full cooperation with voluntary councils, associations and foundations operating at the provincial scale; and *finally*, highly specialized, residual services provided by federal or national agencies, operating largely without advantage of direct contact with the ultimate client."[21]

However, it is clear that in spite of this apparently increasing concensus on roles, we are a long way from seeing this in federal law and it is very unlikely that this will come about in the near future.

Recognizing the "residual principle" in the area of recreation services would inevitably have repercussions on the entire social services field, and the degree to which this could be implemented depends in the first instance on the outcome of the current struggle between the forces of centralization and decentralization which are at work in the Canadian scene. Defining residual roles means that the nature and extent of required services at the municipal and provincial level be identified first before those at the national level can be specified.

This process requires a complex system of consultations, among which those involving all three levels of government must play an important part. And it is here that we run into the first major obstacle. It is highly unlikely that, given present political relationships, the provinces will agree to discussions with the Federal Government in which the municipalities participate. Manitoba expressed the sentiment of a number of the provinces when its Minister of Tourism, Recreation and Cultural Affairs wrote on August 22nd, 1978:

> "it would be the prerogative of the province to determine the method by and through which that (the municipalities) involvement should take place. . . .the tri-level conference process could create unnecessary and undesirable difficulties."[22]

But even if individual provinces with their municipalities were able to agree on their respective roles and therefore would be able to propose to the Federal Government their perspective of residual federal roles, it is inconceivable that all provinces would be able to arrive at a concensus on such roles; cultural, political, economic, geographic and demographic conditions vary too much in a country as diverse as Canada.

Inevitably, a national recreation policy would have to allow and provide for different arrangements and relationships with individual provinces. And, since the emphasis of the federal residual role would undoubtedly be of a financial nature, this means that financial arrangements with the provinces would be central to this type of agreement. This would inevitably affect current arrangements based on equalization payments and it is highly unlikely that a concensus could be found in this area.

But even if such a concensus were possible, the provinces would not know to which agency at the federal level they must address themselves. Essential in the entire process, therefore, is that the Federal Government establish a focal point for its recreation involvement, a place where all threads come together, where real coordination takes place and where meaningful policy development can happen. This obviously means that the federal Cabinet abandon its policy of non-involvement, that it recognizes, as did the provinces, the status of recreation as a "social utility," and become actively involved in the broad spectrum of recreation experiences as part of its concern for human and social development.

Such a move, essential as it may be, seems highly unlikely under present conditions; it would necessitate concensus on the programs that would have to be included, concensus on the principle of residual roles, and concensus on an effective system of coordination by all federal actors involved. Past experiences, interdepartmental jealousies and rivalries and the complexity of the bureaucratic system, make one rather skeptical about the possibilities of all of this coming about in the foreseeable future.

CONCLUSIONS

1. Policy making is not a rational process and should not be primarily entrusted to the bureaucratic system. It must reflect the dominating values of a given social environment, reconcile the often conflicting interests and objectives of all elements concerned and correspond with the political climate of the day.
2. An integrated approach to policy development is probably the most desirable one, in spite of the many difficulties involved.
3. Irrespective of the option selected, serious efforts must be made to achieve conceptual clarity. It is imperative that this not be attempted by the various elements in isolation but, in a multi-disciplinary and multi-agency fashion, resulting in concensus and commitment to the conclusions reached.
4. Free time policy development around the world shows a variety of models, each born from the peculiar situation within the country concerned.
5. In view of the policy options discussed and different models adopted by various countries, the central question appears to be, what difference do these approaches make in the behavior and attitude of individual citizens? Is it true that one option provides better opportunities for human development than another? Or are policies, particularly at the national level, necessarily so broad and general that differences between the philosophies and options are negligible?

REFERENCES

1. Simeon, Richard. "Studying Public Policy," *Canadian Journal of Political Science*, IX:4 (December, 1976). p. 557.
2. Simeon, *Op.Cit.*, p. 557.
3. Thoenes, P. "Congressamenvatting," *Congresverslag Recreatie '98*, (June, 1979). p. 55.
4. Berger, Bennett M. "The Sociology of Leisure." In Smigel, Erwin O. (Ed.), *Work and Leisure*. New Haven, Connecticut: College and University Press, 1963. p. 37.
5. Ministerie Van Cultuur, Recreatie En Maatschappelyk Werk, *Informatie Van De Hoofdafdeling Openluchtrecreatie*, (November, 1978). p. 43.
6. This structure is about to be changed into 16 provinces.
7. Commentaar Van Het Interuniversitair Werkverband Sociologie Van Het Vryetydsgedrag, *Recreatie*, 17:3, (March, 1979). p. 68.
8. The first one of these festivals was held in West Berlin in June 1979, with tens of thousands of people of all ages participating in a large variety of non-competitive, low organizational games. A total of 10 such events is planned for 1979.
9. Nahrstedt, Wolfgang. "Aus-Und Fortbildung Von Mitarbeitern In Freizeiteinrightungen In Der Bundes - Republik Deutschland." *Freizeitpadagogik Und Animation In Europa*. Dusseldorf: Edition Freizeit Verlag GMBH, 1975. p. 43.
10. From a conversation with Dr. A. Ledermann, Zurich, June, 1979.
11. Nahrstedt, Wolfgang. *Freizeit In Schweden*. Dusseldorf: Walter Rau Verlag, 1975. pp. 10-45.
12. Royal Norwegian University of Foreign Affairs, *Norwegian Cultural Policy*. Oslo, May 1977. pp. 1-12.
13. Stundl, Herbert. *Freizeit-Und Erholungssport In Der DDR*. Schorndorf: Verlag Karl Hofmann, 1977. p. 19.
14. Stundl, *Op.Cit.*, p. 21.
15. First National Conference of Provincial Recreation Ministers, *Press Release*. Edmonton, Alberta, (May 27-29, 1974).
16. Campagnolo, Iona, Minister of State for Fitness and Amateur Sport. *Toward a National Policy on Fitness and Recreation*. Ottawa: Minister of Supply and Services, 1979. p. 11.
17. From a letter to the President of the Canadian Parks/Recreation Association from the Right Honorable Pierre Elliot Trudeau, Prime Minister of Canada, July 12th, 1978.
18. Federal-Provincial Conference of Ministers responsible for Fitness, Sport and Recreation, *Press Release*. Montreal, (13 April), 1978.
19. Campagnolo, *Op.Cit.*, p. 6.
20. *Ibid.*, p. 6.
21. Brief submitted to the Task Force on a National Policy on Recreation by the Council of Presidents of Recreation Associations in Ontario. Toronto, February, 1978.
22. Campagnolo, *Op.Cit.*, p. 6.

Chapter Twenty-Eight

Policy Issues in Outdoor Recreation Research

Elwood L. Shafer

We have become rich through the lavish use of our natural resources and we have just reason to be proud of our growth. But the time has come to inquire seriously what will happen when our forests are gone, when the soil has been washed into the streams, and when our rivers become polluted. Although those observations were made by Theodore Roosevelt in 1908 at a conference on the conservation of natural resources, they are even more relevant today because of the impact of man on his environment.

Consider a few facts:

1. Four billion tons of sediment are washed into streams annually as a result of land misuse.
2. Up to now, in only seven states, over 17 million acres of wetlands have been destroyed.
3. Four billion tons of raw materials are presently being consumed annually in U.S. production. Most of this is eventually disposed of as waste.
4. We are taking fresh water out of the ground roughly twice as fast as natural processes can replace it.
5. The demand for electric power is doubling every ten years.
6. We are building 10 million cars a year and the highway systems to accommodate them – that's twice as many cars as we made only 17 years ago.

And, if we think we may be misusing our natural resources today, consider the following Environmental Protection Agency (EPA) projections for the next several decades. EPA's educated guess is that population and market demands between now and the year 2000 will call for the *duplication of everything that has been built in the history of the United States.* For example:

1. Urban sprawl may eat up 19.7 million acres of potential recreation land by the year 2000 – an area equivalent to the states of New

Hampshire, Vermont, Massachusetts, and Rhode Island.

2. Another 3.5 million acres may be paved over for highways and airports.
3. Five million acres of potential hunting and scenic areas may be removed from agriculture for public facilities, second home developments, and waste control projects.
4. Approximately another 2 million acres of right-of-way may be required for 200,000 additional miles of power lines.

At stake are the nation's irreplaceable estuaries, wetlands, beaches, flood plains, river and lake fronts, farms, forests, and scenic uplands. These recreation resources are paramount ingredients of a healthy, vigorous, democratically-oriented, free society. Recreation resource managers, therefore, are being compelled – often unwillingly – to perceive man-environment relationships as complex ecological entities. It is becoming too costly and too dangerous to perceive them any other way.

Until the 1960's, recreation resource management decisions were based on such criteria as highest priority, multiple use, or cost-benefit analyses. Each criterion had its strengths, its weaknesses, and especially its mystique. After 1960, however, a new concept of public responsibility took shape in American society, culminating in January 1970 in the National Environmental Policy Act. The Act signalled the acceptance of man-environment relationships as a legitimate focus for public policy in the United States. But the application of man-environment relationships as a factor in public policy is only now evolving. No doubt many theories of ecosystem administration will be developed in the field of recreation before one is discovered that best relates recreation demands to ecological constraints.

THE ECOSYSTEM CONCEPT

In recreation resource management, the ecosystem is the most fundamental unit for environmental analysis and control. To approach recreation environments as ecosystems means that the totality of the interacting entities and systems, physical and social, that comprise a given environment, must be taken into account in any decision regarding that environment. Of the possible approaches, the ecosystem approach is the most complex and the least easily translated into public policy and management action.

At times, the human mind does not seem able to interpret the complex interaction of social and ecological systems; sometimes human judgment and intuition seem to have been trained to look only in the immediate past for the cause of a problem. The hot stove burns the finger, not the curiosity that made one reach out to touch it. Sometimes, our approaches to problems of providing natural recreation environments tend to be the simplistic. For example, we see thousands of people living in rat-infested, leaky-roofed tenements, with no healthy form of recreation to help relieve their plight. Our traditional answer has been to tear down the tenements and construct large low-income housing projects, with green or open space for recreation separating the housing units. And yet, there are projects that have been boarded up long before they were paid for because vandalism, physical deterioration, and the impossibility of maintaining essential services made them social, architectural and financial disasters.

There is a need for an obvious and persuasive symbol of the ecosystem concept that will help to achieve instant awareness of environmental problems, even though it cannot instill instant understanding. Fortunately, such a symbol has become available. It is the paradigm, or model, of Spaceship Earth. It may be a model of future societies which, incidentally, are expected to have recreation or leisure as a predominant element in their culture. But, the Spaceship Earth model has no analog among present sociopolitical systems.

The Spaceship Earth model implies powerful biological restraints. Most significantly, man must stop multiplying his numbers and gobbling up his natural environment if he wants to continue to use part of it for outdoor recreation. And man must realize this soon, because if the decision isn't made *by* him, it will be made *for* him by the laws of mathematics and nature. A simple experiment shows why. Place a pair of fruit flies in a bottle with a small amount of food. In a matter of days, the flies will multiply to the point where the bottle is black with them. Then the limited food supply and their own effluvia will raise the death rate, and the population will drop suddenly – to zero. After 100,000 years of uninhibited propagation, mankind is just beginning to sense the confines of *its* bottle. And when the crunch for more living space occurs in that bottle, it's often the natural environments in or close to population centers that are utilized first – in the name of progress.

POLITICAL CONSIDERATIONS

Considering the impact of man on our recreation environments in comprehensive biological and ecological terms may lead to fewer errors, but it is not a panacea. Ecological considerations may facilitate, but cannot eliminate, the political necessity to reconcile a great diversity of interests and values. The environmental laws of the last decade have done relatively little to preserve our most precious recreation resource – the land. In the past, laws have dealt almost exclusively with the pollution of air and water and with the management of *publicly*-owned land. These laws have left virtually unregulated the 73.7 percent of the contiguous 48 states that is privately-owned. And it is the possibility of ecologically shortsighted development of at least part of this 73.7 percent that poses one of the threats to the future of natural recreation environments. Public ownership, however, is hardly a panacea either.

The boom in recreational second-homes is a case in point of a problem that is nationwide. Martha's Vineyard, off Cape Cod, is being developed extensively for second-homes, while on the other side of the nation, second-home development along the California coast has cut off all but 25 percent of the state's 1072 miles of shoreline. One of the worst effects of such development oftentimes is the washing away of topsoil – especially where bulldozed areas remain unoccupied for years. And looming behind the development of second-homes is the prodigious impact of the energy crisis. On the prairies of Montana, Wyoming, and the Dakotas, under which lie the country's richest coal deposits, power companies have leased over 1,000 square miles of private land for strip mining.

Why is economic growth eating up recreation opportunities on privately-owned lands? And, why must the growth be so chaotic and destructive to the ecosystem? The answer is simple: the states have delegated their authority to supervise land-use to 78,217 units of local government. These local units support themselves mainly by taxing land. As a consequence, they are constantly searching for opportunities to develop the land, increase its assessed value, and make it produce more in taxes. Thus the basic fact of private land development in the United States today is that some of the very units of government that are charged with controlling land-use may be the ones most susceptible to pressures *not* to control it. A critical question, then, is how to maintain the democratic ideal of local government and at the same time preserve the limited natural environments around towns, cities, and municipalities.

CONTROLLING NATURAL RESOURCE DEVELOPMENT

We are in a period of great ferment, when citizens' groups, the courts, a number of state governments, the national administration, and congressional committees have begun to consider fundamental reforms in the way state and local governments control recreation resource development, as well as the development of other resources. At the heart of the ferment is recognition that land-use decisions affect the interests of people beyond local boundaries, and that decisions must be controlled by the states if critical environments are to be protected, and if development needed by a region is not blocked by local governments.

A precedent-setting law was passed in 1961 by Hawaii – a state that has some of the most valuable recreation resources in the world. The law stated that henceforce, the State of Hawaii would draw up and enforce regulations governing the use of private land. And the state would treat this land not merely as a commodity to be bought and sold but also as a natural resource to be protected. Today, citizens are pressing for similar laws in a dozen other states, and bills have been introduced in Congress to exert pressure on all states to join in land-use planning, especially as it relates to the recreational needs of citizens. Statewide land-use planning is simply an attempt to insure some logical relation between land-use patterns and ecological constraints of the land so that the ecological features required for human needs will be enhanced.

It is imperative, however, that land-use planning should not impede private economic growth. In most instances, laws aimed at protecting the ecology of recreation environments can actually help responsible private development by assuring that the state's natural environment won't disappear down the urban-sprawl drain. In the long run, private investors can afford time and money legally required to protect the natural environment because they know the long-term profit will be there. For example, the Adirondack Park, a magnificent semi-wilderness recreation area in the northeast corner of New York, is managed under a comprehensive land-use plan. The entire region has been classified by land types; soil maps indicate which soils will allow septic tanks and which will not; and slopes have been rated as acceptable for building or too steep. Beautiful views, flood plains, historic sites, hiking trails, and waterfalls have been identified. The plan indicates where the region's growth can be accommodated without destroying the ecological integrity of the area. Similar exciting land-use planning is happening in other states: Vermont, Florida, and Maine, among them.

IMPLICATIONS FOR RESEARCH

The most important research needs concern the quality of our natural recreation environments and the impact of technology on those environments. They are not related solely to the biological aspects of the resource. Rather, research needs are related to the public policy issues that shape our recreation environments. We must abandon the myth that natural resource capability is the sole criterion for recreation land-use planning. Another real issue is the social, political, and economic impact of recreation resources.

Public policy about recreation environments thus emerges as a vast, multidisciplinary field of inquiry in which significant work has been started but where most of the research has been restricted to specific environmental factors – water resources or air pollution, for example. Of course, investigation of specific biological problems is essential to any larger concept of recreation-environment policy – and thus to the quality of natural recreation-environments. Ecological research underpins policy research and forms an important cornerstone of the total recreation research effort. For example, wildlife is a sensitive indicator of a healthy human environment. It has often been likened to the miner's canary for the maintenance of all forms of plant and animal life, not simply because we may be sentimentalists, fishermen, hunters, foresters, or outdoor photographers, but mainly because the presence of flora and fauna is an indication of the quality of our environment.

To lose a single species of plant or animal life means simply that something is wrong. To lose a rare and delicate flower, tree specie, or a songbird's habitat is not important simply because of the anguish of the conservationist, but because songbirds, along with American elms, salmon, grizzly bears, and all other forms of nature *should* be present as part of man's total environment. There is something wrong, for example, with an environment in which indigenous wildlife can no longer live but where rat populations flourish. Therefore, an impact that threatens the existence of natural environmental quality is symptomatic of an environment going downhill, and taking man with it. But ultimately, the accumulation of special ecological studies must relate to a larger order of generalization if comprehensive recreation-environment administration is to become a reality. For it does not follow that if the necessary ecological research is pursued with diligence, the necessary environmental policies will take care of themselves.

The research problem that prevails is: How shall we organize, control, and coordinate public and private recreation development (along with the development of other natural resources) so as to protect, maintain, and improve those environmental features that we value most for recreation? Our research orientation should involve the biological, cultural, and aesthetic characteristics of land: mountains, lakes, streams, forests, fields, grasslands, and wildlife. These are the basic determinants of the quality of our outdoor recreation environments.

We need studies of the ecological carrying capacity of recreation lands, but science has already devoted considerable effort here, so a thorough review of the literature may be sufficient to satisfy at least a part of this research need. We also need studies of how public opinion and preferences in natural recreation environments can be incorporated in recreation resource management decisions. And we need to explore, through gaming techniques and case history studies, the overall results of probable recreation management decisions on the social and political (as well as the ecological) characteristics of a region.

Some broad questions requiring answers are:

1. What kind of quasi-public structure would best meet the needs for effective land-use and reclamation for recreation, as well as other needs of society?

2. What equitable and effective kinds of taxation and zoning would best support a recreation-land-use policy that will meet the needs of the community while preserving the integrity of the environment?

3. What kinds of affirmative action should be taken by individual states to remove potential recreation lands from the commodity market?

4. What are the best means to control population growth and community development so that recreation opportunities can be developed in harmony with the capabilities of natural resources?

5. What kinds of recreation-land classification best meet the needs of recreation planners?

6. What means of public involvement work best in developing recreation-land-use policies?

7. Can recreation-land-use policies be applied equally and vigorously to all with no exceptions?

8. In what areas is compromise most acceptable in conflicts between recreation-environment quality and other social needs?

9. How can recreation-land-use needs be integrated with other land-use goals?

Underlying these broad questions are more specific challenges, such as:

1. What methods can be used to better understand recreation demand and associated underlying benefits and values of recreation?

2. What procedures can be used to inventory, maintain, protect, and augment the supply of recreation environments?

3. How can we design the facilities and preserve the natural environments necessary for integrating supply and demand?

4. How can we coordinate recreation supply-demand relationships with other resource uses?

5. How can we enhance the recreational experiences of individuals?

We are faced with questions, problems, and decisions unprecedented in both magnitude and complexity. They can only be addressed effectively by strengthening the link between research and policy. Each is dependent on the other, but that, too, is part of the concept of an ecosystem and the model of Spaceship Earth.

Chapter Twenty-Nine

The Maturation of Leisure Research

Thomas L. Burton

There is much that is confusing about the state of leisure research and there is a strong feeling of disquiet among researchers and government officials about it. Specifically, two sets of problems are evident: what may be called problems *with* leisure research and problems *of* leisure research.

PROBLEMS WITH LEISURE RESEARCH

The first set of problems has to do with the roles played by leisure research in addressing issues and concerns of North American society. Problems include a perceived lack of communication between researchers and the potential users of research, inadequate communication between researchers and the clients, or sponsors, of research; the lack of a coordinated structure and institutional foundation for the development of leisure research; and unsatisfactory conditions for the funding of research.

The lack of communication between leisure researchers and the potential users of research is one of the primary causes of the attitudes of suspicion towards leisure research that are held by many practitioners and professionals in the parks, recreation, planning and related fields. In recent years, great promises have been held out for leisure research but this has rarely emanated from researchers themselves. When these great promises have turned out to be little more than false expectations, it is the reputation of leisure research which has suffered.

Inadequate communication between leisure researchers and the clients, or sponsors, of research has been a second major cause of suspicion on the part of practitioners and professionals towards leisure research. This has been especially true for research carried out under contract, as distinct from grant-aided research sponsored by foundations and research councils. Once again, false expectations have frequently been generated which, when they have not been met, have triggered disillusionment and lack of confidence in the ability of leisure research and leisure researchers to respond to real-world problems.

The lack of a coordinated structure and institutional foundation for the development of leisure research has served to foster the image of leisure research as being of a generally piecemeal character which, in turn, has served to exacerbate the problems of communication and dialogue between the leisure researcher on the one hand and both the users and the clients, or sponsors, of research on the other. There is a feeling that leisure research, as a field, has no sense of direction and purpose but consists of many people from many disciplines galloping off in all directions simultaneously.

This impression is reinforced by the unsatisfactory conditions for the funding of leisure research which presently prevail throughout North America. Like so many fields of study that transcend disciplinary boundaries, leisure research both suffers and benefits from a situation in which there are many benefactors with a general interest in its development, but none for whom it is a central concern. It benefits because there is a diversity of funding sources to which the researcher can relate. It suffers because there is no central organization concerned about the long term development of the field. Such a situation serves, once more, to exacerbate the piecemeal character of much leisure research.

PROBLEMS OF LEISURE RESEARCH

What may be called the problems *of* leisure research have to do with concerns about the substantive and methodological development of the field itself. Problems include: a lack of intellectual coordination and insufficient cross fertilization of ideas among researchers, an inadequacy of research methodologies and techniques, and a lack of agreement on concepts and codes in the field.

Most leisure research to date has been either disciplinary or multidisciplinary in character. In the latter cases, there has obviously been some intellectual communication and some attempt at cross fertilization of ideas. But true cross fertilization – the kind that comes with interdisciplinary approaches that imply the transfer of disciplinary viewpoints, methods and techniques from one discipline to another – has, it is suggested, been notably absent from the field to this point. Interdisciplinary research in the leisure field is the exception rather than the rule.

The relative inadequacy of leisure research methodologies and techniques reflects, to a considerable extent, this lack of intellectual coordination and poor cross fertilization of ideas among researchers. Methods and techniques that have been developed within specific disciplines to facilitate disciplinary ways of examining and analyzing issues have limited value as means for considering a field of study that transcends disciplinary boundaries, unless they can be altered, adapted and refined so as to be transferable across disciplines. To date, this has not occurred on any significant scale in leisure research.

The lack of agreement on concepts and codes in the leisure field is an almost inevitable consequence of both the lack of intellectual coordination and poor cross fertilization of ideas among researchers, as well as the inadequacy of leisure research methodologies and techniques. Brian Rodgers, one of the pioneers of leisure research in the United Kingdom, expressed this concern aptly when he noted that:

> We have yet to invent even a common language, or an agreed codification of concepts, both necessary preliminaries to interdisciplinary debate. We will not create a valid concept until we define terms. And yet what other facet of human behaviour cries out so insistently for interdisciplinary treatment? If psychologists, sociologists, economists, geographers and planners cannot collaborate in the study of this complex behavioural sub-system, we will never understand it.[1]

An agreed terminology is the first step towards the development of valid concepts. Such concepts require the transfer of methodologies and techniques among and between disciplines. And this requires intellectual communication and the cross fertilization of ideas among researchers. None of these things have occurred to any significant degree in the field of leisure research to the present time.

If these problems and concerns reflect the true state of leisure research in North America – if not wholly, then at least in part – then it would be useful to examine the major trends in leisure research that have occurred during the past two decades or so, which appear to have brought us to this condition, and to suggest directions for the future development and conduct of leisure research. This should help set new directions and goals for leisure researchers themselves, as well as those who use the results of leisure research and those who sponsor it.

THE DEVELOPMENT OF LEISURE RESEARCH

Leisure research experienced a relatively long gestation period. The subject has long been an interest of historians, anthropologists, archaeologists and social commentators. For the most part, however, this interest in leisure was peripheral and can in no way be characterized as leisure research. It did, however, reflect an academic interest in the subject of leisure and thereby served, in a sense, as a precursor of what was to come.

Infancy

The best estimate that can be made suggests that the field of leisure research was born in the 1950's and passed through its infancy during that decade. As recreation departments emerged at the municipal level an interest in leisure and recreation for its own sake began to appear. Leisure was no longer solely of interest to historians, social commentators and the like as an expression or indicator of some greater concern, but became the immediate and primary concern of leisure and recreation professionals. But just as the infant is wholly dependent upon its parents and other adults for the satisfaction of its needs, the new leisure and recreation professionals were fully dependent upon the research activities of historians, anthropologists, sociologists and those in similar disciplines for insights into the emerging phenomenon that was now their responsibility. Leisure research continued to be the *by-product* of investigations into other, "more weighty" concerns, such as economic growth, family structure and social organization. Sport and physical fitness, for purposes of ensuring a healthy and morally sound population, were a special interest of the new municipal departments, and numerous studies on this subject emanated from this period. The same was true of parks, which (at the municipal level at least) were generally seen as a means of reducing crime and delinquency among children and young people, with the result that much parks related research focused upon this concern. The language of leisure and recreation was wholly undeveloped at this time, with communication taking place exclusively in the diverse languages of the adults: sport and physical education, economics, sociology, and the like.

Childhood

During the second stage of development, leisure research began to acquire a language of its own. Unfortunately, however, because it had so many parents, this language did not emerge as a single, cohesive and structured entity but rather as an ill-defined, undisciplined "mish mash" of terms and phrases expropriated from half a dozen or more other languages. Inevitably, there ensued a pre-occupation with language itself, with numerous researchers devoting their attention exclusively to issues of language and terminology, and almost all feeling the need to define their terms before reporting their specific research activities and findings.

In the early 1960's, leisure and recreation became of interest not simply as by-products of greater, more consuming interests but rather as important components of those larger concerns and, therefore, as matters that needed to be investigated and understood if the larger concerns were, themselves, to be understood. In short, leisure advanced from being a mere *by-product* of research into some other concern to being a *dependent variable* in research directed at understanding that greater concern. A good illustration of this is to be found in the attention given to studying the problems of youth. Considerable research was directed toward discovering and analyzing the leisure activities and attitudes of young people, because this was considered to be an important step towards understanding, and thereby coping with, the "Youth Revolution" of that time.

Just as the child learns during this stage of development by imitating the actions of adults, so the field of leisure research imitated its parent fields. But like the child, the leisure research field demonstated considerably lower levels of skill than its parents. The logic and rigor of science were invading the leisure research field's parent disciplines at this time. Sociology, economics, geography, education and public administration, among others, were all adopting increasingly rigorous scientific methods and employing increasingly sophisticated quantitative techniques. Physical education was rapidly changing into what was to become "the sport sciences." The growing field of leisure research, borrowing liberally from these fields, attempted to employ these rigorous methods and quantitative techniques. For the most part, however, these applications were relatively unsophisticated. Most leisure studies were descriptive, employing univariate analyses to derive simple statistical forms such as frequencies, percentages and means.

Those activities which are beyond researchers capabilities are usually performed, or at least completed, by others. Some of the most significant contributions to the field of leisure research during this time were made by the parent disciplines. Economists experimented with methodologies for measuring outdoor recreation demands.[2] Sociologists, psychologists, human geographers and planners developed models for studying behavior patterns, attitudes and perceptions in the leisure field.[3] Other geographers presented formats for measuring recreation site capacities and attractivity.[4] These investigations provided a foundation for the later work of those who classed themselves within the leisure research field, including some of the original investigators themselves. At this time, however, there was no clearly identifiable, independent leisure research field as such. The vast majority of these investigators owed their primary allegiance to their original disciplines and reported their findings to their disciplinary constituencies, thereby strengthening the image of leisure as a dependent variable.

Adolescence

In the 1960's, Canada and the United States experienced a large and rapid growth in the number of organizations and individuals engaged in leisure research, in the volume of funds allocated for such research, and in the number of research studies being carried out at any one time. A major stimulus to this growth was the work of the Outdoor Recreation Resources Review Commission and Jack Knetsch's blueprint for the *Canadian Outdoor Recreation Demand Study* (CORDS).[5] But ORRRC and CORDS were only two of several major leisure studies sponsored and/or carried out by governments during the decade. All were designed primarily to discover patterns of leisure behavior and their associations with selected demographic and socio-economic variables of the population as well as particular indicators of the supply of leisure facilities, services and programs.

In addition to government-related studies, there was a rapid expansion in the numbers of studies undertaken by researchers in universities as well as a less dramatic increase in the numbers carried out by consulting firms and voluntary organizations. The studies by academics were less uniformly dedicated to the task of gathering data about patterns of leisure behavior and their relationships to demographic and socio-economic variables of the population. This kind of study was still evident, but greater attention was clearly given to the development of concepts and theory-building and to hypothesis testing.

But regardless of the orientation of particular studies, the dominant impression which emerges is one of rapid physical growth of the type associated with adolescence. There is a lack of concomitant substantive growth. Almost all of the leisure activity surveys and many of the academic, hypothesis testing studies reflect a tendency for researchers to over-reach themselves, to try to demonstrate that they are fully capable of conducting research on their own. The result was often the collection of data and material that were unrelated to the stated objectives of the research. In some instances, indeed, the research was undertaken without a sound methodological base at all.

A particular characteristic of adolescence which pervaded the field of leisure research during this time was the constant search for personal experience of new ideas and new knowledge. A basic assumption of leisure researchers during this time was that they themselves should collect research data from primary sources. Most studies from this period employed primary data specifically collected by the researcher for the purpose of his or her research. There was a relative dearth of studies involving the analysis of "used" or "second hand" data. New knowledge was equated with the acquisition of new data.

This search for new ideas, new experiences and new knowledge also had its positive aspects, as it led to a multiplicity of different ways of looking at the same problem or concern. This was reflected in the field of leisure research during this period in the growth of multidisciplinary studies. Instead of each discipline considering leisure issues and concerns in its own unique, distinct and self-contained manner, each began to recognize that its own unique and distinct approach was not self-contained, but exists within a broad context which admits of many equally valid ways of viewing the world. It was increasingly recognized that each of the various parent disciplines of leisure research had a valuable contribution to make to the field and, more importantly, that the simultaneous application of several disciplines to an issue or problem might offer insights that each alone could not. Much of the research into the relationships between work and leisure reflects an attempt to develop multidisciplinary perspectives.[6]

Like adolescents there was awkwardness and lack of coordination in the relations between researchers on the one hand and the users and sponsors of research on the other. A common complaint was that researchers were rarely able to focus their work sufficiently to relate it to the specific issue or concern with which the practitioner must cope. In contrast, researchers complained that practitioners, research users and sponsors did not understand the nature of the research process and, consequently, would demand instant and precise solutions to specific problems which were simply unrealistic. Both groups agreed only that there was frequently a significant gap between research and practice. There was a definite sense of isolation between leisure researchers as generators of knowledge, on the one hand, and practitioners and research sponsors as consumers of knowledge on the other.

In summary, during the 1960's there was a rapid growth in the volume of leisure research which, in retrospect, seems little less than amazing. There was a major expansion in the number of organizations and individuals engaged in and/or sponsoring leisure research. Along with both of these developments was a significant increase in the volume of funds provided for leisure research. But with this heady growth came problems. There was a definite lack of intellectual coordination and relatively few examples of the successful cross fertilization of ideas among researchers. Despite the massive volume of research activity, little emerged in the way of universal and generally agreed concepts and codes for the field. New ground was being broken in the parent disciplines in the development of research methodologies and techniques, but their transfer across the wider field of leisure research was fitful at best, Leisure researchers and the users of research were relatively isolated from each other and even tended to watch each other with a certain degree of suspicion and distrust across an imaginary no man's land. It was an exciting period, a busy time of constant action and advance. Yet it would not be unrealistic to suggest that leisure research was in a situation not unlike that of Columbus during his fifteenth century voyages to the New World. When he set out, he didn't know where he was going; when he arrived, he didn't know where he was; and when he returned, he didn't know where he had been. (Moreover, he did it all on government money!)

Young Adulthood

The field of leisure research has now entered young adulthood and is still in this stage. The first major attempts to assess the state of leisure research were in the 1970's. Like Columbus, leisure researchers wanted to know where they had been, where they were and, perhaps most important, where they would like to go next. This process of inquiry is, in fact, still ongoing. Several reviews of leisure research reflect attempts to assess its past and present state. Like the young adult, leisure researchers are looking backwards in an effort to evaluate experience and to use it as a springboard to the future.

The past few years have seen a re-structuring of leisure researchers' attitudes towards the acquisition and development of knowledge in the field.New knowledge is no longer equated exclusively with the acquisition of new data. The development of reference and information retrieval systems reflect an acceptance of the idea that new knowledge can be built upon existing foundations and does not necessarily require that one ignore or break with the past. An increasing number of research projects have consisted in the secondary analysis of previously existing data.

There has been a growing recognition in the leisure research field of the interdependence of research projects and researchers. One reflection of this has been the establishment of reference and information systems and data banks just noted. But it has also been reflected in the establishment of research journals devoted exclusively to the field of leisure research. In Canada the publication, *Recreation Research Review* reflects an increased interest in and concern for research in the field. The UNESCO journal, *Society and Leisure,* became the responsibility of the International Sociological Association. The *Journal of Leisure Research,* and more recently *Leisure Sciences,* have become established international journals. All this indicates that the leisure research field has come of age and is no longer the dependent child of its parent disciplines.

A sense of interdependence has become evident in the growing concern among researchers about the poor quality of their relationships with both the users and the clients of research. All three groups began taking small, but as yet hesitant, steps toward identifying the causes of the problems and potential solutions to it.

Another sign that leisure research has emerged as a field of study in its own right is to be found in the establishment of leisure studies research institutes and centers and the creation of graduate programs in leisure studies. These are in addition to, and distinct from, the many disciplinary and professional graduate degree programs that offer opportunities to specialize in some aspect of leisure studies – programs in departments of Geography, Environmental Studies, Planning, Sociology, and the like.

All of these developments are, in a sense, organizational in character. There is also evidence of a substantive kind to support the contention that the field of leisure research has entered the stage of young adulthood and become a field of study in its own right. Increasing attention has been given by researchers to the search for unifying concepts and codes. There is a long way to travel before uniform concepts emerge; perhaps they never will. But the first steps have clearly been taken towards bringing some degree of commonality to concepts and theories of leisure.

In summary, it is suggested that the field of leisure research entered the stage of young adulthood in the 1970's and is presently still in this stage. The stage is characterized by a search for meaning and identity in the field. Like the young adult, the field of leisure research is in the process of developing balance and direction. There is less emphasis upon the search for new ideas and knowledge through the acquisition of new data and more upon the development of new insights into knowledge through the reexamination of existing information. The field has learned to look backwards to discover where it has been in the past and how it arrived at its present state. Increasing attention has been given to the sharing of research information and experiences, emphasizing the interdependence of both projects and researchers themselves. The field of leisure research has begun the process of establishing a substantial sense of tradition for itself.

TOWARDS MATURITY FOR LEISURE RESEARCH

The growth and development of leisure research have been considered at length here because history offers a yardstick against which to measure the present and, hence, provides a basis for evaluating change, progress and regression.

Perhaps the most important step in the drive to maturity must be the development of an epistemology of leisure, the establishment of a set of unifying concepts and codes for the field. The work begun must be carried forward and expanded. Concomitant with this must be the development of a common language for leisure researchers, a process which has begun in the present stage of young adulthood but which is far from complete. Rodgers' comment, noted earlier, is more critical now than ever: "We will not create a valid concept until we define terms."[7]

One of the key steps along the road to the development of an epistemology of leisure must be the establishment of sound and secure communications links within the leisure research community, not only in Canada and the U.S. but also internationally, for the search for a set of unifying concepts of leisure is not a concern unique to North America. Furthermore, these links must be diverse and multifaceted; a single strand can be too easily broken. The ties that have already been established – the leisure research journals and the organizations – must be refined and reinforced with others.

It is also essential that stable relationships be established between leisure researchers, on the one hand, and the users and sponsors of research on the other. Such relationships must be based upon notions of equality. This implies a recognition and acceptance on the part of each group of the legitimate needs and aspirations of the other. Users and sponsors must recognize and accept that leisure research is not merely the handmaiden or servant of policy. Its *raison d'etre* goes far beyond such a narrow view. On the other hand, leisure researchers must give equal recognition and acceptance to the rights of the users and sponsors of research to influence the design of research studies and to demand and receive practical outputs from problem-oriented projects. Policy formulation may not be the sole objective of leisure research, but it is a legitimate objective of many leisure research projects.

Another important indicator of the move toward maturity will be the development of interdisciplinary research methods and techniques. The leisure research field has passed from a stage when it was merely an interesting by-product of research in the parent disciplines, through a stage in which it consisted essentially of separate disciplinary treatments of the topic, to its present stage which reflects a multidisciplinary perspective. But true intellectual cross fertilization will occur only with the development of interdisciplinary approaches that imply the transfer of disciplinary viewpoints, methods and techniques from one disciplinary boundaries. Yet little research has been interdisciplinary in character. In part, of course, this reflects our conceptual and linguistic poverty for a common language and agreed concepts are both necessary prerequisites to interdisciplinary study and debate.

Finally, a defining characteristic of maturity is the recognition of the condition of scarcity and an acceptance of its consequence, the necessity for choice. For the field of leisure research to reach maturity, it must recognize that it exists in a world of scarce resources, that it cannot do everything that it would like to do (which is not the same thing, however, as becoming everything that it is capable of becoming). The existence of scarce resources implies that choices must be made. This, in turn, implies that priorities must be set. The development of criteria and mechanisms for the setting of priorities in leisure research is a necessary step along the road to maturity for the field.

IMPLICATIONS

This discussion has thus far exhibited an historical bent. The concern has been to chart, in an analogical and admittedly general fashion, the development of leisure research in Canada and the United States and to suggest some preconditions for the maturation of the leisure research field. It is worthwhile, however, to proceed one step further and to discuss briefly some *particular* implications for the immediate future. These implications derive directly from some of the specific conditions that presently characterize the field and which were discussed above.

First, the heavy preponderance of projects carried out directly by the staffs of government departments, or by academics under contract to these departments, has led to a distinct emphasis upon what may be called problem-solving or fact-finding kinds of projects: that is, the types of projects that could be shown to have at least indirect relevance to the program mandates of the sponsoring departments. Approximately half of the more than 100 studies examined in the preparation of this chapter were of the problem-solving or fact-finding kind while one-fifth involved hypothesis testing. Approximately one-quarter dealt in some manner with concept development in some manner with concept development or theory building, and almost all of these were either sponsored by research councils and private research foundations or were undertaken by academics without direct financial support.

Second, in most cases those people in government departments who initiate contract research in the leisure field or who undertake research projects themselves are not the people who manage and operate leisure services and programs. The agencies and people who fund or carry out problem-oriented leisure research often have limited power to initiate and manage practical programs, facilities and services where the results of their research could be applied. In many cases, they are impotent eunuchs when it comes to the implementation of research findings.

A third implication has to do with publications. When projects are undertaken by staff of governments or by academics and others under contract to these departments, there is less likelihood of their reports being published than if they are undertaken by academics with research grants or without direct financial support. Many government reports and articles are available only in typewritten or mimeographed forms. This reduces substantially their communication potential within both the community of leisure researchers and the community of leisure research users and sponsors.

A final implication has to do with coordination. The 1974 report of a panel of British consultants to the government of Canada noted that:

> The major research need as we saw it, and as our Canadian colleagues recognized, is for better coordination of research. It seemed that there was both a duplication of effort and also an unawareness of work being done in other agencies. This is not, of course, a problem peculiar to Canada, for it arises from the nature of recreation and from the fact that some part of it concerns a large number of agencies without being their primary field of responsibility; but it certainly seems more acute in Canada than in the United Kingdom, possibly owing to the scale of funding and to the federal/provincial division of responsibility. As a result, it seemed that the results from research were not always commensurate with the input of effort and resources.

This lack of coordination of research efforts has been noted by many other commentators, though it has seldom been expressed quite so clearly.

CONCLUSION

The coming decade can become as exciting and eventful as the one that has just passed, although perhaps not quite so frantic! The challenge is to move the field of leisure research towards maturity. The fact that it is a young and vigorous field is to our advantage. But it is sobering to reflect upon the words of one anonymous author who remarked: "You are only young once, but you can be immature indefinitely."

REFERENCES

1. Center for Urban and Regional Studies. *An Evaluation of the Development of Recreation Research and Policy*. Birmingham: University of Birmingham, 1977. (Mimeo)
2. Clawson, M. and Knetsch, J. L. *Economics of Outdoor Recreation*. Baltimore: Johns Hopkins University Press, 1966.
3. See, for example: Wolfe, R. I. "Perspectives on Outdoor Recreation." *Geographical Review* (54) 1964. pp. 203-238: Ellis, J. B. *A Systems Theory Model for Recreational Travel in Ontario: A Progress Report*. Toronto: Ontario Department of Highways, 1967. (Mimeo)
4. Robertson, R. W. and Ross, J. H. *Toward a Recreation Feasibility Assessment Model*. Victoria: University of Victoria, 1969.
5. Knetsch, J. L. *A Design for Assessing Outdoor Recreation Demands in Canada*. Ottawa: Department of Indian Affairs and Northern Development, 1967. (Mimeo)
6. The Conference Board in Canada. *The Altered Work-Week*. Ottawa: The Board, 1973.
7. Center for Urban and Regional Studies, *Op. Cit.*
8. Coppock, J. T. et al. *Report on the Development of Recreation Research and Planning in Canada*. Ottawa: Urban Affairs Canada, 1974. (Mimeo)

CONTRIBUTORS

Serena E. Arnold received her doctorate in recreation from Indiana University. Before entering teaching, she served as Superintendent of Parks and Recreation and as a state recreation consultant. For the last 21 years she has been associated with the University of California at Los Angeles as a teacher, researcher, consultant and administrator. Her main interests are in administration and analyzing the conceptual basis of leisure services.

Doyle Bishop, an Associate Professor in the Recreology Department of the University of Ottawa, received his Ph.D. in Psychology at the University of Illinois. He has strong interests in the research of personality as it effects leisure pursuits, creativity, and physical and mental health. He has authored and co-authored many articles in psychology and recreation research journals and is engaged extensively as editor and reviewer of research articles.

Francis J. Bregha, Chairman of the Department of Recreology at the University of Ottawa, was for several years Professor and Chairman of the Community Development and Social Change Program, School of Social Work, University of Toronto. He has been writing about leisure since 1970 when he analyzed the impact of changes in demography, employment and social security on free time. Interested also in social planning and community development, recently he has been examining the philosophical and ethical basis of our ideas about leisure. Member of several federal and provincial commissions and task forces in Canada, he was recently the first Canadian representative of the Inter-American Development Bank in Central America.

Thomas L. Burton is Professor and Chairman, Department of Recreation Administration, University of Alberta. He has taught at universities in England and the United States as well as Canada after receiving a Ph.D. in Resource Economics from Wye College, London, England. He was for three years coordinator and director of programs on the urban environment in the Policy and Research Branch of Canada's Ministry of State for Urban Affairs. Author of seven books in the recreation, resource, planning and research fields and numerous reports and articles, he has served as a consultant to the governments of Ontario, Alberta, Canada, Australia, the United Kingdom, and agencies of the United Nations.

E. Glen Carls is Associate Professor, Department of Recreation and Parks, Texas A. and M. University. Author of many articles on outdoor recreation and the environment, he has served as Supervisor of Systems Research for the Illinois Department of Conservation and was Recreation Research Leader for the New York Sea Grant Institute. He taught at the State University of New York – Cortland and the University of Waterloo after receiving the Ph.D. degree from the University of Illinois.

John R. Crompton is Assistant Professor of Recreation and Parks at Texas A. and M. University. His educational background includes degrees in Physical Education, Geography, Business Administration, Recreation and Parks Administration, and a Ph.D. in Recreation Resource Development from Texas A. and M. University. He served four years as Managing Director of Loughborough Recreation Planning Counsultants, the largest recreation and tourism consulting firm in the United Kingdom. His current research and teaching interests center around financing and marketing leisure and tourism services.

Mary R. Duncan received her Ph.D. from the United States International University and currently Chairs the Recreation Department at San Diego State University. She has published several articles regarding recreation and violence in Northern Ireland and co-authored *Supervision of Leisure Services.* She also wrote *The Underground Guide to Job Interviewing.* She has traveled extensively and lectured in Europe, India and the Arab Gulf as well as at the Smithsonian Institution in Washington, D.C. where she lectured on "Play, Terrorism, Revolution and Radical Politics."

Diana R. Dunn is Head, Department of Physical Education at the University of Arizona, having taught previously at Temple University. She holds degrees in Education and Education Administration and a Ph.D. in Recreation and Park Administration from The Pennsylvania State University. Along with experience in municipal recreation in Ohio and California, she served as Director of Research for the National Recreation and Park Association. She has served as research director and consultant for research for the Department of Housing and Urban Development, Department of Interior, and the World Leisure and Recreation Association and has authored and edited numerous books, articles, monographs and reviews.

John Farina is Professor of Social Work at Sir Wilfred Laurier University, having taught previously at the University of Toronto and the Chinese University of Hong Kong. He earned the Doctor of Social Work degree at Washington University, Saint Louis. Prior to teaching he was Assistant Superintendent of Recreation in Tacoma and Superintendent of Recreation in Edmonton, Alberta and was Executive Secretary for Group Work of the Canadian Welfare Council. He has authored numerous articles and reports on social work and social welfare, as well as leisure and recreation.

Geoffrey Godbey is currently Professor of Recreation and Parks at The Pennsylvania State University. He is the author of *Recreation,*

Park and Leisure Services and co-author, along with Stanley Parker, of *Leisure Studies and Services: An Overview.* He is an associate editor of *Leisure Sciences* and *Review of Sport and Leisure.* His poetry has appeared in many magazines and journals.

Seymour M. Gold is Associate Professor of Environmental Planning at the University of California, Davis. He holds the Ph.D. degree from the University of Michigan and has engaged in teaching and research at Michigan State University and the Universities of Illinois, Michigan, and California-Berkeley. He has extensive experience as a planner at municipal and state levels and as a planning consultant. He is the author of *Recreation Planning and Design* and *Urban Recreation Planning.*

Thomas L. Goodale is Professor, Department of Recreology at the University of Ottawa, having taught previously at the State University of New York-Cortland and the University of Wisconsin-Green Bay. He received the Ph.D. degree from the University of Illinois. The author of numerous articles and reports on recreation and related topics, he has recently completed a report for the Ontario Ministry of Culture and Recreation on the future of municipal recreation services.

Peggy Hutchison teaches in the Department of Recreation at the University of Waterloo, where she is active in research and practice related to community involvement of disabled persons. She previously worked with Canada's National Institute of Mental Retardation. Her most recent publication, which she co-authored with John Lord, is a book entitled *Recreation Integration: Issues and Alternatives in Leisure Services and Community Involvement.*

Claudine Jeanrenaud, currently an Associate Professor in the Department of Recreology, University of Ottawa, earned her Bachelor's of Art Education degree at the University of Lausane, Switzerland; her M.S. and Ph.D. at the University of Illinois, Department of Leisure Studies. Her main interests lie in the area of conceptual and creative development as reflected in graphic expression of adults and children, as well as the environmental and personality determinants of such development.

John R. Kelly is a sociologist who has concentrated his research on leisure in community and family environments. He is currently an Associate Professor at the University of Illinois at Urbana-Champaign in the Leisure Behavior Research Laboratory of the Department of Leisure Studies. His Ph.D. in sociology is from the University of Oregon and he has taught in sociology departments in Oregon, Wisconsin and Virginia. He has recently completed a general introduction to the study of leisure and has published over 30 research-based articles. His current research is on changes and continuities in leisure identities and roles through the life course.

Charles W. Lamb is Associate Professor in the Department of Marketing at Texas A. and M. University. He holds degrees in Business Administration, Management and Marketing, including the Doctorate in Marketing from Kent State University. Co-author of *The Pricing Function: A Pragmatic Approach,* he has published extensively and conducted numerous workshops on marketing. His main teaching and research interest is on service and public sector marketing.

John Lord lives in Kitchener, Ontario where he is currently involved in a number of national and community based advocacy projects. He formerly taught at Dalhousie University in Halifax, Nova Scotia. His most recent publication, which he co-authored with Peggy Hutchison, is a book entitled *Recreation Integration: Issues and Alternatives in Leisure Services and Community Involvement.*

Roger C. Mannell, currently a member of the Department of Recreation, University of Waterloo, is a research psychologist having received a Ph.D. in Psychology at the University of Windsor. Previously he taught in the Departments of Psychology and of Recreation at Acadia University in Nova Scotia where he also directed the government and university sponsored Center of Leisure Studies. His teaching and research interests and his publications focus upon human behavior and experience during free-time as well as personality and social environment influences on experience.

Bill Michaelis is Associate Professor at San Francisco State University and taught previously at California State Polytechnic University-Pomona. He has written extensively on the subjects of games, play, and urban recreation and is the author of *Learning Through Non-Competitive Activities and Play.* He is a member of the Board of Directors of the American Adventure Play Association and serves as Advisory Board member and national trainer for the New Games Foundation.

James F. Murphy is Professor and Chairman of the Department of Recreation and Leisure Studies, Northeastern University having previously taught in the Department of Recreation and Leisure Studies, San Jose State University. He holds a Bachelor's and Master's degree in Recreation and Park Administration and a Ph.D. in Education from Oregon State University. His publications include: *Delivery of Community Leisure Services: An Holistic Approach* (with Dennis Howard), *Recreation and Leisure Service: A Humanistic Perspective, Concepts of Leisure, Leisure Service Delivery System: A Modern Perspective* (with Bill Niepoth, John Williams and Paul Brown).

Francis P. Noe is a Research Sociologist with the Southeast Region of the National Park Service. Since joining the National Park Service he has served at Georgia State University, the National Space Technology Laboratory, and on special assignment to the Countryside Commission, Great Britain. He is involved in initiating research, conducting, contracting, and directing research projects relative to the interest of the National Park Service. He serves as an associate editor for *Journal of Leisure Research.*

Ronald P. Reynolds, currently Associate Professor in the Department of Recreation, Virginia Commonwealth University, completed his Ph.D. degree from the University of Illinois. He was an Assistant Professor at California State University, Chico and at Dalhousie University in Nova Scotia where he also served as a Project Officer with the Recreation Council for the Disabled. His current professional and academic interests include factors affecting the delivery of leisure services to those with special needs and research relating to the acceptance of disabled persons in community leisure settings.

H. Douglas Sessoms is Chairman and Professor of Recreation Administration, University of North Carolina at Chapel Hill. He is a Past President of the Society of Park and Recreation Educators and a Distinguished Fellow of that organization. He is a Member of the Board of Trustees of the National Recreation and Park Association and recipient of the Master Fellow Award of the North Carolina Park and Recreation Society. He has co-authored three texts and published in a number of research and professional journals. His special interests are the sociology of leisure, group dynamics and the conceptual basis of professional preparation of recreation personnel.

Elwood L. Shafer Jr., currently staff assistant to the Deputy Chief for United States Department of Agriculture, Forest Service Research, completed his Bachelor's and Master's degrees in Forestry at The Pennsylvania State University and his Ph.D. degree from the State University of New York College of Environmental Science and Forestry at Syracuse. His experience spans over 20 years of timber, wildlife, recreation, landscape architecture, and urban forestry research with the Forest Service. He has held an adjunct Professorship at Syracuse University and presently is a visiting lecturer at George Washington University.

Stephen L. J. Smith, a faculty member at the University of Waterloo, completed his Bachelor's and Master's degree in Geography and a Ph.D. in Recreation and Resources Development from Texas A and M University. He has taught and researched at Michigan State University. His research activities include the geography and economics of leisure, parks planning, Northern studies, tourism, and the humanities and leisure. He has a special interest in the methods and philosophy of research in these subjects.

Irene M. Spry is Professor Emeritus of Economics at the University of Ottawa. Educated at the London School of Economics, Girton College of Cambridge University and Bryn Mawr, she has taught previously at the University of Toronto and the University of Saskatchewan. She served many years as Administrative Chairman and as Deputy World President of the Associated Countrywomen of the World, an international, non-governmental organization engaged in community development and continuing education activities. Co-editor of *Natural Resource Development in Canada,* she was recently Senior Research Associate with GAMMA, a multi-year, multi-disciplinary study of conservation and resource use in the future.

William Thorsteinson has a varied background in recreation including camping, youth programs, adult education, community work, administration, personnel services and consulting. He has degrees in sociology from Carleton University and McGill University. His early career was with the YMCA in Ottawa, Brantford and Toronto. Since 1974, he has served as Executive Director of the Ontario Recreation Society and has been active as a consultant, particularly in the area of staff training and development. He teaches courses both at York University and the University of Waterloo.

Fred Van Derbeck currently works with the East Mountain Center in Westfield, Massachusetts, where he is involved in policy and advocacy related to child development services for disabled and non-disabled children. He also has an extensive background in political science.

Cor Westland, formerly Director of Recreation Canada in the Department of National Health Welfare is currently Assistant Professor in the Department of Recreology, University of Ottawa. Active in a number of government and non-government organizations at the national and international level, he has been a forceful advocate of recreation planning, programming, coordination, and research. He has presented major papers at national and international conferences as official or unofficial representative of Canada and has published papers and reports on recreation leadership and governments' roles in providing recreation service.

Peter A. Witt is currently a Visiting Distinguished Professor in the Division of Recreation and Leisure Studies, North Texas State University, Denton Texas, having previously taught in the Department of Recreology, University of Ottawa. His Doctorate is from the University of Illinois. He was the first editor of *Leisurability,* conducted the National Study on the Status of Recreation for Special Groups in

Canada, and has authored or co-authored over 35 articles and books. His main areas of interest include the psycho-social determinants of leisure behavior, leisure counseling/leisure education, future recreation perspectives, and recreation services for special groups.

Jiri Zuzanek is currently Associate Professor in the Departments of Recreation and of Sociology, University of Waterloo and Chairman of the Research Group on Leisure and Cultural Development at the same University. He is author of *Leisure and Social Change,* (forthcoming) *Work and Leisure in the Soviet Union: A Time-Budget Analysis* (forthcoming) and many other publications.

CREDITS

While nearly every chapter was prepared especially for this book, a few are revised or expanded versions of papers or articles initially prepared for another forum. We, and the authors noted below, believed the subject matter timely and pertinent to the issues orientation we have tried to develop, and we wish to cite and thank those for whom the subject matter was initially developed. The chapter by Doyle Bishop and Claudine Jeanrenaud is an expanded version of a chapter in *Play and Human Settlements* (1979) and appears here with the kind permission of the editor of that volume. Thomas Burton's chapter is a revised and edited version of addresses delivered at the Second Canadian Congress on Leisure Research (1978). The chapter by John Kelly was initially prepared for presentation at the Third Van Cle World Congress on Leisure (1979) and Jiri Zuzanek's chapter was also developed for presentation at a conference in England in 1978. Finally, Seymour Gold's chapter is an expanded version of an article reprinted from the May, 1979 issue of Parks and Recreation by special permission© 1979, National Recreation and Park Association.